First as a theologian, then bishop and later the Prefect of the Congregation for the Doctrine of the Faith, Joseph Ratzinger is often thought to have moved steadily to the right. In this collection, Gerard Mannion and Lieven Boeve dispel such easy generalizations. With judiciously chosen and suitably lengthy extracts from Ratzinger's writings, accompanied by helpful editorial comments, these two leading European Catholic theologians demonstrate the continuity of the one Ratzinger and consequently shed light on the complexity of his present-day role as Pope. Anyone who wishes to understand better the current face of Roman theology is greatly in their debt.

Paul Lakeland, Fairfield University, CT, USA.

An indispensable guide for understanding the theology of Joseph Ratzinger. Belgian Lieven Boeve and Irish Gerard Mannion have charted the theological journey of this German figure who has cast a long shadow for more than fifty years on the church and the world as university professor, expert at Vatican II, but above all as prefect of the Congregation of the Doctrine of the Faith for more than twenty years and now as Pope Benedict XVI. Ratzinger insists that his theological opinions are distinct from his official positions as prefect and pope, but this collection shows otherwise. A very personal theology has become the official theology of the church. This book offers the most comprehensive selection of writings from the various stages of Ratzinger's career arranged according to central topics, which Boeve and Mannion introduce by identifying crucial contexts and critical issues informing these texts.

Bradford Hinze, Fordham University, New York, USA.

Anyone attempting to gain serious familiarity with the theology of Joseph Ratzinger will find this book invaluable. Through a judicious selection of texts that represent Ratzinger's thinking in the areas of theology to which he has paid most attention, the editors provide a reliable overview of his thought. They offer informed introductions to each theme that they highlight and to each text that they choose, alerting readers to the context and the main preoccupation of Ratzinger in each of their selections, as well as to possible alternative viewpoints in many cases. This book is not just a conventional reader but a uniquely structured, signposted guide through the terrain of Ratzinger's theology as a whole. It comes at exactly the right time in emerging Ratzinger scholarship, providing a pathway for the uninitiated as well as a compact one-volume resource for those who are further along the road. I recommend it highly.

James Corkery, S.J., Milltown Institute of
Theology and Philosophy, Dublin, Ireland.

This Reader, helpfully subtitled, Mapping a Theological Journey, is a valuable contribution to the exposition of and debate about the theological positions of Theologian Joseph Ratzinger, and how far they have changed over the half-century since his years as expert theological advisor (peritus) to Cardinal Frings of Cologne through the Second Vatican Council. The structure of the book is interesting in itself as the editors each select central themes with their sub-themes from Ratzinger's theological writings. With a short evaluative introduction from the individual editor (and further evaluation for the sub-themes) each chapter is mainly devoted to extended texts by Ratzinger himself on theme and subthemes. The three popular questions: Did Ratzinger change his theology over the fifty years from mildly 'liberal' to strongly 'restorationalist?' Did he correctly or incorrectly interpret Vatican II, in which way and at what stage? Is he now leading the Catholic Church back or forward to a pre/post Vatican II condition? However the book is much more than any set of popular comments on these questions with its substantial exposition of Ratzinger's theology through all the major themes of theology. Supporters and critics alike of his theology will learn much from this work and will have much both to agree and disagree with. A must for every theologian's and theological library.

Enda McDonagh, Saint Patrick's College, Maynooth,
Ireland's National Seminary and Pontifical University,
Ireland.

THE RATZINGER READER

Mapping a Theological Journey

JOSEPH RATZINGER

edited by

LIEVEN BOEVE

GERARD MANNION

t&t clark

Published by T&T Clark International
A Continuum Imprint
The Tower Building, 11 York Road, London SE1 7NX
80 Maiden Lane, Suite 704, New York, NY 10038

www.continuumbooks.com

British Library Cataloguing-in-Publication Data
A catalogue record for this book is available from the British Library

ISBN13: 978-0-567-03213-3 (Hardback)
ISBN13: 978-0-567-03214-0 (Paperback)

Typeset by Pindar NZ, Auckland, New Zealand
Printed and bound in Great Britain by the MPG Books Group

LIST OF CONTENTS

Acknowledgments   ix

Volume Format and Guidance to the Reader   xi

Preface: Mapping a Theological Journey   xiii
Gerard Mannion

Introduction: Joseph Ratzinger: His Life, Thought
and Work   1
Lieven Boeve

Joseph Ratzinger: Prolific Theologian and Outspoken
Church Leader   1
'Only the truth will set you free'   7
Both Church Leader and Theologian Concurrently?   9
Is there a Ratzinger I and a Ratzinger II? The
Question of the Theological 'Volta-faccia'   11

1 Theological Foundations: Revelation, Tradition and
Hermeneutics   13
Lieven Boeve

Introduction   13
1.1 Revelation, Scripture and Tradition   13
1.2 The Formation of Tradition   18
1.3 Christian Faith Challenged by a Modern Context   28

2 Christ, Humanity and Salvation   51
Lieven Boeve

Introduction   51

2.1 Christian Faith is About Conversion: 'It is no
   longer I who live, but Christ who lives in me'
   (Gal 2:20a)   53

2.2 Salvation   57

2.3 Salvation in Christ: 'I am the way, the truth and
   the life' (John 14:6)   65

2.4 Salvation in Christ Includes the Hope of
   Resurrection and Eternal Life   72

2.5 The Historical and Bodily Human Being
   Before God: A Sacramental Anthropology   75

3 Understanding the Church: Fundamental Ecclesiology   81
   Gerard Mannion

   Introduction   81

   3.1 The Essential Nature of the Church   87

   3.2 The Babylonian Captivity of the Post-Conciliar
      Church   94

   3.3 Reinterpreting the Ecclesiology of Vatican II:
      The Ontological Priority of the Universal
      Church   100

   3.4 The Fullness of the Church: Discerning the
      Meaning of 'Subsistit in'   108

   3.5 A Normative Ecclesiology of Communion:
      A Project on the Way   113

4 Christian Faith, Church and World   119
   Lieven Boeve

   Introduction   119

   4.1 The Dialogue of the Church with the Modern
      World   119

   4.2 The Christian Soul of Europe   125

   4.3 Christian Faith and Politics   133

5 Christian Unity and Religious Dialogue: On
   Ecumenism and Other Faiths   139
   Gerard Mannion

   Introduction   139

   5.1 Christianity and World Religions   148

   5.2 No Salvation Outside the Church?   154

5.3 Discerning the 'Ecumenical Dispute' between
    Orthodoxy, Catholicism and Protestantism   160
5.4 Ecumenical Realities Today   167
5.5 Against Pluralism and Relativism   172

6 Teaching and Authority: Dimensions of Magisterium   179
  Gerard Mannion
  Introduction   179
  6.1 The Relationship between the Bishops and the
      Papacy   187
  6.2 The Structure and Task of the Synod of Bishops   201
  6.3 Free Expression and Obedience in the Church   207
  6.4 The Vocation of the Catholic Theologian   212
  6.5 Magisterium and Morality   218

7 Liturgy, Catechesis and Evangelization   225
  Gerard Mannion
  Introduction   225
  7.1 Change and Permanence in the Liturgy   233
  7.2 The Crisis of Catechesis   240
  7.3 The Teaching Office of the Bishop   246
  7.4 The New Evangelization   251

8 Interpreting the Second Vatican Council   257
  Lieven Boeve
  Introduction   257
  8.1 *Aggiornamento* and Vatican II   258
  8.2 The Reception of Vatican II: 'The Real Time
      of Vatican II is Still to Come'   264
  8.3 Interpreting Vatican II: Between the Spirit and
      the Letter   272
  Postscript: Which 'hermeneutics of reform'?   276

Index of Names   281
Index of Subjects   284

ACKNOWLEDGMENTS

The editors wish to express their sincere gratitude to a number of individuals who have helped make the publication of this volume possible. Special thanks are due most of all to Terence Bateman for his extensive assistance throughout much of its production. Our deep gratitude is also due to Gregory Grimes and Anneleen Decoene for their invaluable assistance with the gathering together of the definitive texts, and also to David Kirchhoffer for his dedicated work in producing original translations of hitherto untranslated texts by Ratzinger from the original German into English. We also wish to express our sincere thanks to the Faculty of Theology, Katholieke Universiteit Leuven, to the Flemish Fund for Scientific Research, and to the Research Fund Katholieke Universiteit Leuven, who all helped to sponsor the sterling team of people who worked with us on this project. All Ratzinger scholars will be forever grateful to Father Idahosa Amadasu who provided the equally invaluable service of compiling the index.

We are especially indebted to Dr Francesca Angeletti and Prof Dr Giuseppe Costa SDB of Librice Editrice Vaticana, for permission to reproduce the theological texts of Joseph Ratzinger here. A deep debt of gratitude, as always, to Tom Kraft, Anna Turton, Dominic Mattos, and all at Continuum for their encouragement, patience and belief in this project, with especial thanks due to Kim Pillay, Tessa King and Diane Lowther.

VOLUME FORMAT AND GUIDANCE
TO THE READER

The volume opens with an introductory essay briefly charting the life and career of Joseph Ratzinger. This is followed by eight chapters focused on specific theological themes and areas of debate. Each individual chapter is prefaced by a brief introduction to its context and background, themes and debates, as well as a sampling of some of the discussion points to which the chapter gives rise.

The beginning of each reading is indicated by an indentation of the text and change of font. As a rule, the footnotes from the original sources have been retained where they are referential. Where supportive and/or expansive, it has been mostly left to the individual editor's discretion whether to retain or omit further footnotes. Decisions in this respect have been dictated by the chapter editor's opinion of the need for detailed footnotes to aid exposition relevant to the nature of the topic, or where he has felt that their omission will bring greater clarity to the reader's study of the text. Where original footnotes have been retained which do not contain the full publication details, these have been added, where possible, although such additions are not marked as editorial interpolations.

All text in [square brackets] constitutes an editorial interpolation. All text in the readings which is in italics or with particular emphasis, has been represented as in the original. An ellipsis [. . .] indicates where material has been omitted – normally for the sake of abbreviation, but on occasion also for stylistic purposes. Where the journals *Concilium* and *Communio* are referred to or cited, this will refer to the English editions except where otherwise indicated.

The chapters are by no means intended to be exhaustive nor even definitive, but rather to be indicative of the nature of Ratzinger's thought in relation to each topic.

PREFACE: MAPPING A THEOLOGICAL JOURNEY

Gerard Mannion

Joseph Ratzinger was formally announced to the world as Pope Benedict XVI from the balcony above St Peter's Square on April 19th 2005. This moment which marked the completion of his long journey from being a pastor-theologian to the Chair of Peter. Unlike either of his two immediate predecessors (indeed, in a global sense, any of his predecessors), the world already knew a great deal about him. For the first time in history, here was a pontiff whose books were read across the globe, whose ideas were widely known, who even had his own online 'fan club'. So, too, were there many books and articles, both popular and scholarly about him. And all this, *prior* to his elevation to Peter's chair.

Of course, the attention afforded him since his election to the Pontificate has multiplied enormously, and the number of books about him is legion. So there are many volumes about Joseph Ratzinger the theologian in print already, including collections of his own writings. Exhaustive bibliographies have been produced[1] and many are available freely on the World Wide Web. A complete edition of his entire published corpus is also presently in production.[2] So why another book about Ratzinger?

This volume hopes to offer something different and its subtitle – *Mapping a Theological Journey* – offers the key to understanding the intentions behind this work. The volume brings together a collection of key texts by Joseph Ratzinger, from his earlier writings, to the 'transition period' following his disillusionment with developments in the church in the aftermath of Vatican II, to his pioneering and frequently polemical writings as part of the *Communio* project, to his debates and disagreements with fellow theologians and schools of theology. Representative writings

---

1   A definitive bibliography has been recently produced by the Ratzinger Schülerkreis, *viz.,* V. Pfnür (ed.), *Joseph Ratzinger/Papst Benedikt XVI. Das Werk: Bibliographisches Hilfsmittel zur Erschließung des literarisch-theologischen Werkes von Joseph Ratzinger bis zur Papstwahl,* (mit CD-Rom), Augsburg: Sankt Ulrich Verlag, 2009.

2   Joseph Ratzinger *Gesammelte Schriften,* Freiburg, Herder, with the first volume (Band XI) appearing in 2008.

contemporaneous to his time as Prefect of the Vatican's Congregation for
the Doctrine of the Faith (CDF) are naturally included, but the emphasis
in this volume is upon Joseph Ratzinger as 'private theologian'. The time
for a compilation of his papal writings lies in the future.

Here we focus on his writings as a private theologian partly because
his many writings released in a personal capacity chart the formation of
and comment on the official statements and texts released under his name
in a more informative fashion than the simple inclusion of the formu-
laic 'official texts' themselves. But, more significantly, we wish to offer
a comprehensive portrait of the scope of Ratzinger's theological vision,
charting the core themes that have preoccupied him over the decades
and illustrating his theological sources, methods and styles. We therefore
hope that this volume will afford general readers, students, scholars and
Ratzinger specialists alike, a synoptic perspective on the nature and
substance of the theology of Joseph Ratzinger. Finally, as Ratzinger has
frequently said himself, his writings as a private theologian carry no
official ecclesial authority and therefore are entirely open for debate,
discussion and questioning.[3] Therefore all readers can fruitfully explore
the various perspectives and conclusions that such a synoptic portrait
might bring to light.

This volume is the product of a three-year collaboration between two
theologians from differing contexts and methodological backgrounds.
A chance meeting at a Vatican conference on *Gaudium et Spes* in March
2005 and a long conversation over an ice cream while walking around
the entire perimeter of the Vatican complex (on a day of searing heat!)
led to the realization of a shared conviction that the familiar picture
of Ratzinger as a theologian whose mind had somehow dramatically
changed along the way, was a misleading one.

We had both earlier and independently come to the same conclusion
that the familiar picture of a once-liberal turned arch-conservative is
thus misleading. If anything, the shifts in Ratzinger's thinking have been
more subtle than often presumed and suggest a more pragmatic personal
character than his doctrinal pronouncements indicate. Thus the seemingly
more progressive tone adopted during the Second Vatican Council and
(in relation to some areas of doctrine and theology) in the immediate

3   As will become evident, there are many periods throughout the career of Ratzinger when the
     dividing line between the private theologian and the public church leader becomes significantly
     blurred. This occurs especially during his time as Prefect of the Congregation for the Doctrine of
     the Faith. Thus there are times when his private theological writings either shape official church
     pronouncements or reflect the same. This is especially evident, as we shall see, in relation to his
     writings on ecclesiology, ecumenical and inter-faith relations and, perhaps above all else, in relation
     to church teaching authority and the role of the Catholic theologian.

years following its end should be interpreted not, as is often presumed, as the revolutionary zeal of a young man that transforms into mature realism with the benefit of increased wisdom and experience. Rather those earlier flashes of progressiveness might better be interpreted, if one is going to be generous, as the workings of a young and talented scholar and priest finding his way in the church and academy alike. Surrounded by the progressive giants, not least of all his fellow Deutsche-phones, such as Karl Rahner and Hans Küng, and considering his role as a conciliar advisor to Cardinal Frings, it is little wonder that Ratzinger may have chosen to proceed more tentatively during that period, allowing himself and his ideas alike to be caught up in and swept along in the *aggiornamento*, and hence progressiveness, that seemed destined to be the consensus that would emerge from the Council. We must also remember that his career as an academic theologian was then still in its formative stages, thus pragmatism might have been deemed prudent with regard to certain debates and issues during the conciliar period.

But, whichever picture is the more accurate, or whatever alternative might prove to be more so, there is more consistency to the thinking of Joseph Ratzinger than has often been the impression given in Catholic periodicals and both popular and scholarly volumes alike. Hence, as Michael Fahey illustrated as long ago as 1981, a perusal of the writings of Joseph Ratzinger demonstrates this one characteristic, above all else:

> His thought shows an amazing consistency. The emergence of cautious writings in recent years is not based on some new dramatic conversion but is the logical conclusion of years of reflection. Prior to Vatican II he expressed impatience with the lack of vitality in Catholic theology and wrote critically about procedures in the Roman Curia. Shortly after the Council he grew more and more convinced that its real goals had been misunderstood or distorted by certain theologians.[4]

In compiling our collection, the editors of this volume have also sought to remain true to their own methodological, contextual and disciplinary backgrounds. We have consciously chosen to avoid trying to offer a uniform and standardized approach to introducing and analyzing the writings of Ratzinger included here. In common, we share the fact that we are both systematic theologians with ongoing interests in theology's interaction with wider culture, particularly with philosophical schools of thought and with public issues and contexts. With regard to more distinctive areas of focus, one of us is a specialist in fundamental theology,

---

4   Michael Fahey (1981), 'Joseph Ratzinger as Ecclesiologist and Pastor', in Gregory Baum and Marcus Lefébure (eds), *Neo-Conservatism: Social and Religious Phenomenon*, vol. 141. Edinburgh, T&T Clark, pp. 76–83.

the other has dual specialisms in ecclesiology and ethics. One hails from continental Europe and is steeped in the approaches to Ratzinger from within the heart of Europe, the other is an Irish citizen with particular familiarity with the Anglophone reception of Ratzinger on both sides of the Atlantic, alongside the wider European responses to his theological vision. Together we hope our differing backgrounds, styles and approaches (and occasionally even conclusions) will prove complementary and offer some further stimulation to reflection and discussion for the reader.

Obviously, in seeking to craft a one-volume resource for those wishing to delve deeper into the thought of Ratzinger, we have had to be selective, as a complete collection of Ratzinger's theological writings alone would run to many, many volumes. Thus we have selected but representative texts. An exhaustive sampling would have made this book unaffordable for most readers, especially in the current economic climate. So we have tried to discern which texts might best, together in a single volume, offer the reader the most appropriate and synoptic account of Ratzinger's thought.

Given the importance of hermeneutical principles and practice to the rationale behind not simply this volume, but also as a key to understanding the thought of its subject as well, one third of this book necessarily takes the form of editorial introduction and commentary – in this Preface and the General Introduction to the volume as a whole, to each broad thematic area in the chapter introductions and to each reading in its own right as a particular manifestation of the thoughts, methods and *modus operandi* of Joseph Ratzinger. Where appropriate, we have also sought to point the reader in the direction of questions that other schools of thought, method and even critics of Ratzinger might raise.

Some will no doubt ask, where are Ratzinger's writings on subject x or topic y or controversy z? We have focused on the topics that this theologian, himself, has most often chosen to write and speak about. We are confident that readers will find the other issues, either referred to in the context of his wider 'core foci' or else alluded to in the broader debates each chapter enters into.

It was also a priority for us to provide readings of a substantive length, as opposed to brief 'bite-size' readings. Most readings are thus between two and three thousand words in length unless the especial significance or particular pertinence of a text of greater or, indeed, lesser length demands its inclusion. We hope readers will particularly appreciate the fact that a number of the readings are here appearing in English translation and hence English printed publication for the first time.

This volume is therefore about two theologians seeking to map the theological journey of a third practitioner of their shared craft. We hope this book will offer something different to the accounts of Ratzinger's thought that appear in the existing textbooks, hagiographies and polemical critiques. To our mind, nothing of the exact sort of this project, combining these particular areas of focus and treating these issues in the suggested manner, has been attempted thus far. In one of Ratzinger's writings included here (in relation to the scriptural testimony to the emergence of the church), he advises us that in approaching a broad and intricate subject, '[W]hat is needed first of all is a kind of aerial photograph of the whole: when our gaze ranges over a larger expanse of terrain, it is also possible to find our bearings'.[5] Such an aerial perspective, Ratzinger continues, might furnish us with a 'hermeneutic compass' that points towards the 'internal continuity' of that scriptural testimony. We sincerely hope that the volume will provide an analogous aerial perspective and thus hermeneutic compass to the theological journey of Joseph Ratzinger and that it will demonstrate a greater 'internal continuity' (by intention if not always in substantial terms) to his theology, allowing readers both to discern and to evaluate the developments, level of consistency, abiding character and tone of Ratzinger's writings at various points of his career, as well as on the whole.

Feast of St Bonaventure, 2009

5   See reading 3.1, below, p. 89.

INTRODUCTION

JOSEPH RATZINGER: HIS LIFE, THOUGHT AND WORK

Lieven Boeve

The purpose of this introduction is to offer a concise biography of Joseph Ratzinger, with particular attention to his theological and ecclesial career,[1] followed by an equally brief summary of his theological position. Finally, we address two particular questions that have accompanied the study of the theology of Joseph Ratzinger over the years. First, is there a significant difference between Ratzinger the theologian and Ratzinger the Church leader? Second, did Ratzinger's theological position change in a dramatic sense in the post-conciliar period, i.e. in his theological career, should one distinguish between a Ratzinger I and Ratzinger II (with the 1968 student revolt in Tübingen as the symbolic event between the two)?

Joseph Ratzinger: Prolific Theologian and Outspoken Church Leader

On 16 April 1927, Joseph Ratzinger was born in the Bavarian town of Marktl am Inn, the youngest of three children of a policeman and his wife. He felt an attraction to the priesthood from an early age, but was unable to pursue this interest owing to the fact that, at the age of 16 in 1943, he was conscripted into the German army to fulfil his military service. After about a year attached to an anti-aircraft battery near Munich, he was sent to the Hungarian front as an infantryman and was eventually captured by the American forces. After six months as a prisoner of war in Ulm, he was finally released in the summer of 1945.

In 1946, the then nineteen-year-old Joseph entered the seminary at Freising and a year later, embarked upon his philosophical studies at the University of Munich, where he also continued his theological formation. Among his professors were Romano Guardini, Michael Schmaus

---

1   This introduction is drawn from L. Boeve, 'Kerk, theologie en heilswaarheid. De klare visie van Joseph Ratzinger', in *Tijdschrift voor theologie* 33 (1993) pp. 139–165; and L. Boeve, 'Europe in Crisis. A Question of Belief or Unbelief? Perspectives from the Vatican', in *Modern Theology* 23 (2007) pp. 205–227.

and Gottlieb Söhningen. He was ordained priest on 20 June 1951 and appointed as assistant at a parish in the Archdiocese of Munich, while continuing with his university studies. In 1953, he graduated as a doctor of theology with a dissertation on the concept of the people and house of God in Augustine.[2] A few years later, he obtained – not without some difficulty[3] – his 'habilitation', with a research project on the theology of history in St. Bonaventure.[4] This latter qualification was, in effect, a kind of second doctoral thesis that is required as a 'licence' to teach in German universities.

On completion of his formal education, he taught dogmatic theology at the Freising seminary (1958), fundamental theology at the University of Bonn (1959–63) and dogmatic theology and the history of dogma in Münster (1964–66). His publications during this period included studies on Christian fraternity, questions in ecclesiology, particularly on the relation between the episcopate and papal primacy (together with K. Rahner[5]), on authority in the Church, and on revelation, tradition, and hermeneutics.

During this time, he participated in the Second Vatican Council, first as the personal advisor of Cardinal Josef Frings of Cologne – an undaunted critic of Cardinal Ottaviani, the Prefect of the Holy Office at the time – and later as an official *peritus*. At this time, he was also instrumental in the founding of the international journal *Concilium* and became an influential member of the group of forty theologians who comprised the initial membership of the International Theological Commission. During his time as chair of dogmatic theology at Tübingen (1966–69), he composed his widely read and translated book on the content of the Christian faith and also produced his first collection of essays on ecclesiology.[6] Both these works already indicate a prudent caution in the interpretation of the Council, with the central thrust of Ratzinger's position that Vatican II's *aggiornamento* must not be allowed to lapse into a modernization of the

2   J. Ratzinger, *Volk und Haus Gottes in Augustins Lehre von der Kirche* (Münchener Theologische Studien, 2. Systematische Abteilung 7). München: Zink, 1954.
3   See his report on this in *Aus meinem Leben. Erinnerungen (1927–1977).* Stuttgart: DVA, [1-3]1998 (E.T.: *Milestones. Memoirs (1927–1977).* San Francisco: Ignatius Press, 1998).
4   Idem, *Die Geschichtstheologie des heiligen Bonaventura.* München: Schnell & Steiner, 1959. (cf. *Die Geschichtstheologie des heiligen Bonaventura* (1959). St. Ottilien: EOS Verlag, 1992 (E.T.: *The Theology of History in St. Bonaventure.* Chicago: Franciscan Herald Press, 1971, 1989). The 'habilitation' (qualification) is a postdoctoral degree that is a prerequisite for teaching at a German university.
5   K. Rahner and J. Ratzinger, *Episcopat und Primat* (QD 11). Freiburg: Herder, 1961 (E.T.: K. Rahner and J. Ratzinger, *The Episcopate and the Primacy.* New York: Herder and Herder, 1962).
6   Cf. J. Ratzinger, *Einführung in das Christentum. Vorlesungen über das Apostolische Glaubensbekenntnis.* München: Kösel-Verlag, 1968 (E.T.: *Introduction to Christianity.* London, 1969, [2]1985); *Das neue Volk Gottes. Entwürfe zur Ekklesiologie.* Düsseldorf: Taschenbuchausgabe, 1969.

faith, the Church, and of theology itself. Furthermore, his experiences with the 1968 student generation seem to have shocked him. These students were reading the works of Herbert Marcuse, Theodor Adorno, and other neo-Marxists.

Ratzinger was particularly disturbed by the student riots of 1968 and the associated wave of anti-authoritarian feelings. In 1969 he decided to return to Bavaria and to take up a position at the newly erected theological faculty of the University of Regensburg. His initial openness to the achievements of modernity and his willingness to enter into dialogue with the world now rapidly disappeared and his writings began to display increasingly polemical features. In particular, Ratzinger consistently opposed a tendency, which he believed was prevalent at that time, that understood human salvation as a phenomenon that is merely internal and subjective. Furthermore, political theology in particular came under fire.[7] It was also during this period that he vigorously began to question the reception of *Gaudium et Spes*, a document with which he never appeared fully at ease, seeing in its interpretive reception a license to an unlimited adaptation of the Christian faith to the world. He suspects that this could offer a key to understanding the malaise in the Church at that time.[8]

In the early seventies, Ratzinger found an ally in Hans Urs von Balthasar, with both theologians convinced that the Catholic Church had entered into a period of serious difficulty.[9] In 1972, they founded, together with Karl Lehman, Henri de Lubac and other theologians, a new theological journal: *Internationale Katholische Zeitschrift/Communio*, as a counter movement that would provide a corrective influence on *Concilium*, which, according to them, had gone astray.[10]

Communio would become and remain the primary platform from which Ratzinger would express his theological ideas. In this period after the Council he published – along with his *Einführung in das Christentum (Introduction to Christianity)*, *Das neue Volk Gottes* and some shorter essays

---

7   Cf. U. Hommes and J. Ratzinger, *Das Heil des Menschen. Innerweltlich – Christlich*. München: Kösel-Verlag, 1975.

8   Cf. J. Ratzinger, *Weltoffene Kirche? Überlegungen zur Struktur des Zweiten Vatikanischen Konzils*, in T. Filthaut (ed.), *Umkehr und Erneuerung. Kirche nach dem Konzil*. Mainz: Grünewald, 1966, pp. 273–291 (*Das neue Volk Gottes*, 281-301); and especially the revised version of *Angesichts der Welt von heute. Überlegungen zur Konfrontation mit der Kirche im Schema XIII* (originally in *Wort und Wahrheit* 20 (1965) pp. 493–504) in *Dogma und Verkündigung*. München, Wewel, 1973, pp. 183–204.

9   J. Ratzinger and H. U. von Balthasar, *Zwei Plädoyers. Warum ich noch ein Christ bin. Warum ich noch in der Kirche bin*. München: Kösel-Verlag, 1971 (E.T.: *Two say why. Why I am still a Christian. Why I am still in the Church*. Chicago: Franciscan Herald Press, 1973).

10   Later, Ratzinger wrote that *Concilium* wanted to form a second magisterium and as such had become sectarian. Simultaneously, he no longer found in it the Council's authentic spirit, but rather the illusion of an imaginary Vatican III: "It is not I who have changed, but others" (from J. Ratzinger and V. Messori, *The Ratzinger Report*. San Francisco: Ignatius Press, 1985, p. 18).

in a 1973 collection, *Dogma und Verkündigung.*[11] In 1977 a further monograph appeared, *Eschatologie – Tod und ewiges Leben.*[12]

On 24 March 1977, Ratzinger succeeded Cardinal Döpfner as archbishop of Munich-Freising and on June 27 of the same year, was elevated
to the Cardinalate by Pope Paul VI. For his episcopal motto, he chose
Cooperatores Veritatis (co-workers of the truth). In this period, Ratzinger
became involved with the well-known 'Hans Küng case'. In support of
Cardinal Höffner, he urged the removal of Küng's *missio canonica* (canonical approval to teach at a pontifical theology faculty). The document
that enacted this extraordinary disciplinary measure was promulgated
on 15 December 1979. Ratzinger also came into conflict with Karl
Rahner concerning the successor of Heinrich Fries at the theology faculty of the University of Munich. At the request of Cardinal Ratzinger,
the Bavarian education minister Hans Maier bypassed the candidate
whose name appeared at the top of the shortlist for the chair, John
Baptist Metz, and appointed the second-named candidate, Heinrich
Döring. Rahner reacted with his famous *'Ich protestiere'* ('I protest') on
16 November 1979, in which he suggested that the cardinal's aversion
to political theology was the true reason behind his unwillingness to
appoint Metz.[13]

On 25 November 1981, at the request of Pope John Paul II, Cardinal
Ratzinger succeeded Cardinal Seper as Prefect of the Congregation for
the Doctrine of the Faith. From this position, he would acquire enormous
influence on the Vatican's theological and institutional outlook and policy.
Henceforth, Ratzinger would reveal himself as a vigorous champion of
orthodoxy, gaining himself the nickname 'der Pantzerkardinal'. In word,
text, and deed he would defend a tightening of discipline in matters
of faith and morals. Alongside his numerous responsibilities, he would
frequently address episcopal conferences.

As Prefect of the Congregation for the Doctrine of the Faith, and
therefore also head of the International Theological Commission, he
issued numerous further documents[14] that addressed theological 'abuses'.
He never hesitated in disciplining those theologians whom he perceived

---

11   Cf. J. Ratzinger, *Einführung in das Christentum. Vorlesungen über das Apostolische Glaubensbekenntnis.*
      München: Kösel-Verlag, 1968 (E.T.: *Introduction to Christianity.* London, 1969, ²1985); *Das neue Volk
      Gottes. Entwürfe zur Ekklesiologie.* Düsseldorf:Taschenbuchausgabe, 1969; and, Cf. J. Ratzinger, *Dogma
      und Verkündigung.* München:Wewel, 1973 (which has been translated only partially in English: *Dogma
      and Preaching.* Chicago: Franciscan Herald Press, 1985).

12   Cf. J. Ratzinger, *Eschatologie – Tod und ewiges Leben.* Regensburg: Pustet, 1977 (E.T.: *Eschatology, Death
      and Eternal Life.* Washington D.C.: Catholic University of America Press, 1988).

13   Cf. *Publik-Forum* 8 (1979) 23; *Ratzingers Antwort auf Rahner,* in *Publik-Forum* 9 (1980) 4, p. 16–17.

14   For the texts of the under-mentioned documents, cf.: www.vatican.va/roman_curia/congregations/
      cfaith/

to be dissident, for example, E. Schillebeeckx, L. Boff, C. Curran and J. Dupuis. Instructions appeared on topics such as liberation theology (*Libertatis Nuntius* [1984] and *Libertatis Conscientia* [1986]), and on medical ethics concerning human reproduction (*Donum Vitae* [1987]). He also reacted sharply to the reports of the Anglican-Roman Catholic International Commission ecumenical dialogue with the Anglicans (ARCIC I & II [resp. 1982 and 1988]). He formulated a mandatory profession of faith and an accompanying oath of fidelity for those who sought to take up a particular office on behalf of the Church (1988 and 1998). In 1990 he emphasized, in *Donum Veritatis*, the ecclesial vocation of the theologian in response to the 1989 Cologne Declaration and other theological protests against restorative tendencies in the church.

Ratzinger also issued documents on the pastoral care of homosexuals in the Church (1986), on the correct nature of Christian meditation (1989) and ones concerning the differing understandings of the Church as *communio* (1992). Further documents followed offering considerations about the Petrine office and the mystery of the Church (1998), and a note on the precise use of the term 'sister church' (2000). Also in 2000, the declaration *Dominus Iesus* appeared, addressing the topic of the unicity and salvific universality of Jesus and the Church. Later documents would feature guidelines on the participation of Christians in political life (2003), address legal initiatives concerning unions between homosexual persons (2003), and the collaboration between men and women in the Church and the world (2004). He was also president of the preparatory commission of the Catechism of the Catholic Church, which was finally promulgated in 1992 on the authority of Pope John Paul II.

Unlike his predecessors at the CDF, Ratzinger remained an active theologian in his own right. His most important theological publications from this time include *Theologische Prinzipienlehre* (1982), *Kirche, Ökumene und Politik* (1987), *Wesen und Auftrag der Theologie* (1993), *Der Geist der Liturgie* (2000) and *Werte in Zeiten des Umbruchs* (2005).[15] Furthermore, many of his publications as private theologian were intended to clarify

---

15 *Theologische Prinzipienlehre. Bausteine zur Fundamentaltheologie.* München: Wewel, 1982 (E.T.: *Principles of Catholic Theology: Building Stones for a Fundamental Theology.* San Francisco: Ignatius Press, 1987); *Kirche, Ökumene und Politik. Neue Versuche zur Ekklesiologie.* Einsiedeln, Freiburg im Breisgau: Johannes Verlag, [1-2]1987 (E.T.: *Church, Ecumenism and Politics. New Essays in Ecclesiology.* New York: Crossroad 1988 and also San Francisco, Ignatius Press, 2008 and, with a different trans., Slough: St. Paul Publications, 1988); *Wesen und Auftrag der Theologie* Einsiedeln, Freiburg im Breisgau: Johannes Verlag, 1993 (E.T.: *The Nature and Mission of Theology: Essays to Orient Theology in Today's Debates.* San Francisco: Ignatius Press, 1995); *Der Geist der Liturgie. Eine Einführung.* Freiburg im Breisgau: Verlag Herder, [1-2-3-4-5]2000, [6]2002 (E.T.: *The Spirit of the Liturgy.* San Francisco: Ignatius Press, 2000); *Werte in Zeiten des Umbruchs. Die Herausforderungen der Zukunft bestehen.* Freiburg im Breisgau: Verlag Herder, 2005 (E.T.: *Values in a Time of Upheaval.* San Francisco: Ignatius Press, 2006).

and defend magisterial positions, for example, his vigorous defence of the two documents of the CDF on liberation theology and also of that on medical ethics.[16]

Through such private publications, he also explained his difficulties with the ARCIC documents and offered his reflections on the role of the woman in the Church on the occasion of the apostolic letter, *Ordinatio Sacerdotalis* (1994). In addition, the encyclicals *Splendor Veritatis* (1993), *Evangelium Vitae* (1995) *Fides et Ratio* (1998), *Ecclesia de Eucharistia* (2003), as well as the publication of the Catechism (1992) among others, enjoyed his full support. At the same time, he attempted to counter the steady erosion of Vatican authority. Some of the favourite themes of his writings on ecclesiology include: the primacy of the Pope, unity and plurality, magisterium and theology, the formation of priests, the statutes of the synod of bishops and the pastoral significance of the bishops conference, the relation between Church and politics and – in relation to interreligious dialogue – the uniqueness of Christ and the salvific necessity of the Church.

In the meantime, he also repeatedly stressed the necessity for a correct interpretation of the Second Vatican Council. These issues, particularly his assessment of the situation of the contemporary Church, also became the subject of regular and invited interviews, in which he spoke with outspoken candour. A number of these interviews have been published in book form.[17]

Throughout this period, he received several honorary doctorates, from, amongst others, the Catholic universities of Lima (1986), Eichstätt (1987), Lublin (1998), and Navarra (1999). His 'Schülerkreis' (scholarly circle comprising his former students), still meets regularly to this day and in 1987, they honoured him with the publication of the festschrift: *Weisheit Gottes – Weisheit der Welt*.[18] In 1998, Pope John Paul II appointed him Vice-Dean of the College of Cardinals; in 2002 he became Dean of the same College.

On 19 April 2005, Joseph Ratzinger was elected Pope during the

16   Cf. J. Ratzinger, *Vi spiego la teologia della liberazione*, in *30 Giorni* (March 1984) pp. 48–55; *Der Mensch zwischen Reproduktion und Schöpfung. Theologische Fragen zum Ursprung des menschlichen Lebens*, in *Internat. Kath. Zeitschr.* 18 (1989) 1, pp. 61–71.

17   Cf. J. Ratzinger and V. Messori, *Rapporto sulla fede*. Torino: Edizioni Paoline, 1985. (E.T.: *The Ratzinger Report*. San Francisco: Ignatius Press, 1985); J. Ratzinger, *Salz der Erde: Christentum und katholische Kirche an der Jahrtausendwende. Ein Gespräch mit Peter Seewald*. Stuttgart: DVA, [1-5]1996, [6-9]1997, [10]1998 (E.T.: *Salt of Earth: Christianity and the Catholic Church at the End of the Millenium. An Interview with Peter Seewald*. San Francisco: Ignatius Press, 1997); see also the autobiographical *Aus meinem Leben. Erinnerungen (1927–1977)*. Stuttgart: DVA, 1998 (E.T.: *Milestones. Memoirs (1927–1977)*. Ignatius Press: San Francisco, 1998).

18   W. Baier, *et al.*, (eds) *Weisheit Gottes – Weisheit der Welt*. St. Ottilien: EOS Verlag, 1987 (with as an annex an exhaustive bibliography: pp. 1–77).

fourth ballot in the Sistine Chapel. He chose the name Benedict XVI, signalling the tone of his pontificate as a continuation of that of the Pope of peace, Benedict XV, and to the patron saint of Europe and founder of the Benedictine order, Benedict of Nursia. His first two encyclicals were *Deus Caritas Est* (December 25, 2005) and *Spes Salvi* (30 November 2007). An encyclical on social teaching appeared in the summer of 2009: *Caritas in Veritate* (28 June 2009). Even as Pope, he has remained theologically active. For example, he has published a further monograph titled *Jesus of Nazareth*,[19] wherein he stresses the distinction between his public role as teacher and his personal theological work. 'It goes without saying that this book is in no way an exercise of the magisterium, but is solely an expression of my personal search "for the face of the Lord" (cf. Ps 27:8)'.[20] Many of his earlier works have been and continue to be republished, and many previously published articles have been edited into collections and published in various forms. In addition, there are references to publications and available texts on the internet, for example on his 'fan club' pages.[21]

'Only the truth will set you free'

There are perhaps many ways in which Joseph Ratzinger's theological position can be summarized, depending on the place from which one starts. For our part, we start with the soteriological impetus of his theology: it is only the truth of God that sets human beings free.

According to Ratzinger, to live a life of holiness is to live from the truth that God revealed through Jesus Christ. A Christian submits him or herself to the salvific truth, which is sanctifying in itself.[22] Whoever lives like this conforms themselves to the pre-ordained order of things and realizes that the human person is already constituted in an original

---

19   Cf. Joseph Ratzinger – Benedikt XVI, *Jesus von Nazareth: Von der Taufe im Jordan bis zur Verklärung.* Freiburg: Verlag Herder, 2007 (E.T.: Joseph Ratzinger – Benedict XVI. *Jesus of Nazareth: From the Baptism in the Jordan to the Transfiguration.* New York: Doubleday, 2007).

20   Ibid, p. xxiii.

21   Cf. http://www.popebenedictxvifanclub.com/

22   Ratzinger returns several times very explicitly to this point, in, among others: J. Ratzinger, 'Vorfragen zu einer Theologie der Erlösung', in L. Scheffczyk (ed.), *Erlösung und Emanzipation* (QD, 61). Freiburg: Herder, 1973, pp. 141–155; J. Ratzinger and U. Hommes, *Das Heil des Menschen. Innerweltlich – christlich* München: Kösel, 1975; and especially after 1983 in the discussion on liberation theology, in *Politik und Erlösung. Zum Verhältnis von Glaube, Rationalität und Irrationalem in der sogenannten Theologie der Befreiung.* Opladen: Rheinisch-Westfälische Akademie der Wissenschaften Vorträge G 279, 1986. See also his *Jesus Christus heute*, in *Internat. Kath. Zeitschr. Communio* 19 (1990) 56–70.

and fundamental relationship. This requires a rejection of human hubris, of the unjust prerogative of absolute self-determination, which leads to the principle of 'the subject's own truth'.[23]

It presupposes a true metanoia[24]: opening up in an attentive way to that which exceeds the human person and makes room for that One who is so much greater. In this way, discerning reason discovers the truth as love, as a person.[25]

Salvific truth was definitively revealed in Jesus Christ, the Son of God, as personal love beyond death and is articulated in the Christian tradition.[26] This truth is entrusted to the Church, the subject of faith. The human person cannot grant faith to him or herself, but receives it from the Church, which in turn does not have faith from herself. The Church watches over it that the truth remains the truth and that it is never lost sight of in the flow of time.[27] Finally, it is precisely in the sacraments, and more accurately in the sacramental structure of reality, that the unity of salvation and truth is expressed and realized.[28]

Ratzinger is acutely aware that the contemporary situation gives rise to many questions when it comes to living according to an already given truth. He also sees here a fundamental conflict between Christian faith and the foundations of modern thinking. After all, the latter is not the only one to claim the prerogative of absolute self-determination. Moreover, as he writes in his *Theologische Prinzipienlehre*, where previously the problem of the relation between 'being' and 'time' was solved in favour of 'being', after Hegel the case is that 'being' is 'time'. Truth becomes a function of time.[29] What was constitutive yesterday exists today only as that which

---

23 This means, among other things, that Ratzinger, in his reflections on salvation and truth, resolutely reacts against positivism, the liberal thinking on freedom, and Marxism; and later, after 1989, increasingly against libertarianism and relativism. Each time, it is about arbitrary attempts by the human person to self-realize truth, happiness, future, salvation, etc. and to pass over the truth of faith that all these elements are to be received in the first place (alongside the already cited sources, see also: J. Ratzinger, *Die christliche Brüderlichkeit*. München: Kösel-Verlag, 1960; *Entretien sur la foi*. Paris: Fayard, 1985; *Werte in Zeiten des Umbruchs. Die Herausforderungen der Zukunft bestehen*. Freiburg im Breisgau: Herder, 2005).

24 Cf. J. Ratzinger, *Theologische Prinzipienlehre*, pp. 57–69. Published earlier as: *Metanoia als Grundbefindlichkeit christlicher Existenz*, in E. C. Suttner (ed.), *Busse und Beichte. Drittes Regensburger Ökumenisches Symposion*. Regensburg, 1972, pp. 21–37.

25 Cf. J. Ratzinger, *Interpretation – Kontemplation – Aktion. Überlegungen zum Auftrag einer Katholischen Akademie*, in *Internat. Kath. Zeitschr. Communio* 12 (1983), p. 170.

26 Cf. J. Ratzinger, *Eschatologie – Tod und ewiges Leben* (Kleine Katholische Dogmatik, 9). Regensburg: Pustet, 1977.

27 Ratzinger develops this last point forcefully in his previously mentioned *Principles of Catholic Theology*.

28 Here, see J. Ratzinger, *Die sakramentale Begründung christlicher Existenz*. Meitingen: Kyrios, 1966.

29 The *Logos* finds itself again, becomes itself in history. All truth unfolding in history is understood as a single moment of the whole truth. Particular unfoldings are true during the time span of their unfolding and can only remain true if one leaves them at the end of that time and integrates it

has been assimilated into today's truth. Ratzinger sets himself the task of demonstrating that the human person is given an original truth that, despite all cultural mediations, always *remains* true because s/he *is* true.

In his reflections on this problem, he provides concrete answers to two sets of questions. On the one hand, how does the eternally and universally valid truth relate to the form in which it took shape in history and its subsequent transmissions? And, what has been the role of the cultural baggage that converts from diverse cultures contributed? What should a responsible hermeneutics that wants to preserve the specifics of Christianity look like? On the other hand, what is the role of the Church and, more particularly, of its teaching authority, in all of this? What is the particular task of theology in this regard? The first set of questions occupied Ratzinger primarily in the first period of his theological career.

As Prefect of the Congregation for the Doctrine of the Faith, he has a particular interest in the second set of questions. He dedicates a great deal of time to clarifying the function of the papal teaching authority and, consequently, limits the competence of bishops, bishops' conferences, and theologians.[30] What remains is the basic conviction that it is about salvific truth, granted by God and not given over to the free disposal of the human person. This is truth to live from, leading to eternal life. The only suitable response to this is an attitude of diffidence. One should never forget what is really at stake: the salvation of the believing person.

This broad but nevertheless focused and consistent theological spectrum will be dealt with in this book through a selection of carefully chosen texts.

Both Church Leader and Theologian Concurrently?

In this book, we above all intend to bring to the fore the main lines of the work of Ratzinger, the theologian. Hence, as already mentioned in the Preface, we have drawn nothing from the documents that he prepared and/or signed in his offices as Archbishop, Prefect, and Pope. Clearly, it is worth questioning whether this distinction, and particularly that of Prefect and theologian, can be so strictly demarcated. The then cardinal

---

into the whole that continually reconstructs itself – Cf. J. Ratzinger, *Principles of Catholic Theology: Building Stones for a Fundamental Theology*. San Francisco: Ignatius Press, 1987, pp 16–17. The original title of these contributions (pp. 15–27): "Was ist für den christlichen Glauben heute konstitutiv?", in H. Rossmann and J. Ratzinger (eds), *Mysterium der Gnade*. Regensburg: Pustet, 1975, pp. 11–19.

30   See among others his: J. Ratzinger, *Kirche, Ökumene und Politik. Neue Versuche zur Ekklesiologie*. Einsiedeln: Johannes Verlag, 1987; Idem, *Wesen und Auftrag der Theologie*. Einsiedeln: Johannes Verlag, 1993.

Ratzinger himself said in an interview with *Herder Korrespondenz* that there is a real danger that a prefect, who also wishes to be a theologian, confuses the roles.[31] Nevertheless, he explained that two things help to resolve this: first, by not publishing in a personal capacity anything related to the subject matter of a case pending at the congregation, and second, by strictly adhering to the objectivity of the procedures to be followed, e.g. in investigations of the work of theologians.

It is not quite clear if the distinction of prefect–theologian is here accurately delimited. Two examples might indicate the blurring of the distinction. In an interview the cardinal permitted to Vittorio Messori, Ratzinger spoke, according to Pope John Paul II at least, as a theologian and not in his capacity as prefect.[32] However, the journalist recounts at the beginning the unparalleled opportunity of being granted this interview: after all 'it should be considered that no other personage in the Church – apart from the Pope, of course – could answer our questions with greater authority'.[33] Moreover, if we take into consideration the fact that this book appeared right before the special synod of bishops, which convened in 1985 to evaluate Vatican II after twenty years, then a little doubt is somewhat justified.

Our second example concerns his personal reflections on liberation theology. The text of the first instruction on liberation theology was leaked to the press and published in *Trenta Giorni* prior to its official promulgation, thereby revealing the Prefect's position in the document.[34] Moreover, we have already indicated that many of Ratzinger's later articles dealt with theological issues, but especially with problems of internal ecclesial politics, in which he quite clearly stated his position on specific issues. A perusal of his publications from this period offers a behind-the-scenes insight into the dynamics of Church politics and a deeper insight into the context and the general vision '. . . that lies behind the individual, official pronouncements and bans'.[35]

31   Cf. D. Seeber, "Gesicht und Aufgabe einer Glaubensbehörde. Ein Gespräch mit Joseph Kardinal Ratzinger über die römische Glaubenskongregation", in *Herderkorrespondenz*, 38 (1984), p 364.

32   Cf. P. Hebblethwaite, *Synod Extraordinary. The Inside Story of the Roman Synod November-December, 1985*. Doubleday, 1986, p. 52: 'Pope John Paul said in the plane on the way back from Africa on August 19 (1985): "What Cardinal Ratzinger says is his own opinion. He is free to express his own opinion"'.

33   J. Ratzinger and V. Messori, *The Ratzinger Report*. San Francisco: Ignatius Press, 1985, p. 10; and in this text, Messori goes further: '. . . the Congregation for the Doctrine of the Faith is the instrument through which the Holy See promotes the deepening of faith and watches vigilantly over its purity. Accordingly, it is the custodian proper of Catholic orthodoxy'.

34   J. Ratzinger, *Vi spiego la teologia della liberazione*, in *30 giorni* (Marchaart 1984) pp. 48–55, taken over in a slightly altered version in the previously mentioned *The Ratzinger Report*, pp. 24–234.

35   P. Hebblethwaite, *Inside the Vatican*. London: Sidgwick and Jackson, 1986, p. 89.

The question about the appropriateness of a bishop, prefect, and pope who remains a theologian at the same time is not easy to answer. The disadvantages are obvious: under the pretext of rendering a strictly personal opinion, a number of pronouncements are given greater authority than they deserve. On the other hand, the personal, theological expressions nonetheless offer a backdrop to how official Roman decisions and certain positions are arrived at. Moreover, it makes it possible to enter into a discussion on a theological level and even exert criticism of his opinions, which the Pope went so far as to invite in his introduction to *Jesus of Nazareth*.

Is there a Ratzinger I and a Ratzinger II? The Question of the Theological 'Volta-faccia'

In 1978, Roberto Tura was already dividing Ratzinger's theological work into two periods: he talks about *un primo Ratzinger* and *un secondo Ratzinger*.[36] Others present it as if he made a 180-degree turn. It is certainly true that in the second half of the 1960s Ratzinger's theological position is somewhat adjusted, and that shifts appear over the years. It is also certain that Ratzinger at the time of the Council took positions that he later no longer holds. Nevertheless, in our opinion, a fundamental continuity is noticeable. Rather, it is the severe tone and polemical writing style that distinguish a number of his later works from the earlier writings.

His earliest articles are clearly characterized by a certain openness to Church reform and to *rapprochement* with the world. He spoke about how Christian life in the Church should be determined by the basic polarities of, on the one hand, the forthrightness to testify to the purity of the Church – which can include condemnation – and on the other, obedience to the Church.[37] He wrote articles on collegiality; did not exclude the idea of a permanent bishops' council, yet framed it strictly within the hierarchical-sacramental framework.[38]

Concerning the *rapprochement* with the world, even in his early

---

36 R. Tura, 'Joseph Ratzinger', in P. Vanzan and H. J. Schultz (eds), *Lessico dei Teologi del seculo XX* (Mysterium Salutis: Supplementum). Brescia, 1978, pp. 750–752.

37 Cf. J. Ratzinger, *Freimut und Gehorsam. Das Verhältnis des Christen zu seiner Kirche*.

38 Cf. J. Ratzinger, *Die bischöfliche Kollegialität. Theologische Entfaltung*, in G. Barauna (ed.), *De Ecclesia. Beitrage Zur Konstitution "Uber de Kirche" des.* 2 *Vatikanischen Konzils*. Bd. II. Herder: Freiburg/Frankfurt, 1966, pp. 44–70; *Die pastoralen Implikationen der Lehre von der Kollegialität der Bischöfe*, in *Concilium* 1 (1965) pp. 16–29 (both included in *Das neue Volk Gottes*, resp. pp. 171–200 and 201–224); as the idea of a bishops' council did not appear before 'Primat und Episkopat', in *Das neue Volk Gottes*, pp. 121–146, 143–144. E.g. 'Bischofsrat und andere Formen der Kollegialität bieten die Möglichkeit, die Erfordernisse der Pluralität und der Einheit möglichst einander anzunähern', among others.

writings, one hears the warning that the theology of the incarnation can never be regarded without the theology of the cross.[39] Very soon after the Council, Ratzinger became suspicious of his fellow theologians and the post-conciliar developments in theology and the Church and his pessimism increased over the years. This is underscored by his recounting of the story of 'Clever Hans' (who loses a gold nugget on his way home), to represent the state of the Christian faith in the modern era.[40] Furthermore, his continuous and ever more severe assessment of the content and reception of *Gaudium et Spes* in the post-conciliar Church also demonstrates this progression.[41]

Nonetheless, as claimed in our summary of his thinking, Ratzinger's theological insights have not fundamentally changed, but have rather demonstrated a firm internal consistency throughout more than fifty years. With the choice of the texts in this book, we hope to underline this point further. His early researches on Augustine and Bonaventure and the deepening of the underlying thoughts he developed then can be said to be determinative of the way in which he understands the relation between God and humanity, Church and world, faith and reason, truth and time, tradition and history. However, over the course of time he does stress different accents, particularly concerning his conviction that Vatican II has been interpreted and put into practice in an erroneous fashion. For Ratzinger, the Council has been used as a license for far too extensive changes.

Once he came to be convinced of this position, Ratzinger abandoned his attitude of moderate reformist and took up the defence of a Catholicism under threat that, in his opinion, has sold out to modernity. As has been said, from this point on, he began to articulate his views more sharply and radically, and he explicitly sought to express his thoughts and convictions in a polemical fashion. Precisely because of this style, his positions on ecclesial governance, structures and authority have been transformed as well.[42] The Church must defend itself with ever-greater force against the threat of modernity.

39   Cf. J. Ratzinger, 'Sentire Ecclesiam', in *Geist und Leben* 36 (1963) pp. 321–326.
40   Cf. his preface to the previously mentioned *Einführung in das Christentum*.
41   In this regard, see Chapter Four of this volume.
42   See Chapter Three of this volume.

CHAPTER 1

THEOLOGICAL FOUNDATIONS: REVELATION, TRADITION AND HERMENEUTICS

Lieven Boeve

Introduction

In this chapter, we first shed some light on the concept of revelation that Ratzinger developed at the time of the Second Vatican Council. Afterwards we will present his thoughts on the development of tradition and the hermeneutics of scripture and tradition. We will pay special attention to his elaborations on the creative, providential synthesis Christianity established during the patristic period between Christian faith and Hellenistic thinking, and the problems for biblical and theological hermeneutics that occur when Christianity (including this synthesis) is confronted with modernity.

1.1 Revelation, Scripture and Tradition

In one of his earliest articles in 1958, which stemmed from the period after he finished his doctoral dissertation on Augustine and the conclusion of his habilitation thesis on Bonaventure, Joseph Ratzinger was already speaking about revelation, scripture, and tradition.[1] Beginning with a reflection on Bonaventure, and in dialogue with Thomas Aquinas, the rule of Benedict, and the works of Augustine, Ratzinger takes a position in the discussion concerning the material sources of revelation. He raises questions concerning the idea that tradition would be the second material principle next to scripture. To that end, he turns to Bonaventure's concept of dynamic revelation. After all, revelation cannot be fixed and objectified from outside but is an (at least partially – he carefully adds) internal event.[2] Revelation, as the turning of God toward humanity, effectively continues to this day – even after the closure of objective revelation. It is therefore

---

1 Cf. J. Ratzinger, 'Offenbarung – Schrift – Überlieferung. Ein Text des heiligen Bonaventura und seine Bedeutung für die gegenwärtige Theologie', in *Trierer Theologische Zeitschrift* 67 (1958), pp. 13–27.
2 Ibid., p 26.

necessary to understand scripture and tradition from this dynamic concept of revelation. Only in this way can the theological discussions mired in controversy productively gain new perspectives necessary for creative development.

Ratzinger adopts a similar position during the Council in his booklet *Revelation and Tradition*,[3] published with Karl Rahner in 1965. Here he again advocates that only when scripture and tradition as 'positive' sources are brought into relation with their 'internal source' (revelation) can the pre-conciliar questions influenced by the controversies with the protestants be answered. To this end, he unfolds five theses, concisely presented below. In the following we quote from this booklet, and for the sake of the argument, we have integrated the fragments into an overall presentation of the structure of the text.

Thesis 1: According to Ratzinger, the Christian tradition exists by the grace of the fact that there is incongruence between revelation and scripture. Scripture is exceeded by revelation in a twofold manner: from above by God's speaking and acting; from below by what revelation realizes in the faith event itself, beyond the boundaries of scripture.

> A first thesis on this set of problems might be formulated as follows, bearing in mind the patristic conception of scripture and revelation. The fact that 'tradition' exists is primarily based on the non-identity of the two realities, 'revelation' and 'scripture'.[4] Revelation means God's whole speech and action with man; it signifies a reality which scripture makes known but which is not itself simply identical with scripture. Revelation, therefore, is more than scripture to the extent that reality exceeds information about it.[5] It might also be said that scripture is the material principle of revelation (perhaps the only one, perhaps one side by side with others – a question that can be left open for the moment), but that it is not revelation itself. [. . .]

3   Cf. K. Rahner and J. Ratzinger, *Offenbarung und Überlieferung* (QD 25). Freiburg: Herder, 1965 (E.T.: *Revelation and Tradition*. New York: Herder and Herder, 1966). After a first contribution by Rahner, Ratzinger develops, as a second part (pp. 25–49), a systematic theological reflection on the concept 'tradition'. For the third part, which is a rather historical-theological contribution, he writes 'On the Interpretation of the Tridentine Decree on Tradition' (pp. 50–66).

4   [Selection of texts from K. Rahner and J. Ratzinger, *Revelation and Tradition*. New York: Herder and Herder, 1966, pp. 35–37, 40–41, 45–46].

5   This statement is not meant in a sense that would make scripture simply an unsubstantial report of facts that remain entirely external to it. On the contrary, it should remain abundantly clear (as we hope what follows will show) that the reality of revelation is a 'word-reality', and that in the word of preaching the reality of revelation comes to the individual. The fact remains, however, that the mere presence of the word of scripture is not the reality of revelation itself, which is never simply 'there'. The above remark is simply meant to draw attention to the difference between scripture and the reality, which makes itself known in scripture, a difference which is not annulled by the verbal character of revelation.

There can be scripture without revelation. For revelation always and only becomes a reality where there is faith. The unbeliever remains under the veil of which Paul speaks in 2 Corinthians 3⁶. He can read scripture and know what it contains. He can even understand, purely conceptually, what is meant and how its statements cohere, yet he has no share in the revelation. Revelation is in fact fully present only when, in addition to the material statements which testify to it, its own inner reality is itself operative in the form of faith. Consequently revelation to some degree includes its recipient, without whom it does not exist. Revelation cannot be pocketed like a book one carries around. It is a living reality which calls for the living man as the location of its presence.

In view of what has been said, we may, therefore, affirm that revelation goes beyond the fact of scripture in two respects: as a reality deriving from God it always extends upwards into God's action; as a reality which makes itself known to man in faith, it also extends beyond the fact of scripture which serves to mediate it.

This non-coincidence of scripture and revelation makes it clear that quite apart from the question whether scripture is the sole material source or not, there can never really, properly speaking, be a sola scriptura in regard to Christianity. As we have already said, that was still clear in principle to the great Reformers, and only fell into oblivion in what has been called Protestant orthodoxy. Scripture is not revelation but at most only a part of the latter's greater reality.

Thesis 2: For the early Christians the Old Testament remains scripture, but is read from the perspective of the Christ event, which is experienced as the fulfillment of scripture. In Jesus Christ, scripture is completed and exceeded. It ceases to exist as *gramma*, i.e. objectifiable, closed, and completed revelation. Christ, as *pneuma*, reveals its true and living content and meaning.[7]

Thesis 3: In the strict sense, only Jesus Christ is the revelation of God. To receive revelation then means to enter into the reality of the Christ-mystery. Scripture is not revelation but testifies that revelation essentially has to do with faith and the Church.

The actual reality which occurs in Christian revelation is nothing and no other than Christ himself. He is revelation in the proper sense: 'He who has seen me, has seen the Father', Christ says in John (14:9). This means that the reception of revelation is equivalent to entering into the Christ-reality, the source of that double

---

6   Cf. on this point the important article by A. Oepke, 'ἀποχαλύπτω', in *Theologisches Worterbuch zum Neuen Testament*, vol. III (1938), pp. 565–597.

7   In this regard, Ratzinger refers to 2 Cor 3:6-18. Paul argues that scripture – the law – kills exactly because of this objectification. The *pneuma* causes life, 'for the letter kills, but the Spirit gives life' (2 Cor 3:6).

state of affairs which Paul alternately describes with the words 'Christ in us' and 'we in Christ'. [. . .]

The reception of revelation, in which the Christ-reality becomes ours, is called in biblical language 'faith'. From this point of view perhaps it is clearer why, for the New Testament, faith is equivalent to the indwelling of Christ. If we firmly hold that for scripture the presence of revelation is equivalent to the presence of Christ, a further step follows. We find the presence of Christ designated in two further ways. It appears on the one hand, as we have already seen, identical with the faith (Eph 3:17), in which the individual encounters Christ and in him enters the sphere of influence of his saving power. But it is also hidden under the Pauline term of 'Body of Christ' which of course implies that the community of the faithful, the Church, represents Christ's continued abiding in this world in order to gather men into, and make them share, his mighty presence.[8] These two aspects taken together mean, therefore, that faith is entry into Christ's presence, into the abiding reality of Christ to which scripture bears witness but with which scripture itself is not simply and solely identical. It also follows that the presence of revelation is essentially connected with the two realities 'faith' and 'Church', which themselves, as is now clear, are closely connected. This in turn leads back to what was stated in the first thesis, that revelation goes beyond scripture in two respects, in relation to God and in relation to its human recipient. That statement, which at first was rather indefinite, is now found to possess an essentially concrete meaning in relation to actual Christian realities.

Thesis 4: What then is tradition? This is essentially the explanation of the 'Christ-reality' in a twofold way: an explanation of the Old Testament from the Christ-event and of the Christ-event itself from the *pneuma*, i.e. from the ecclesial present. After all, Christ lives in his Church, which is his body, and in which his Spirit works. From this follows that there are three sources and four levels of tradition.

Summarizing what has been said, we can now observe several sources of the reality called 'tradition' and, consequently, several strata within it.

First source: The extent to which the reality of 'revelation' is more than 'scripture'.

Second source: The specific character of New Testament revelation as pneuma, as opposed to gramma, and consequently what one might call in Bultmann's terminology, the impossibility of objectivizing it. This state of affairs has been expressed in the Church's practice and, as a consequence, in mediaeval theology, by the placing of fides above scriptura, that is to say, of the creed as rule of faith above the details of what is written.[9] The creed appears as the

8   H. Schlier, 'Die Kirche nach dem Brief an die Epheser' in *Die Zeit der Kirche* (3, 1962), pp. 159–186.
9   On this question, the best that has been said as regards to the Fathers will still be found in A.V. Harnack, *Lehrbuch der Dogmengeschichte*, v. 2. Freiburg: Akademische Verlagsbuchhandlung von

hermeneutical key to scripture which without interpretation must ultimately remain dumb.

Third source: The character of the Christ-event as present and the authoritative enduring presence of Christ's Spirit in his Body the Church and, connected with this, the authority to interpret Christ yesterday in relation to Christ today, the origin of which we have observed in the Church's reinterpretation by the apostles of the message of the kingdom.

Corresponding to these three sources of the concept of tradition (or, better, of the reality which we term tradition), the following strata in tradition can perhaps be discerned.

(i) At the beginning of all tradition stands the fact that the Father gives the Son over to the world and that the Son for his part allows himself to be given over to the 'nations', as a sign. This original *paradosis*, in its character as judgment and gift of salvation, is continued in the abiding presence of Christ in his Body, the Church. To that extent the whole mystery of Christ's continuing presence is primarily the whole reality which is transmitted in tradition, the decisive fundamental reality which is antecedent to all particular explicit expressions of it, even those of scripture, and which represents what has in fact to be handed down.

(ii) Tradition then exists concretely as presence in faith, which again, as the in-dwelling of Christ, is antecedent to all its particular explicit formulations and is fertile and living, thus developing and unfolding throughout the ages.

(iii) The organ of tradition is the authority of the Church, that is, those who have authority in it.[10]

(iv) Tradition also exists, however, as actually expressed in what has already become a rule of faith (creed, *fides quae*), by the authority of faith. The question whether certain express affirmations were transmitted from the beginning side by side with scripture, whether, therefore, there is a second

J.C.B. Mohr, [5]1931, pp. 84–116. Harnack actually says, p. 87, note 3: 'The "Canon" was originally the rule of faith; scripture has in truth intervened, yet in such a way that its authority had a significance lying still further back, namely, in the Old Testament and the words of the Lord'. I have tried to show that this was still true in the Middle Ages, and that here (together with the concept of *revelatio*, which will be dealt with in the next chapter) the placing of '*fides*' (the creed) higher than *scriptura* represents the essential form of the idea of tradition. See my essay: 'Wesen und Weisen der auctoritas im Werk des heiligen Bonaventura' in Corsten, Frotz and Linden (eds), *Die Kirche und ihre Ämter und Stände, Festgabe Kardinal Frings*. Köln: Bachem, 1960, pp. 58–72.

10   This line of thought cannot be developed in greater detail here, as it really needs to be, for we are only concerned with indicating the basis of the concept of tradition. In view of the limitation of the theme, I have been content in the preceding theses to develop the matter to the point where it becomes evident that tradition is concerned with the 'Church' (cf. theses 4 and 5). What that means could only be explained in more precise terms by an analysis of the concept of the Church, which must be taken for granted here. Cf. my article on ministry and unity of the Church mentioned in note 6 above; in it I attempted a few observations on the matter.

material principle besides scripture, independent from the beginning, becomes quite secondary in comparison; but it would probably have to be answered negatively.

Thesis 5: The function of exegesis has to be seen from the given that tradition, within whose authority the Church participates, is essentially an explanation 'according to scripture.' Concerning the ecclesial explanation of scripture in tradition, there exists, complementary to the 'safeguarding function of the Church and her witness under the Spirit', the safeguarding function of exegesis. Ratzinger even sees therein an expression of the autonomy of scripture vis-à-vis the ecclesial teaching office, since what can be demonstrated univocally through scientific exegesis should be seen as a criterion of truth that the magisterium should also take into account.

1.2 The Formation of Tradition

We now go deeper into Ratzinger's vision of the concrete form that tradition has adopted and its significance for faith and theology today. (a) First, we discuss the question of how far the Hellenistic culture in which the Christians of the first century lived co-determined the specific form of Christianity. Especially important in this regard is the conversation with Greek philosophy. (b) Then we investigate the significance of the Church Fathers for contemporary theology. (c) Finally, we look at dogma and Ratzinger's view on dogmatic hermeneutics.

(a) The God of Faith and the God of the Greek Philosophers

In Chapter 3 of his *Introduction to Christianity*, Ratzinger recounts how Jewish-Christian faith and Greek thinking found each other in the first centuries of Christianity. Christianity chooses the God of reason over the gods of mythology. In its conversation with reason, Christian theology not only borrows from Greek thought about God but also changes it to suit its purposes: to assist faith in the biblical God by reason. For Ratzinger, the decision of the early Christians is still of major importance, and is therefore to be qualified as providential.[11]

11   Ratzinger already begins to develop this idea in 1959 in his 'Antrittsvorlesung' in J. Ratzinger, *Der Gott des Glaubens und der Gott der Philosophen. Ein Beitrag zum Problem der theologia naturalis.* Leutesdorf: Johannes, 2nd edn. 2005 (1959), pp. 11–35.

1. The decision of the early church in favour of philosophy[12]

[. . .] Christianity boldly and resolutely made its choice and carried out its purification by deciding *for* the God of the philosophers and *against* the gods of the various religions. Wherever the question arose as to which god the Christian God corresponded, Zeus perhaps or Hermes or Dionysus or some other god, the answer ran: To none of them. To none of the gods to whom, you pray but solely and alone to him to whom you do not pray, to that highest being of whom your philosophers speak. The early Church resolutely put aside the whole cosmos of the ancient religions, regarding the whole of it as deceit and illusion, and explained its faith by saying: When we say God, we do not mean or worship any of this; we mean only Being itself, what the philosophers have expounded as the ground of all being, as the God above all powers – that alone is our God. This proceeding involved a choice, a decision, no less fateful and formative for ages to come than the choice of El and *yah* as opposed to Moloch and Baal had been in its time, with the subsequent development of the two into Elohim and toward Yahweh, the idea of Being. The choice thus made meant opting for the *logos* as against any kind of myth; it meant the definitive demythologization of the world and of religion.

Was this decision for the *logos* rather than the myth the right one? To find the answer to this we must keep in view all our previous reflections on the inner development of the biblical concept of God, the last stages of which had in essentials already determined that the position to be taken up by Christianity in the Hellenistic world should be this one. On the other side, it must be noted that the ancient world itself knew the dilemma between the God of faith and the God of the philosophers in a very pronounced form. Between the mythical gods of the religions and the philosophical knowledge of God there had developed in the course of history a stronger and stronger tension, which is apparent in the criticism of the myths by the philosophers from Xenophanes to Plato, who even thought of trying to replace the classical Homeric mythology with a new mythology appropriate to the *logos*. Contemporary scholarship is coming to see more and more clearly that there are quite amazing parallels in chronology and content between the philosophers' criticism of the myths in Greece and the prophets' criticism of the gods in Israel. It is true that the two movements start from completely different assumptions and have completely different aims; but the movement of the *logos* against the myth, as it evolved in the Greek mind in the philosophical enlightenment, so that in the end it necessarily led to the fall of the gods, has an inner parallelism with the enlightenment that the prophetic and Wisdom literature cultivated in its demythologization of the divine powers in favor of the one and only God. For all the differences between them, both movements coincide in their striving toward the *logos*. [. . .]

---

12   [Selection from J. Ratzinger, *Introduction to Christianity*. San Francisco: Ignatius Press, 2004, pp. 137–141, 143–144, 147–148.]

The opposing fates of myth and Gospel in the ancient world, the end of myth and the victory of the Gospel, are fundamentally to be explained, from the point of view of intellectual history, by the opposing relationship established in either instance between religion and philosophy, between faith and reason. The paradox of ancient philosophy consists, from the point of view of religious history, in the fact that intellectually it destroyed myth but simultaneously tried to legitimize it afresh as religion; in other words, that from the religious point of view it was not revolutionary but, at the most, evolutionary, that it treated religion as a question of the regulation of life, not as a question of truth. [. . .]

Religion did not go the way of the *logos* but lingered in myths already seen to be devoid of reality. Consequently its decline was inevitable; this followed from its divorce from the truth, a state of affairs that led to its being regarded as a mere *institutio vitae*, that is, as a mere contrivance and an outward form of life. The Christian position, as opposed to this situation, is put emphatically by Tertullian when he says with splendid boldness: 'Christ called himself truth, not custom.'[13] In my view this is one of the really great assertions of patristic theology. In it the struggle of the early Church, and the abiding task with which the Christian faith is confronted if it is to remain itself, is summed up with unique conciseness [. . .]

2. The transformation of the God of the philosophers

Of course, the other side of the picture must not be overlooked. By deciding exclusively in favour of the God of the philosophers and logically declaring this God to be the God who speaks to man and to whom one can pray, the Christian faith gave a completely new significance to this God of the philosophers, removing him from the purely academic realm and thus profoundly transforming him. This God who had previously existed as something neutral, as the highest, culminating concept; this God who had been understood as pure Being or pure thought, circling around forever closed in upon itself without reaching over to man and his little world; this God of the philosophers, whose pure eternity and unchangeability had excluded any relation with the changeable and transitory, now appeared to the eye of faith as the God of men, who is not only thought of all thoughts, the eternal mathematics of the universe, but also *agape*, the power of creative love. In this sense there does exist in the Christian faith what Pascal experienced on the night when he wrote on a slip of paper that he henceforth kept sewn in the lining of his jacket the words: 'Fire. "God of Abraham, God of Isaac, God of Jacob", not "of the philosophers and scholars".'[14] He had encountered the burning

13   1 'Dominus noster Christus veritatem se, non consuetudinem cognominavit.' De virginibus velandis I, 1, in Corpus Christianorum seu nova Patrum collection (CChr) 2:1209.

14   The text of the 'Mémorial', as this slip of paper is called, is quoted in R. Guardini, *Christliches Bewusstsein* (2nd edn.). Munich: Kösel, 1950, pp. 47f.; on p. 23 there is a facsimile, reduced in size, of the original; cf. also Guardini's analysis on pp. 27–61. This is supplemented and corrected by

bush experience, as opposed to a God sinking back completely into the realm of mathematics, and had realized that the God who is the eternal geometry of the universe can only be this because he is creative love, because he is the burning bush from which a name issues forth, through which he enters the world of man. So in this sense there is the experience that the God of the philosophers is quite different from what the philosophers had thought him to be, though he does not thereby cease to be what they had discovered; that one only comes to know him properly when one realizes that he, the real truth and ground of all Being, is at one and the same time the God of faith, the God of men. [. . .]

To sum up, we can say that, in the deliberate connection with the God of the philosophers made by the Christian faith, purely philosophical thinking was transcended on two fundamental points:

a. *The philosophical God is essentially self-centered*: thought simply contemplating itself. The God of faith is basically defined by the category of relationship. He is creative fullness encompassing the whole. Thereby a completely new picture of the world, a completely new world order is established: the highest possibility of Being no longer seems to be the detachment of him who exists in himself and needs only himself. On the contrary, the highest mode of Being includes the element of relationship. It is hardly necessary to say what a revolution it must mean for the direction of man's existence when the supreme Being no longer appears as absolute, enclosed autarchy but turns out to be at the same time involvement, creative power, which creates and bears and loves other things [. . .]

b. *The philosophical God is pure thought*: he is based on the notion that thought and thought alone is divine. The God of faith, as thought, is also love. His image is based on the conviction that to love is divine.

The *logos* of the whole world, the creative original thought, is at the same time love; in fact this thought is creative because, as thought, it is love, and, as love, it is thought. It becomes apparent that truth and love are originally identical; that where they are completely realized they are not two parallel or even opposing realities but one, the one and only absolute. At this point it also becomes possible to glimpse the starting point of the confession of faith in the triune God.

H. Vorgrimler, 'Marginalien zur Kirchenrrommigkeii Pascals' in J. Daniélou and H. Vorgrimler (eds), *Sentire Ecclesiam*. Freiburg: Herder, 1961, pp. 371–406.

(b) *The Enduring Importance of the Fathers of the Church*

The establishment of the original and creative synthesis between Christian faith and Hellenistic philosophy, and thus of theology, is only one of the accomplishments of the Fathers of the Church. They are also responsible for the canon of scripture, the first creeds, and the constitutive forms of the liturgy. Because of these accomplishments, they have a lasting influence and normative importance for Christian faith and theology. The Fathers of the Church have indeed offered a first and constitutive 'response' to the offer of revelation ('the Word') in Christ as witnessed to in scripture. The following text illustrates this point.

> Word and response: the content of this formula by which we have attempted to express the relationship between scripture and the Fathers can be made more concrete from the perspective of history.[15] At the same time, it will become even clearer wherein lies the permanent value, the indispensability, of these ecumenical teachers of the faith whom we call Fathers of the Church. The uniqueness of their proto-response can be summarized in four fundamental facts.

> (a) The canon of Holy Scripture can be traced back to them, or, at least, to the undivided Church of the first centuries of which they were the representatives. It is through their efforts that precisely those books that today we call the 'New Testament' were chosen as such from among a multitude of other available literary texts, that the Greek canon of the Jewish Bible was joined to them as the 'Old Testament', that it was interpreted in terms of them and that, together, the two Testaments came to be known as 'Holy Scripture'. The establishment of the canon and the establishment of the early Church are one and the same process but viewed from different perspectives. A book was recognized as 'canonical' if it was sanctioned by the Church for use in public worship. By the Church: that meant that the numerous Eastern Churches which, in the beginning, each had her own custom with regard to liturgical reading, all came, in the end, to accept this one book.[16] The fact that a given book was selected while another was rejected presumes, however, a process of intellectual winnowing and deciding and a dramatic tension such as we can hardly conceive today when we read, on the one hand, the Gnostic gospels that aspired to become scripture and, on the other hand, the anti-Gnostic writings of the Fathers in which what seems to us such a clearly drawn dividing line then divided the Church in two and for the recognition of which she had to struggle and suffer.

15 [Selection from J Ratzinger *Principles of Catholic Theology: Building Stones for Fundamental Theology* (San Francisco, Ignatius Press, 1987), 148–152].

16 Cf. Alfred Adam, *Lehrbuch der Dogmengeschichte*. Gütersloh: Mohn, 1965, pp. 87–91.

By the end of the second century, this process of winnowing and deciding—Augustine compares it to the dividing of the waters above from the waters below by the vault that turned chaos into cosmos[17]—had already more or less come to an end, although its offshoots extended far into the following centuries, which expanded, deepened and gave final form to the earlier decisions. This means that the canon, as canon, would be inconceivable without the intellectual movement to which patristic theology bears witness. The canon is the product of this movement: to accept it is, therefore, of necessity to accept also those basic intellectual decisions that formed it. Word and response are here inseparably united—and this despite the fact that the Fathers were always careful to keep their response distinct from the proclaimed word in contrast to the intermingling of the two that was so characteristic of *gnosis* and appears, in a particularly classic manner, in the mixture of tradition and interpretation in the so-called Gospel of St. Thomas.[18] Where the writings of the New Testament are read as canon and the Old Testament is read as the Christian Bible, there we find ourselves in the intellectual ambience of the struggle of the first centuries; there we have as Fathers those who were then teachers of the Church.

(b) In selecting the writings that were to be recognized as constituting the Bible, the early Church made use of a norm that she designated, in her own words, as the κανὼν τῆς πίστεως, *regula fidei*. Certainly not the least of the functions of this canon was to lead to a discrimination between false and genuine sacred writings and, in this way, to help establish the canon of 'the' Scripture. The *regula*, for its part, continued to function in the many different *symbola*, whether conciliar or extraconciliar, in which the effort of the ancient Church to determine what actually constituted Christianity found its binding expression. In addition to her role in laying down the canon of the Bible, then, the Church of the Fathers may also be characterized as the time that gave birth to the fundamental *symbola* of all Christendom. As long as these *symbola* continue to be prayed, as long as Christianity continues to confess Jesus Christ as both God and man and to worship God as one God in three Persons, just as long are these Fathers its Fathers. When the 'basis' of the ecumenical council of the Church of Jesus Christ speaks of Jesus as 'God and Savior' and determines the mission of the Church as being, in the language of the doxology, 'to the glory of God the Father, the Son and the Holy Spirit',[19] the heritage of the great early Christian *symbola* is present in and basic to this new attempt at

17   St. Augustine, 'Confessionum Libri XIII', bk. 13, chap. 15, sec. 18 (pp. 251–252) and sec. 22 (pp. 253–254) in CChr 27 (1981); 'Enarratio in Ps. CIII', 8, in CChr 40 (1956): 1479.

18   Cf. J. B. Bauer, 'Echte Jesusworte?' in W. C. Ulnik (ed.), *Evangelien aus dem Nilsand*. Frankfurt: Verlag Heinrich Scheffler, 1960, pp. 108–150.

19   Wolfdieter Theurer, *Die trinitarische Basis des Ökumenischen Rates der Kirchen*. Bergen-Enkheim: Kaffke, 1967.

a kind of minimum-*symbolum*. Whenever the Church confesses her Lord in the words of the *symbolum*, she is always reminded of those who first made this confession of faith and, in the affirmation of faith that it signifies, likewise formulated the renunciation of a faith that was false.

(c) In the ancient Church, the reading of scripture and the confession of faith were primarily liturgical acts of the whole assembly gathered around the Risen Lord. That brings us to our third point: the ancient Church created the fundamental forms of the Christian liturgical service, which are to be regarded as the permanent basis and indispensable reference point of every liturgical renewal. The liturgical movement between the two world wars, which, in Catholic as well as in Protestant Christianity, led to a new concentration on the nature and form of the Christian liturgy, resulted, on both sides, in a decisive orientation toward the great liturgies of the ancient Church. Today, however, when so much of what was then hoped for has become a reality, a new tendency is making itself felt: the desire to compose for this technical age a liturgy that will not only transcend the exuberance of the Middle Ages but will also consider it necessary to begin again from the beginning and to free itself from the heritage of the ancient Church. If war is thereby declared on a certain archaism, a romantic glorification of antiquity that certainly existed in the liturgical movement, and, in its place, a spiritual freedom is proposed that would not be bound to antiquity and would not feel compelled to adopt what is old—if all this is true, we can only applaud it. But if the bond with the basic forms of ancient Christian prayer and ecclesial prayer through the centuries is thereby to be severed, we must be firm in our resistance. The findings of Protestant liturgists of our own time, who have long since made similar experiments and can speak from their own experience, can stand us in good stead here. Of the many judgments available to us, two will suffice. First, that of so unromantic a theologian as Wellhausen, who came to the conclusion that the Protestant liturgical service is, at bottom, Catholic, but with the heart cut out.[20] Secondly, the opinion of A. Benoît: 'The sixteenth century was too brutal in destroying the bridges that linked it to the past, and the liturgical tradition of Protestantism found itself, in consequence, not merely impoverished but reduced almost to nothing.'[21] Liturgical renewal that does not seek to disintegrate and destroy or to replace the unifying power of the liturgical service by a general antagonism cannot ignore the liturgical heritage of the patristic age. Benoît is right in summarizing his reflections on patrology and liturgy in the words: 'The return to the ancient tradition, to the tradition of the as yet undivided Church, is one of the ways that lead to unity.'[22]

---

20 Quoted in Wilhelm Averbeck, *Der Opfercharakter des Abendmahls in der neueren evangelischen Theologie.* Paderborn: Verlag Bonifacius Druckerei, 1967, p. 151.

21 Ibid., p. 75.

22 Ibid., p. 77.

(d) To these three facts—that we owe to the Church of the Fathers the canon of Scripture, the *symbola* and the basic forms of liturgical worship—a final comment may be added as a kind of appendix. By comprehending faith as a *philosophia* and placing it under the rubric *Credo ut intelligam*, the Fathers acknowledged their rational responsibility for the faith and thus created theology as we understand it today, despite all the differences in individual methodologies. This turning to a rational responsibility, moreover, is not to be regarded lightly. It was, in fact, the precondition for the survival of Christendom in the ancient West, and it is the precondition for the survival of the Christian way of life today and tomorrow. This 'rationalism' of the Fathers has been often enough criticized, but its critics have, nevertheless, been unable to abandon the course it set, as we see most clearly in the work of Karl Barth, with its radical protest against every effort to find rational explanations and its simultaneous and fascinating struggle to find a deep-rooted understanding of what God has revealed. Thus, by its very existence, theology will always be indebted to the Fathers and will have cause to return again and again to these masters. We have now considered the most important formal perspectives on which is based the lasting significance of the Fathers for contemporary theology and for every theology of the future. In many respects, it would be desirable now to begin again from the beginning in order to make the whole content as concrete as possible. We should discuss the problem of patristic exegesis;[23] we should comment on the structure of patristic thought, its unique union of biblical, liturgical and theological attitudes; we should deal with the question of the relationship between critical thinking and thinking based on faith. Some secondary, but not therefore unimportant, aspects of the questions should be included, for instance, the fact that, even in a purely historical way of thinking, no satisfactory conclusion can be reached if we place a vacuum between ourselves and the Bible and try to forget that the Bible comes to us by way of history. Only by acknowledging history can we transcend it. If we try to ignore it, we remain entangled in it;[24] we cannot possibly read the Bible in a way that is truly historical however much we may seem to be applying historical methods. In reality, we remain bound to the horizon of our own thinking and reflect only ourselves. But to do all this would be to exceed by far the limits of this small work. Instead, I should like to conclude these

---

23   Cf. especially, in this context, the various writings of Henri de Lubac and Jean Daniélou (especially *Sacramentum futuri*. Paris: Beauchesne, 1950); Rolf Gögler, *Zur Theologie des biblischen Wortes bei Origenes*. Düsseldorf: Patmos, 1963. See also the bibliographical material in all of the above.

24   Cf. A. Benoît, *L'Actualite des Peres de l'eglise*. Neuchatel: Delachaux & Niestle, 1961, pp. 29–30; pp. 56–57: 'Elle (= the Church) peut, par suite de l'ignorance de son histoire, se croire libre, libre d'entamer un dialogue immédiat et direct avec l'Écriture. Mais en fait parce que, sans qu'elle s'en rende compte, son passé pèse sur elle, elle en dependra presque totalement. Et plus cette dependance sera inconsciente, plus elle sera lourde et pesante' (p. 57).

reflections with the thought with which André Benoît concludes his important study of the relevance of the Fathers and with which I am in total agreement. He says there: 'The patrologist is, without doubt, the individual who studies the first centuries of the Church, but he should likewise be the individual who prepares the future of the Church. That, at least, is his mission.'[25] Indeed, working with the Fathers is not just a matter of cataloguing in a museum dedicated to what has been. The Fathers are the common past of all Christians. And in the rediscovery of this common possession lies the hope for the future of the Church, the task for her—and our—present.

(c) Doctrine and History: Dogma as a Community Constituting Linguistic Phenomenon

The unfolding of the truth revealed by God through Jesus Christ continues even after the period of the Church Fathers. Revelation takes on an historical character; is contained in human language and limited by the possibilities of that language.[26] However, the character of this truth possesses an eternal dimension; her historical shape is always conditioned by space and time. As such, this truth knows its own historical unfolding in tradition. 'The timeless is realized for men [sic] existing in time only through constantly renewed bonds with time . . . . The true task of the Church is to restate the timeless in the up-to-date conditions of time'.[27] At this point, it is interesting to recall Ratzinger's 1968 reflections on the status of dogmas and the task of dogmatic hermeneutics: dogma is a linguistic phenomenon that, as in every faith language, functions as a symbol – it refers to the other and as such, makes unity possible. At the same time, dogmas are linguistic phenomena formed throughout history and for that particular reason they cannot be put aside or changed by the faithful or by theologians; change becomes irreducibly part of a process through which the faith community ultimately mediates and is mediated.

'On the question concerning the historicity of dogmas'
We can very succinctly say what ['historicity of dogma'] entails in four summarising

25 Ibid., p. 84. In this connection, reference must be made again to the interesting reflections on the contemporary function of patrology in U. Wickert, 'Glauben und Denken bei Tertullian und Origenes', in *Zeitschrift für Theologie und Kirche 62* (1965) pp. 153–177.
26 [Selection from J. Ratzinger, 'Zur Frage nach der Geschichtlichkeit der Dogmen' in *Martyria, Leiturgia, Diakonia: FS Hermann Volk*. Oskar Semmelrotz (ed.), Mainz: Matthias-Grünewald, 1968, pp. 69–70. Translated by David Kirchhofer].
27 'The Changeable and Unchangeable in Theology', *Theological Digest* 10 (1962), p. 76.

theses that highlight the fruits of the previous considerations.

1. Dogma is essentially a phenomenon of language. Because its job is to bring about the community of the intellect through the community of the word, its emphasis lies just as much on the word as on the idea; the word is not an incidental and random accoutrement of dogma, but rather dogma is precisely there for the sake of the word, as the idea having its say.[28] This linguistic character of dogma simultaneously and inseparably establishes both dogma's particular form of historicity and its particular form of immutability.

2. Human language exists as a process of the history of language. As the self-expression of the historically existing human mind, language likewise needs tense-overlapping continuity through which it can effect understanding and facilitate the intellect's communication from the past, via the present, into the future, like change whose power is testified to in the language of each generation and in which it leaves its traces. Language without continuity would lose its function, as would language without the timeliness of new speech developments. At the same time it is true that language precludes the caprice of the individual while still needing and thriving on the individual's living, personal, speaking-with.[29]

3. As a phenomenon of language, dogma participates in the dual nature of language: continuity and identity. But it must also be a forward-looking proc-ess of new adoption and transformation. Thus, dogma is 'historical' in the twofold sense of this word: history implies continuity and unity as well as the open-ended process of progress and its transformations.

4. The boundaries of historicity, and of the possibility of transformation, thus lie (a) in the fact that Faith itself is only one and that therefore the language of Faith can only ever refer to that one, the one of which it is the language. They lie (b) in the fact that in cases where the modification of language may be necessary, not only can this not happen without the common struggling and shared suffering of individuals, but on the other hand it can also never happen as a result of just the caprice of the individual. The unifying function of the word can only be preserved if it is not left to private caprice, i.e., such a modification can only happen through the community, and then not without the individual, his courage and his patience. We need both of these in equal measure today in a situation in which, together with an epoch of the human intellect, an epoch of human language also seems to be coming to an end. Patience without courage remains without a future, and a courage that loses

---

28   Translator's comment: Ratzinger uses a play on words here in the German. Literally translated, dogma is for the sake of the word, as the coming-to-word (*Zu-Wort-Kommen*) of the idea.

29   Translators comment: The substantive of the verb *mitspreche*, is here literally translated as 'speaking-with' to preserve the reference to language. However, the noun *mitsprache* means co-determination, and so this meaning should be understood as implied in the term 'speaking-with'.

patience becomes destructive and cheats itself of its own work. To remain patient in courage and courageous in patience, this appears to be the real task of the hour. Only in this way can what Paul proclaimed to be Faith's perpetual mission also be fulfilled in our generation: 'so that together you may with one voice glorify the God and Father of our Lord Jesus Christ' (Rom 15:6).

According to Ratzinger, ecclesial dogmatic formulations thus form a community-shaping language phenomenon. The shape that the inaccessible has adopted in language can be coincidental; however, through its community-shaping character it has also become binding even if it needs to be explained repeatedly. A hermeneutics of tradition should therefore distinguish between what essentially belongs to the salvific truth – to be preserved in the received historical shape of the deposit of faith – and what can be ascribed to cultural mediation.

In interpreting the salvific truth, theology should not allow itself to be carried along by modern forms of tradition criticism that, in the name of enlightened reason, sanitize the tradition of all so-called irrational elements or that even reject all of tradition's authority. In the following, we elaborate on Ratzinger's critical observations in this regard.

1.3 Christian Faith Challenged by a Modern Context

The Scandal of Christian Faith in a Modern Context

'For people of all ages, the Christian faith is a scandal: that the eternal God concerns himself with us people and knows us, that the intangible has in the man Jesus become tangible, that the immortal one has suffered on the cross, that resurrection and eternal life awaits us mortals: this belief is an exhilarating prospect for humanity'.[30] It is because of this scandal that Christianity will be met by the criticisms of modernity.

Joseph Ratzinger becomes increasingly aware of the irreconcilability of a number of modernity's premises and the structure of Christian faith. In the following chapters of this reader, and particularly Chapter Two, this point will be the focus of attention. Ratzinger's great fear consists in the fact that because of this irreconcilability on the one hand, and the all-too-eager willingness of the faithful and theologians to adapt faith to modernity on the other, eventually Christian faith will be eroded. Much

---

30   Translated from J. Ratzinger, *Einführung in das Christentum* (*Introduction to Christianity*) – *Das neue Volk Gottes*, p. 317. This text (pp. 302–319), titled *Der Katholizismus nach dem Konzil – Katholische Sicht*, was Ratzinger's lecture at the *Katholikentag* in Bamberg in 1966, and was later published in *Auf Dein Wort hin. 81. Deutscher Katholikentag*. Paderborn, Bonifacius, 1966, 245-266.

of his work can therefore be understood as an ongoing concern and effort to defend the integrity of faith against modern adaptation.

An example that illustrates this concern of the loss of (the core of) tradition, which was previously mentioned in the Introduction of this volume, is found in Ratzinger's *Introduction to Christianity*, where he uses the fairy tale of 'Clever Hans' to underscore the threat for the Christian tradition in a modern context.

> The question of the real content and meaning of the Christian faith is enveloped today in a greater fog of uncertainty than at almost any earlier period in history.[31] Anyone who has watched the theological movement of the last decade and who is not one of those thoughtless people who always uncritically accept what is new as necessarily better might well feel reminded of the old story of 'Clever Hans'. The lump of gold that was too heavy and troublesome for him he exchanged successively, so as to be more comfortable, for a horse, a cow, a pig, a goose, and a whetstone, which he finally threw into the water, still without losing much; on the contrary, what he now gained in exchange, so he thought, was the precious gift of complete freedom. How long his intoxication lasted, how somber the moment of awakening from the illusion of his supposed liberation, is left by the story, as we know, to the imagination of the reader. The worried Christian of today is often bothered by questions like these: Has our theology in the last few years not taken in many ways a similar path? Has it not gradually watered down the demands of faith, which had been found all too demanding, always only so little that nothing important seemed to be lost, yet always so much that it was soon possible to venture on the next step? And will poor Hans, the Christian who trustingly let himself be led from exchange to exchange, from interpretation to interpretation, not really soon hold in his hand, instead of the gold with which he began, only a whetstone that he can safely be advised to throw away?
>
> To be sure, such questions are unfair if they are posed in too general terms. It is simply not correct to assert that 'modern theology' as a whole has taken a path of this sort. But it is just as undeniable that there is widespread support for a trend that does indeed lead from gold to whetstone. This trend cannot be countered, it is true, by merely sticking to the precious metal of the fixed formulas of days gone by, for then it remains just a lump of metal, a burden instead of something offering by virtue of its value the possibility of true freedom. This is where the present book comes in: its aim is to help understand faith afresh as something that makes possible true humanity in the world of today, to expound faith without changing it into the small coin of empty talk painfully laboring to hide a complete spiritual vacuum.

31   [Selection from J. Ratzinger, *Introduction to Christianity*. San Francisco: Ignatius Press, 2004, pp. 31–32].

The Dissonance Between Faith and Modernity.

What then is the real problem with Christian faith? Why is the plausibility of Christian faith the subject of discussion? Ratzinger seems to believe the fundamental issue is with its particular features, which he sees as being at odds with modern sensibilities. Firstly, Christian faith is about an invisible God in a world marked by visibility, and secondly, it is its past that is constitutive for the present. It is here that the peculiarity of the Christian scandal becomes all too apparent: the very positivity of Christian faith, of revelation, the fact that it is in the concrete history of a particular human being that God has comprehensively communicated and revealed in fullness Godself.

On top of the gulf between 'visible' and 'invisible' there comes, to make things harder for us, the gulf between 'then' and 'now'.[32] The basic paradox already present in belief as such is rendered even more profound by the fact that belief appears on the scene in the garb of days gone by and, indeed, seems itself to be something old-fashioned, the mode of life and existence current a long time ago. All attempts at modernization, whether intellectual, academic 'demythologiza-tion', or ecclesiastical, pragmatic *aggiornamento*, do not alter this fact; on the contrary, they strengthen the suspicion that a convulsive effort is being made to proclaim as contemporary something that is, after all, really a relic of days gone by. It is these attempts at modernization that first make us fully aware just how old-fashioned what we are being offered really is. Belief appears no longer as the bold but challenging leap out of the apparent 'all' of our visible world and into the apparent 'void' of the invisible and intangible; it looks much more like a demand to bind oneself to yesterday and to affirm it as eternally valid. And who wants to do that in an age when the idea of 'tradition' has been replaced by the idea of 'progress'?

We touch here on a specific element in our present situation that is of some importance to our question. For intellectual circles in the past, the concept of 'tradition' embraced a firm program; it appeared to be something protective on which man could rely; he could think himself safe and on the right lines if he could appeal to tradition. Today precisely the opposite feeling prevails: tradition appears to be what has been laid aside, the merely out-of-date, whereas progress is regarded as the real promise of life, so that man feels at home, not in the realm of tradition, of the past, but in the realm of progress and the future . . ... From this point of view, too, a belief that comes to him under the label 'tradition' must appear to be something already superseded, which cannot disclose the proper

32 [Selections from J. Ratzinger, *Biblical Interpretation in Crisis: the Ratzinger Conference on Bible and Church.* Grand Rapids: Wm. B. Eerdmans, 1989, pp. 4–5, 18–23].

sphere of his existence to a man who has recognized the future as his real obligation and opportunity. All this means that the primary stumbling block to belief,
the distance between the visible and the invisible, between God and Not-God,
is concealed and blocked by the secondary stumbling block of Then and Now,
by the antithesis between tradition and progress, by the loyalty to yesterday that
belief seems to include.

That neither the subtle intellectuals of demythologization nor the pragmatism of
the *aggiornamento* can supply a convincing solution certainly makes it clear that
this distortion of the basic scandal of Christian belief is itself a very far-reaching
affair that cannot be easily settled either by theories or by action. Indeed, in
one sense it is only here that the peculiarity of the specifically *Christian* scandal
becomes visible; I refer to what might be termed Christian positivism, the ineradicable positivity of Christianity. What I mean is this: Christian belief is not merely
concerned, as one might at first suspect from all the talk of belief or faith, with
the eternal, which as the 'entirely Other' would remain completely outside the
human world and time; on the contrary, it is much more concerned with God in
history, with God as man. By thus seeming to bridge the gulf between eternal
and temporal, between visible and invisible, by making us meet God as a man,
the eternal as the temporal as one of us, it understands itself as revelation. [. . .]

At first glance this really seems to be the maximum degree of revelation, of
the disclosure of God. The leap that previously led into the infinite seems to have
been reduced to something on a human scale, in that we now need only take the
few steps, as it were, to that person in Galilee in whom God himself comes to
meet us. But things are curiously double-sided: what at first seems to be the most
radical revelation and to a certain degree does indeed always remain revelation,
the revelation, is at the same moment the cause of the most extreme obscurity
and concealment. The very thing that at first seems to bring God quite close to
us, so that we can touch him as a fellow man, follow his footsteps and measure
them precisely, also becomes in a very profound sense the precondition for the
'death of God', which henceforth puts an ineradicable stamp on the course of
history and the human relationship with God. God has come so near to us that
we can kill him and that he thereby, so it seems, ceases to be God for us. Thus
today we stand somewhat baffled before this Christian 'revelation' and wonder,
especially when we compare it with the religiosity of Asia, whether it would not
have been much simpler to believe in the Mysterious Eternal, entrusting ourselves
to it in longing thought; whether God would not have done better, so to speak,
to leave us at an infinite distance; whether it would not really be easier to ascend
out of the world and hear the eternally unfathomable secret in quiet contemplation
than to give oneself up to the positivism of belief in one single figure and to set
the salvation of man and of the world on the pinpoint, so to speak, of this one
chance moment in history. Surely a God thus narrowed down to one point is
bound to die definitively in a view of the world that remorselessly reduces man
and his history to a tiny grain of dust in the cosmos, that can see itself as the center

of the universe only in the naive years of its childhood and now, grown out of childhood, ought finally to have the courage to awake from sleep, rub its eyes, shake off that beautiful but foolish dream, and take its place unquestioningly in the huge context in which our tiny lives have their proper function, lives that should find new meaning precisely by accepting their diminutiveness?

It is only by putting the question in a pointed form like this and so coming to see that behind the apparently secondary stumbling block of 'then' and 'now' lies the much deeper difficulty of Christian 'positivism', the 'limitation' of God to one point in history, that we can plumb the full depths of the question of Christian belief as it must be answered today. Can we still believe at all? Or rather – for the question must be posed in a more radical fashion – is it still permissible to believe? Have we not a duty to break with the dream and to face reality? The Christian of today must ask himself this question; he is not at liberty to remain satisfied with finding out that by all kinds of twists and turns an interpretation of Christianity can still be found that no longer offends anybody. When some theologian explains that 'the resurrection of the dead' simply means that one must cheerfully set about the work of the future afresh every day, offense is certainly avoided. But are we then really still being honest? Is there not serious dishonesty in seeking to maintain Christianity as a viable proposition by such artifices of interpretation? Have we not much rather the duty, when we feel forced to take refuge in solutions of this sort, to admit that we have reached the end of the road? Are we not then bound to emerge from the fog and to face straightforwardly the abiding reality? Let us be quite plain about it: An 'interpreted' Christianity of this kind that has lost all contact with reality implies a lack of sincerity in dealing with the questions of the non-Christian, whose 'perhaps not' should worry us as seriously as we want the Christian 'perhaps' to worry him.

Dimensions of the Theological Conflict with Modernity

In the modern context, it is indeed the survival of Christian faith and tradition that is at stake, and on many occasions, in many of his speeches and publications on diverse topics, Ratzinger warns of the dangers of a too-easy adaptation to modernity, which puts the very integrity of the truth of Christian faith at risk. In this regard he is highly critical of many modern theological developments that would seem to measure Christian faith by the normativity of modernity (and especially the modern scientific method and worldview), rather than the opposite. The same concerns have preoccupied Ratzinger with regard to contemporary exegesis. In the following, we first present his criticisms in this regard (a). Then we present his comments regarding the deplorable state of theology today, and the remedies he proposes: theology needs to reconsider its relation to philosophy (b), it should be more aware of the limits of theological hermeneutics (c), and it should remember its ecclesial embodiment, and thus its relation to the magisterium (d).

(a) Biblical Interpretation in Crisis

While in 1965 Ratzinger still pleads for the safeguarding function of exegesis, from the 1980s his trust in historical-critical exegesis is thoroughly shocked. He complains that the Bible is no longer read; there is no room for faith in the exegetical method; God is not assigned a role in historical events. The exegete tries to distill the 'real' out of the stories by applying source criticism, but eventually one does not hear the text speak anymore but rather the one who explains the text, based on hypothetical sources behind the biblical writings that serve as his or her criterion. Other symptoms of the decay of exegesis are the so-called 'materialist', 'feminist' and 'psychoanalytic' approaches to scripture. These forms of exegesis do not ask for the truth anymore but arbitrarily seek in the texts elements to underpin a self-chosen praxis.

If Rudolph Bultmann used the philosophy of Martin Heidegger as a vehicle to represent the biblical word, then that vehicle stands in accord with his reconstruction of the essence of Jesus' message.[33] But was this reconstruction itself not likewise a product of his philosophy? How great is its credibility from a historical point of view? In the end, are we listening to Jesus or to Heidegger with this approach to understanding? Still, one can hardly deny that Bultmann seriously grappled with the issue of increasing our access to the Bible's message. But today certain forms of exegesis are appearing which can only be explained as symptoms of the disintegration of interpretation and hermeneutics. Materialist and feminist exegesis, whatever else may be said about them, do not even claim to be an understanding of the text itself in the manner in which it was originally intended. At best they may be seen as an expression of the view that the Bible's message is in and of itself inexplicable, or else that it is meaningless for life in today's world. In this sense, they are no longer interested in ascertaining the truth, but only in whatever will serve their own particular agendas. They go on to justify this combination of agenda with biblical material by saying that the many religious elements help strengthen the vitality of the treatment. Thus historical method can even serve as a cloak for such maneuvers insofar as it dissects the Bible into discontinuous pieces, which are then able to be put to new use and inserted into a new montage (altogether different from the original biblical context).

---

33   Cf. R. Guardini, *Das Christusbild. der paulinischen und johanneischen Schriften* Würzburg: Im Werkbund-Verlag, 1961, p. 14.

What the exegete forgets here is that the application of the historical-critical method needs to be complemented with an understanding of the text for today. An exegesis should search for the internal coherence between historical analysis and hermeneutical synthesis. Moreover, a real synthesis is possible only if one begins to see the Bible again in close connection with the living Church community. Synthesis needs to have as a point of departure the fact that the faith of the Church be in sympathy with the text, without which there is no opening to its real significance. There can be no conflict between the interpretation of scripture and of tradition. The connection with dogma is no threat but rather a guarantee of a correct exegesis. In our following text, again taken from *Biblical Interpretation in Crisis*, Ratzinger reflects on the relation between 'event' and 'word', and develops the biblical view on it as normative for contemporary exegesis. Finally, he also formulates five hopes, which are in fact five conditions that enable a correct hermeneutics of scripture.

The exegete should not approach the text with a ready-made philosophy, nor in accordance with the dictates of a so-called modern or 'scientific' worldview, which determines in advance what may or may not be. He may not exclude a priori that (almighty) God could speak in human words in the world. He may not exclude that God himself could enter into and work in human history, however improbable such a thing might at first appear.

He must be ready to learn from the extraordinary. He must be ready to accept that the truly original may occur in history, something which cannot be derived from precedents but which opens up out of itself.[34] He may not deny to humanity the ability to be responsive beyond the categories of pure reason and to reach beyond ourselves toward the open and endless truth of being.

We must likewise reexamine the relationship between event and word. For Dibelius, Bultmann, and the mainstreams of modern exegesis, the event is the irrational element. It lies in the realm of mere facticity, which is a mixture of accident and necessity. The fact as such, therefore, cannot be a bearer of meaning. Meaning lies only in the word, and where events might *seem* to bear meaning, they are to be considered as illustrations of the word to which they have to be referred. Judgments which derive from such a point of view are certainly persuasive for people of today, since they fit nicely into their own patterns of expectations. There is, however, no evidence in reality to support them. Such evidence is admissible only under the presupposition that the principle of scientific method, namely

---

34   Cf. also J. Bergmann, H. Lutzmann, W. H. Schmidt, 'dabar', in G. J. Botterweck and H. Ringgren (eds), *Theologisches Wörterbuch zum Alten Testament* 2. Stuttgart: W. Kohlhammer, 1977, pp. 89–133; O. Proksch, 'lego', in *Theologisches Wörterbuch zum Neuen Testament* 4, Stuttgart: W. Kohlhammer, 1932-79, esp. pp. 91–97. On the unity of word and event in Thomas, cf. M. Arias-Reyero, *Thomas von Aquin als Exeget*. Einsiedeln: Johannes-Verlag, 1971, pp. 102, 246f., *et passim*.

that every effect which occurs can be explained in terms of purely immanent relationships within the operation itself, is not only valid methodologically but is true in and of itself. Thus, in reality there would be only 'accident and necessity,' nothing else, and one may only look upon these elements as brute facts.

But what is useful as a methodological principle for the natural sciences is a foregone banality as a philosophical principle; and as a theological principle it is a contradiction. (How can any or all of God's activity be considered either as accidental or necessary?) It is here, for the sake of scientific curiosity, too, that we must experiment with the precise contrary of this principle, namely, that things can indeed be otherwise.

To put it another way: the event itself can be a 'word,' in accord with the biblical terminology itself.[35] From this flow two important rules for interpretation.

(a) First, both word and event have to be considered equally original, if one wishes to remain true to the biblical perspective. The dualism which banishes the event into wordlessness, that is meaninglessness, would rob the word of its power to convey meaning as well, for it would then stand in a world without meaning.

It also leads to a docetic Christology in which the reality, that is the concrete fleshly existence of Christ and especially of man, is removed from the realm of meaning. Thus the essence of the biblical witness fails of its purpose.

(b) Secondly, such a dualism splits the biblical word off from creation and would substitute the principle of discontinuity for the organic *continuity* of meaning which exists between the Old and New Testaments. When the continuity between word and event is allowed to disappear, there can no longer be any unity within the Scripture itself. A New Testament cut off from the Old is automatically abolished since it exists, as its very title suggests, because of the unity of both. Therefore the principle of discontinuity must be counterbalanced by the interior claim of the biblical text itself, according to the principle of the *analogia scripturae*: the mechanical principle must be balanced by the teleological principle.[36]

Certainly texts must first of all be traced back to their historical origins and interpreted in their proper historical context. But then, in a second exegetical operation, one must look at them also in light of the total movement of history and in light of history's central event, Jesus Christ. Only the *combination* of *both* these

---

35   For a correct understanding of teleology, see R. Spaemann and R. Löw, *Die Frage Wazu? Geschichte und Wiederentdeckung des Teleo-logischen Denkens*. Munich and Zürich: Piper Verlag, 1981.

36   'Officium est enim boni interpretis non considerare verba sed sensum', in R. Cai (ed.) *Matthaeum* 27, no. 2321. Rome: Marieti, 1951, p. 358; cf. M. Arias-Reyero, *Thomas von Aquin als Exeget*. Einsiedeln: Johannes-Verlag, 1971, p 161.

methods will yield understanding of the Bible. If the first exegetical operation by the Fathers and in the Middle Ages is found to be lacking, so too is the second, since it easily falls into arbitrariness. Thus, the first was fruitless, but the rejection of any coherence of meaning leads to an opinionated methodology.

To recognize the inner self-transcendence of the historical word, and thus the inner correctness of subsequent rereadings in which event and meaning are gradually interwoven, is the task of interpretation properly so-called, for which appropriate methods can and must be found. In this connection, the exegetical maxim of Thomas Aquinas is quite to the point: 'The duty of every good interpreter is to contemplate not the words, but the sense of the words.'[37]

In the last hundred years, exegesis has had many great achievements, but it has brought forth great errors as well. These latter, moreover, have in some measure grown to the stature of academic dogmas. To criticize them at all would be taken by many as tantamount to sacrilege, especially if it were to be done by a nonexegete. Nevertheless, so prominent an exegete as Heinrich Schlier previously warned his colleagues: 'Do not squander your time on trivialities.'[38] Johann Gnilka gave concrete expression to this warning when he reacted against an exaggerated emphasis by the history-of-traditions school.

Along the same lines, I would like to express the following hopes:

(a) The time seems to have arrived for a new and thorough reflection on exegetical method. Scientific exegesis must recognize the philosophic element present in a great number of its ground rules, and it must then reconsider the results which are based on these rules.

(b) Exegesis can no longer be studied in a unilinear, synchronic fashion, as is the case with scientific findings which do not depend upon their history but only upon the precision of their data. Exegesis must recognize itself as a historical discipline. Its history belongs to itself. In a critical arrangement of its respective positions within the totality of its own history, it will be able, on one hand, to recognize the relativity of its own judgments (where, for example, errors may have crept in). On the other hand, it will be in a better position to achieve an insight into our real, if always imperfect, comprehension of the biblical word.

(c) Philological and scientific literary methods are and will remain critically important for a proper exegesis. But for their actual application to the work of criticism—just as for an examination of their claims—an understanding of the philosophic implications of the interpretative process is required. The

37   H. Schlier, 'Was heisst Auslegung der Heiligen Schrift?' in *Besinnung auf das Neue Testament Exegetische Aufsätze und Vorträge* 2. Freiburg: Herder, 1964, pp. 35–62, esp. 62; cf. J. Gnilka, 'Die biblische Exegese im Lichte des Dekretes über die göttliche Offenbarung' in *Münchnere Theologische Zeitschrift* 36 (1985) p. 14.

38   Gnilka, 'Die biblische Exegese im Lichte des Dekretes über die göttliche Offenbarung', in *Münchnere Theologische Zeitschrift* 36 (1985) p. 14.

self-critical study of its own history must also imply an examination of the essential philosophic alternatives for human thought. Thus, it is not sufficient to scan simply the last one hundred and fifty years. The great outlines of patristic and medieval thought must also be brought into the discussion. It is equally indispensable to reflect on the fundamental judgments made by the Reformers and the critical importance they have had in the history of exegesis.

(d) What we need now are not new hypotheses on the *Sitz im Leben*, on possible sources or on the subsequent process of handing down the material. What we *do* need is a critical look at the exegetical landscape we now have, so that we may return to the text and distinguish between those hypotheses which are helpful and those which are not. Only under these conditions can a new and fruitful collaboration between exegesis and systematic theology begin. And only in this way will exegesis be of real help in understanding the Bible.

(e) Finally, the exegete must realize that he does not stand in some neutral area, above or outside history and the church. Such a presumed immediacy regarding the purely historical can only lead to dead ends. The first pre-supposition of all exegesis is that it accepts the Bible as a book. In so doing, it has already chosen a place for itself which does not simply follow from the study of literature. It has identified *this particular literature* as the product of a coherent history, and this history as the proper space for coming to understanding. If it wishes to be theology, it must take a further step. It must recognize that the faith of the church is that form of "sympathia" without which the Bible remains a *closed* book. It must come to acknowledge this faith as a hermeneutic, the space for understanding, which does not do dogmatic violence to the Bible, but precisely allows the solitary possibility for the Bible to be itself.

(b) The Need for a New Relationship between Philosophy and Theology

The rise of modern thought has put the original synthesis between faith and reason as established in the patristic era under pressure. Philosophy and theology have become two disciplines, each having gone its own way. Moreover, new philosophical approaches that are extremely critical of ontological thinking make fruitful engagement between philosophy and theology much more difficult, and this is to the detriment of the latter. In his reflections on the current crisis of theology, Ratzinger sees the need for establishing a new relationship between theology and philosophy, because both suffer from the modern antithesis between the two. It is again his former work on Bonaventure that offers the inspiration to establish a way out: apart from the problem of death and the question of God, it is especially love, and in particular the love for truth, at the heart of Christian faith, which makes room for an intimate relationship between philosophy and theology. In short: against the developments of modern philosophy and theology, Ratzinger pleads for what one could legitimately call a restoration of the original synthesis between faith and reason.

In the foregoing, we began by giving a rough sketch of the distinction between philosophy and theology.[39] While we did so, it became apparent that in the history of the two disciplines this distinction has increasingly tended to take the form of an antithesis. It also became clear, however, that the development of an opposition between philosophy and theology has itself transformed the two sciences. In the wake of this evolution, philosophy tends more and more to cast off ontology, that is, its own primordial question, while theology discards the fundamental principles which originally made it possible, in its characteristic double tension between revelation and reason. In contrast, we affirmed that philosophy as such cannot do without ontology and that theology is no less obliged to have recourse to it. The exclusion of ontology from theology does not emancipate philosophical thinking but paralyzes it. The extinction of ontology in the sphere of philosophy, far from purifying theology, actually deprives it of its solid basis. Contrary to the common hostility toward ontology, which is apparently becoming the sole link between contemporary philosophers and theologians, we held that both disciplines need this dimension of thought and that it is here that they find themselves indissolubly associated.

We must now render this general diagnosis somewhat more precise and concrete. After having thoroughly investigated the *aporia* of the antithesis, we must frame the question positively: In what sense does faith need philosophy? In what way is philosophy open to faith and oriented from within toward dialogue with its message? I would like to sketch very briefly three levels of an answer to these queries.

a. We have already encountered a first level of correlation between philosophical and theological inquiry in our glance at the earliest images of faith: both faith and philosophy confront the primordial question which death addresses to man. Now, the question of death is only the radical form of the question about how to live rightly. It asks whence man comes and whither he is going. It seeks an origin and a destination. Death, the one question which it is impossible to ignore forever, is thus a metaphysical thorn lodged in man's being. Man has no choice but to ask what might be the meaning of this

39   [Selection from J. Ratzinger, *The Nature and Mission of Theology: Approaches to Understanding Its Role in the Light of Present Controversy*. San Francisco: Ignatius Press, 1995, pp. 22–27].

final limit. On the other hand, it is clear to every thinking person that only someone with firsthand knowledge of what lies beyond death could give a well-founded answer to that question. In consequence, if faith knows that such an answer has in fact been given, it demands the attention and joint reflection which are the special activities of questioning inquiry. Such an answer by no means causes the shipwreck of inquiry, as Jaspers opines. On the contrary, questioning founders when there is no hope of finding an answer. Faith hears the answer because it keeps the question alive. It can receive the answer as such only if it is able to understand its relevance to the question. When faith speaks of the resurrection of the dead, what is at stake is not a more or less abstruse assertion about an unverifiable future place and an unknown future time but the comprehension of man's being within the whole of reality. The fundamental problem of justice is therefore also in play, and this is inseparable from the problem of hope. The central concern is the relationship between history and ethos, between human action and the unmanipulable character of reality. The sort of questions involved here, which, though formulated diversely from period to period, remain essentially the same, can mark progress only in the exchange between question and answer, philosophical and theological reflection. This dialogue of human thought with the prior givens of faith will have one aspect when it is conducted in strictly philosophical terms and another when it is expressly theological. But both kinds of dialogue must maintain a mutual relationship, and neither can wholly dispense with the other.

b. We have likewise already alluded to the second level of correlation in the preceding reflections: faith advances a philosophical, more precisely, an ontological claim when it professes the existence of God, indeed, of a God who has power over reality as a whole. A powerless God is, in fact, a contradiction in terms. If he cannot act, cannot speak and be spoken to, he may be considered the concluding hypothesis of the reasoning process but has nothing to do with what the religious belief of mankind means by 'God'. The scope of the assertion that there is a God who is the creator and savior of the whole universe reaches beyond the religious community which makes it. It is not intended as a symbolic representation of the un-nameable, which looks one way in this religion and another in that, but as a statement about reality as it is in itself. This breakthrough in thinking about God to a fundamental claim on human reason as such is wholly evident in the religious critique of the prophets and the biblical wisdom literature. If the prophets ridicule man-made idols with mordant acerbity and set the only real God in contrast to them, in the wisdom books the same spiritual movement is at work as among the pre-Socratics at the time of the early Greek enlightenment. To the extent that the prophets see in the God of Israel the primordial creative ground of all reality, it is quite clear that what is taking place is a religious critique for the sake of a correct understanding of this reality itself. Here the faith of Israel unquestionably steps beyond the limits of a single people's peculiar worship: it puts forth a universal claim, whose universality has to do with its being rational. Without the prophetic religious critique, the universalism of Christianity would have been unthinkable. It was this critique which, in the very heart of Israel itself, prepared that synthesis of Hellas and the Bible which the Fathers labored to achieve. For this reason, it is incorrect to reduce the concepts *logos* and *aletheia*, upon which John's Gospel centers the Christian message, to a strictly Hebraic interpretation, as if *logos* meant 'word' merely in the sense of God's speech in history, and *aletheia* signified nothing more than 'trustworthiness' or 'fidelity'. For the very same reason, there is no basis for the opposite accusation that John distorted biblical thought in the direction of Hellenism. On the contrary, he stands in the classical sapiential tradition. It is precisely in John's writings that one can study, both in its origins and in its outcome, the inner movement of biblical faith in God and biblical Christology toward philosophical inquiry.[40]

Is the world to be understood as originating from a creative intellect or as arising out of a combination of probabilities in the realm of the absurd? Today as yesterday, this alternative is the decisive question for our comprehension of reality; it cannot be dodged. Whoever, on the other hand, would draw faith back into paradox or into a pure historical symbolism fails to perceive its unique historical position, whose defense engaged both the prophets and the apostles in equal measure. The universality of faith, which is a basic presupposition of the missionary task, is both meaningful and morally defensible only if this faith really is oriented beyond the symbolism of the religions toward an answer meant for all, an answer which also appeals to the common reason of mankind. The exclusion of this common appeal inevitably puts an end to any communication to men which touches upon ultimate realities. The question of God, therefore, obliges theology to take a position in the philosophical debate. When it gives up the claim to the reasonability of its fundamental assertions, it does not return to a purer attitude of belief but rather betrays a fundamental element of its own constitution. By the same token, a philosophy which wishes to remain true to its object must open itself to faith's claim on reason. The coordination of philosophy and theology is indispensable on this second level as well.

c. Finally, I would like to suggest a few remarks on the controversy which this issue aroused in medieval theology. In the works of Bonaventure there are two principal answers to the question whether and why it is legitimate to attempt a comprehension of the biblical message using methods of philosophical

---

40   Important observations on these questions are offered by H. Gese, 'Der Johannesprolog' in *Zur biblischen Theologie*. Munich: Kaiser, 1977, pp. 155–201.

reasoning. The first answer relies on a statement from 1 Peter 3:15, which in the Middle Ages was the *locus classicus* for the justification of systematic theology in general: 'Always be prepared to make a defense to anyone who calls you to account for the hope that is in you.'[41] The Greek text is by far more expressive than any translation. Believers are enjoined to give an *apo-logia* regarding the *logos* of our hope to whoever asks for it. The *logos* must be so intimately their own that it can become *apo-logia*; through the mediation of Christians, the Word [*Wort*] becomes response [*Antwort*] to man's questions. At first glance, this seems to be a justification of theology purely for its apologetical value: one must be able to explain before others why one believes. This point is quite significant in its own right. Faith is not pure private decision, which as such does not really concern anyone else. It will and can show its credentials. It wishes to make itself understandable to others. It lays claim to being a *logos* and, therefore, to the never-failing capacity to become apo-logy. But at a deeper level, this apologetic interpretation of theology is a missionary one, and the missionary conception, in its turn, brings to light the inner nature of faith. Faith has the right to be missionary only if it truly transcends all traditions and constitutes an appeal to reason and an orientation toward the truth itself. However, if man is made to know reality and has to conduct his life, not merely as tradition dictates, but in conformity to the truth, faith also has the positive duty to be missionary. With its missionary claim, the Christian faith sets itself apart from the other religions which have appeared in history; this claim is implicit in its philosophical critique of the religions and can be justified only on that basis. The fact that today missionary dynamism threatens to trickle away into nothing goes hand in hand with the deficit in philosophy which characterizes the contemporary theological scene.

But we can identify another justification of theology in Bonaventure's work; though it seems at first to point in an entirely different direction, its inner tendency is to merge with what has been said so far. The Saint is aware that the citizenship of philosophy in theology is a contested issue. He concedes that there is a violence of reason which cannot be brought into harmony with faith. Nevertheless, he affirms that there is also an inquiry inspired by another motive. Faith can wish to understand because it is moved by love for the One upon whom it has bestowed its consent.[42] Love seeks understanding. It wishes to know ever better the one whom it loves. It 'seeks his face', as Augustine never tires of repeating.[43] Love is the desire for intimate knowledge, so that the quest for intelligence can even be an inner requirement of love. Put another way, there is a coherence of love and

41   Bonaventura, *Sent*, proœm, q, 2 sed, contra 1.
42   Ibid., q. 2 and 6.
43   See, for example, *En. in ps. 104, 3* CChr XL p. 1,537.

truth which has important consequences for theology and philosophy. Christian faith can say of itself, I have found love. Yet love for Christ and of one's neighbor for Christ's sake can enjoy stability and consistency only if its deepest motivation is love for the truth. This adds a new aspect to the missionary element: real love of neighbor also desires to give him the deepest thing man needs, namely, knowledge and truth. In the first part we took as our starting point the problem of death considered as the philosophical thorn in the side of faith. We then discovered in the second part that the God question, together with its universal claim, is the place of philosophy in theology. We can now add a third element: love, the center of Christian reality on which 'depend the law and the prophets', is at the same time eros for truth, and only so does it remain sound as agape for God and man.

(c) Realizing the Theological Limits of the Hermeneutics of Tradition

All too easily are elements of the faith tradition that offend modern human beings considered as belonging to an out-of-date worldview and thus not binding for today's believer. A radicalized hermeneutics panders to these circumstances: theologians try their utmost to interpret away elements that contradict the modern *Zeitgeist* and the mood of the marketplace. One example of this, according to Ratzinger, is *Abschied vom Teufel (Farewell to the Devil)* by Herbert Haag, an Old Testament exegete from Tübingen University.[44] For Haag, 'Satan', 'devil', and 'demon' are framed in the outdated Jewish worldview and are, in terms of the contemporary worldview, images for evil and sin. For Ratzinger, Haag does not come to this position as an exegete but as a contemporary; the modern worldview cannot accept the existence of the devil. In his critique, Ratzinger outlines several criteria for dealing with the conflict between worldviews and for maintaining a respect for the integrity of the tradition.

> This raises the question: How can one resolve this [conflict]? How can one avoid a repetition of false and harmful encounters such as the Galileo controversy?[45] Conversely, how can one prevent Faith being amputated for the sake of Modernity . . . .. There are no standards that one can apply immediately and with absolute

44   H. Haag, *Abschied vom Teufel (Farewell to the Devil)*. Einsiedeln: Benziger, 1969.
45   [Selection from J. Ratzinger, 'Abschied vom Teufel? (Farewell to the Devil)', in *Dogma und Verkündigung*. München/Freiburg: Wewel, 1973, pp. 221–234, 223–224, 226, 227, 228–230. Translation by David Kirchhoffer. Originally appeared as: J. Ratzinger, 'Abschied vom Teufel?', in *Bistumsblatt Aachen*, Aachen: Einhard-Verlag, 1973, nr 11 & 12].

certainty to every case that arises; the demarcation of the boundaries remains a challenge that time and time again requires mental exertion. And so one can have an appreciation for a struggle for the boundaries of Faith, as long as, in the process, a preparedness to be corrected by clearly demonstrated knowledge remains on the one hand, and the understanding that Faith can only be realised by believing *with* the Church—and is not subordinated to the directives of private decisions about what may or may not be considered defensible at any one time—remains on the other.

Thus, even if there is no standard that, in every instance, respectively shows where Faith ends and worldview begins, there are a series of judgement aids that guide us in our search for clarifications. I shall name four of these. The first standard presents itself in the relationship of the two Testaments. The Bible, after all, exists not as a uniform entity, but rather in the harmony of the Old and the New Testament, which, in their respective counterparts and in their unity, interpret each other. Above all, it must be said that the Old Testament is only valid when unified with the New, under its sign, by means of its proportionateness throughout, just as, indeed, the New Testament only reveals the richness of its content through its constant reference to the Old. [. . .]

This already leads to a second standard. In each instance, the question must be asked as to the way in which a proposition relates to the inner practice of Faith and the life of Faith. Propositions that just remain theoretical points of view, but that do not become part of the actual living-out of existence, do not normally become the core of what could be counted as Christian. By contrast, that which does not just arise as a theoretical point of view, but instead falls within the realm of Faith experience, appearing in the Faith-life as a datum of experience, is of an entirely different status. Thus, even if the idea of the rising and setting of the sun, of the Earth as the centre, may be a self-evident and manifoldly analysable Faith perspective, it does not belong to Faith's specific experiences. Mysticism, with its path of unification, sooner leads to the relativisation of all worldview schemata. [. . .]

Closely associated with this is the third standard. The Bible without the Church would just be an anthology of literature. Hence, where, beyond the necessary scientific investigation of the strictly historical, the Bible is questioned as a book of Faith, and the difference is sought between what is Faith and what is not, this association of Bible and Church must come into play. Faith can only be realised, as we have already said, through believing *with* the whole; it dissolves when it is transferred to the arbitrariness of the individual. Thus, as a further standard, one should inquire as to the extent to which propositions have been absorbed into the Faith of the Church. Now, the Faith of the Church is no unequivocally definable thing, otherwise everything would be easy. One must, therefore, try to more carefully analyse and find out the extent to which something has become part of the actual inner practice of Faith, of the foundational forms of prayer and life, even beyond the idiosyncrasies of the tradition. Thus, for example, the conflicts over the status of Jesus as God's Son, over the divinity of the Holy Spirit, over the Trinity, are guided by their consequences for the Baptismal liturgy, for the Eucharistic liturgy, and hence for the significance, announced in Baptism, of Christian conversion. [. . .]

Finally, as the last standard regarding the issue of 'worldview', compatibility with scientific knowledge must be mentioned. Though Faith will always become a critique of that which, at the time, is held to be modern and, though uninter-rogated, to be certain, it cannot contradict established scientific knowledge, which thus sets up some boundaries worth paying attention to [. . .]. That [the idea of the Devil] opposes mainstream tastes is clear. That it finds no support in a functionalistically viewed world is likewise obvious. But in a pure functionalism, there is also no place for God, or for people as persons; there is only place for people as function. Therefore, a great deal more collapses here than just the idea of the 'Devil' [. . .]. The Between[46] is a destiny-determining power which is in no way at the complete disposal of our I. To think this is to accept the rationalism of an almost seemingly adventurous naivety. Here, it seems to me, modern thought puts at our disposal a category that can help us to understand again more pre-cisely the power of the Demons whose existence is indeed independent of such categories. They are a power of the "Between" that confronts the human being at every turn without him being able to pin it down. This is exactly what Paul means when he speaks of the 'powers of this darkness'; when he says that it is against them, the spiritual forces of evil, not against flesh and blood that our struggle is directed (Eph 6:12). It is directed against that firmly established 'Between' that simultaneously chains people together and cuts them off from one another, that assaults them while it masquerades as freedom. Here, a very specific characteristic of the demonic is made clear: its facelessness, its anonymity. When one asks whether the Devil is a person, then the correct answer should surely be that he is the un-person, the disintegration, the dissolution of personhood, and therefore that it is typical that he should appear without a face, that unrecognisability should be his ultimate strength. Whatever the case may be, this Between is a real power, or better yet, it is a collection of powers and not just an aggregation of human I's. Incidentally, the category of the Between, which thus helps us to understand the nature of the Demon anew, renders yet another parallel service: it makes it possible to better explain what is actually the countervailing power, which has likewise become ever more strange to occidental theology: the Holy Spirit. Here would could say: There is that Between in which the Father and the Son are one

---

46   [Translators comment: Ratzinger uses the substantive of the word *zwischen*, which is usually used as a preposition or adjective. As a preposition it can mean among, amongst, between, or in-between. As an adjective it can mean inside, temporary, or intermediate. In part of the chapter omitted for this translation, Ratzinger makes it clear what he means by '*das Zwishcen*': deeper forms of personalism make it clear that one cannot explain all of reality with just the categories 'I' and 'thou' – that the 'Between' that binds the two poles to each other is a reality in its own right and with its own power].

as the one God; in the power of this Between, the Christ counters that demonic Between that stands 'in between'[47] and hinders unity.

(d) The Ecclesial Character of Theology and the Role of the Magisterium

As we have already seen, Ratzinger repeatedly affirms the ecclesial character of Christian truth in the discussions about the state of Christian faith and theology in the modern context. An all-too-easy post-conciliar theology accommodates modernity and forgets its ecclesial vocation. With a starting point rooted in a concern for unity between faith and the totality of truth, he tries therefore to define the correct relationship between magisterium and theology.[48] After all, the Church is the subject bearer of faith and therefore speaks the voice of faith. Under the guise of a 'scientific' theology, however, far too many theologians proclaim opinions that deviate from what the magisterium teaches – a magisterium they do not consider the mouthpiece of the faith of the Church but rather an exponent of the archaic, Roman theology.[49] Others, who are somewhat more careful and who present themselves as ecclesial theologians, attempt to stretch the interpretations to achieve just the opposite of what is posited in the doctrinal texts. Both attitudes go against the apostolicity of the Church from which the teaching authority receives its mandate to make authoritative pronouncements on matters of faith and morals. Moreover, such a 'loose' theology imposes itself as a parallel magisterium and causes confusion among believers.

Therefore, Ratzinger stresses that it is one of the magisterium's main tasks to defend orthodoxy, especially for the sake of the simple faithful who remain in the cold in the midst of all this intellectual discussion. In this way, the magisterium fulfils an essentially social and democratic function.[50] Theology then is the scientific reflection on the faith of the

---

47   [Translators comment: Here Ratzinger uses *dazwischen*, thereby creating a wordplay with *das Zwischen*.]

48   Cf. J. Ratzinger, 'Kirche und wissenschaftliche Theologie', in W. Sandfuchs (ed.) *Die Kirche*, Würzburg: Echter Verlag, 1978, pp. 83–95; Idem, 'Theologie und Kirchenpolitik', in *Internat. Kath. Zeitschr.* 9 (1980) pp. 425–434 (*Communio. International Catholic Review* 7 (1980) pp. 332–342); Idem, 'Theologie und Kirche', in *Internat. Kath. Zeitschr.* 16 (1986) pp. 515–533. The English version is in fact the first section of part two of *The Nature and Mission of Theology*, pp. 45–72, from which an excerpt is taken for this section of our volume.

49   Cf. Ratzinger, *The Ratzinger Report*, p. 26.

50   Ratzinger stresses this repeatedly in *Theologische Prinzipienlehre*. Augsburg: Sankt Ulrich Verlag, 2005, pp. 340–341, 348; *Entretien sur la foi*. Paris: Fayard, 1985, p. 25; and in 'Theologie und Kirche', in *Internat. Kath. Zeitschr.* 16 (1986), p. 527. Hence, the ultimate yardstick for all theology is respect

Church. Its task is to discern and explain the rationality inherent in faith, and which determines its own coherence. It can only do this by conforming to the faith of the Church, of which it is the bearer. In other words, theologians can only perform theology if they undergo a conversion, if they too go through a metanoia, and in this way open themselves to the truth that comes to them. Therefore, the theologian must in the first place be a believer.

In what follows we present a text that explores the ecclesial context of theology and that elaborates more concretely on the magisterium's normative role for theology, which comes from the mission of the Church to proclaim the faith.[51]

> The Church is not an authority which remains foreign to the scientific character of theology but is rather the ground of theology's existence and the condition which makes it possible.[52] The Church, moreover, is not an abstract principle but a living subject possessing a concrete content. This subject is by nature greater than any individual person, indeed, than any single generation. Faith is always participation in a totality and, precisely in this way, conducts the believer to a new breadth of freedom. On the other hand, the Church is not an intangible spiritual realm in which everyone can pick what suits him. She is endowed with a concreteness rooted in the binding Word of faith. And she is a living voice which pronounces itself in the organs of the faith.[53] [. . .]
>
> It is not necessary at this time to expound in detail the theory of the Magisterium and its forms which follows from what we have just said. Nevertheless, we must still deal with a few concrete issues which crop up continually in this context. For the problems lie in the concrete. It is not at all difficult to acknowledge in theory that theology is ecclesial by its very nature; that the Church does not merely provide theology with an organizational framework but is its inner foundation and its immediate wellspring; that, in consequence, the Church cannot be incompetent in matters of content or theologically mute but must have a living voice, that is, the faculty to speak bindingly even for the theologian. However,

for the faith of the simple. According to Ratzinger, the gospel of Mark articulates this clearly: 'If anyone causes one of these little ones who believe in me to sin, it would be better for him if a large millstone were hung around his neck and he were thrown into the sea' (Mk 9:42) (ibid., p. 530).

51   While the remainder of this chapter explores Ratzinger's understanding of the relationship between theology and the teaching authority of the church, i.e., magisterium, Chapter Six of this volume deals more specifically with his thinking on the role of the official magisterium in relation to teaching and authority in the church.

52   [Selection from J. Ratzinger, *The Nature and Mission of Theology: Approaches to Understanding Its Role in the Light of Present Controversy*. San Francisco: Ignatius Press, 1995, pp. 61–65].

53   R. Guardini developed the idea of the Church as the subject of theology in his Bonn inaugural lecture, published here: 'Anselm von Canterbury und das Wesen der Theologie', in *Auf dem Wege*. Mainz: Versuche, 1923.

another means of escaping this concreteness, an expedient which increasingly finds public advocates today, insinuates itself here. The pastoral office, it is said, is entrusted to the Church; she preaches for the faithful but does not teach for the theologians. But such a divorce of preaching and teaching is most profoundly opposed to the essence of the biblical message. It merely rehashes that division between psychics and gnostics whereby the so-called gnosis of antiquity had already tried to secure for itself a free zone, which in reality placed it outside of the Church and her faith. This division, in fact, presupposes the typically pagan way of conceiving the relationship between myth and philosophy, religious symbolism and enlightened reason. Christianity's critique of religion ran counter to this scheme and was accordingly also a critique of a certain religious class mentality. It achieved the emancipation of the simple and credited even them with the capacity to be philosophers in the true sense of the word, that is, to lay hold of the essential dimension of man's being, and to do so as well as or even better than the learned. Jesus' words concerning the incomprehension of the wise and the understanding of the 'babes' (especially Mt 11:25, par.) are pertinent precisely to this situation, inasmuch as they establish Christianity as a popular religion, as a religious creed without any two-caste system.

As a matter of fact, proclamation in the form of preaching does teach bindingly; such is its essence. For it does not suggest some sort of pastime or a kind of religious entertainment. Its aim is to tell man who he is and what he must do to be himself. Its intention is to disclose to him the truth about himself, that is, what he can base his life on and what he can die for. No one dies for interchangeable myths; if one myth leads to difficulties, there is always another to select in its place. Nor is it possible to live on hypotheses: after all, life itself is no hypothesis but rather unrepeatable reality upon which rides an eternal destiny.[54] But how could the Church teach bindingly if at the same time her teaching remained without binding force for theologians? The essence of the Magisterium consists precisely in the fact that the proclamation of the faith is also the normative criterion of theology: indeed, this very proclamation is the object of theological reflection. In this sense, the faith of the simple is not a sort of theology whittled down to the measure of the layman, a kind of 'Platonism for the people'. On the contrary, things stand in precisely the reverse relationship: proclamation is the measure of theology, and not vice versa. This primacy of simple faith, moreover, is also in perfect accord with a fundamental anthropological law: the great truths about human nature are grasped in a simple apprehension which is in principle available to everyone and which is never wholly retrieved in reflection. One could say—somewhat carelessly—that the Creator has, as it were, proceeded in a thoroughly democratic fashion. Though not all men can be professional theologians, access to the

---

54   R. Spaemann offers a brilliant analysis of the civilization of hypothesis, 'Die christliche Religion und das Ende des modernen Bewußtseins', in *IKZ* [Internationale Katholische Zeitschrift:] *Communio* 8 (1979) pp. 251–270, esp. 264–268.

great fundamental cognitions is open to everyone. In this sense, the Magisterium has something like a democratic character: it defends the common faith, which recognizes no distinction of rank between the learned and the simple. It is indeed true that in virtue of her pastoral office the Church is empowered to preach and not to teach scientific theology. The point, however, is that the very office of preaching the gospel is the teaching office even for theology.

    This observation already touches upon an aspect of the question which was raised earlier. We had said that it is not difficult to accept the Magisterium in theory. But the passage from theory to practice immediately arouses a grave misgiving: Is it not the case that this transition unduly restricts thought's freedom of movement? Does it not inevitably give rise to a minute supervision which takes up the breathing space needed for great thought? Must we not fear that the Church may also interfere beyond the confines of preaching in the proper business of the scholar and thus overreach herself? These questions must be taken seriously. In consequence, it is legitimate to seek to regulate the relationship between theology and the Magisterium in such a way as to guarantee that the inherent responsibility of theology have its due sphere of action. Yet, however warranted this procedure may be, the limitations of such ways of framing the issues must be borne in mind. In reality, whoever sees ecclesial identity as nothing but a fetter is already operating on a false conception of theology. This was the insight which had dawned upon Guardini in the encounter with his professors, who, though personally orthodox, in their scholarly work were emulators of liberalism. This insight led him to a radically new beginning: If theology considers its own specific property only as an obstacle, how can it possibly yield any fruit? We must factor Church and dogma into the theological equation as a generative power rather than as a shackle. Indeed, only this 'energy source' discloses to theology its grand perspectives.[55] As an example, let us take exegesis, which even today is considered to be the classic illustration of the fact that the Church is a mere hindrance to theology. What, then, does a theology which emancipates itself from the Church actually achieve? In what sort of freedom does it then find itself? It becomes antiquarianism. It limits its researches to the past and advances varying hypotheses regarding the origin of individual texts and their relationship to the historical facts. These hypotheses interest us more than other literary theories only because the Church still asserts that these books document not merely past events but what is true. Neither does the attempt to make the Bible relevant by means of some personal philosophy improve matters, for there are better philosophies which nonetheless leave us cold. But how exciting exegesis becomes when it dares to read the Bible as a unified whole. If the Bible originates from the one subject formed by the people of God and, through it, from the divine subject himself, then it speaks of the present. If this is so, moreover, even what we know about the diversity of its underlying historical

55   Cf. R. Guardini, *Berichte über mein Leben*, Dusseldorf: Patmos Verlag, 1984 p. 86 and *passim*.

constellations yields its harvest; there is a unity to be discovered in this diversity, and diversity appears as the wealth of unity. This opens up a wide field of action both to historical research and to its hypotheses, with the sole limit that it may not destroy the unity of the whole, which is situated on another plane than what can be called the 'nuts and bolts' of the various texts. Unity is found on another plane, yet it belongs to the literary reality of the Bible itself.

CHAPTER 2

CHRIST, HUMANITY AND SALVATION

Lieven Boeve

Introduction

With his theological project, Joseph Ratzinger wants in the first place to offer an answer to the human quest for meaning, the search of the human person for wholeness and fulfillment. The background to this consists of the situation of emptiness, meaninglessness, alienation. The modern person, after all, suffocates in a world that offers everything except answers to the deeper 'why?' questions. Moreover, the modern context leads to a vacuum of meaning that sharply brings to the fore the urgency of the question of salvation. In the 1970s and 80s Ratzinger articulates this in three different ways, each responsive to the shift in the mood of the time. In 1971, for instance, he treats this problem from the perspective of the question of the future[1], in 1975, from the question of happiness,[2] and from 1983 on, the question of the pursuit for freedom[3] as the fulfillment of the highest human possibilities and a way out of alienation. 'The fundamental experience of our epoch is precisely the experience of "alienation": that is, the condition which Christianity expresses traditionally as the *lack of redemption*', he writes in 1985.[4] At the same time, Ratzinger detects an alarming shift in the nature of the answer that people attempt to give to their deepest questions. After all, the quest for salvation today is all too often translated into the search for an inner-worldly happiness in the future; redemption is seen as liberation. The fulfillment of life is not so much an expectation after death, in eternal life, but rather here in the earthly life. As years go by, Ratzinger's evaluation of the modern person

---

1   Cf. J. Ratzinger, *Glaube und Zukunft*. München: Kösel, 1970, ²1971 (E.T.: *Faith and Future*. Chicago: Franciscan Herald Press, 1971). Chapter two, with the title 'Faith and Existence', treats this problem from an existential angle.
2   J. Ratzinger and U. Hommes, *Das Heil des Menschen. Innerweltlich – christlich*. München: Kösel, 1975, pp. 33–34.
3   Ratzinger treats the question about freedom as a starting point for theology, among other things, in studies on liberation theology.
4   J. Ratzinger and V. Messori, *The Ratzinger Report*. San Francisco: Ignatius Press, 1985, p. 172.

and society becomes more and more negative. The pervasive sense of alienation finds expression in an anti-culture of death, in opposition to the Christian faith.[5]

A short note concerning the style of Ratzinger's theological argument is fitting here.[6] In his reflections about the actual situation of godlessness and especially his criticism of false paths to salvation, Ratzinger generally makes sharp distinctions between truth and error, good and evil, holiness and godlessness. He certainly does not avoid polemic. In language that is often quite vehement, he first criticizes false paths or flawed theological perspectives, after which he provides his own explanation, most often presented in sharp contrast to the ideas he has subjected to criticism. This first part is not always sufficiently argued for and firmly established, and appears mainly intended to give his own ideas added force. In this way he criticizes ideological tendencies like liberalism, positivism, scientism, Marxism and later, also postmodern libertarianism and relativism.[7] Likewise, he subjects contemporary theological thought such as political theology, liberation theology, and pluralistic theologies of religions, which often emerge out of dialogue with the aforementioned ideologies, to criticism. Moreover, to his dismay, he notes that the disastrous influence on Christianity of paths to salvation offered by these theological movements has implications for the whole of theology, particularly – so he writes in 1989 – on Christian theologies of creation, Christology, and eschatology.[8]

From the perspective of the human quest for salvation, we now present a few basic elements of Ratzinger's theological answer. We begin with his vision of the structure of faith itself that, determined as it is by *metanoia*, already provides part of the answer to the actual salvation quest. That is why it is necessary to unfold this aspect – the anthropological structure of the Christian faith – prior to discussing the specific Christian offer of salvation in terms of content.[9] Thereafter, helped by extracts from Ratzinger's writings, we examine four criteria to which a theology

5   J. Ratzinger, 'Jesus Christus heute', in *Internat. Kath. Zeitschr.* 19 (1990) p. 68. (E.T.: 'Jesus Christ Today', in *Communio* 17 (Spring 1990) pp. 68–87). Cf. his *Abbruch und Aufbruch: die Antwort des Glaubens auf die Krise der Werte.* München: Minerva, 1988.

6   We shall see the distinctive characteristics of Ratzinger's style of theological prose and argumentation unpacked and illustrated throughout each chapter of this volume.

7   Ratzinger's positions on these central issues in his theological thought will be dealt with in greater depth throughout subsequent chapters in this volume.

8   Cf. J. Ratzinger, 'Moeilijkheden met betrekking tot het geloof in Europa vandaag', in *Emmaüs* 20 (1989) pp. 145–154, 148–153 (E.T.: 'Difficulties Confronting the Faith in Europe Today', in *L'Osservatore Romano* [English edition], July 24, 1989, p 6.).

9   For instance, Ratzinger also uses this distinction between formal principles and contents of Christian faith in his *Theologische Prinzipienlehre.* Munich: Wewel, 1982.

that speaks about salvation should conform. These are: universal truth, freedom and love, which find their norm in Jesus Christ, and typically for Christian faith, the expectation of life after death. Finally, we briefly explore Ratzinger's view on the sacramental structure of Christian existence.

2.1 Christian Faith is About Conversion: 'It is no longer I who live, but Christ who lives in me' (Gal 2:20a)

The Christian answer to the quest for salvation carries in it a certain human image that is clearly visible in the structure of Christian faith. This structure itself belongs to salvific truth and is to an important degree constitutive of it. After all, faith means *metanoia*, the conversion from an I-involvement to a relationship of trust and to being included in a relationality that precedes the human being; a relationality that touches the human being so much that it changes the horizon of meaning of his or her existence. This inclusion in the meaningful whole to which one wants to entrust oneself is experienced personally and lived out communally. However, the word *metanoia* sounds strange. As with concepts such as 'sin' and 'penance', it too has disappeared from contemporary human discourse and become a new taboo. Yet herein is the key to a proper understanding of salvation.

> Any attempt to translate the word 'metanoia' runs immediately into difficulty:[10] repudiation, change of mind, repentance, atonement, conversion, reformation – all these suggest themselves, but none of them exhausts the word's full meaning. 'Conversion' and 'reformation' [of one's whole life: *Be-kehrung*], however, perhaps best reveal its radical character, what it really is: a process that affects one's entire existence – and one's existence entirely, that is, to the full extent of its temporal span – and that requires far more than just a single or even a repeated act of thinking, feeling or willing. Perhaps the difficulty of linguistic interpretation is linked to the fact that the whole concept has become strange to us, that we know it only in isolated bits and pieces and no longer as a comprehensive whole. And there is a strangeness even about the pieces that remain. Probably no one today would echo Nietzsche's comment: '"Sin" . . . is a Jewish feeling, a Jewish invention, and, in view of this background, . . . Christianity has actually attempted to "judaize" the whole world. How far it has succeeded in Europe is best seen in the degree of strangeness that Greek antiquity – a world without the feeling of sin – still has for

---

10   [Selection from J. Ratzinger, *Principles of Catholic Theology: Building Stones for Fundamental Theology.* San Francisco: Ignatius Press, 1987, pp. 55–60].

our sensibilities [. . .]. "Only when thou repentest is God gracious to thee" – for a Greek, such a concept would be both laughable and shocking [. . .].'[11]

But if the notion of sin and repentance is, understandably enough, no longer ridiculed as Jewish, the basic statement itself still stands with unabated force even today. A second comment of Nietzsche's, which I should like to quote in this context, might well have been spoken by any modern theologian: 'The concept of guilt and punishment is lacking in the whole psychology of the "gospel" . . .; "sin", indeed every distance between God and man, has been done away with – precisely that is the "glad tidings".'[12]

The attempt to give Christianity a new publicity value by putting it in an unqualifiedly positive relationship to the world – by actually picturing it as a conversion to the world – corresponds to our feeling about life and hence continues to thrive. Many a false anxiety about sin, created by a narrow-minded moral theology and all too often nourished and encouraged by spiritual advisers, avenges itself today by leading people to regard the Christianity of the past as a kind of harassment that kept man constantly in opposition to himself instead of freeing him for open and anxiety-free cooperation with all men of good will. One might almost say that the words sin-repentance-penance belong to the new taboos with which the modern consciousness protects itself against the powers of those dark questions that could be dangerous to its self-assured pragmatism. [. . .]

Those who live vigilantly in the world of today, who recognize its contradictions and its destructive tendencies – from the self-destruction of technology by the destruction of the environment to the self-destruction of society by racial and class struggles – such people do not look to Christianity for approbation but for the prophetic salt that burns, consumes, accuses and changes. Nevertheless, a basic aspect of metanoia comes thereby into view – for it demands that man change if he is to be saved. It is not the ideology of adaptation that will rescue Christianity, although adaptation is still operative wherever, with sycophantic zeal or tardy courage, those institutions are criticized which, in any event, have become the powerless butt of world publicity . . .;[13] nothing can rescue it but the prophetic courage to make its voice heard decisively and unmistakably at this very hour.

If the social and public components of metanoia come once again to the fore, there is, nevertheless, no lack of signs to remind us of the inevitability of conversion, of reformation and of its visible marks in the individual. Like Protestant Christianity,

11   Friedrich Nietzsche, 'Die frohliche Wissenschaft 3:135', in *Nietzsche's Werke* 5. Leipzig: Naumann, 1908, pp. 169–70. (E.T.: Friedrich Nietzsche, *The Gay Science*. Trans. Walter Kaufmann. New York: Random House, 1974.)

12   Friedrich Nietzsche, 'Der Antichrist', in *Werke in zwei Bänden* 2. Munich: Carl Hanser, 1967, sec. 33, p. 511 (E.T.: 'The Antichrist', in Walter Kaufmann (ed. and trans.), *The Portable Nietzsche*. New York: Viking Press, 1954, pp. 565–656).

13   Cf. Hans Urs von Balthasar, *Klarstellungen*. Freiburg: Herder, 1971, pp. 94–99 (E.T.: Hans Urs von Balthasar, *Elucidations*. London: SPCK, 1975).

Frank Buchmann has discovered anew, for the movement of moral rearmament that he founded, the necessity of the confession [of faith] as an act of liberation, of renewal, of surrendering the past and the destructive concealment of one's own guilt; in the secular sphere, psychology has come, in its fashion, to the realization that guilt, if unmastered, divides a man, destroys him physically and eventually also corporally, but that it can be mastered only by a confrontation that releases into the consciousness what has been suppressed and is festering within for an outlet: the increasing number of such secular confessors should show even a blind man that sin is not a Jewish invention but the burden of all mankind. The true burden from which, above all, man must be freed if he wants and is to be free.

On the basic biblical meaning of metanoia

Because secular components of the fundamental state of metanoia are so much in evidence today, the question of the real meaning of a properly Christian metanoia acquires, for the first time, a degree of urgency. Nietzsche, as we saw, represented sin and repentance as something typically Jewish, in contrast to which he ascribed to the Greeks the noble virtue of finding even crime beautiful and of regarding repentance as something to be scorned. For the close observer, Greek tragedy, which he offered as evidence, reveals exactly the opposite tendency: dread in the face of a curse that not even the gods can ward off.[14] Anyone who looks, however briefly, at the history of religion will learn to what extent it is dominated by the theme of guilt and atonement, with what abstruse and often strange efforts man has attempted to free himself from the burdensome feeling of guilt without being able actually to do so. To demonstrate the special nature of biblical metanoia, I shall limit myself here to two brief observations. The word metanoia has no special significance in classical or Hellenistic Greek. The verb μετανοιεῖν means 'to perceive afterward, to change one's mind, to regret, to experience remorse, to repent'; correspondingly, the noun means 'change of mind, regret, repentance'. 'For the Greek, μετάνοια does not suggest a transformation of one's whole moral attitude, an effectual change in the whole direction of one's life, a conversion that determines the whole course of one's subsequent behavior. Before himself as well as before the gods, the Greek is able to repent, μετανοιεῖν, a sin in actu . . ., but μετάνοια as penance or conversion in the sense of the Old and New Testaments . . . is unknown to him.'[15] Individual acts of metanoia remain separate acts of repentance or regret; they never combine into a single whole – a single permanent and total turning of one's whole existence

---

14 Cf., for example, Gilbert Murray's searching analyses in *Euripides and His Age*. London: Oxford University Press, 1965; Hans Urs von Balthasar, *Herrlichkeit. Eine theologische Ästhetik 3.1: Im Raum der Metaphysik*. Einsiedeln: Johannes Verlag, 1965, pp. 94–142.

15 Johannes Behm, 'μετανοέω, μετάνοια', in *Theologisches Wörterbuch zum Neuen Testament* 4, Stuttgart: W. Kohlhammer, 1932, pp. 972–1004. For the passage quoted in the text, see pp. 975–976; on the meaning of the word, see esp. pp. 972–975.

into a new way; metanoia continues to be just repentance; it does not become conversion. The notion never suggests itself that one's whole existence, precisely *as a whole*, has need of a total conversion in order to become itself. One might perhaps say that the difference between polytheism and monotheism is silently at work here: an existence that is oriented toward many divine powers, that seeks to affirm itself in their confusion and rivalries, is never more than a many-sided gamble with the powers that be, whereas the one God becomes the one way that places man before the Yes or No of acceptance or rejection, that unifies his existence around a single call.

An objection arises at this point that will, at the same time, help to clarify our meaning. For it might be said that the arguments thus far adduced are relevant only as long as they are applied exclusively to the words μετάνοια and μεταωοεῖε; they become untenable if they are applied to the Greek word for conversion, namely, ἐπιοτροφή-ἐπιοτρέφειν (the word generally used in this sense in the Septuagint to translate the Hebrew šūb).[16] Plato uses the word στρέφειν to designate circular movement, that is, the perfect movement that is proper to the gods, the heavens and the world. The circle, at first a cosmic sign, becomes also an existential symbol: a sign for the return of existence to itself. From this origin, ἐπιστροφή – a return to the oneness of reality, incorporation into the circular form of the world – becomes for the Stoa and for Neoplatonism the central ethical postulate.[17] Then follows the realization that, to be truly himself, man, as a whole, has need of the comprehensive movement of conversion [*Umkehr:* turning away] and self-communion [*Einkehr:* turning within], which, as the never-ending task of metanoia, requires that he turn his life away from dissipation in external matters and direct it within, where truth dwells. In my opinion, there is no need to deny, out of false anxiety about the originality of the Bible or naive counterpoising of biblical and Greek thought, that philosophical thought is here close to Christian belief and offers a formula by which the Fathers of the Church were able to express the ontological depths of the historical process of Christian conversion. Let us not hesitate to say that advance has been made here. But we must add that with this reference to man's communion with himself we have not encompassed the whole range of the conversion demanded by the Bible. The Greek ἐπιστροφή is a turning within to that innermost depth of man that is at once one and all. It is idealistic: if man penetrates deeply enough, he reaches the divine in himself. Biblical belief

16   Johannes Behm, 'μετανοέω, μετάνοια', in *Theologisches Wörterbuch zum Neuen Testament* 4, pp. 985–994. Granted, Behm does not see the significance of this fact. His whole presentation is based on the antithetical relationships: biblical–Greek, legal-prophetic, cultic-religious (personal), and is consequently open to question despite the comprehensive body of material in the evaluations and the ordering of the matter under consideration. P. Hoffmann, 'Umkehr', in Heinrich Fries (ed.), *Handbuch theologischer Grundbegriffe 2*. Munich: Kösel, 1963, pp. 719–724 has simply appropriated the plan of Behm's article.
17   Cf. Pierre Hadot, 'Conversio', in Joachim Ritter (ed.), *Historisches Wörterbuch der Philosophie I*. Darmstadt: Wissenschaftliche Buchgesellschaft, 1971, pp. 1033–1036.

is more critical, more radical. Its criticism is directed not just to the outer man. It knows that danger lurks precisely in man's arrogance of spirit, in the most inward depths of his being. It criticizes not just half but all of man. Salvation comes not just from inwardness, for this very inwardness can be rigid, tyrannical, egoistical, evil: 'It is what comes out of a man that makes him unclean' (Mk 7:20). It is not just the turning to oneself that saves but rather the turning away from oneself and toward the God who calls. Man is oriented, not to the innermost depths of his own being, but to the God who comes to him from without, to the Thou who reveals himself to him and, in doing so, redeems him. Thus metanoia is synonymous with obedience and faith; that is why it belongs in the framework of the reality of the Covenant; that is why it refers to the community of those who are called to the same way: where there is belief in a personal God, there horizontality and verticality, inwardness and service, are ultimately not opposites. From this fact, it is immediately clear that metanoia is not just any Christian attitude but the fundamental Christian act per se, understood admittedly from a very definite perspective: that of transformation, conversion, renewal and change. To be a Christian, one must change not just in some particular area but without reservation even to the innermost depths of one's being.

2.2 Salvation

In the same way in which faith is structurally marked by *metanoia*, so too should salvation be understood. In a 1973 article, considered as programmatic, Ratzinger described the conditions to which salvation has to measure up if it really wants to be considered as salvation according to Christian theology.[18] To this end, he formulates four theses from which a Christian theology of redemption or teaching on salvation should find its point of departure.

Preliminary Questions Concerning a Theology of Redemption . . .[19]

The most serious challenge to the Christian faith lies in its historical ineffectiveness. It has not changed the world, or at least so it seems. All theoretical difficulties are trivial in comparison to this dismal record, because it means that the central tenet of Christianity, the message of redemption, is empty. It is only words. When, however, through faith, nothing happens, then everything else that it may otherwise say is also just an empty theory, beyond verification or falsification, and hence irrelevant. [. . .]

In this situation, it might have seemed like an escape to seek to simply explain

18 [Selection from J. Ratzinger, 'Vorfragen zu einer Theologie der Erlösung', in: L. Scheffczyk, *Erlösung und Emanzipation*. Freiburg: Herder, 1973, pp. 141–155. Trans. by David Kirchhoffer].
19 Cf. Ibid.

redemption using the traditional vocabulary of theology, which was certainly once a verbal and conceptual expression of religious experience, but which today no longer reveals these experiences, so that its words have become, for a start, doctrinal formulae that must first be reopened to the experiences that they contain. The powerlessness, not only of theology, but indeed of the word, including the primal word of the Christian message itself, is at the same time the reason why theology today desperately seeks to attach itself to those actualities that appear to offer hope of transforming the world—the reason, therefore, why it becomes political and emancipatory. One can understand this attempt to find a connection to reality, but it is hardly convincing. One has the impression that theology, since it can present no facts of its own, now seeks to claim facts established elsewhere as its own reality by spelling them out using a theological vocabulary—with considerable intellectual skill, and yet nevertheless without credibility, because neither were the facts considered from the perspective of their origin, nor was this vocabulary originally intended for such a statement.[20] More serious for the human being than the failure of theology is the fact that even in the new attempts at changing the world, a salvation is nowhere in sight that would deserve this name; instead, the human being is getting increasingly lost in the contradiction between his expectations and his possibilities. What should one say? In principle, we can only stutteringly try to find the reality that is in faith, and to make this suggestively accessible using words; ultimately, the words can only encourage one to search, and no more. With this in mind I would like to develop, in four theses, a view of what salvation [das Heil][21] should be that deserves this name, and how this expectation relates to the testimony of Christian faith.

First Thesis:

Only universal salvation can be labelled as salvation.
Salvation is bound to universality. [. . .]
Why should two people, who have found one another in fulfilling love, not

---

20 This does not dismiss the important issue of the political dimension of Christianity, but rather its transformation into a purely worldly doctrine of salvation.

21 [Translator's note: *Das Heil* is obviously a very important concept in this document. A note of clarification may be helpful. *Das Heil*, certainly in religious terms, is usually translated as salvation. Nevertheless, it shares a root with the verb to heal, *heilen* (salus, well-being, fulfillment). *Heil* in German also carries with it the connotation of fullness or completeness. Finally, *das Heil* can also mean well-being and happiness, hence, though in English we use salvation, or to be saved, it lacks the quality of fullness, completeness, health, flourishing, or happiness that is implied in the German. It may be that at times, Ratzinger intentionally relies on this double meaning. For example, when Ratzinger talks of the *Heil* of two lovers in the first thesis below, the notion of well-being or happiness is obviously very strong. Therefore, though this translation will, as a rule, use salvation for *das Heil*, and insert in square brackets German terms that are derived from the word *Heil* in order to allow the reader to see links that may not be otherwise apparent in the English translation, the reader should bear in mind that *das Heil* can have a less religious connotation. The context will help to make the difference clear].

have also found salvation, even if the all the rest of the world is in misery?

If one follows this question, it leads to our thesis. For, salvation that is only in the moment is no salvation. Salvation demands security, freedom from fear. It demands a future. It demands the fullness of the human being as time. This raises, first of all, the problem of death. Does death, as the end of human time, as the continuous threat to human time, as its ever present opponent in sickness and life-threatening circumstances, not fundamentally call every salvation into question? This includes however the fact that the fullness experienced in the depth of the soul is insufficient, as much as it outweighs the weakness of the body and helps it to exist. Where sickness strikes people down, and where it at the same time leads the other to suffer with them; that is where the abundance of salvation is shattered. Where hunger tortures, where social dangers make the future uncertain, where injustice endangers the existence of the lovers; in all these circumstances there is an innermost that cannot be destroyed, which they alone can claim for themselves, but the fullness of salvation is missing.

Thus it becomes clear that there is no such thing as the isolated happiness of a few lovers, that they are dependent upon the society in which they stand and are also dependant on the powers of the world over which neither they nor the others have control. This idea can be further deepened: can love actually be reliance when one does not know whether one can indeed rely on a human being? Whether he, the other, or I are capable of faithfulness and reliability? And can one be happy with others, if one does not know if humanity should be happy about its existence at all?[22] Whether some people can be happy ultimately depends on the context of the society and the world of values in which they live—only they can empower them to be happy, but then the problem again arises as to who empowers this society to be happy. [. . .]

In the background of such considerations, the question of God automatically arises. For, if it is as depicted, if human happiness is so demanding, then only a God could in principle grant it. Because only he could give certainty that the world and its time, its still unknown future, are worth saying yes to. The empowerment to be happy could ultimately only come from him. For, only he can answer even the most powerful opponent of happiness, death, in all its manifold presence.

In a world in which there is no universal salvation, there must certainly be the beginnings of salvation, fragments of salvation. These appear where love appears in one of its forms. They are the foundation that allows the human being to hope for salvation at all, that encourages him to resist despair. But they are fragments of salvation, not salvation itself. For this requires universality. Absolute wholeness.

---

22   The seriousness of this question is intensely brought to light by Sartre and Camus. Cf. Camus, 'Le mythe de Sisyphe', in *A. Camus: Essais*. Paris: Gallimard, 1965, p. 89–211. Regarding Camus, cf. also G. Linde, 'Das Problem der Gottesvorstellungen im Werk von Albert Camus' (unpublished masters/doctoral dissertation, 1972).

Second Thesis:

Salvation is bound to freedom.

The universality of salvation compels the human being to seek the salvation of others, because his salvation lies in the salvation of others. He must try to make them happy in order to be happy. He must deliver them, in order to be delivered. This leads to the question as to what the conquerable causes of suffering [das Unheil] are. The person is thus led to cultural, social, and political activity. The society attempts to become the locus of salvation. Historically, this can take on various forms. In classical Latin, the word redeemer [der Heiland][23] means 'conservator.' Those who conserve the perfect order of the world, who protect it from war and barbarism, warrant salvation. The advent of Christianity changed the situation and no longer simply identified salvation with the conservation of what had been achieved, and could also thus no longer refer to the redeemer using the term conservator, but rather created a new word, salvator.[24] Christianity found its chance, to begin with, amongst the many who were not favoured by the current system and who could hence not rely on the conservator. Finally, in the perspective opened up by the French Revolution, no longer the conservator, but the revolutionary is the translation of 'redeemer;' salvation is no longer seen in conservation, but in change.

In both cases, in the socio-political idea of salvation, there is also a religious factor. The emperor is the conservator not only of the momentary political achievement, but, by virtue of his proximity to the divine powers, also the conservator of the cosmos. Only if he can be that, only if he is something like a god, can he provide that security that salvation signifies. And the revolutionary also does not promise just another government, but another person, and another world: when the revolution has run its course, the human being will be another, and therefore his relationship to the world and thus the world itself will be another. And that is why there will be salvation.

Both cases overlook the fact that one cannot simply externally decree salvation for a human being. This is above all impossible because salvation is not based on having[25] but on being.[26] The inadequacy, and indeed the irredeemabilty, of having has become similarly clear in all cultures and under all ideological systems.

23 [Translator's note: *Der Heiland* is usually translated as redeemer or saviour and typically refers to Jesus Christ. This seems not to be the intended meaning in this context, however, as Ratzinger appears to be working with the dual meaning of *das Heil* (see note above). In this sense, *der Heiland* is the one who brings happiness or well-being (*das Heil*). This translation has nevertheless opted for the classical translation but the reader is advised to bear the nuances in mind].

24 H. U. Instinsky, *Die alte Kirche und das Heil des Staates.* München: Kösel, 1963, p. 28 ff.

25 [Translator's comment: Ratzinger uses *Haben*, the substantive of the verb *haben* (to have). The same applies to *Sein*, the substantive of *sein* (to be). This substantive usage is indicated here by capitalizing the first letter].

26 Regarding being and having, see esp. Gabriel Marcel, *Être et avoir.* Paris: Éditions Aubier-Montaigne 1935.

The attempt to attain salvation through having has been sufficiently disproved that it must be dismissed as a serious alternative. A minimum of having can be a condition of salvation, but it can never be salvation itself. Salvation is not based on having, but on being, which means it is based on an interpretive faculty [*Sinngebung*: literally meaning-giving][27] that decides on the value or disvalue of having or not having.

The definition 'salvation is tied to meaningful interpretation [*Sinngebung*]', is only apparently in contradiction to the first attempt at a definition 'salvation [*Heil*] is attached to love'. For love heals [*heilt*][28] because it gives meaning [*ist sinngebend*: is meaning-giving], and interpretation [*Sinngebung*] has in some sense to do with love, with the creative affirmation of the being given to me, a being based on certitude. This will be dealt with in more detail shortly.

First, however, it must be said that the attempt to produce salvation, be it by the conservator, or be it by the revolutionary, can initially still indeed claim that it offers to give meaning [*Sinngebung*]: the salvation of this society. In reality, an interpretation [*Sinngebung*] that is based on conserving or changing the circumstances of the world ultimately still remains limited to having, and therefore does not even begin to enter into the area in which meaning [*Sinn*] indeed only truly reveals itself.

That salvation is connected to meaning [*Sinn*] and hence proceeds in the manner of love, ultimately has as a consequence that it can only come about where the freedom of the human being reveals meaning-giving [*sinngebenden*] salvation. A politically enacted salvation is no salvation. And an emancipation that only happens from the outside does not free the person. They can establish conditions of freedom, fragments of freedom, but not be freedom themselves. Freedom can only come from freedom. Only where the human being allows himself to be freed for love and meaning [*Sinn*], does he touch the realm of salvation. However, where his being is hidden by his focus on having, he is only pushed ever further away from freedom, and hence also from the possibility of salvation.

At this point, the God-question sails back into view. In principle, only a God can reach into the freedom of the human being. Only God can offer to give the human being's freedom the significance [*Sinngebung*] that again both is freedom and creates freedom. But, at the same time, herein lies also the barrier for God: he too can only touch freedom in freedom. He too cannot force salvation. Because, one who is forced is not free. And only the free are saved [or complete: *Heil*].

Third Thesis:
Salvation is bound to love

---

27   [Translator's comment: This could possibly also be translated as a *hermeneutic*, i.e. a life-orienting interpretive framework].

28   [Translator's comment: Salvation (*das Heil*) shares a root with the verb to heal (*heilen*). See previous note on the meanings associated with the German word *das Heil*].

The content of this statement, which has increasingly revealed itself to be the central point of our considerations, must now be examined more closely. What is love? Why does the human being need it to the extent that his salvation substantially depends on it and everything else appears to be only a condition of salvation, but not its actual content?

Here, I rely heavily on Josef Pieper's analysis of love, which seems to me to convincingly clarify its anthropological character and its theological depth.[29] So what is love? To love someone means, first, allowing someone to be there. Accepting his being. More—willing it. 'It is good that you are'—this is the character of love. Love means standing up for the being of the beloved. At the same time, love, of its own accord, once more affords being to the beloved, justifies this being as good; indeed, as necessary.

[. . .] To put it differently, love has to do with truth, with that which is truly good for a human being. When put this way, however, the question arises as to what actually is good for the other. What is the truth of the human being? Is this truth really good at all? Is the truth salvation? Or is the truth of the human being ultimately just a dark meaninglessness that one would be better off not asking about? Could human salvation just be a forgetting, a superficial façade in the midst of what is actually absurdity? In other words, love ultimately faces emptiness if there is no truth that saves [or no truth that is complete: *die Heil ist*]. The human affirmation of the existence of the other, the human 'good' regarding the existence of the other, remains superficial and tragic if this good is only spoken about by people, if this good is not also objectively true. Truth needs the human being in order to be creative, but the human being also needs truth so that what he creates does not become a lie.[30]

Thus, behind the idea of the hope-giving, transformative human 'good,' lies the question as to whether this good is true, and only if it is true does it hold. Related to this fact is the fact that the human being always wants to see his salvation as having been achieved independent of the acceptance of the other, of love; he would like it autonomously. This is true for the Stoic idea of salvation. This is largely true also for modern consciousness.

[. . .] To me it would appear incontrovertible that in the call for emancipation, in the way that it has today become almost a religious confession, one can also hear to a large extent the longing for emancipation from the highest Love, which seems like an aggressive primeval father, because it hinders the human being's autarchy, because it seems to make his salvation dependent on the unenforceable nature of the love for another and its truth. But, is not humourlessness, the grim seriousness of people, which is taken to be the inner foundation of their being,

29 J. Pieper, *Über die Liebe*. Munich: Kösel-Verlag, 1972, pp. 38–105. Cf. also the well-thought-out analysis of the concept of salvation by K. Hemmerle, 'Der Begriff des Heils', in *Internat. Kath. Zeitschr.* 1 (1972), p. 210–230.
30 Cf. J. Pieper, *Über die Liebe*. Munich: Kösel-Verlag, 1972, p. 67 ff.

and whose freedom is at the same time a liberation from the ground of their own being, without which nothing can be grounded, valuable or meaningful, rooted in this kind of emancipation? Without which [the seriousness, or the foundation it seems to supply], only inconsolability still remains. Freud himself admits, with staggering openness, at the end of his considerations regarding the problem of conscience, that he does not know how to offer his fellow human being any consolation.[31] Perhaps the liberation of the human being is not really his emancipation from the highest love, not the ability to (in a Marxist or Freudian way) see through love as in illusion, but the received assurance that it really does exist and that it is the unshakeable locus of my being and the being of all people? It would be appropriate for theology critically to examine contemporary liberation (emancipation) ideas where it encounters them. It is not uncommon for them to aim for a freedom that is void, and is hence itself a nothing that offers nothing to the human being. Where reverence, love, and faithfulness are said to come from the vocabulary of the un-human (as happens), the human being has not become free, but has become trapped by a lie that can only destroy him.[32]

Fourth Thesis:
Salvation is bound to universal love, which, however, calls for particular human love and makes it possible in faith.

The third thesis led us back to the first: human love remains questionable as the medium of salvation, and indeed ultimately a tragic temerity, if its 'being called good' [*Gutheißung*][33] is not true, if its 'being called good' is not based on a genuine endorsement [*Gutheißung*], issuing from it, of people and the world. At this point, to me, it seems the liberating power of faith becomes apparent: faith is assurance that the truth is good. Assurance that 'one's own existence indeed says nothing else than that one is loved by the Creator.'[34] It is entering

---

31   S. Freud, 'Das Unbehagen in der Kultur', in S. Freud, *Gesammelte Werke XIV*. London: Hogarth Press, 1955, p. 506.

32   With regard to the problematic of the concept of emancipation, cf. G. Rohrmoser, *Emanzipation und Freiheit*. Munich: Goldmann, 1970; R. Spaemann, "Autonomie, Mündigkeit, Emanzipation. Zur Ideologisierung von Rechtsbegriffen", in *Erziehungswissenschaft. Zwischen Herkunft und Zukunft der Gesellschaft. In memoriam Ernst Lichtenstein*, Siegfried Oppolzer (ed). Wuppertal: Bergische Universität Wuppertal, 1971, pp. 317-324.

33   [Translator's note: *Gutheißen* means to endorse, but when literally translated it is 'to name good'. This is important because Ratzinger seems to be using a wordplay when he refers to the goodness of creation (see below). Hence, this translation notes where he uses *Gutheißen* or its substantive *Gutheißung*: endorsement, in order to bring this nuance to the reader's attention].

34   J. Pieper, *Über die Liebe*. Munich: Kösel-Verlag, 1972, p. 56 ff. [Translated here from the original German as quoted in the present text.] This connection is also rightly noted by H. Keßler, *Erlösung als Befreiung*. Düsseldorf: Patmos, 1972. p 90: 'This certainty of being accepted completely is the one moment in Jesus' experience of God, and that which this experience historically mediates—that which breaks forth from Jesus. The other moment, the direct turning to the other, indeed belongs so essentially to this that without it, it does not add up to Jesus' experience of God . . .'. Translated

into the liberating endorsement [*Gutheißung*] of the seventh day, which first and foremost legitimises all human endorsement [all human 'being called good': *Gutheißung*].

But the issue doesn't end there, because the human being has his history, which disconnects him from the Creation. He is a fallen and fragmented creature, who cannot manage to be one with himself. He does not reflect God, he reflects humankind and their messed-up world. One can absolutely not endorse him the way he is; he himself cannot declare himself good [*sich gutheißen*] in this situation; he can only affirm himself, against his empirical presence, as that which he could be and is not. The discrepancy that disconnects him from his salvation, from his being one with himself, and all that is, does not only come about as a result of the tragedy of the world, it is also called guilt. The human being does not in fact just need to be called good [or endorsed: *Gutheißung*], he needs endorsement [*Gutheißung*] in the form of forgiveness. Forgiveness that leaves the truth intact, that plainly reveals guilt as guilt, but that opens up the possibility of conversion. He needs the goodness of truth in a deeper sense, with which we are confronted in the idea of creation: he needs truth not only as the good [*Gute*] of being, but as the goodness that bears that which has become untrue. Human existence not only becomes irredeemable where the endorsement [*Gutheißung*] of being is denied it, or where it conceals this from itself, but also there where there is no forgiveness, or where the human being rejects forgiveness.

The crucified Christ is, for the believer, the assurance of a universal love that is simultaneously a very concrete love for him, for all people. He is the assurance of God's love that lasts even into death; of a 'being called good' [*Gutheißung*] that does not deviate from the truth—otherwise God did not need to die—and which nevertheless in the truth persists in being unconditional, reliable goodness [or benevolence] that reaches to the deepest end of human existence (εἰς τέλος! John 13:1). The crucified Christ is God's concrete promise, valid for every human being, that makes him certain that he, the human being, is such a serious concern [*Ernstfall*][35] for God, that he gives up his own life for him. This 'being taken seriously' is part of 'being called good' [*Gutheißung*]. The crucified

here from the German as quoted in the present text. Keßler, after this positive start, then blocks his own way to an adequate doctrine of salvation, first due to the fact that he hardly takes the problem of guilt and forgiveness into account, and second with an anthropology in which there is little room for substitution in the full sense of the word, so that practically only the association of example and imitator remains as a Christological foundation. At the same time, despite usable approaches, the fact that, in the Christology itself, a strict interconnection between theology and anthropology is not achieved takes its toll. With respect to the philosophy of substitution, it would be particularly useful to analyze the work of E. Levinas, esp. *Totalité et Infini. Essai sur l'Extériorité*. La Haye: Nijhoff, 1971. Cf. also the reference made by K. Hemmerle, 'Der Begriff des Heils', in *Internat. Kath. Zeitschr.* 1 (1972), p. 210–230, esp. p. 228 ff.

35 [Translators comment: The word used in the German is *Ernstfall*, which means emergency. 'Serious concern' here is used for stylistic purposes].

God is the event that expresses the seriousness [*Ernstfall*] of the 'good-calling' [*Gutheißung*] of the seventh day of creation. The cross says, there is a truth of the human being that is good [*gut*] and that is benevolent [*gütig*]—that is his redemption. [. . .]

The salvation of the world exists, paradoxically, in the crucified one. Only in the cross, in freedom that leaves itself, that can leave itself in the assurance of His love, does the freedom arise that can be redemption. The cross is the ultimate challenge to risk a love that changes the privation and the injustice of the world. But it is also the most definitive rejection of a producible redemption, which cannot affect being; the locus of a meaning and a love that donates itself—has donated itself and indeed for this reason is redemption.[36]

Only at this point does it become possible to enter into the classical themes of the theological tradition, such as the relationship between 'redemption' and 'sanctification.' I stop here, in order to make a final comment with regard to the question that we started with. To he who feels tormented by his self-love, by the narcissism of an emancipation that aims at nothingness through ethics, it may appear as if his salvation could only come about through being released *from* ethics. To he who has experienced the shadows of his own ego and the destructiveness of a freedom of nothingness, it can become clear that he is nevertheless not delivered *from* ethics, but *by* ethics—of course on the precondition that there is really forgiveness by the final authority. Both together—ethics and forgiveness, law and good news, deliver him, break through the fatal darkness of a love that is not directed by truth, and open up that love that grants salvation.

With this last thesis, we have obviously arrived at Christ, in whom the link between universality, truth, freedom and love has been concretely revealed, as an offer of salvation to humanity. In the third section of this chapter, we continue this reflection.

2.3 Salvation in Christ: 'I am the way, the truth and the life' (John 14:6)

Salvific truth has indeed been revealed to us in and through Jesus Christ. This constitutes the core of Christian faith: everything that is believed is Christologically tinted. Christ teaches us to know God in an unsurpassable way. 'I believe in Jesus Christ' means that one accepts that in the human being, Jesus, is the deepest meaning that is encountered. In him, God personally comes near to the human person. Even more, he is the

---

36 Cf. K. Hemmerle, 'Der Begriff des Heils', in *Internat. Kath. Zeitschr.* 1 (1972), p. 221, 226.

God-become-human.[37] 'Anyone who has seen me, has seen the Father'
(John 14:9). Jesus' life shows us what God is like, how people should see
him, and how they can live meaningfully.[38] In Christ, God's love becomes
visible and as such, he signifies hope for all believers.[39] His death on the
cross and resurrection – as seen in the previous section – gives the human
being the certainty of God's love to the utmost.[40] In the following, we
will present sections from an article published in 1990, which is typically
representative of Ratzinger's view on how, from a Christological perspective, freedom, truth and love are united in Christ.[41]

In fact, Ratzinger observes that images of Christ that have no connection with the Christ we know from tradition abound – some appear
to create their own Christ nowadays. Still others, especially since the
enlightenment, are fixated with the past: only the historical Jesus is the
true Jesus. These two dead-end paths stand in the way of a real encounter
with Jesus Christ.

> Whoever wants to see only the Christ of yesterday will not find him; and[42]
> whoever wants to have him only today will likewise not encounter him. From the
> very beginning it is proper to him that he was, he is, and he will come. As the
> living one, he was always already the one who is to come. The message of his
> coming and remaining belongs essentially to the image of himself: this claim on
> all the dimensions of time rests again upon the claim that he understood his earthly
> life as a going forth from the Father and a simultaneous remaining with him, thus
> bringing eternity into relation with time. [. . .]
>
> The first encounter with Jesus Christ takes place in today; in fact one can only
> encounter him because he truly has a today. But in order for me to come close to
> the whole Christ and not to some coincidentally perceived part, I must listen to the
> Christ of yesterday, as he shows himself in the sources, especially in Holy Scripture.
> If at the same time I listen carefully, and do not, because of some dogmatizing
> world-view, cut off essential parts of his self-revelation, I see him open to the future,

37   Cf. J. Ratzinger, *Theologische Prinzipienlehre*. Munich: Wewel, 1982, p. 191: here, Ratzinger goes
       deeper into the divinity: the statement 'Jesus, the man, is God' has a metaphysical nature; it is
       an ontological statement. However, this does not lead to a denial of the historical dimension of
       Christianity, but it is the condition to speak of *sarks egeneto*.
38   Cf. Idem, *Introduction to Christianity*. San Francisco: Ignatius Press, 2004, p 50: 'the discovery of God
       in the countenance of the human being Jesus from Nazareth'.
39   Cf. Idem, *Dogma und Verkündigung*. München/Freiburg: Wewel, 1973, p. 455.
40   Cf. Idem, 'Vorfragen zu einer Theologie der Erlösung', in L. Scheffczyk, *Erlösung und Emanzipation*.
       Freiburg: Herder, 1973, p. 152–155.
41   Cf. J. Ratzinger, *Jesus Christus heute*, in *Internat. Kath. Zeitschr.* 19 (1990) pp. 56–70 (E.T.: 'Jesus Christ
       Today', in *Communio* 17 (Spring 1990) pp. 68–87).
42   [Selections from J. Ratzinger, 'Jesus Christ Today', in *Communio* 17 (Spring 1990) pp. 68–87, 69–70,
       71–72, 74–81 and 84–86].

and see him coming toward us from eternity, which encompasses past, present, and future at once. Precisely wherever such holistic understanding has been sought out and lived, there Christ has always become completely 'today,' for only that which possesses roots in yesterday and the power of growth for tomorrow and for all time has true power over today and in today, and stands in contact with eternity. Thus have the great epochs of the history of the faith each brought forth their own image of Christ, as they were able to see him anew from their own today, and thus recognized 'Christ yesterday, today, and forever.' [. . .]

From considerations of the experiences and hardships of our time, contemporary theology has proposed fascinating images of Christ today: Christ the Liberator, the new Moses in a new Exodus; Christ the poor among the poor, as he shows himself in the beatitudes; Christ the completely loving one, whose being is being for others, who in the word 'for' expresses his deepest reality. Each of these images brings forth something essential to the image of Jesus; each of them presupposes basic questions: What is freedom, and where does one find the road that leads not just anywhere but to true freedom, to the real 'Promised Land' of human existence? What is the blessedness of poverty, and what must we do that others and we ourselves arrive at it? How does Christ's 'being-for' reach us, and where does it lead us? On all these questions there is today a lively debate, which will be fruitful if we do not try to solve it only out of the present, but also keep our gaze on the Christ of yesterday and of eternity. Within the limits of a single article it is impossible to enter into this debate, even though as background it gives the leading perspectives. Starting with our methodological considerations, I would like to choose a different route: to take our current question and thinking and connect them to a biblical theme, and thus draw it into our consideration of the tension of Yesterday-Today-Eternity. I am thinking of the fundamental saying of the Johannine Christ, 'I am the way and the truth and the life' (John 14:6). The idea of the way is clearly connected with the Exodus. Life has become a key word of our time in view of the threats of a 'civilization' of death, which is in truth the loss of all civilization and culture; the motif 'being-for' is obvious here. On the other hand, truth is not a favorite notion of our time; it is associated with intolerance, and is thus perceived more as threat than promise. But precisely for this reason it is important that we ask about it, and allow ourselves to be questioned about it from the perspective of Christ.

Christ the way—Exodus and liberation

Jesus Christ today—the first image in which we can see him in this our time is that of the *Way*, which from the history of Israel we call the Exodus: as the way out into the open. [. . .]

We can say then, that the 'departure' of Jesus in Jerusalem is the real and definitive exodus, in which Christ treads the path into freedom and becomes himself the way to freedom for mankind. Let us add that for Luke the entire public life of Jesus is depicted as a going up to Jerusalem, and so the life of Jesus as a whole is an exodus in which he is like Moses and Israel. To grasp all the dimensions of this way, we must also look at the Resurrection; the Epistle to the Hebrews describes the exodus of Jesus as not ending in Jerusalem: 'He has opened for us a new and living way through the curtain, that is, through his flesh' (Heb. 10:20). His exodus leads beyond all things created, to the 'tent not made by human hands' (Heb. 9:11) into contact with the living God. The promised land to which he comes and to which he leads us is the act of sitting 'at the right hand of God' (cf. Mk. 12:36; Acts 2:33; Rom. 8:34, etc.). There lives in every human the thirst for freedom and liberation; at each step reached along this way we are also conscious that it is only a step, and that nothing which has been reached fulfills our desire. The thirst for freedom is the voice of the image of God within us; it is the thirst 'to sit at God's right hand,' to be 'like God.' A liberator who wishes to deserve the name must open the door to this, and all empirical forms of freedom must be measured against this. [. . .]

We must of course not construe the notion of following as the core of New Testament exodus too narrowly. A correct understanding of the following of Christ depends on a correct understanding of the figure of Jesus Christ. The following cannot be narrowed down to morality. It is a Christological category, and only then does it flow over into a moral charge. And so following says too little if one thinks too narrowly of Jesus himself. One who sees Jesus only as a pioneer for a freer religion, for a more open morality, or for a better political structure, must reduce the following to the acceptance of specific programmatic ideas. The result of this is that one then ascribes to Jesus the beginnings of a program which one has oneself further developed, and whose use can then be interpreted as joining oneself to him. Such a following through participating in a program is as arbitrary as it is insufficient, for the empirical situations then and now are all too different; what one thinks to be able to take over from Jesus does not extend beyond quite general intentions. Recourse to such a diminution of the notion of following, and thus of the message of exodus, rests often on a logic that at first seems enlightening: Jesus was, it is true, God and man, but *we* are only human; *we* cannot follow him in his being God, but only as humans. In such an explanation we think all too little of mankind, of our freedom, and fall completely away from the logic of the New Testament and its bold statement, 'Be imitators of God' (Eph. 5:1).

No, the call to the following concerns not just some human program, or the human virtues of Jesus, but his *entire* way, 'through the curtain' (Heb. 10:20). What is essential and new about the way of Jesus Christ is that he opens *this* way for us, for only thus do we come into freedom. The dimension of the following is: to enter into communion with God, and thus it is bound up with the Paschal mystery.[43] Thus the summons to following which comes after Peter's confession

---

43   This interpretation, taken for granted by the Fathers, can be found in brief in one of the unsurpass-able sayings of Augustine: *Ascendit Christus in caelum: sequamur eum.* Sermon 304.4, PL: 38.1397. Still important in this connection is E. Peterson, 'Zeuge der Wahrheit', in *Theologische Traktate*. Munich:

says: 'If anyone will come after me, let him deny himself and take up his cross, and so follow me' (Mk. 8:34). That is not just a bit of moralizing, which sees life primarily from the negative side, nor is it masochism for those who dislike themselves. One does not come near the true meaning of the saying if one twists it as a stern morality for heroic temperaments who decide for martyrdom. The call of Jesus is only to be understood from the great Easter context of the entire exodus, which 'goes through the curtain.' It is from this goal that the fundamental human wisdom gets its meaning: only the one who loses self finds self; only the one who gives life receives it (Mk. 8:35). [. . .]

To put it straightforwardly, Christian exodus involves a conversion which accepts the promise of Christ in its entire breadth, and is prepared to lose one's self, and life itself, therein. To this conversion belong therefore the overcoming of self-reliance and the entrusting of one's self to the mystery, to the sacrament in the community of the Church, where God as the agent enters my life and frees it from its isolation. To this conversion belongs, with faith, that losing of self in love which is resurrection because it is a dying. It is a cross contained in an Easter, which for all that is not necessarily less painful.

Christ the truth – truth, freedom, and poverty

Let us now attempt at least a short glance at the other two terms which belong with 'Way': Truth and Life. [. . .]

Of course when we talk today of knowledge as liberating us from the slavery of ignorance, we usually do not think of God, but of mastery, the knowledge of dealing with art, with things, with people. God remains out of the picture; for questions of getting along he seems unimportant. First one must know how to assert oneself; once that is secured, one wants room for speculation. In this shrinking of the question of knowledge lies not only the problem of our modern idea of truth and freedom, but *the* problem of our time altogether, for it presumes that for the shaping of things human and the fashioning of our lives it is indifferent whether or not there is a God. God seems to lie outside the functioning relationships of our lives and our society, the well-known *Deus otiosus* (superfluous God) of the history of religions.[44] A God who is insignificant for human life is no God at all, since he is powerless and unreal. But if the world does not come from God, and is not influenced by him even in the smallest things, then it does not come out of freedom, and freedom is thus not a power in it; it is merely a conglomerate of necessary mechanisms, and any freedom is only appearance. And so from

Kösel, 1951, pp. 165–224.

44 Helpful is A. Brunner, *Die Religion: eine philosophische Untersuchung auf geschichtlicher Grundlage.* Freiburg: Herder, 1956, pp. 67–80. Cf. also A. Dammann, *Die Religionen Afrikas.* Stuttgart: Verlag Kohlhammer, 1963, p. 33; G. van der Leeuw, *Phänomenologie der Religion.* Tübingen: J. C. B. Mohr, 1956, p. 180 ff. (E.T.: G. van der Leeuw, *Religion in Essence and Manifestation.* Princeton, N.J.: Princeton University Press, 1986).

another angle, we once more come up against the notion that freedom and truth are inseparable. If we can know nothing of God, and he cares to know nothing of us, we are not free beings in a creation opening toward freedom, but parts in a system of necessities, in whom the call for freedom, however, will not be quenched. The question about God is simultaneous and one with the question about freedom and about truth.

Basically we have arrived again at that point where once Arius and the Church split, the question of what is distinctively Christian, and of the human capacity for reaching truth. The real kernel of Arius's heresy consists in holding fast to that notion of the absolute transcendence of God which he acquired from the philosophy of late antiquity. This God cannot communicate himself; he is too great, man is too small; there is no meeting of the two. 'The God of Arius remains locked up in his impenetrable solitariness; he is incapable of imparting his own life fully to the Son. Out of care for the transcendence of God, Arius makes of the one and exalted God a prisoner of his own greatness.'[45] So the world is not God's creation; this God cannot operate outwardly, he is closed up in himself, just as, consequently, the world is closed in on itself. The world proclaims no creator, and God cannot proclaim himself. Man does not become a 'friend'; there is no bridge of trust. In a world estranged from God we remain without truth, and thus remain slaves.

Here a saying of the Johannine Christ is of great importance: 'He who sees me, sees the Father' (John 14:9). Christoph Schönborn has shown penetratingly how in the battle over the image of Christ a deeper wrestling with the divine capability of man, that is, his capacity for truth and freedom, was being mirrored. What does he see, who sees the man Jesus? What can an image that represents this man Jesus show? According to one, we see there only a man, nothing more, since God cannot be captured in a likeness. His divinity lies in his 'person,' which as such cannot be 'delineated' nor brought into a picture. The exact opposite view has managed to prevail as orthodox in the Church, that is, as the proper explanation of Holy Scripture: He who sees Christ, truly sees the Father; in the visible is seen the invisible, the invisible one. The visible figure of Christ is not to be understood as static, one dimensional, belonging only to the world of the senses, for the senses themselves are for movement and starting points beyond themselves. The one who looks upon the figure of Christ enters into his exodus, of which the Church Fathers speak expressly in connection with the experience of Mount Tabor. He is led along the Easter road of going beyond, and learns in the visible to see more than the visible.[46] [. . .]

45   Christoph Schönborn, *Die Christus-Ikone. Eine theologische Hinführung.* Schaffhausen: Novalis Verlag, 1984, p. 20 (E.T.: *God's Human Face: The Christ-Icon.* Trans. by Lothar Krauth. San Francisco: Ignatius Press, 1994).

46   C. Schönborn, *Die Christus-Ikone. Eine theologische Hinführung.* Schaffhausen: Noralis Verlag, 1984, p. 30–54.

Christ the life – pre-existence and love

Our closing reflection must take up at least briefly the third word of Jesus' self-proclamation: Jesus the life. The fanatical eagerness for life which we meet on all continents today has sprouted an anti-culture of death, which is becoming more and more the physiognomy of our time. The unleashing of sexual desires, drugs, and the traffic in arms have become an unholy triad, whose deadly net stretches ever more oppressively over the continents. Abortion, suicide, and collective violence are the concrete ways in which the syndicate of death is effective. AIDS has become a portrait of the inner sickness of our culture. There is no longer an immune factor for the soul. Positivistic intelligence offers the soul's organism no ethical immune power; it is the ruin of the soul's immune system, and thus the defenseless surrender to the lying promises of death which appear in the guise of more life. [. . .]

In this situation the realism of the Christian must be found anew; Jesus Christ must be found in today; we must grasp anew what it means to say 'I am the way, the truth, and the life.' For this it would be proper to offer an exact analysis of the sickness, but that is impossible here. Let us be satisfied with the fundamental question: Why do people flee into drugs? In general terms we can say they do it because the life that is offered them is too insipid, too scanty, too empty. After all the pleasures, after all the liberations and hopes that one has pinned on these, there remains a 'much-too-little.' To endure and accept life as hardship becomes insufferable. Life itself should be an inexhaustibly giving, unbounded joy. Two other things are also in play: for one, the desire for completeness, for infinity, which contrasts with the limitations of our life; for another, the wish simply to have all this without pain, without effort. Life should give to us, without our self-giving. Thus we could also say that the reality of the whole process is the denial of love, which leads to flight into lies. But behind this is a false view of God, that is, the denial of God and the worship of an idol. For God is understood in the way of the rich man: he could yield nothing to Lazarus because he wanted to be a god himself, and for that reason even the much that he had was always too little. Thus, God is understood in the manner of Arius, for whom God can have no external relationships because he is only entirely himself. Man desires to be such a god, one to whom everything comes and who gives nothing. And therefore the true God is the real enemy, the competition for a man so innerly blind. Here is the real core of his sickness, for then he is settled in the lie and turned aside from love, which even in the Trinity is a boundless, unconditional self-giving. Thus it is that the crucified Christ—Lazarus—is the true picture of the trinitarian God. In him, this trinitarian being, the whole of love and the whole of selfgiving is seen undimmed.[47]

---

47   Cf. Kolvenbach, *Der österliche Weg:Exerzitien zur Lebenserneuerung.* Freiburg: Herder, 1988, pp. 133–142.

2.4 Salvation in Christ Includes the Hope of Resurrection and Eternal Life

The thesis 'salvation demands universality', quoted in the second section of this chapter, contains a question for the future. Salvation that does not exceed the present moment is not authentic salvation. Salvation requires eternity. God's answer in Jesus Christ announces to us his eternity in saving love. To believe that Jesus Christ is risen implies that Ratzinger believes that we too, the Christian faithful, will rise some day. This 'rising' – he also speaks with confident ease about 'immortality'[48] – is the final salvation of all people. If true human life is rooted in relation to God, then the completion of this life is to arrive at an immediate encounter with God, which is traditionally expressed as the attainment of the beatific vision (*visio beatifica*).

All too often, according to our theologian, this critical faith element is neglected. Belief in eternal life hardly plays any role in contemporary proclamation of the faith.[49] If traditional terms such as resurrection, immortality, eternal life, heaven, hell and purgatory are mentioned, they soon are adapted hermeneutically and completely translated to '*das Diesseitige*', the temporal realm, without offering any perspective on a real life after this earthly life. Then the kernel of faith disappears 'in the clouds of hermeneutics'. Faith in a realistically considered hereafter then testifies to a hermeneutical naïveté typical for simple believers while the 'hermeneutici' claim to possess true '*gnosis*'.[50]

Ratzinger does not accept this reduction of Christian hope and eschatological expectation. The reality of the resurrection event cannot be interpreted away. To this end, he refers to the fifteenth chapter of Paul's first letter to the Corinthians, in which the apostle defends the essentials of Christian faith lived over and against all Greek *sophia*. What is revealed in Christ's resurrection is the belief that God brings life out of death and this is the revelation of salvation. A faith that has not established the content of this belief primarily and substantially is not Christian faith.

48   Cf. J. Ratzinger, *Eschatologie – Tod und ewiges Leben* (Kleine Katholische Dogmatik IX) Regensburg: Pustat Verlag, 1977 (E.T.: *Eschatology, Death and Eternal Life*. Chicago: Franciscan Herald Press, 1988).
49   Cf. J. Ratzinger, *Moeilijkheden met betrekking tot het geloof in Europa vandaag*, in *Emmaüs* 20 (1989), p. 152. (E.T.: 'Difficulties Confronting the Faith in Europe Today', in *L'Osservatore Romano* [English edition], July 24, 1989, p. 6).
50   Cf. J. Ratzinger and U. Hommes, *Das Heil des Menschen*. München: Kösel, 1975, p. 42–43.

Let us . . . take up the question that has been largely left out of the spirit of modern times [*die Neuzeit*], namely, the nature of the salvation of which Faith speaks.[51] In order not to conduct our discussion in a limitless void, it would be good to narrow it down and define it as precisely as possible, even if in so doing, due to the vastness of the issue, some things will be lost. Our question, on the whole, focuses on the comparison of inner-worldly and Christian expectation of salvation. Thus, it stands to reason that we should now ask, in comparison to secular hope in the future, which is what was discussed so far, what hope faith actually has to offer. What does humankind have to hope for after the message of the New Testament? [. . .]

[. . .] and if Christ has not been raised, then our proclamation has been in vain and your faith has been in vain. We are even found to be misrepresenting God, because we testified of God that he raised Christ—whom he did not raise if it is true that the dead are not raised. For if the dead are not raised, then Christ has not been raised. If Christ has not been raised, your faith is futile . . . . Then those also who have died [*die Entschlafenen*: fallen asleep] in Christ have perished [*sind verloren*: are lost]. If for this life only we have hoped in Christ, we are of all people most to be pitied . . . . If the dead are not raised, 'Let us eat and drink, for tomorrow we die.' Do not be deceived: 'Bad company ruins good morals [*das Gute*: good].' Come to a sober and right mind, and sin no more; for some people have no knowledge of God. I say this to your shame (1 Cor 15:14-19, 32-34).

The answer given here is clear: The Christian hopes for the resurrection of the dead. This must, first of all, be said unequivocally, even if today it may sound like naive belief in myths and everything pushes us to weaken and change the interpretation of the statement, even before it is stated. Where this is not done, one has already paved the way for excuses. For Paul, the significance of the Christian proclamation rests on this expectation; without it, faith and testimony are futile, Christian life pointless.[52] In the history of dogma, this statement has been developed in two ways:

(a) Captured in the belief in the resurrection of the dead is the expectation of a new Heaven and new Earth, i.e., the assurance of a positive fulfilment of the purpose of the cosmos and of history, the assurance that both do not end up as a heap of rubbish that, finally, calmly buries the blood and tears of this age as an empty illusion.[53] The image of a 'new Heaven and the new Earth' envisions much more, in the end, a holistic meaning into which all partial meanings enter. They are enclosed in it, belong to it, but it is neither their sum nor their product. It is

51 [Selection from J. Ratzinger, in J. Ratzinger and U. Hommes, *Das Heil des Menschen. Innerweltlich – christlich*. München: Kösel, 1975, pp. 42–49. Trans. by David Kirchhoffer].

52 As to the question, beyond the scope of this discussion, of how 'Resurrection of the Dead' can be appropriately understood from the text and in light of contemporary knowledge, may I refer you to my *Einführung in das Christentum*. München,: Kösel, [10]1970, pp. 289–300.

53 Cf. J. Ratzinger, *Dogma und Verkündigung*. München/Freiburg: Wewel, 1973, pp. 301–314.

precisely the reduction of reality to the relationship between matter and product
that took place in the philosophy of modern times [*der Neuzeit*] and translates
into the praxis of the technical age that has become the undoing of the human
being, who, therein, only completely experiences the discrepancy between desire
[*Wollen*] and work. Under the universal domination of this schema of thought
and life, something that is not a product, and therefore cannot be brought about
by calculated effort, seems to be totally negated. And yet, hope only appears
again in its true sense when we have something more to expect than just our
production. In this way, the reference to the new Heaven and the new Earth is
an acknowledgment of the fact that the human being may hope at all, and that
it is this that then also gives his productions meaning.[54]

(b) A second aspect has been ever more clearly articulated in the history of
Dogma, namely that the Christian promise also entails the fulfilment of every
individual, in which life continues after death. Pope Benedict XII explicitly formulated this in 1336 in his *Bulle Benedictus Deus*: 'The souls . . . of the faithful
who have died, . . . who are in need of no further purification, . . . already
before the resurrection and the general judgement are . . . in Heaven . . . and
see God's essence face to face.'[55] One must say it clearly: the Christian expects
Heaven—even today. In a world that is familiar with the law of the conservation of energy, it does not surprise him that that mysterious energy that we call
'spirit', 'soul' does not get lost and, through all the shadows, it finally sees its
ground, communicates with it and, precisely in this way, communicates with all of
Creation.

In this context, an additional comment is necessary. In reference to the question
that death poses for every human hope, we named 'Heaven', but we did not
speak of Hell, which is no 'hope', but rather the end of hope and in this way the
radicalisation of the phenomenon of death. [. . .] Again: the Christian hope is
called Heaven; even though Christian doctrine is familiar with the word Hell, this
means to say that Christian Hope is the assurance of true justice, which can also
be a curse where human life is unjust to the core.

In the light of such information, which comes from the documents of the faith,
the question is unavoidable: But is there then nothing promised for this world, for
this time? This leads us to a third point:

(c) The hope in a definitive progression in history, and in a historically situated

54   Cf. R. Schaeffler, *Die Religionskritik sucht ihren Partner*. Freiburg: Herder, 1974, esp. pp. 47–57, where,
under the title 'Jenseitskritik und Ressentimentverdacht' these problems are presented in a very
illuminating way.

55   'Die Seelen . . . der verstorbenen Gläubigen, . . . die keiner weiteren Reinigung bedürfen,. . . sind
noch vor der Auferstehung und dem Allgemeinen Gericht . . . im Himmel . . . und schauen Gottes
Wesenheit von Angesicht.' Denzinger-Schönmetzer, *Enchiridion Symbolorum* pp. 1000–1002; cf. my
article 'Benedictus Deus', in *Lexikon für Theologie und Kirche II*. Freiburg im Breisgau: Herder, 1957–
1968, pp. 171 ff.

society that is definitively perfect belongs nowhere in Christian expectation. The idea of progress did indeed develop from Christian ideas, but is, as the idea of a cumulative and fixable worldly growth of salvation, itself not Christian. Its date of origin can be fixed with some certainty: it lies in the work of the Calabrian abbot Joachim of Fiore (ca. 1130-1202), who projected the Christian belief in the Trinity onto history, and as such expected a rising line through history from the Age of the Fathers (Old Testament), through the Age of the Son (New Testament), to the Age of the Holy Spirit. [. . .]

One can very well understand this transformation of the Trinitarian creed into a stepwise logic of history: the dissatisfaction with the world as it is has always awoken a longing for a Golden Age; the difference between the prophetic promises of the ancient covenant and the actual reality of the Church had to, after the weakening of the expectation that Christ would return in the short term, formally provoke such concepts of a true Church and a definitively redeemed world. The Church, nevertheless, condemned this as a misinterpretation of its meaning in the dramatic conflict of the 13th and 14th centuries, and rightly so. The Christian expectation for this world should be understood completely differently in light of the Bible and the supporting creeds: this world will always be a world of tribulation [*Drangsal*] and toil. In order to support this statement, one need not refer to the Apocalypse, because this conviction is among the perennial assertions of the whole New Testament. Perhaps, it is most penetratingly formulated in Jesus' farewell speech in the Gospel of John. The last sentence before the so-called High Priestly Prayer reads: 'I have said this to you, so that *in me* you may have peace. *In the world* you face persecution [*Drangsal*]. But take courage; I have conquered the world!' (16,33).

2.5 The Historical and Bodily Human Being Before God: A Sacramental Anthropology

We conclude this chapter with some reflections from 1967 from Joseph Ratzinger on the sacramental nature of being a Christian. Again, he first elaborates on the crisis of the sacramental structure of reality and the sacraments due to modern presuppositions, after which he gives his views on the meaning of the sacraments today. Against idealism and materialism, Ratzinger shows how a Christian sacramental understanding of humanity's relation to God draws upon how human beings really are, as bodily and historically situated beings, in relation to their fellow human beings. It is as such that they live their relation to God. God can only be encountered in a human way — the same God who has revealed Godself in Jesus Christ in the same human, bodily and historical way.

I believe that the sacrament-wary attitude held by the average mentality today stems from a twofold anthropological error, which has sunk deep into the general consciousness as a result of the givens of our time (i.e., as a result of the view of history we have inherited).[56] First, in this regard, the idealistic misjudgement of the nature of the human being, which has reached the height of excess in Fichte's work, still applies, i.e., that every person is an autonomous mind[57] that constructs itself completely according to its own decisions, and is entirely the product of its own choices—nothing other than Will and Freedom that accepts nothing that is not of the mind, and instead constitutes itself entirely in itself. This creative 'I' that Fichte describes is based on, to put it mildly, a confusion of the human being with God by equating them with each other, which is what he in fact does, is a thoroughly consequent expression of his approach, and is indeed at the same time ground for its categorical condemnation, because the human being is not God. To know this, one basically only needs to be a human being oneself. As absurd as this idealism may be in the end, it is nevertheless still deeply ingrained in the European (at least the German) consciousness. When Bultmann says that the mind cannot be fed by material goods and believes he has thereby dealt with the sacramental principle, the same naïve conception of human beings' mental autonomy is, however, ultimately still at work. It seems a bit strange that just in the period that believes it has rediscovered the incarnated-ness of the human being, that thinks that the human being can only be a mind through corporeality, a metaphysics of the mind based on the negation of this relationship continues to have influence, or indeed is just reaching the fullness of its influence. In all fairness, we must indeed admit that Christian metaphysics, long before Fichte, received an excessive dose of Greek idealism, and as a result considerably paved the way for this misunderstanding. It [i.e. Christian metaphysics] considered human souls to already be substantially atomised, edifying themselves in a historical freedom; in so doing, it could barely still explain the wholly historically defined assertions of the Christian faith concerning original sin and redemption; the sacraments, which are the expression of the historical embeddedness of man, became the soul-nourishment for the individual mind existing only for itself. And then one can indeed really ask oneself why God, as mind, does not choose an easier way to encounter the mind of man, and to accord him his mercy [or grace: Gnade]. If it were only about the solitary soul, as individual, being addressed by its God and receiving mercy [or grace: Gnade], then indeed it would be impossible to see what, in this highly intimate,

---

56   [Selection from J. Ratzinger, *Die sakramentale Begründung christlicher Existenz* (Meitingen, Kyrios, 1967), pp. 22-27. Translation by David Kirchhoffer].

57   [Translator's comment: *Geist* in German can mean mind or spirit. When speaking of the philosophy of idealism, it is usually taken to mean mind. A notable exception is Hegelian idealism in which spirit is more common. Hence, *Geist* is usually translated in this text, which addresses idealism, as mind].

totally internal and spiritual process, the intervention of the Church and the material media of the sacraments could actually mean. If, however, there is no such
thing as the autonomy of the human mind, if it is not a relationshipless mental
atom [*Geistatom*], but rather, as a human being, lives only in an incarnated
and historical way, with other human beings, then the question poses itself in
a fundamentally different way. Then, his relationship to God, if it should be a
human relationship to God, must be just as the human being is: incarnate, historical, with other human beings. Otherwise there is no relationship. The error of the
anti-sacramental [*sakramentsfeindlichen*: literally sacrament-hostile] idealism is
that it wants to make man a pure mind before God. Instead of a human being,
only a phantom remains here, a phantom that does not exist, and a religiosity
that would build on such foundations, builds on treacherous[58] sand. Today, the
idealistic heresy (if we want to call it that) is joined in a peculiar way by the
Marxist [heresy], of which Heidegger sagely said, materialism is not materialism
because it classifies all being as matter, but rather because it considers all matter
to be just the mere material of human work. Indeed, here, in the anthropological
extension of the ontological approach, lies the real core of the heresy: in the
reduction of the human being to homo faber, who is not concerned with things
in themselves, but rather only regards them as functions of work, whose function-
ary he has himself become. Here, the perspective of symbolism and the human
being's visual aptitude for the eternal are lost, he is incarcerated in his work
world, and his only hope is that subsequent generations might find more comfortable working conditions than he, when he himself has sufficiently laboured for
the establishment of such conditions. Truly slim consolation for an existence that
has become extremely narrow!

    With these perspectives, we have come full circle, returning to the starting
point of our considerations. What—we may ask once more—is the human
being who celebrates the services of the Church, the sacraments of Jesus Christ,
actually doing? He does not abandon himself to the naïve notion that God,
the omnipresent one, would only inhabit this particular space, represented by
the tabernacle in the church. That would already be contradicted by the most
superficial knowledge of the inventory of dogmatic assertions, because what is
specific to the Eucharist is not the presence of God in general, but rather the
presence of the person of Jesus Christ, which points to the horizontal, historically
bound character of man's encounter with God. He, who goes into the church
and celebrates its sacraments, if he understands the whole issue properly, also
does not do it because he thinks that the spiritual [*geistige*] God needs material

---

58   [Translator's comment: Ratzinger may be using a wordplay here. The adjective *trügerisch* can mean
      treacherous and deceptive, or it can mean delusive, illusory, or even phantasmal. The latter, of course,
      would imply a wordplay referring to his earlier statement that idealism reduces the human being
      to a phantom].

media in order to be able to touch the human spirit [or mind: *Geist*].[59] Rather, he does it because he knows that as a human being he can only encounter God in human ways; but 'in human ways' means in the form of incarnatedness, historicity and being with other people. And he does it because he knows that as a human being he cannot himself control when and how and where God should show himself to him, that he is rather the receiver dependent upon the prevailing power [*Vollmacht*], a power that he cannot produce of his own accord, and which constitutes a sign of God's sovereign freedom, who alone determines the manner of his presence.

No doubt, our piety has often been a little superficial here, which has led to various misunderstandings. In this regard, the critical question of modern consciousness could provoke a healthy purification of religious self-understanding. It may help, finally, to give an example through which the crisis becomes particularly clear and through which the meaning of the purification that is necessary can once more be concisely brought to light. With regard to meaningfulness, Eucharistic adoration, or silent visits to the Eucharist in the Church, cannot just be a conversation with the God thought to be present in a locally circumscribed way.[60] Statements like 'God lives here', and conversations with the God thought to be locally present on the basis of such statements, express a disregard, for both the Christological mystery and the concept of God, that is off-putting to thinking people who know about God's omnipresence. If one were to justify going to church by arguing that one ought to visit the God who is present only there, then this would indeed be an argument that made no sense and that would be rightly rejected by modern man. Eucharistic adoration is in truth based on the Lord who, through his historical life and suffering, has become 'bread' for us, i.e. he who, through his incarnation and sacrificial death, has become open for us. Such prayer is, therefore, based on the historical mystery of Jesus Christ, on God's with humankind, the history that comes to us in the sacrament. And is it based on the mystery of the Church: as it is based on God's history with humankind, it is based on the entire 'body of Christ', on the community of believers in which and through which God comes to us. Thus, praying in church and in the vicinity of the Eucharistic sacrament means that we are situating our relationship to God in the mystery of the Church as the concrete locus where God meets us. And this is ultimately the meaning of going to church: situating my self in God's history with humankind, where alone I have my true human existence as a human being, and which therefore opens up for me the true space for my encounter with God's eternal love. For this love does not just seek an isolated mind, which (as we have said already) would merely be a phantom in comparison to the reality of man, but rather, man in his entirety, in the body of his historicity; and this love gives him the guarantee of a divine answer in

---

59   [Translator's comment: See earlier note on the use of *Geist*].
60   [Cf. Chapter Seven of this volume (7.1) for a more detailed exploration of Ratzinger on the Eucharist and Eucharistic devotion].

the sacred signs of the sacraments, an answer in which the open-ended question of human existence finds its end and its fulfilment.

CHAPTER 3

UNDERSTANDING THE CHURCH: FUNDAMENTAL ECCLESIOLOGY

Gerard Mannion

Introduction

Ecclesiology is a theme that runs throughout the entire corpus of writings by Joseph Ratzinger the theologian.[1] His understanding of and writings on the church raise particular questions of continuity and about whether or not any changes of great significance have arisen over the course of the maturation of his ecclesiological thinking. Essentially, a synoptic examination of his writings indicates that there is much continuity across the decades, despite some fluctuation in his written views concerning areas such as Episcopal conferences and the Synod of Bishops. Nonetheless, new themes, concerns and motifs emerge at various stages.

Ratzinger's theological explorations took on an ecclesiological flavour from the very beginning, with his doctoral dissertation exploring the themes of the people and household of God in the writings of Augustine of Hippo.[2] Ratzinger's essential Christian anthropology, along with his understanding of the interrelation between nature and grace, are influential upon his writings upon the Church. So, too, is his Bavarian

---

1   There are few writings by Ratzinger that do not have relevance for understanding his ecclesiological thought in some way, but among his books available in English that are more explicitly focused upon ecclesiology (either *in toto* or significant parts thereof), the following offer a good representative sampling of Ratzinger's thoughts on the church: *The Episcopate and the Primacy* (co-authored with Karl Rahner). New York: Herder and Herder, 1962; *Theological Highlights of Vatican II*. New York: Paulist Press, 1966; *Principles of Catholic Theology: Building Stones for a Fundamental Theology*. San Francisco: Ignatius Press, 1982; *Church, Ecumenism, Politics: New Essays in Ecclesiology*. New York: Crossroad, 1988, also under a different translation: Slough: St. Paul Publications, 1988; *Called to Communion: Understanding the Church Today*. San Francisco: Ignatius Press, 1996; *Pilgrim Fellowship of Faith: the Church as Communion*. San Francisco: Ignatius Press, 2005. Cf., also, the interviews: *The Ratzinger Report: An Exclusive Interview on the State of the Church* (with Vittorio Messori). San Francisco: Ignatius Press, 1983, and *Salt of the Earth: The Church at the End of the Millennium: An Interview with Peter Seewald*. San Francisco: Ignatius Press, 1997, esp. parts 2 and 3. Ratzinger's *Das neue Volk Gottes: Entwürfe zur Ekklesiologie*, Düsseldorf: Patmos, 1969 (2nd edn., 1977), awaits full translation still, although the present volume includes some translated sections of that study. His autobiographical *Milestones: Memoirs 1927–1977*. San Francisco: Ignatius Press, 1998, is also instructive here.

2   Joseph Ratzinger, *Volk und Haus Gottes in Augustins Lehre von der Kirche*, München: K. Zink, 1954.

background, with the strong sense of the role of the Church being at the heart of the local community and the positive sense of ecclesial tradition that accompanies such also shaping his ongoing understanding of the Church. But his theological education and his initial ecclesiological explorations emerged during a time of upheaval for both the Church and wider European society as a whole. And soon afterwards, of course, the monumental ecclesiological 'revolution' of Vatican II[3] would also have a profound effect upon Ratzinger's ecclesiology in both a formative and reactive sense.

That doctoral student of Augustine (who also became very familiar with the ecclesiological writings of Martin Luther) maintains a preoccupation with core ideas and themes throughout all his ecclesiological writings. His studies for his habilitation on Bonaventure's theology of history would also leave a deep impact upon his own ecclesiological thinking. Ratzinger's own formative researches are particularly reflected in the fact that, above all else, the fundamental understanding of the relationship of the Church to the wider world offers a key to understanding his ecclesiology. Indeed, a pessimistic assessment of the state of contemporary culture and the contemporary world vis-à-vis the Church has been one of the most consistent elements of his writings and addresses throughout much of his career.[4]

Related to this is his assessment of the ills and challenges of modernity and later postmodernity vis-à-vis that world. The idea that the Church finds itself in a 'situation of Babylonian captivity' in the modern and contemporary world would come to have a profound effect upon his fundamental ecclesiology. Ratzinger also seeks to relate his ecclesiology to the scriptural testimonies – with his ecclesiologically-attuned exegesis engaging with both the Hebrew Bible and the New Testament.

As a basic synthesis we might say that, for Ratzinger, the Church and the faith it safeguards constitute the definitive and pre-eminent means

3   Not that Ratzinger would understand the council in revolutionary terms as such.
4   This is further evidenced throughout Chapters One, Four and Seven of this volume. Cf., also, John Allen, *Pope Benedict XVI*. New York: Continuum, 2001, esp. pp. 78–81; Gerard Mannion, *Ecclesiology and Postmodernity: Questions for the Church in our Time*. Minnesota: Michael Glazier Books, 2007, esp. chapters 3 (43-74) and 4 (75-101). Also, cf. the early Eamon Duffy, 'Urbi, but not Orbi . . . The Cardinal, the Church and the World', in *New Blackfriars*, vol. 66, no. 780 (June 1985), 272-278. There Duffy describes Ratzinger's view of the church-world relationship as Manichean in character (274). Duffy questions 'the lurid and simplistic world of easy dualisms from which Cardinal Ratzinger's oracular voice seems to emanate. For him history, the world outside the Church, is the place of the demonic', 273. Finally, Charles Curran, one of Ratzinger's long-standing theological interlocutors summarizes the issue in hand as follows: 'Ratzinger is a theological Augustinian who equates the heavenly city with the church and the earthly city with the world; hence the strong opposition between the church and the world in his thinking', Charles E. Curran, 'A Place for Dissent: My Argument with Joseph Ratzinger', in *Commonweal* 132 no. 9 (May 6, 2005), 18-20, at 18

to salvation for human beings. The Church is called to gather all into the Body of Christ, to be a sacrament of unity. Its mission is to announce and witness to the incarnation of God in Christ, the universal call to communion with God's very self. Thus the Church mediates and makes present the grace of God in the world and guides and informs, through its teaching and leadership, the day-to-day existence of Christians. Thus the areas of both faith and morals serve as the remit for the Church's concern in a single continuum. Ratzinger's ecclesial writings contain a preoccupation, also, with *pastoral* matters: he constantly returns to a concern for the 'simple faithful.' Though it should be noted that critics believe this pastoral concern is more a rhetorical feature than a substantial one, particularly given Ratzinger's own limited pastoral experience in his clerical career.

The notion of communion – developed in the Patristic writings and rediscovered anew by Catholic scholars in the middle decades of the twentieth century – whereby the salvific bonds between Christians in any particular local community are microcosmic reflections of the wider bonds of communion between Christians of all churches within the embrace of the universal church, is another key theme. For Ratzinger, this all has a profound effect upon our understanding of the importance of the ecclesial hierarchy, papal primacy and indeed ecclesial organisation in general. His understanding of what criteria must be met in order for a Christian community to actually be considered a 'valid church' centres around the essential prerequisites of valid ministerial orders, including a valid episcopate, and the celebration of a valid Eucharist.[5] Communion with Rome is also seen as a prominent defining feature, except for the churches of the Orthodox traditions.

All this also pertains to the understanding of the dynamics of the relationship between the local and the universal church. Although some of his writings around the end of Vatican II appear to suggest otherwise, in the main, and with a renewed emphasis in later years, Ratzinger has steadfastly championed the primacy of the universal church over and against the local: a local community is a church only insofar as it is part of the (authentic) universal church. Following Vatican II, and his various deliberations on the ecclesiological debates and documents of the Council, including fundamental considerations over the meaning and implications of the Council's two ecclesial constitutions, Ratzinger's ecclesiology develops in a direction that many have considered to be a negative reaction

---

5   Ratzinger speaks about the profound relation between Eucharist, catholicity and apostolicity in *Principles of Catholic Theology: Building Stones for a Fundamental Theology*. San Francisco: Ignatius Press, 1982, pp. 295–296 ff.

to certain developments that Vatican II unleashed in the Church.[6] As part of this reactionary movement, he played a central role in the founding of the journal *Communio*, which, as he later said, was much more than a journal; it was an (ecclesiological, indeed ecclesial) *project*.

Ratzinger's increasingly vociferous assertions of the priority of the universal church and of its authority led, at the beginning of the twenty-first century, to a protracted debate between himself and Cardinal Walter Kasper, later to be president of the Pontifical Council for the Promotion of Christian Unity. In a series of exchanges,[7] the latter stated his belief that the position adopted by Ratzinger actually reversed the traditional order of priority between the local and the universal church (in constitutive terms). Cardinal Kasper asserted that: 'The local Church is neither a province nor a department of the universal church: it is the Church at a given place.'[8]

Another constant theme, increasingly so from the 1990s onwards, is the crucial importance of the role the Church has played in the cultural development of the wider societies in which it lives, particularly in Europe,[9] and the continuing importance of this role in the future: the Church has much to teach the world still, just as it has done so historically. Ratzinger has much to say on what the Church can and must offer the postmodern world. His critics argue that he sees only a one-way relationship: the Church can teach the world but, seemingly, the 'fallen' world cannot teach the Church.

As we shall see throughout this volume, another subject to occur

6   One recent study of Ratzinger's ecclesiology with particular focus upon its relation to Vatican II suggests the alternative perspective that Ratzinger is in fact offering a more faithful interpretation of the true intentions behind the conciliar documents. This study carries an approving foreword by Ratzinger himself: Maximilian Heinrich Heim, *Joseph Ratzinger: Life in the Church and Living Theology: Fundamentals of Ecclesiology with Reference to Lumen Gentium*. San Francisco: Ignatius Press, 2007 (the original German edition appeared in 2005). Heim argues that not only did Ratzinger have a significant impact upon the conciliar ecclesiological outcomes, but that he was also deeply influenced by them and continued to reflect that influence throughout his own ecclesiological writings. Also offering some additional insights into Ratzinger's ecclesiology are Ratzinger's commentaries on the Vatican II documents in the Vorgrimler edited commentary (Herbert Vorgrimler (ed.), *Commentary on the Documents of Vatican II*. 6 vols. New York: Herder and Herder, pp. 1967–1969). Aspects of the latter are discussed elsewhere in this volume.

7   Ratzinger, in the view of many, had famously changed his mind on this issue, given the position he took in the very first issue of *Concilium* – 'The Pastoral Implications of Episcopal Collegiality', in *Concilium*, vol. 1. Glen Rock, NJ: Paulist, 1964, pp. 39–67.

8   Walter Kasper, 'On the Church', *America* vol. 184 no. 14 (23-30 April 2001), 8-14 at 9 (originally in *Stimmen der Zeit* (December 2000), with a different translation appearing in *The Tablet* (23 June 2001), pp. 927–30). With regard to this debate see Kilian McDonnell, 'The Ratzinger/Kasper Debate: The Universal and the Local Churches', in *Theological Studies* 63 (2002) pp. 1–24 and Robert Leicht, 'Cardinals in Conflict', in *The Tablet* (28 April 2001), 607-608..

9   See, also, Chapter Four of this volume.

in numerous writings and addresses is Ratzinger's attempt to offer a particular and 'authentic' interpretation of Vatican II, and particularly of its ecclesiological documents and implications. Ratzinger's preference is for an emphasis upon the Council's dogmatic constitutions with *Lumen Gentium* being the fundamental document, ecclesiologically-speaking.[10] Ratzinger finds *Gaudium et Spes* more problematic, as we see elsewhere in this volume. In more frank or, depending upon one's interpretation, less guarded addresses, his criticisms of some of the developments unleashed after the Council have been stringent.

Ratzinger's ecclesiology seeks to paint a more harmonious, if not quite seamless, ecclesiological picture of transition from an emphasis upon the Church as the Mystical Body of Christ, through an understanding of the Church as sacrament of salvation and hence the importance of the Eucharist as a foundational element for understanding the nature and purpose of the Church.[11] This leads naturally into the priority of a particular understanding of the ecclesiology of *communio*. Ratzinger does not so much reject the Vatican II emphasis upon the Church as the people of God outright, he rather says that he seeks to offer correctives to erroneous understandings of this notion – particularly the sociological and political versions of this concept. Nonetheless, the outcome is that the notion has become distinctly sidelined in favour of that particular understanding of the ecclesiology of *communio*.

Ratzinger has frequently spoken of the possible need for the Church to become smaller, but purer. He has equally, therefore, served as a rallying figure and champion for many reactionaries and conservatives – including those opposed to Vatican II itself. This helps to account for the foundation of his very own 'fan club'. Critics suggest he represents a backward-looking and intransigent form of ecclesiology that is exclusivistic and life-denying. Nonetheless, Ratzinger maintains, like both Augustine and Luther before him, that the Church is a company *always* in need of constant renewal.[12]

Ratzinger's ecclesiology is distinctly normative in character – by and large the vision of the Church that he is in favour of is one he believes should be applicable to the entire Church. Critics speak of an ecclesiological

---

10   Again, cf. Maximilian Heinrich Heim, *Joseph Ratzinger: Life in the Church and Living Theology: Fundamentals of Ecclesiology with Reference to Lumen Gentium.* San Francisco: Ignatius Press, 2007, *passim*, and also Chapter Eight of the present volume.

11   Here see, also, Chapter Seven of the present volume.

12   Indeed, 'A Company in Constant Renewal' is the title of the final section of his *Called to Communion: Understanding the Church Today.* San Francisco: Ignatius Press, 1996, pp. 133–156. The crux of the matter centres, of course, on what form of renewal serves the church best.

'restorationism' throughout his writings and speeches.[13] Although it is important to appreciate here that the fundamental understanding of the Church that we find in the works of Ratzinger is motivated, to a large extent, by his perception of how the Church needs to respond to those challenges posed by social, cultural and intellectual challenges in the late modern and the postmodern eras, some critics view the developments within the official Roman Catholic Church in recent decades as increasingly reactionary. This has included a hardening of the stance of that Church in relation to those who disagree with its teachings both within and without its walls. Hence, the critical voices suggest, not only has the *openness* to the world that Vatican II proclaimed been transformed, firstly, into a much more cautious approach, it has also, in recent decades, been supplanted by a more hostile and antagonistic attitude towards the world and those Catholics who believe in greater dialogue than the official paradigm currently in vogue appears to allow for. Such critics believe that Ratzinger's ecclesiological vision has been a decisive influence upon such developments.

David Tracy has suggested that there are parallels to be drawn between such developments within Roman Catholic theology and those in other denominations. 'Indeed, this new kind of post-Vatican II Catholic theology of Balthasar and Ratzinger is remarkably similar in method to the claim in American Protestant theology proposed by the neo-Barthian anticorrelational theologians',[14] although he qualifies this by going on to state that 'The differences are also, of course, notable: the Protestant theologians, in fidelity to the theology of the Word, emphasize the intertextual developments; the Catholics, in fidelity to the sacramental vision of Catholicism, emphasize the "ecclesial sense" (Ratzinger) or the importance of the incarnational-sacramental "visible form" (Balthasar)'.[15] Subsequently, further parallels still can be identified alongside a wider range of trends that have emerged throughout many Christian churches since Tracy's article was written.[16]

---

13   In J. Ratzinger and V. Messori, *The Ratzinger Report*. San Francisco: Ignatius Press, 1985, Ratzinger clarifies how he understands the term 'restoration' to mean not so much a turning back but rather, true to its semantic roots, 'a recovery of values within a new totality', 38n.5 and also 'But if by restoration we understand the search for a new balance after all the exaggerations of an indiscriminate opening to the world, after the overly positive interpretations of an agnostic and atheistic world, well, then a restoration understood in this sense (a newly found balance of orientations and values within the Catholic totality) is altogether desirable and, for that matter, is already in operation in the Church. In this sense it can be said that the first phase after Vatican II has come to a close', ibid., pp. 37–38.

14   David Tracy, 'The Uneasy Alliance Reconceived: Catholic Theological Method, Modernity and Postmodernity', in *Theological Studies* 50 (September 1989), 548–570, at 555.

15   Ibid., p. 555, n. 27.

16   Cf. Gerard Mannion, 'Postmodern Ecclesiologies', in Gerard Mannion and Lewis Mudge (eds), *The Routledge Companion to the Christian Church*. New York and London: Routledge, 2007 and 2010,

Indeed, it could be argued that the writings of Joseph Ratzinger prior to his becoming Supreme Pontiff display an ecclesiological mindset that is similar to that found in the works of various scholars and ecclesial groups across the Christian church in general. To come full circle, it is an understanding of the Church that appears to accentuate the distinctive nature of the Church vis-à-vis the world. Such an ecclesiology therefore fosters an exclusivistic mentality anew in the Church.[17] In other words, the Church and world are separate entities and the Church must work hard to resist being 'tainted' by the ways of the world. Ratzinger's supporters, however, would counter that both he and like-minded theologians in other denominations are simply trying to preserve the Church as it moves through the eye of the postmodern storm. He subscribes, so the arguments go, to an ecclesiology that stands fast against the pernicious cultural, moral and intellectual developments of the present age.

3.1 The Essential Nature of the Church

In the essay which follows below, Ratzinger explores the origins and essence of the Church by considering differing perspectives of the biblical sources. He examines various schools of biblical interpretation with regard to the understanding of the relationship between the kingdom of God, the Church and Jesus. Thus he seeks to offer an 'aerial picture of the exegetical hypotheses of a century'. He rejects liberal and socialist-informed interpretations and denounces Alfred Loisy's 'modernist' separation of kingdom and Church and later forms of the same understanding. Instead, Ratzinger prefers to see Jesus as the answer to the yearning for the kingdom and, therefore, his prime mission was a gathering of an eschatological community for that kingdom, which brought the Church into being. Christ is the 'point of convergence' of the drawing near of people to God.

Ratzinger proposes a negative and positive means of discerning an 'authentic' ecclesiology. On the one hand, he points out that the leading exegetical models of any period 'are borrowed from the thought pattern of the respective period'. He argues for the need to remove elements of 'contemporary ideology' from any such interpretations. His 'positive' maxim is that 'compatibility with the base memory of the Church is the standard for judging what is to be considered historically and objectively accurate'. Thus Ratzinger seeks continuity as opposed to any

pp. 127–152. An informative study of related interest here is Richard Lennan, *Risking the Church: the Challenges of Catholic Faith*. Oxford: OUP, 2005, *passim*.

17   Again, cf. Mannion, *Ecclesiology and Postmodernity*, especially Part I, pp. 3–40.

interpretations that divides the 'true' Church from its institutional form. This second criterion he terms 'basic ecclesial memory'.

He offers an ecclesiological interpretation of the synoptic gospels, Paul and Acts that seeks to illustrate that an ecclesiology of communion has good grounding in the biblical testimonies. Ratzinger here argues that the Last Supper and the words of the institution of the Eucharist are the moment that the Church came into being. Paul's notion of the 'body of Christ' further underpins this interpretation and ecclesiology. Themes of union relate to unity and thus Ratzinger is able to privilege the preservation of the unity of the Church (implicitly understood as conforming to the authority of the universal Church) on biblical grounds. The connection between Eucharist and Church permeates many of Ratzinger's writings in relation to numerous themes. Our extract charts the main elements of Ratzinger's argument.

The critic of Ratzinger would here point towards the selective and rhetorical nature of the exegesis that he employs here. The absence of scriptural evidence that the Church as it later came into being was something intended by Jesus remains an obstacle that here he passes over by largely ignoring the question. Furthermore, if the models of exegesis owe much to the thought patterns of the period in which they arise then, by the same token, so, also, must the prevailing ecclesiological models. All schools of theology and exegesis are shaped by their cultural and intellectual contexts, bar none. Noting how Ratzinger labels as 'ideology' any school of thought he is opposed to, critics would also argue that what is required is not the privileging of one normative ecclesiological model (utilizing alternative and preferred schools of thought) over another but rather a comparative method to discern which models and visions seem to offer the most promising means of proclaiming and putting into practice the gospel in particular contexts at particular times. Such critics would claim that the sense of continuity offered here is exaggerated.

1. Preliminary considerations on method[18]

The questions that occupy today's discussion of the Church are mostly of a practical nature: What is the responsibility of the bishop? What is the significance of the particular Churches in the whole of the Church of Jesus Christ? What is the raison d'être of the papacy? How should the bishops and the pope, the particular Church and the universal Church work together? What is the status of the layman in the Church? In order to be able to respond correctly to these practical problems, we must premise the fundamental question: What is the Church in the

18 [Sections from J. Ratzinger, 'The Origin and Essence of the Church', in *Called to Communion: Understanding the Church Today*. San Francisco: Ignatius Press, 1996, pp. 13–45].

first place? What is the purpose of her existence? What is her origin? Did Christ actually will her, and, if so, how did he intend her to be? Only if we are able to reply properly to these basic questions do we have any chance of finding an adequate answer to the particular practical problems mentioned above. Yet the very question about Jesus and the Church, as well as about the initial form of the Church in the New Testament itself, is so overgrown by the tangled thicket of exegetical hypotheses that there is seemingly next to no hope of finding any sort of adequate answer to it. There thus exists the dangerous temptation to pick out the solutions that appear most congenial or else to skip over the problem entirely in order to plunge immediately into practical matters. [. . .]

[. . . W]hat is needed first of all is a kind of aerial photograph of the whole: when our gaze ranges over a larger expanse of terrain, it is also possible to find our bearings . . . . [W]e can distinguish three generations of exegetes and, corresponding to these, three great principal changes in the history of biblical interpretation in our century. At the beginning of this history stands liberal exegesis, which regards Jesus according to the liberal world picture as the great individualist who liberates religion from cultic institutions and reduces it to ethics, which for its part is founded entirely upon the individual responsibility of conscience. Such a Jesus, who repudiates cultic worship, transforms religion into morality and then defines it as the business of the individual, obviously cannot found a church. He is the foe of all institutions and, therefore, cannot turn around and establish one himself.

The First World War brought with it the collapse of the liberal world and a resulting aversion to its individualism and moralism. The great political bodies, which had relied entirely on science and technology as carriers of the progress of humanity, had failed as forces of ethical order. So the yearning for communion in the sacred was reawakened. There was a rediscovery of the Church, even in the domain of Protestantism. Scandinavian theology witnessed the development of a cultic exegesis, which, in strict antithesis to liberal thought, no longer saw Jesus as a critic of cultic worship but rather understood this worship as the intimate, vital atmosphere of the Bible, in both the Old and the New Testament. Such exegesis, therefore, also attempted to interpret Jesus' words and intentions themselves in the light of the great stream of the lived liturgy. Similar tendencies appeared in the English-speaking world. But even in German Protestantism, a new sense of Church had arisen: there was a growing awareness that the Messiah is unthinkable with-out his Church.[19] With this renewal of interest in the sacrament, the significance of Jesus' Last Supper as forming communion was now also recognized; the thesis was formulated that Jesus had founded a new community by means of the Last

19   At the end of this movement, F.M. Braun presented a summary of its most significant developments in his still valuable book: *Neues Licht auf die Kirche. Di protestantische Kirchendogmatik in ihrer neuesten Entfaltung.* Einsiedeln: Benziger & Co, 1946 [original French edition: *Aspects nouveaux du problème de l'église*, 1942].

Supper itself and that the Last Supper is the origin of the Church and her permanent rule.[20] Exiled Russian theologians active in France developed the same idea on the basis of the Orthodox tradition into the model of a eucharistic theology that after the Second Vatican Council also came to exercise a powerful influence in Catholicism.[21] After the Second World War, humanity was divided ever more sharply into two camps: into a world of affluent peoples, who for the most part were once more living according to the liberal model, and into the Marxist block, which conceived of itself both as the spokesman of the poor nations of South America, Africa and Asia and as their model for the future. Correspondingly, there arose a twofold division of theological tendencies.

In the neoliberal world of the West, a variant of the former liberal theology now became operative in a new guise: the eschatological interpretation of Jesus' message. Jesus, it is true, is no longer conceived as a pure moralist, yet he is once again construed in opposition to the cult and the historical institutions of the Old Testament. This interpretation was a revamping of the old framework that breaks up the Old Testament into priests and prophets: into cult, institution and law, on the one hand, and prophecy, charism and creative freedom, on the other. In this view, priests, cult and institution appear as the negative factor that must be overcome. Jesus, on the other hand, supposedly stands in the prophetic line and fulfills it in antithesis to the priesthood, which is said to have done away with him as it had the prophets.

A new variety of individualism thus comes into being: Jesus now proclaims the end of the institutions. Though his eschatological message may have been conceived according to the mentality of the time as an announcement of the end of the world, it is retrieved for our day as the revolutionary breakthrough from the institutional realm into the charismatic dimension, as the end of the religions, or, in any case, as 'unworldly faith' that is ceaselessly re-creating its own forms. Once again there can be no question of the foundation of a Church; such an act would, in fact, contradict this eschatological radicalness.

But this new version of liberalism was quite susceptible to being converted into a Marxist-oriented interpretation of the Bible. The opposition between priests and prophets becomes a cipher for the class struggle, which is taken to be the law of history. Accordingly, Jesus lost his life engaged in combat against the forces of oppression. He is thus transformed into the symbol of the suffering and struggling proletariat, of the 'people', as is now more commonly said. The eschatological character of the message then refers to the end of the class-society;

20   To my knowledge, this idea was first worked out with full clarity by F. Kattenbusch, 'Der Quellort der Kirchenidee', in *Harnack-Festgabe* (1921), pp. 143–172.

21   Cf., inter alia, P. Evdokimov, *L'Orthodoxie*. Paris: Delachaux et Niestlé, 1959; N. Afanasieff *et al.*, *La Primauté de Pierre dans l'Église orthodoxe*. Neuchatel: Delachaux et Niestlé, 1960. On the Catholic side: O. Saier, '*Communio' in der Lehre des Zweiten Vatikanischen Konzils*. Munich: Max Hueber Verlag, 1973; J.-M. Tillard, *Église d'églises: L'ecdésiologie de communion*. Paris: Editions du Cerf, 1987.

the prophet-priest dialectic expresses the dialectic of history, which comes to its final conclusion with the victory of the oppressed and with the emergence of the classless society. The fact that Jesus hardly mentioned the Church, but spoke repeatedly of the Kingdom of God, can be very easily integrated into this view: the 'Kingdom' is the classless society, which is held out as the objective toward which the downtrodden people struggles; it is considered as already existing wherever the organized proletariat, that is, its party, socialism, has triumphed.

Ecclesiology now becomes newly significant: it is fitted into the dialectical framework already set up by the division of the Bible into priests and prophets, which is then conflated with a corresponding distinction between institution and people. In accordance with this dialectical model, the 'popular Church' is pitted against the institutional or 'official Church'. This 'popular Church' is ceaselessly born out of the people and in this way carries forward Jesus' cause: his struggle against institutions and their oppressive power for the sake of a new and free society that will be the 'Kingdom'. [. . .]

What does this aerial picture of the exegetical hypotheses of a century show us? Above all it makes evident that the chief exegetical models are borrowed from the thought pattern of the respective period. Thus, we get at the truth by extracting from the individual theories their element of contemporary ideology – this is, so to say, the hermeneutic compass with which our aerial photograph furnishes us. By the same token, we also gain new confidence in the internal continuity of the Church's memory. In both her sacramental life and in her proclamation of the Word, the Church constitutes a distinctive subject whose memory preserves the seemingly past word and action of Jesus as a present reality. This does not imply that the Church has nothing to learn from the historically evolving currents of theology. Every new situation of humanity also opens new-sides of the human spirit and new points of access to reality. Thus, in her encounter with the historical experiences of humanity, the Church can be led ever more deeply into the truth and perceive new dimensions of it that could not have been understood without these experiences. But skepticism is always in order where new interpretations assail the identity of the Church's memory and replace it with a different mentality, a move that is tantamount to attempting its destruction as memory. We have thereby gained a second criterion of discernment. We were saying just now that it is necessary to remove from the dominant interpretations of a given epoch that element that originates from contemporary ideology. We can now lay down the converse: compatibility with the base memory of the Church is the standard for judging what is to be considered historically and objectively accurate, as opposed to what does not come from the text of the Bible but has its source in some private way of thinking. Both criteria – the negative criterion of ideology and the positive criterion of the basic ecclesial memory – complement each other and can help us remain as close as possible to the biblical text without disregarding whatever real addition to knowledge the endeavor of the present can have in store for us.

2. The witness of the New Testament regarding the origin and essence of the Church

[. . .] Let us take as our starting point the fact that what Jesus' message immediately announced was not the Church but the kingdom of God (or 'the Kingdom of the Heavens'). This can be demonstrated statistically alone by the fact that of the 122 mentions of the Kingdom of God in the New Testament, ninety-nine belong to the synoptic Gospels, of which another ninety uses of the term occur in the sayings of Jesus. One can thus understand the dictum of Loisy, which has since gained popular currency: 'Jesus proclaimed the Kingdom; what came was the Church.'[22] But a historical reading of the texts reveals that the opposition of Kingdom and Church has no factual basis. For, according to the Jewish interpretation, the gathering and cleansing of men for the Kingdom of God is part of this Kingdom. [. . .] Jeremias goes so far as to formulate the following conclusion: 'We must reduce the whole question quite sharply to a single point: the *sole* meaning of the entire activity of Jesus is the gathering of the eschatological people of God.'[23]

Jesus speaks of this people using many images, particularly in the parables having to do with growth. Yet as he does so, it becomes apparent that the 'soon' of the imminent eschatology characteristic of John the Baptist and Qumran passes over with Jesus into the 'now' of Christology. Jesus himself is God's action, his coming, his reigning. In Jesus' mouth, 'Kingdom of God' does not mean some thing or place but the present action of God. One may therefore translate the programmatic declaration of Mark 1:15, 'the Kingdom of God is near at hand', as 'God is near.' We perceive once more the connection with Jesus, with his person; he himself is God's nearness. Wherever he is, is the Kingdom. In this respect we must recast Loisy's statement: The Kingdom was promised, what came was Jesus. Only in this way can we understand aright the paradox of promise and fulfillment.

But Jesus is never alone. For he came in order to gather together what was dispersed (cf. Jn 11:52; Mt 12:30). His entire work is thus to gather the new people. Hence, this early stage is already marked by the appearance of two elements that are essential for the future understanding of the Church. First, the dynamism of unification, in which men draw together by moving toward God,

---

22 E. Peterson, in his famous short treatise of 1929, *Die Kirche* (reprinted in: *Theologische Traktate*. Munich: Kösel, 1951, pp. 409–429), had been the first to take up this thesis and give it a Catholic twist. I myself probably contributed to its spread by treating it in my lessons and by adopting it from Peterson and Schlier, though in a substantially modified form, in my article 'Kirche' in *LThK* [*Lexikon für Theologie und Kirche*, 2nd edn., Freiburg: Herder, 1957-68, 6: 172-183]. Unfortunately, these alterations have been wiped away in the process of popularization; the maxim was lined with an interpretation that found no support even in Loisy's original meaning. See, for example, L. Boff, *Chiesa, carisma e potere*. [Edizioni Borla] Rome: 1983 [E.T.: *Church, Charism and Power*, London: SCM, 1985].

23 J. Jeremias, *Neutestamentliche Theologie*. Gütersloh: Gütersloher Verlagshaus Gerd Mohn, 1979, 1971, 1:167.

is a component of the new people of God as Jesus intends it. Second, the point of convergence of this new people is Christ; it becomes a people solely through his call and its response to his call and to his person.

[. . . T]he disciples ask Jesus for a special prayer for their community. [. . .] The request for a prayer thus expresses the disciples' awareness of having become a new community that has its source in Jesus. They appear as the primitive cell of the Church, and they show us at the same time that the Church is a communion united principally on the basis of prayer – of prayer with Jesus, which gives us a shared openness to God . . ..

The common prayer that the disciples received from Jesus leads us onto a further track. During his earthly life, Jesus had taken part with the Twelve in the temple worship of Israel. The Our Father was the first stage on the way toward a special communion of prayer with and from Jesus. On the night before his Passion, Jesus took another decisive step beyond this: he transformed the Passover of Israel into an entirely new worship, which logically meant a break with the temple community and thereby definitively established a people of the 'New Covenant'. The words of institution of the Eucharist, whether read in the Markan or in the Pauline tradition, always have to do with the covenant event; they refer backward to Sinai and forward to the New Covenant announced by Jeremiah. Moreover, both the Synoptics and John's Gospel, though each in a different way, make the connection with the events of Passover. Finally, there is also an echo of Isaiah's words regarding the suffering servant of God. With Passover and the Sinaiatic covenant ritual, the two founding acts whereby Israel became and ever anew becomes a people are taken up and integrated into the Eucharist. The association of this primordial cultic basis, upon which Israel was founded and by which it lived, with the core words of the prophetic tradition fuses past, present and future in the perspective of a new covenant. [. . .]

What conclusion emerges from all the foregoing considerations? The institution of the most holy Eucharist on the evening before the Passion cannot be regarded as some more or less isolated cultic transaction. It is the making of a covenant and, as such, is the concrete foundation of the new people: the people comes into being through its covenant relation to God. We could also say that by his eucharistic action, Jesus draws the disciples into his relationship with God and, therefore, into his mission, which aims to reach 'the many', the humanity of all places and of all times. These disciples become a 'people' through communion with the Body and Blood of Jesus, which is simultaneously communion with God. The Old Testament theme of covenant, which Jesus incorporates into his preaching, receives a new center: communion with Christ's Body. It could be said that the people of the New Covenant takes its origin as a people from the Body and Blood of Christ; solely in terms of this center does it have the status of a people. We can call it 'people of God' only because it is through communion with Christ that man gains access to a relationship with God that he cannot establish by his own power.

Looking ahead to our principal theme – the local Church and the universal Church – we can say that the Eucharist, seen as the permanent origin and center of the Church, joins all of the 'many', who are now made a people, to the one Lord and to his one and only Body. This fact already implies that the Church and her unity are but one. It is true that the many celebrations in which the one Eucharist will be realized also point ahead to the multiformity of the one Body. Nevertheless, it is clear that these many celebrations cannot stand side by side as autonomous, mutually independent entities but are always simply the presence of one and the same mystery.

3.2 The Babylonian Captivity of the Post-Conciliar Church

In the early 1970s, Ratzinger painted a bleak picture of the challenges facing the church in our times. He argued that the church was in 'a situation of Babylonian captivity', where division and mistrust ruled. Declaring that too many rush to divide those within the church into progressives and conservatives, the then Professor Ratzinger went on to suggest attention would be better focused on other themes – ones which would increasingly come to dominate his own thinking down to the present day. These are 'the Church's true mission' vis-à-vis the prayer life of the 'ordinary' faithful, the disillusionment that set in amongst many in the Church after Vatican II when so many had felt a new Pentecost was about to dawn, and a return to a focus upon the fundamentals of the faith that had been clouded by obsession with those ways of the contemporary world and with cultural as well as intellectual novelty and fashion. The final fundamental theme of the professor would be a renewed emphasis upon the universal Church and, in particular, upon a renewal of its teaching authority over all believers. Naturally, this also focused attention upon those Catholic theologians deemed to be espousing ideas that prolonged this 'Babylonian captivity'. These themes would become increasingly familiar ones in Ratzinger's theological corpus.

Here, as throughout his writing, Ratzinger displays dismay at and, indeed, disdain for those whom he perceives to be allowing the Church itself, and theology, alike, to be led astray by secular ideas and trends. As indicated, he has consistently been keen to preserve the 'purity' of both.

Ratzinger speaks of guarding against ossification in the Church, here echoing sentiments of his earlier writings as well as those of his co-author in the volume from which our reading comes, Hans Urs von Balthasar. But he goes on to state (something echoed again in the final chapter of his later book, *Called to Communion*) that 'true reform' attends to repentance, to matters of faith. 'False reform' seeks change, indeed, salvation even, 'merely by changing others, by creating ever fresh forms, and by accommodation to the times'. Too many, he continues, have become obsessed with changing church structures, patterns of ministry and the like, so that the Church itself becomes of secondary importance. Ecclesiology becomes bogged down in a 'battle about machinery'. The 'real problem', however, is the 'crisis of faith'.

Ratzinger continues by asserting that instead of renewing the Church in order for it to speak all the more effectively the gospel of love to the world, the aftermath of Vatican II saw a blurring of distinctions between belief and unbelief. Those outside the Church applauded the Council because it seemed to take the Church in the direction of their own ways and views, rather than the other way around. Addressing the theological ebb and flow of the 1960s and early 70s, Ratzinger thus offers a lament at the current 'state of the Church' and especially of theology.

His conclusion is that unbelief has taken a firm foothold in the Church, thanks to this blurring of distinctions. Tellingly, he laments that elements of the vision for the Church that were pronounced at Vatican I have been lost. The lament continues: the theology of the Church espoused by many in the post-conciliar age seeks to turn away from the Church's theological attributes towards its political ones, whereby sociological theory dictates ecclesial organization and the sacramental principle is replaced by 'democratic control'.

This writing reflects many of the key concerns of Ratzinger and those who shared his worries about the direction in which the Church was moving post-Vatican II. But critics would point out that here again Ratzinger is employing rhetorical flourishes to promote the 'restorationist' agenda of the then fledgling *Communio* project.[24] His assertions concerning theology, the Church and Vatican II would be contested by many, all offering markedly different interpretations. His well-known anti-ideological bias is again to the forefront here.

The blueprint offered in this text would be replicated in each analysis concerning the state of the Church offered by Ratzinger in the years to come. The schools of thought and the trends he attacks would change as Ratzinger turned his attentions over the years to new perceived threats, with forms of religious pluralism and moral relativism being the foremost amongst them. But the essential thesis and preferred solution would remain the same and the essential ecclesiological picture would remain constant. Critics would suggest that the latter does not become more nuanced, but simply more assertive and more all-encompassing in its ecclesial and theological remit. Even those critical of Ratzinger's

---

24 See reading no. 3.5, below. The work it appeared in was produced along with Hans Urs von Balthasar, one of Ratzinger's key collaborators in the *Communio* project.

stewardship of the Congregation for the Doctrine of the Faith (CDF)
would acknowledge that many of the 'enemies' he identifies in this text
would be dealt with one by one during his time at the CDF – the private
theological vision being brought to bear upon the future direction of the
Church and theology alike.

The Church now finds itself in a situation of Babylonian captivity, in which the
'for' and 'against' attitudes are not only tangled up in the oddest ways, but seem
to allow scarcely any reconciliation.[25] Mistrust has emerged, because being in
the Church has lost straightforwardness and no one any longer risks attributing
honesty to another.

Romano Guardini's hopeful observance of 1921 (A process of great moment
has begun, the Church is coming to lie in the souls of men) seems to run thus:
Indeed, momentous things are in progress, the Church is becoming extinguished
in men's souls, and Christian communities are crumbling. In the midst of a world
striving for unity the Church is falling apart in nationalistic partisanship, in calumni-
ation of the alien and glorification of self.

There seems to be no middle way between the iconoclasts and a reaction
that clings too much to externals and what always has been, between contempt
of tradition and a mechanical dependence on the letter. Public opinion places
everyone inexorably in his precise category, for it needs to have clear-cut rules,
and admits of no nuances: a person has to be either a progressive or a conservative. But reality, however, is different.

Silently, with no voice to speak for them, even at this time of confusion, the
simple faithful carry on fulfilling the Church's true mission: prayer, bearing daily
life with patience, always listening to the word of God. But they do not fit into
the picture that people want to see; and so, for the most part, they remain silent,
although this Church is by no means invisible, though hidden deep beneath the
powers of this world.

So far we have discovered our first clue about the background against which
we must ask: Why am I still in the Church? In order to find a meaningful answer
we have first of all to scrutinize this background, which is linked directly to our
topic by the little word 'today', and, having described the situation, go on further
to seek for its causes.

How was it possible for this Babylonian captivity to arise at a moment when
we had been hoping for a new Pentecost? How was it possible that just when the
Council seemed to have reaped the ripe harvest of the last decades, instead of
enjoying the riches of fulfilment we found only emptiness? How could disintegration emerge from a great surge towards unity?

25   [From Joseph Ratzinger, 'Introductory Thoughts on the State of the Church', in *Two Say Why. Why
      I Am Still a Christian, by Hans Urs von Balthasar, and Why I Am Still in the Church, by Joseph Ratzinger.*
      Trans. John Griffiths. London: Search Press, Chicago: Franciscan Herald Press, 1973, pp. 67-75].

For a start, I shall try to reply with a metaphor designed both to clarify the task before us and to begin to reveal how it is possible for every No to contain a Yes.

It would seem that in our efforts to understand the Church, efforts which at the Council finally developed into an active struggle for the Church, and into concrete work upon the Church, we have come so close to the Church that we can no longer see it as a whole: we cannot see the city for the houses, or the wood for the trees.

The situation into which science has so often led us in respect of reality seems now to have arisen in respect of the Church. We can see the detail with such precision that we cannot see the whole thing. As in scientific study, so here, an increment in exactitude represents loss in truth. Indisputably precise as is all that the microscope shows when we look through it at a section from a tree, it may obscure truth if it makes us forget that the individual is not just an individual, but has life within the whole, which is not visible under the microscope and yet is true – truer, indeed, than the isolation of the individual.

The perspective of the present day has distorted our view of the Church, so that in practice we see the Church only under the aspect of adaptability, in terms of what can be made of it. Intensive efforts to reform the Church have caused everything else to be forgotten.

For us today the Church is only a structure that can be changed, and which constantly causes us to ask what can be altered, in order to make the Church more efficient for the functions that someone or other thinks appropriate. In all this questioning the concept of reform as it occurs in the popular mind has largely degenerated and lost its essence.

Reform originally meant a spiritual process, very much akin to repentance. A man becomes a Christian only by repenting; and that applies throughout his life; it applies to the Church throughout its history. The Church, too, keeps alive as the Church by turning again and again to its Lord, by fighting ossification and comfortable habits which so easily fall into antagonism to the truth.

When reform is dissociated from the hard work of repentance, and seeks salvation merely by changing others, by creating ever fresh forms, and by accommodation to the times, then despite many useful innovations it will be a caricature of itself. Such reform can touch only things of secondary importance in the Church.

No wonder, then, that in the end it sees the Church itself as of secondary importance. If we become aware of this, the paradox that has emerged apparently with the present efforts at reform becomes intelligible: the attempt to loosen up rigid structures, to correct forms of Church government and ministry, which derive from the Middle Ages, or, rather, the age of absolutism, and to liberate the Church from such encrustations and inaugurate a simpler ministry in the spirit of the Gospel – all these efforts have led to an almost unparalleled over-emphasis on the official elements in the Church.

It is true that today the institutions and ministries in the Church are being criticized more radically than ever before, but in the process they attract more exclusive attention than ever before.

For not a few people the Church today seems to consist of nothing but these. And so, questions about the Church exhaust themselves in a battle about machinery; one does not want to leave such an elaborate piece of mechanism lying about idle, yet finds it wholly unsuited to the new functions it is expected to fulfil.

Behind this the real problem appears: the crisis of faith which is the true heart of the process. The socio-logical radius of the Church still extends far beyond the circle of the genuine faithful.

The publicity effect of the Council and the apparent possibility of *rapprochement* between belief and unbelief – an illusion fostered almost inevitably by the popular new coverage given to the Church – pushed this alienation to the limit.

Applause for the Council came in part from those who had no intention of becoming believers, in the traditional Christian sense, but who hailed the 'progress' of the Church in the direction of their own views, taking this as a corroboration of their way of life. It is true that at the same time in the Church itself faith is in a state of ferment.

The problem of historical transmission sets the ancient creed in a doubtful twilight in which outlines become blurred; the objections of science or, rather, of what people think is the modern view of the world, play a part in making the process worse.

The boundary-line between interpretation and falsification, even at the very heart of things, becomes more and more confused. What do we really mean by 'resurrection from the dead'? Who is believing, who is interpreting, who is falsifying? The countenance of God rapidly disappears behind this argument about the limits of interpretation. The 'death of God' is a very real process, and today reaches right into the heart of the Church. It looks as if God were dying within Christianity. For where the resurrection becomes the experience of a message that is felt to be cast in out-of-date imagery, God ceases to be at work.

Does he work at all? This is the question that follows immediately. But who is so reactionary as to insist upon a realistic 'He is risen'? And what one sees as progress another thinks of as unbelief, and what was for aeons inconceivable is now usual: men who have long since given up the Church's creed, in good conscience regard themselves as genuine progressive Christians.

For them the one standard by which to judge the Church is the efficiency with which it operates. Obviously we have to ask what efficiency is, and what the end is which it subserves. Is it supposed to provide a critique of society, to assist evolution, or to inaugurate revolution, or is it there to promote community celebrations? At all events we have to start again from the ground floor, for the Church was originally designed for none of these things, and in its present form really is not adapted to these functions at all.

Discontent grows among believers and unbelievers alike. The foothold gained by unbelief within the Church makes the situation seem intolerable to both parties;

most of all, these circumstances have given the reform programme a certain notable ambiguity, which to many seems almost irremovable – at least for the time being.

Quite obviously this is not the whole story. In recent years many positive things have happened, about which we must not keep silent: the new accessibility of the liturgy,[26] an awareness of social problems, a better understanding between separated Christians, the removal of much anguish that had arisen from a false and liberalistic faith, and many other things.

All this is true and not to be minimized. But these things are not the distinguishing features of the general climate in the Church. On the contrary, all of this has in the meantime passed into the twilight created by the blurring of the lines of demarcation between faith and unbelief. Only at the beginning did this blurring look like a liberation. Today it is clear that, in spite of all signs of hope, the Church that has emerged from this process is not a modern but a thoroughly shaky and deeply divided Church.

Let us put it very crudely: the first Vatican Council described the Church as a '*signum levatum in nationes*', as the great eschatological banner that was visible from afar and called and united men. It was (so said the Council of 1870) that for which Isaiah had hoped (Is. 11, 12): the universally visible sign that every man could recognize and that pointed the way unequivocally to all men. With its astounding expansion, superb holiness, fecundity in all goodness, and invincible stability, it was supposed to be the real miracle of Christianity, its permanent authentication – replacing all other signs and miracles – in the eyes of history.

Today everything seems to have turned to the opposite. There is no marvellous expansion, but only a small-scale, stagnating association that cannot seriously overstep the boundaries of Europe or of the spirit of the Middle Ages; there is no superb holiness, but a collection of all human sicknesses besmirched and humiliated by a history from which no scandal is absent – the persecution of heretics and witch-hunting, persecution of the Jews and violation of conscience, self-dogmatizing and opposition to scientific evidence – so that anyone who listens to this story can only cover his head in shame; there is no stability, but only involvement in all the streams of history, in colonialism and nationalism, and the beginnings of adaptation to, and even identification with, Marxism. These are not signs that evoke faith, but seem to constitute a supreme obstacle to it.

A true theology of the Church would seem to consist in denuding the Church of all theological attributes and looking on it as a wholly political entity. Then it is no longer seen as a reality of faith, but as a purely accidental – even if indispensable – organization of the faithful, which ought as quickly as possible to be remodelled according to the most recent sociological theory. Trust is good, but

---

26   [But contrast this with Ratzinger's position in reading no. 1, Chapter Seven, below].

control is better – after all our disillusionment with the official Church; this is now our slogan. The sacramental principle is no longer self-evident; the only reliable thing is democratic control.

Ultimately we come to the point where the Holy Spirit himself is also incomprehensible. Anyone who is unafraid to look back into the past is aware, of course, that the scandals of history arose from the conviction that man must always seize power, that only the achievements of power are real.

3.3 Reinterpreting the Ecclesiology of Vatican II: The Ontological Priority of the Universal Church

In September 2001, Ratzinger was invited by the Archbishop of Milan to address the opening of the Pastoral Congress of the Diocese of Aversa. The focus of his lecture here was to be the ecclesiology of Vatican II. This would prove to be one of a number of addresses and writings in which we see Ratzinger seeking to offer an interpretation of the Council's vision of Church through his attention to a particular group of themes, issues and perspectives.

His address first of all deals with conceptions of the Church in the decades prior to the Council, particularly the pre-conciliar emphasis upon the Church as the mystical body of Christ. He then revisits familiar themes from many of his talks and writings, such as the Last Supper interpreted as the beginning of the Church, itself (see reading 3.1, above), and the implications of 'Eucharistic ecclesiology.' The latter, he believes, serves as a key to understanding Vatican II's conception of the local Churches.

Here Ratzinger places the emphasis upon what counts as a 'legitimate' local Church and the criteria that need to be met to ensure this. The remainder of his address simply repeats much of what he had said about the 'ecclesiology of communion' in an address the year before (which forms the earlier parts of our next reading).

This core issue of the relations between local Churches and the universal Church would preoccupy not only many of Ratzinger's personal theological writings and addresses, but also numerous documents that were issued by the CDF during Ratzinger's time as its Prefect.[27] These range from the CDF document against Leonardo Boff in 1985 to *Communionis notio* (1992) and *Dominus Iesus* (2000). Hence this lecture is given in the context of the controversy that followed the release of the latter document, in particular.

Critical voices would point out, first, that Ratzinger makes a number of historical and theological generalizations, some of which prove

27   Cf. the Introduction to this Chapter, p. 81-87.

misleading. Second, they would suggest what is offered here is, once again, not so much an explication of Vatican II as a reinterpretation, with the emphasis placed upon different concepts and aspects than those actually intended by the Council Fathers. Hence what is offered is a different ecclesiological perspective to that intended by the council itself.

[. . .] To understand Vatican II one must look back on this period and seek to discern, at least in outline, the currents and tendencies that came together in the Council.[28] I will present the ideas that came to the fore during this period and then describe the fundamental elements of the Council's teaching on the Church.

I. The Church, the Body of Christ
The Image of the Mystical Body
[. . .] The Church is much more than an organization: it is the organism of the Holy Spirit, something that is alive, that takes hold of our inmost being. This consciousness found verbal expression with the concept of the 'Mystical Body of Christ', a phrase describing a new and liberating experience of the Church. [. . .]

Today, it is difficult to communicate the enthusiasm and joy this realization generated at the time. In the era of liberalism that preceded the First World War, the Catholic Church was looked upon as a fossilized organization, stubbornly opposed to all modern achievements. Theology had so concentrated on the question of the primacy as to make the Church appear to be essentially a centralized organization that one defended staunchly but which somehow one related to from the outside. Once again it became clear that the Church was more than this – she is something we all bring forward in faith in a living way, just as the Church brings us forward. It became clear that the Church has experienced organic growth over the centuries, and continues to grow even today. Through the Church the mystery of the Incarnation is alive today: Christ continues to move through time. If we were to ask ourselves what element present from the very beginning could still be found in Vatican II, our answer would be: the Christological definition of the Church. [. . .]

The Second Vatican Council placed this concept masterfully at the pinnacle of its deliberations; the fundamental text on the Church begins with the words: *Lumen gentium cum sit Christus*: 'since Christ is the Light of the World . . . the Church is a mirror of His glory; she reflects His splendour'. If we want to understand the Second Vatican Council correctly, we must always go back to this opening statement.

Next, with this point of departure, we must establish both the feature of her

28   [Sections from the published lecture, Joseph Ratzinger, 'Conference of Cardinal Ratzinger at the opening of the Pastoral Congress of the Diocese of Aversa (Italy)', *L'Osservatore Romano*, English edition no. 4 (23 January 2002), pp. 5-8].

interiority and of her communitarian nature. The Church grows from within and moves outwards, not *vice-versa*. Above all, she is the sign of the most intimate communion with Christ. She is formed primarily in a life of prayer, the sacraments and the fundamental attitudes of faith, hope and love. Thus if someone should ask what must I do to become Church and to grow like the Church, the reply must be: you must become a person who lives faith, hope, and charity. What builds the Church is prayer and the communion of the sacraments; in them the prayer of the Church comes to meet us. [. . .]

[T]he concept of the development and therefore of the historical dynamic of the Church belongs to this theme. A body remains identical to itself over the course of its life due to the fact that in the life process it constantly renews itself. For the great English Cardinal, Newman, the idea of development was the true and proper bridge to his conversion to Catholicism. I believe that the idea of development belongs to those numerous fundamental concepts of Catholicism that are far from being adequately explored. Once again it is Vatican II to which we owe the first solemn formulation of this idea in a Magisterial document. Whoever wants to attach himself solely to the literal interpretation of the Scriptures or to the forms of the Church of the Fathers imprisons Christ in 'yesterday'. The result is either a wholly sterile faith that has nothing to say to our times, or the arrogant assumption of the right to skip over 2,000 years of history, consign them to the dustbin of mistakes, and try to figure out what a Christianity would look like either according to Scripture or according to Jesus. The only possible result will be an artificial creation that we ourselves have made, devoid of any consistency. Genuine identity with the beginning in Christ can only exist where there is a living continuity that has developed the beginning and preserved the beginning precisely through this development.

Eucharistic ecclesiology

Let us go back and look at developments in the pre-Conciliar era. Reflection on the Mystical Body of Christ marked the first phase of the Church's interior re-discovery; it began with St Paul and led to placing in the foreground the presence of Christ and the dynamics of what is alive (in Him and us). Further research led to a fresh awareness. Above all, more than anyone else, the great French theologian Henri de Lubac in his magnificent and learned studies made it clear that in the beginning the term '*corpus mysticum*' referred to the Eucharist. For St Paul and the Fathers of the Church the idea of the Church as the Body of Christ was inseparably connected with the concept of the Eucharist in which the Lord is bodily present and which He gives us His Body as food. This is how a Eucharistic ecclesiology came into existence.

What do we mean today by 'Eucharistic ecclesiology'? I will attempt to answer this question with a brief mention of some fundamental points. The first point is that Jesus' Last Supper could be defined as the event that founded the Church. Jesus gave His followers this Liturgy of Death and Resurrection and at the same time, He gave them the Feast of Life. In the Last Supper he repeats the covenant of Sinai – or rather what at Sinai was a simple sign or prototype, that becomes now a complete reality: the communion in blood and life between God and man. Clearly the Last Supper anticipates the Cross and the Resurrection and presupposes them, otherwise it would be an empty gesture. This is why the Fathers of the Church could use a beautiful image and say that the Church was born from the pierced side of the Lord, from which flowed blood and water. When I state that the Last Supper is the beginning of the Church, I am actually saying the same thing, from another point of view. This formula means that the Eucharist binds all men together, and not just with one another, but with Christ; in this way it makes them 'Church'. At the same time the formula describes the fundamental constitution of the Church: the Church exists in Eucharistic communities. The Church's Mass is her constitution, because the Church is, in essence, a Mass (sent out: 'missa'), a service of God, and therefore a service of man and a service for the transformation of the world.

The Mass is the Church's form, that means that through it she develops an entirely original relationship that exists nowhere else, a relationship of multiplicity and of unity. In each celebration of the Eucharist, the Lord is really present. He is risen and dies no more. He can no longer be divided into different parts. He always gives Himself completely and entirely. This is why the Council states: 'This Church of Christ is truly present in all legitimate local communities of the faithful which, united with their pastors, are themselves called Churches in the New Testament. For in their locality these are the new People called by God, in the Holy Spirit and with great trust (cf. 1 Thes. 1,5). [. . .] In these communities, though frequently small and poor, or living in the diaspora, Christ is present, and in virtue of His power there is brought together one, holy, catholic and apostolic Church' (Lumen Gentium, n. 26). This means that the ecclesiology of local Churches derives from the formulation of the Eucharistic ecclesiology. This is a typical feature of Vatican II that presents the internal and sacramental foundation of the doctrine of collegiality. [. . .]

Vatican II was aware of the concerns of both Orthodox and Protestant theology and integrated them into a more ample Catholic understanding. In Orthodox theology the idea of Eucharistic ecclesiology was first expressed by exiled Russian theologians in opposition to the pretensions of Roman centralism. They affirmed that insofar as it possesses Christ entirely, every Eucharistic community is already, in se, the Church. Consequently, external unity with other communities is not a constitutive element of the Church.

Therefore, they concluded that unity with Rome is not a constitutive element of the Church. Such a unity would be a beautiful thing since it would represent the fullness of Christ to the external world, but it is not essential since nothing would be added to the totality of Christ. The Protestant understanding of the Church was moving in the same direction. [. . .]

If we go back now to the Council text certain nuances become evident. The text does not simply say, 'The Church is entirely present in each community that celebrates the Eucharist', rather it states: 'This Church of Christ is truly present in *all legitimate local communities of the faithful which, united with their pastors,* are themselves called Churches'. Two elements here are of great importance: to be a Church the community must be 'legitimate'; they are legitimate when they are 'united with their pastors'. What does this mean? In the first place, no one can make a Church by himself. A group cannot simply get together, read the New Testament and declare: 'At present we are the Church because the Lord is present wherever two or three are gathered in His name'. The element of 'receiving' belongs essentially to the Church, just as faith comes from 'hearing' and is not the result of one's decision or reflection. Faith is a converging with something I could neither imagine nor produce on my own; faith has to come to meet me. We call the structure of this encounter, a 'Sacrament'. It is part of the fundamental form of a sacrament that it be received and not self-administered. No one can baptize himself. No one can ordain himself. No one can forgive his own sins. Perfect repentance cannot remain something interior – of its essence it demands the form of encounter of the Sacrament. This too is a result of a sacrament's fundamental structure as an encounter (with Christ). For this reason communion with oneself is not just an infraction of the external provisions of Canon Law, but it is an attack on the innermost nature of a sacrament. [. . .]

One cannot make the Church but only receive her; one receives her from where she already is, where she is really present: the sacramental community of Christ's Body moving through history. It will help us to understand this difficult concept if we add something: 'legitimate communities'. Christ is everywhere whole. This is the first important formulation of the Council in union with our Orthodox brothers. At the same time Christ is everywhere only one, so I can possess the one Lord only in the unity that He is, in the unity of all those who are also His Body and who through the Eucharist must evermore become it. Therefore, the reciprocal unity of all those communities who celebrate the Eucharist is not something external added to Eucharistic ecclesiology, but rather its internal condition: in unity here is the One. This is why the Council recalls the proper responsibility of communities, but excludes any self-sufficiency. The Council develops an ecclesiology in which being Catholic, namely being in communion with believers in all places and in all times, is not simply an external element of an organizational form, it represents grace coming from within and is at the same time a visible sign of the grace of the Lord who alone can create unity by breaching countless boundaries.

II. The Church, as the People of God

After the initial enthusiasm that greeted the discovery of the idea of the Body of Christ, scholars analyzed and gradually began to refine the concept and make corrections in two directions. We have already referred to the first of these corrections in the work of Henri de Lubac. He made concrete the idea of the Body of Christ by working out a Eucharistic ecclesiology and opened it in this way to concrete questions about the juridical ordering of the Church and the reciprocal relations between local Churches and the universal Church. The other form of correction began in Germany in the 1930's, where some theologians were critical of the fact that with the idea of the Mystical Body certain relationships were not clear between the visible and the invisible, law and grace, order and life. They therefore proposed the concept of 'People of God', found above all in the Old Testament, as a broader description of the Church to which one could more easily apply sociological and juridical categories. While the Mystical Body of Christ would certainly remain an important 'image', by itself it could not meet the request of theology to express things using 'concepts'.

Initially this criticism of the idea of the Body of Christ was somewhat superficial. Further study of the Body of Christ uncovered its positive content; the concept of 'People of God', along with the concept of the Body of Christ, entered the ecclesiology of the Council. One wondered if the image of the Mystical Body might be too narrow a starting point to define the many forms of belonging to the Church now found in the tangle of human history. If we use the image of a body to describe 'belonging' we are limited only to the form of representation as 'member'. Either one is or one is not a member, there are no other possibilities. One can then ask if the image of the body was too restrictive, since there manifestly existed in reality intermediate degrees of belonging. The Constitution on the Church found it helpful for this purpose to use the concept of 'the People of God'. It could describe the relationship of non-Catholic Christians to the Church as being 'in communion' and that of non-Christians as being 'ordered' to the Church where in both cases one relies on the idea of the People of God (Lumen Gentium, nn. 15, 16).

In one respect one can say that the Council introduced the concept of 'the People of God' above all as an ecumenical bridge. It applies to another perspective as well: [. . .] The Christological distinction had to be clearly emphasized: the Church is not identical with Christ, but she stands before Him. She is a Church of sinners, ever in need of purification and renewal, ever needing to become Church. The idea of reform became a decisive element of the concept of the People of God, while it would be difficult to develop the idea of reform within the framework of the Body of Christ.

There is a third factor that favoured the idea of the 'People of God'. [. . .] : the Church has not yet reached her goal. Her true and proper hope still lies ahead of her. The 'eschatological' import of the concept of Church became clear. The phrase conveys the unity of salvation history which comprises both Israel and the Church in her pilgrim journey. [. . .] It describes the unity of the People of God amid the variety, as in all peoples, of different ministries and services; yet above and beyond all distinctions, all are pilgrims in the one community of the pilgrim People of God. In broad outline, if one wants to sum up what elements relating to the concept 'People of God' were important for the Council, one could say that the phrase 'People of God' conveyed the historical nature of the Church, described the unity of God's history with man, the internal unity of God's people that also goes beyond the frontiers of sacramental states of life. It conveys the eschatological dynamic, the provisional and fragmentary nature of the Church ever in need of renewal; and finally, it expresses the ecumenical dimension, that is the variety of ways in which communion and ordering to the Church can and do exist, even beyond the boundaries of the Catholic Church.[29]

However, commentators very soon completely handed the term 'people' in the concept 'People of God' to a general political interpretation. Among the proponents of liberation theology it was taken to mean 'people' in the Marxist sense, in opposition to the ruling classes, or more generally, it was taken to refer to popular sovereignty at long last being applied to the Church. This led to large-scale debates on Church structures. On occasion the expression was understood in a peculiarly Western sense as 'democratization' or more in the sense of the so-called Eastern 'People's Republics'. [. . .] The discussion is brought back to the essential point: the Church does not exist for herself; rather, she is God's instrument to gather mankind in Himself and to prepare for that time when 'God will be all in all' (I Cor 15:28). The very concept of God was left out of all the 'fireworks' surrounding this expression, thus depriving the expression of its meaning. A Church which existed only for herself would be useless. People would realize this immediately. The crisis of the Church reflected in the expression 'People of God' is a 'crisis of God'. It derives from our abandoning the essential. All that remains is a struggle for power. This sort of thing is already abundantly present in the world – there is no need for the Church to enter this arena.

III. The Ecclesiology of Communion[30]

Around the time of the extraordinary Synod of 1985 which attempted to make an assessment of the 20 years since the Council there was a renewed effort to synthesize the Council's ecclesiology. The synthesis involved one basic concept: the ecclesiology of communion. I was very much pleased with this new focus in ecclesiology and I endeavoured, to the extent I was able, to help work it out. First of all one must admit that the word 'communio' did not occupy a central place in the Council. All the same if properly understood it can serve as a synthesis of the essential elements of the Council's ecclesiology. All the essential elements of the Christian concept of 'communio' can be found in the famous passage from the First Letter of Saint John (1:3); it is a frame of reference for the correct Christian understanding of 'communio'. 'That which we have seen and heard we proclaim also to you, so that you may have fellowship (communio) with us; and our fellowship is with the Father and with his Son Jesus Christ. And we are writing this that our joy may be complete'. The point of departure of communio is

29 [Cf. the following reading's focus on the notion of *subsistit in*].
30 [This notion is treated in extended form in reading 3.5, below].

clearly evident in this passage: the union with the Son of God, Jesus Christ, who comes to mankind through the proclamation of the Church. Fellowship (*communio*) among men is born here and merges into fellowship (*communio*) with the One and Triune God. One gains access to communion with God through the realization of God's communion with man – it is Christ in person. [. . .] The ecclesiology of communion at its very foundation is a Eucharistic ecclesiology. It is very close to that Eucharistic ecclesiology that Orthodox theologians so convincingly developed during the past century. In it – *as we have already seen* – ecclesiology becomes more concrete while remaining totally spiritual, transcendent and eschatological. [. . .] Without any possible doubt one could say that this concept conveys a synthesis of ecclesiology which combines the discourse of the Church with the discourse of God, and to life through God and with God. This synthesis assembles all the essential intentions of Vatican II ecclesiology and connects them with one another in an appropriate fashion.

For these reasons I was both grateful and happy when the 1985 Synod placed '*communio*' at the centre of their study. The following years demonstrated the fact that no word is safe from misunderstanding, not even the best and most profound word. To the extent that '*communio*' became an easy slogan, it was devalued and distorted. As happened to the concept 'People of God', one must point to a growing horizontal understanding that abandoned the concept of God. The ecclesiology of communion was reduced to a consideration of relations between the local Church and the universal Church; this in turn was reduced to the problem of determining the area of competence of each. Naturally the egalitarian thesis once more gained ground: only full equality was possible in '*communio*'. [. . .]

This does not mean that there should be no discussion of good government and the division of responsibility in the Church. It is certainly true that there are imbalances that need correcting. We should watch for and root out an excessive Roman centralization that is always a danger. But questions of this sort ought not to distract us from the true mission of the Church: the Church should not be proclaiming herself but God. It is only to assure that this is done in the purest possible way, that there is criticism within the Church. Criticism should insure a correlation between discourse on God and common service. [. . .]

Faced with the post-1985 reduction of the concept of '*communio*', the Congregation for the Doctrine of the Faith thought it appropriate to prepare a 'Letter to the Bishops of the Catholic Church on Some Aspects of the Church Understood as Communion'. The Letter was issued on 28 May, 1992. [. . .] Our Letter met with a storm of criticism—very few parts of the text met with approval. The phrase that provoked the most controversy was this statement: 'The universal Church in her essential mystery is a reality that ontologically and temporally is prior to every particular Church' (cf. n. 9). There was a brief reference to this statement being based on the Patristic notion that the one, unique Church precedes the creation of particular Churches and gives birth to them. The Fathers were reviving a rabbinical concept that the Torah and Israel were pre-existent. Creation was conceived as providing space for the Will of God. This Will needed a people who would live for the Will of God and would make it the Light of the world. Since the Fathers were convinced of the final identity of the Church and Israel, they could not envision the Church as something accidental, only recently created; in this gathering of people under the Will of God the Fathers recognized the internal theology of creation. Beginning with Christology this image was amplified and deepened: they explained history—under the influence of the Old Testament—as a story of love between God and man. God finds and prepares a Bride for His Son—the unique Bride who is the unique Church. In the light of Genesis 2,24, where man and woman become 'two in one flesh' the image of the Bride merges with the idea of the Church as the Body of Christ—an analogy derived from the Eucharistic liturgy. The unique Body of Christ is prepared; Christ and the Church will be 'two in one flesh', one body and in this way 'God will be everything to everyone'. The ontological priority of the universal Church—the unique Church, the unique Body, the unique Bride—vis-à-vis the empirical, concrete manifestations of various, particular Churches is so obvious to me that I find it difficult to understand the objections raised against it. These objections only seem possible if one will not or cannot recognize the great Church conceived by God—possibly out of despair at her earthly shortcomings. These objections look like theological ravings. All that would remain is the empirical image of mutually related Churches and their conflicts. This would mean that the Church as a theological theme is cancelled. [. . .]

3.4 The Fullness of the Church: Discerning the Meaning of 'Subsistit in'

Here we continue with the themes of our previous reading but turn to explore a more nuanced aspect of those debates in greater depth. In November 2000, Rome staged a symposium on the Second Vatican Council at which Ratzinger gave a long presentation that explored his interpretation of the background to and character of the Council in general, the ecclesiology of the Council (in particular that of *Lumen Gentium*), the subsequent interpretation of the conciliar ecclesiology by the CDF and the emergence of the particular form of *communio* ecclesiology that Ratzinger gives preference to. Something, then, of a prelude to the address included in our previous reading,[31] albeit with significantly different areas of emphasis,

---

31 As with many of Ratzinger writings and addresses, there is considerable overlap and repetition between these two full texts – for example, echoing the end of our previous reading, here he also states '. . . [The] ontological precedence of the universal Church, the one Church, the one body, the one bride, over the concrete empirical realizations in the particular Churches seems to me so obvious that I find it hard to understand the objections to it [. . .]. Resistance to the affirmations of the pre-eminence of the universal Church in relation to the particular Churches is difficult to

as well. In particular, his address stressed how, although the Council was primarily an ecclesiological council, first and foremost the Fathers were concerned with God and then questions concerning the Church. Here he characteristically challenges ecclesiological 'horizontalism' and sociological and relativistic understandings of the Church. He demonstrates unease with how the conciliar phrase 'people of God' has subsequently been understood, hence his preference for the notion of communion, with its Trinitarian and Eucharistic overtones – which, as we have already seen, are all familiar themes in Ratzinger's ecclesiological writings.

In our extract, which opens by picking up on the theme of *communio*, Ratzinger expounds an interpretation of the famous passage from *Lumen Gentium* concerning the definition of the Church and the now famous phrase employed in the Latin text, '*subsistit in*'. The core question here is once again concerning the relationship between the universal Church and local, particular Churches, as well as the relation between the Roman Catholic Church and other Christian communities.

In addition to featuring as the subject of the intense focus of Ratzinger's own theological reflections, a great deal of debate has been generated over the meaning of this concept in the wider theological and ecclesial world. Indeed, a number of documents from the CDF, both during Ratzinger's time as Prefect and since, can be interpreted as an attempt to declare a normative and 'definitive' interpretation of a term that many other scholars, bishops and faithful believe is significantly different to the intentions and meaning that the Council Fathers had in mind at the time. So, also, have the debates concerning the relation between the local and universal Church continued apace.[32] Not least of all, the aforementioned and now much-discussed exchange on the subject between then Cardinal Ratzinger and Cardinal Kasper on the subject, throughout 2001. We will see these themes explored further still in Chapter Five of this volume.

[. . . W]e find ourselves concretely [. . .] facing the question of the interpretation of the Council.[33] We now ask the following question: what really was the idea of

understand and even impossible to understand theologically [. . .]' (see footnote 33, below, this passage is found on pp 6-7 of the original text). Here we include some of the most significantly distinctive sections from the 2001 text.

32 Cf. Francis Sullivan, 'The Meaning of *subsistit in* as Explained by the Congregation for the Doctrine of the Faith', in *Theological Studies* 69.1 (March 2008), 116–124,. See the historical survey by Karim Schelkens, 'Lumen gentium's "*subsistit in*" Revisited: the Catholic Church and Christian Unity after Vatican II', in *Theological Studies* (I December 2008), pp. 875–893.

33 [Sections on 'Subsistit in' from Joseph Ratzinger, 'The Ecclesiology Of The Constitution On The Church, Vatican II, "*Lumen Gentium*"', in *L'Osservatore Romano* English edition, no. 38 (19 September 2001), pp. 5–8. A different translation also appears in Ratzinger's *Pilgrim Fellowship of Faith: the Church as Communion*. San Francisco: Ignatius Press, 2005, 123-152].

the Council on the universal Church? [. . .] The first sentence of the Constitution on the Church immediately explains that the Council does not consider the Church as a reality closed in on herself, but sees her in a Christological perspective: 'Christ is the light of the nations; and it is, accordingly, the heartfelt desire of this sacred Council, being gathered together in the Holy Spirit, that [. . .] the light of Christ, reflected on the face of the Church, may enlighten all men'. With this background we can understand the image used in the theology of the Fathers, who see the Church as the moon that does not shine with its own light, but reflects the light of Christ the sun. Ecclesiology is shown to be dependent upon Christology and con- nected with it. But since no one can speak correctly of Christ, of the Son, without at the same time speaking of the Father, and, since it is impossible to speak correctly of the Father and the Son without listening to the Holy Spirit, the Christological vision of the Church necessarily expands to become a Trinitarian ecclesiology (Lumen Gentium, nn. 2-4). The discourse on the Church is a discourse on God, and only in this way is it correct. In this Trinitarian ouverture, which offers the key to a correct interpretation of the whole text, we learn what the one, holy Church is, starting with and in all her concrete historical phenomena, and what 'universal Church' should mean. This is further explained when we are subsequently shown the Church's inner dynamism towards the kingdom of God. Precisely because the Church is to be theologically understood, she is always transcending herself; she is the gathering for the kingdom of God, the breaking-in of the kingdom. Then the different images of the Church are briefly presented, which all describe the unique Church, whether she is described as the bride, the house of God, his family, the temple, the holy city, our mother, the Jerusalem which is above or God's flock, etc. This, ultimately, becomes even more concrete. We are given a very practical answer to the question: what is this, this one universal Church which ontologically and temporally precedes the local Churches? Where is she? Where can we see her act? [. . .]

At this point I would like to interrupt my analysis of the concept of communio and at least briefly take a stance regarding the most disputed point of Lumen gentium: the meaning of the disputed sentence of Lumen gentium, n. 8, which teaches that the unique Church of Christ, which we confess in the Creed as one, holy, catholic and apostolic, 'subsists' in the Catholic Church, which is governed by the Successor of Peter and by the bishops in communion with him. In 1985 the Congregation for the Doctrine of the Faith was forced to adopt a position with regard to this text, because of a book by Leonardo Boff in which he supported the idea that the one Church of Christ as she subsists in the Roman Catholic Church could also subsist in other Christian Churches. It is superfluous to say that the statement of the Congregation for the Doctrine of the Faith was met with stinging criticism and then later put aside.

In the attempt to reflect on where we stand today in the reception of the Council's ecclesiology, the question of the interpretation of the subsistit is inevitable, and on this subject the postconciliar Magisterium's single official pronouncement, that is, the Notification I just mentioned, cannot be ignored. Looking back from the perspective of 15 years, it emerges more clearly that it was not so much the question of a single theological author, but of a vision of the Church that was put forward in a variety of ways and which is still current today. The clarification of 1985 presented the context of Boff's thesis at great length. We do not need to examine these details further, because we have something more fundamental at heart. The thesis, which at the time had Boff as its proponent, could be described as ecclesiological relativism. It finds its justification in the theory that the 'historical Jesus' would not as such have conceived the idea of a Church, nor much less have founded one. The Church, as a historical reality, would have only come into existence after the resurrection, on account of the loss of the eschatological tension towards the immediate coming of the kingdom, caused in its turn by the inevitable sociological needs of institutionalization. In the beginning, a universal *Catholic* Church would certainly not have existed, but only different local Churches with different theologies, different ministers, etc. No institutional Church could, therefore, say that she was that one Church of Jesus Christ desired by God himself; all institutional forms thus stem from sociological needs and as such are human constructions which can and even must be radically changed again in new situations. In their theological quality they are only different in a very secondary way, so one might say that in all of them or at least in many, the 'one Church of Christ' subsists; with regard to this hypothesis the question naturally arises: in this vision, what right does one have to speak at all of the one Church of Christ?

Instead, Catholic tradition has chosen another starting point: it puts its confidence in the Evangelists and believes in them. [. . .] Christ's Church is not hidden invisibly behind the manifold human configurations, but really exists, as a true and proper Church which is manifest in the profession of faith, in the sacraments and in apostolic succession.

The Second Vatican Council, with the formula of the *subsistit* in accord with Catholic tradition wanted to teach the exact opposite of 'ecclesiological relativism': the Church of Jesus Christ truly exists. He himself willed her, and the Holy Spirit has continuously created her since Pentecost, in spite of being faced with every human failing, and sustains her in her essential identity. The institution is not an inevitable but theologically unimportant or even harmful externalization, but belongs in its essential core to the concrete character of the Incarnation. [. . .]

At this point it becomes necessary to investigate the word *subsistit* somewhat more carefully. With this expression, the Council differs from the formula of Pius XII, who said in his Encyclical *Mystici Corporis Christi*: 'The Catholic Church "is" (*est*) the one mystical body of Christ'. The difference between *subsistit* and *est* conceals within itself the whole ecumenical problem. The word *subsistit* derives from the ancient philosophy as later developed in Scholastic philosophy. The Greek word *hypostasis* that has a central role in Christology to describe the union of the divine and the human nature in the Person of Christ comes from that vision. *Subsistere* is a special case of *esse*. It is being in the form of a subject who has an autonomous existence. Here it is a question precisely of this. The Council wants to tell us that the Church of Jesus Christ as a concrete subject in this world can be found in the Catholic Church. This can take place only once, and the idea that the *subsistit* could be multiplied fails to grasp precisely the notion that is being intended. With the word *subsistit*, the Council wished to explain the unicity of the Catholic Church and the fact of her inability to be multiplied: the Church exists as a subject in historical reality.

The difference between *subsistit* and *est* however contains the tragedy of ecclesial division. Although the Church is only one and 'subsists' in a unique subject, there are also ecclesial realities beyond this subject – true local Churches and different ecclesial communities. Because sin is a contradiction, this difference between *subsistit* and *est* cannot be fully resolved from the logical viewpoint. The paradox of the difference between the unique and concrete character of the Church, on the one hand, and, on the other, the existence of an ecclesial reality beyond the one subject, reflects the contradictory nature of human sin and division. This division is something totally different from the relativistic dialectic described above in which the division of Christians loses its painful aspect and in fact is not a rupture, but only the manifestation of multiple variations on a single theme, in which all the variations are in a certain way right and wrong. An intrinsic need to seek unity does not then exist, because in any event the one Church really is everywhere and nowhere. Thus Christianity would actually exist only in the dialectic correlation of various antitheses. Ecumenism consists in the fact that in some way all recognize one another, because all are supposed to be only fragments of Christian reality. Ecumenism would therefore be the resignation to a relativistic dialectic, because the Jesus of history belongs to the past and the truth in any case remains hidden.

The vision of the Council is quite different: the fact that in the Catholic Church is present the *subsistit* of the one subject the Church, is not at all the merit of Catholics, but is solely God's work, which he makes endure despite the continuous unworthiness of the human subjects. They cannot boast of anything, but can only admire the fidelity of God, with shame for their sins and at the same time great thanks. But the effect of their own sins can be seen: the whole world sees the spectacle of the divided and opposing Christian communities, reciprocally making their own claims to truth and thus clearly frustrating the prayer of Christ on the eve of his Passion. Whereas division as a historical reality can be perceived by each person, the subsistence of the one Church in the concrete form of the Catholic Church can be seen as such only through faith.

Since the Second Vatican Council was conscious of this paradox, it proclaimed the duty of ecumenism as a search for true unity, and entrusted it to the Church of the future [. . .].

3.5 A Normative Ecclesiology of Communion: A Project on the Way

In each or our readings in this chapter thus far, we have encountered the notion of *communio*. How did this ecclesiological concept come to be in vogue once again during the decades of Ratzinger's theological and ecclesial career? In our next reading, Ratzinger supplies the background answers to such a question himself. In the mid-1960s a new international journal was founded to continue and promote the spirit of Vatican II. It was entitled *Concilium*, with the name reflecting the theological and ecclesiological method and approach of the founding editors and indeed of the Council itself.[34] Ratzinger was among the contributors to the very first volume. But in the following years he would gradually find himself at odds with other contributors and their ecclesiological perspectives. He was drawn more towards a group of theologians who were becoming increasingly critical of how the Council was being implemented and interpreted. This group's leading light was the Swiss theologian, Hans Urs von Balthasar. This group founded its own journal to promote a different theology, ecclesiology and form of understanding the Church's interaction with wider culture.

Our extract comes from a paper delivered by Ratzinger to mark the anniversary of the founding of the journal. He charts the story of its conception, how its name came to be chosen and, both explicitly and implicitly, how this turned into a project and programme for the church. The paper is more about the project or programme than the actual journal. His own contribution to helping ensure that this theological and ecclesiological outlook would prevail at the very highest levels of decision-making in the Church cannot be underestimated. This form of 'communio' ecclesiology became the normative 'official' ecclesiology of the Church during Ratzinger's time as Prefect of the CDF.

The paper covers the key debates and is rich in rhetorical argument and retrospective assessment. We see the usual targets for Ratzinger attacked here once more: the notion of a 'horizontal' and sociological over and against a hierarchical ecclesiology is critiqued, as is the use of the phrase 'people of God' in the post-conciliar period. Again, the prioritizing of the local over the universal Church is challenged. An ecclesiology 'from below' is rejected and a 'theological' ecclesiology 'from above' – in a 'real' sense – is privileged. Ratzinger offers a synthesis of

---

34   See, also, Ratzinger's 'Eucharist, Communion and Solidarity': A Lecture Given at the Eucharistic Congress of the Archdiocese of Benevento, Italy, (June 2, 2002), especially §2, available at: www. vatican.va/roman_curia/congregations/cfaith/documents/rc_con_cfaith_doc_20020602_ratzinger-eucharistic-congress_en.html (accessed 1 March 2009).

the ecclesiological 'discontents' of the *communio* project. Many have taken great encouragement from the *communio* project, finding in it a steadfast refuge in turbulent ecclesial and societal times. They believe it works towards a restoration of theological faithfulness and a vision for a renewed Christendom. For such, it promotes renewal through heart and head, as well as through particular ecclesial movements. But critics would argue that the paper is prone to stereotypes and embellished 'straw man' arguments against opposing perspectives – again, familiar features that appear in the style of various parts of Ratzinger's theological corpus. Note, also, that there are numerous and widely differing versions and conceptions of '*communio* ecclesiology', in addition to that associated with Ratzinger and the project in question.[35]

> When the first issue of the *International Catholic Review: Communio* appeared at the beginning of 1972, there were two editions, one in German and one in Italian . . ..[36] Common to the two editions was the fundamental theological contribution of Hans Urs von Balthasar, 'Communio: A Programme.' When we read these pages twenty years later, we are astonished at the relevance of what was then said. Its effect could still be explosive in the contemporary theological landscape. [. . .]

> *The origins of the review* Communio
> [. . .] At the beginning, Hans Urs von Balthasar's initiative was not aimed at founding a journal. The great theologian from Basel had not participated in the event of the Council. Considering the contribution that he could have made, one must admit a great loss. But there was also a good side to his absence. Balthasar was able to view the whole from a distance, and this gave him an independence and clarity of judgment which would have been impossible had he spent four years experiencing the event from within. He understood and accepted without reservation the greatness of the conciliar texts, but also saw the round-about fashion to which so many small-minded men had become accustomed. They sought to take advantage of the conciliar atmosphere by going on and on about the standard of faith. Their demands corresponded to the taste of their contemporaries and appeared exciting because people had previously assumed that these opinions were irreconcilable with the faith of the Church. Origen once said: 'Heretics think

---

35   Cf. Dennis M. Doyle, *Communion Ecclesiology: Visions and Versions*. Maryknoll, NY: Orbis, 2000, and Gerard Mannion, *Ecclesiology and Postmodernity – Questions for the Church in our Times*. Collegeville: Liturgical Press, 2007, pp. 32–74.

36   [From Joseph Ratzinger, 'Communio: A Program', *Communio: International Review*. Vol. 19, no. 3 (1992), pp. 436–449, (English trans. by Peter Casarella of 'Communio – Ein Programm', *Internationale Katholische Zeitschrift* 21 (1992) pp. 454–463; English version also available online: www.communio-icr.com/articles/ratzingerprogram.html (accessed 1 October 2008)].

more profoundly but not more truly.'[37] For the postconciliar period I think that we must modify that statement slightly and say: 'Their thinking appears more interesting but at the cost of the truth.' What was previously impossible to state was passed off as a continuation of the spirit of the Council. Without having produced anything genuinely new, people could pretend to be interesting at a cheap price. They sold goods from the old liberal flea market as if they were new Catholic theology.

From the very beginning, Balthasar perceived with great acuity the process by which relevance became more important than truth. [. . .] He had made himself vulnerable with the hope that these trumpet blasts would herald a return to the real subject matter of theological thinking. Once theology was no longer being measured according to its content but rather according to the purely formal categories of conservative and progressive, the learned man from Basel must have seen very quickly that his own voice alone was not sufficient. What was classified as conservative in this situation was immediately judged to be irrelevant and no further arguments were required.

So Balthasar went about seeking allies [. . .]. Thus the idea for a journal occurred to him, an idea which took shape in conversation with the first session of the International Theological Commission (1969) [. . .]. Balthasar, de Lubac, L. Bouyer, J. Medina, M. J. Le Guillou, and I arranged to meet in the fall of 1969 apart from the official consultations of the Commission. There the project took on concrete form. [. . .]

Obviously, it took a long time for the idea to be realized . . . . There was also the question of the title. Many different possibilities were tested . . . . I no longer remember exactly when the name Communio first entered into the conversation, but I believe it occurred through contact with Communione e Liberazione. The word appeared all of a sudden, like the illumination of a room. It actually expressed everything we wanted to say. [. . .]

The name as a program
When our journal started out twenty years ago, the word *communio* had not yet been discovered by progressive postconciliar theology. At that time everything centred on the 'people of God,' a concept which was thought to be a genuine innovation of the Second Vatican Council and was quickly contrasted with a hierarchical understanding of the Church. More and more, 'people of God' was understood in the sense of popular sovereignty, as a right to a common, democratic determination over everything that the Church is and over everything that she should do. God was taken to be the creator and sovereign of the people because the phrase contained the words 'of God,' but even with this awareness

---

37 Origen, *Commentary on the Psalms*, 36, 23 (PG [J-P. Migne, ed: *Patrologia Graeca*, 161 vols. (1857ff)] 17, 133 B), quoted in Hans Urs von Balthasar, *Origenes, Geist und Feuer.* Einsiedeln/Freiburg: Johannes Verlag, 1991, p. 115 [for an English translation, see *Origen: Spirit and Fire.* Washington, D.C.: Catholic Univeristy of America Press, 1984. Trans. by Robert J. Daley].

he was left out. He was amalgamated with the notion of a people who create and form themselves.[38] The word *communio*, which no one used to notice, was now surprisingly fashionable—if only as a foil. According to this interpretation, Vatican II had abandoned the hierarchical ecclesiology of Vatican I and replaced it with an ecclesiology of *communio*. Thereby, *communio* was apparently understood in much the same way the 'people of God' had been understood, i.e., as an essentially horizontal notion. On the one hand, this notion supposedly expresses the egalitarian moment of equality under the universal decree of everyone. On the other hand, it also emphasizes as one of its most fundamental ideas an ecclesiology based entirely on the local Church. The Church appears as a network of groups, which as such precede the whole and achieve harmony with one another by building a consensus.[39]

This kind of interpretation of the Second Vatican Council will only be defended by those who refuse to read its texts or who divide them into two parts: an acceptable progressive part and an unacceptable old-fashioned part. In the conciliar documents concerning the Church itself, for example, Vatican I and Vatican II are inextricably bound together. It is simply out of the question to separate an earlier, unsuitable ecclesiology from a new and different one. Ideas like these not only confuse conciliar texts with party platforms and councils with political conventions, but they also reduce the Church to the level of a political party. After a while political parties can throw away an old platform and replace it with one which they regard as better, at least until yet another one appears on the scene.

The Church does not have the right to exchange the faith for something else and at the same time to expect the faithful to stay with her. Councils can therefore neither discover ecclesiologies or other doctrines nor can they repudiate them. In the words of Vatican II, the Church is 'not higher than the Word of God but serves it and therefore teaches only what is handed on to it.'[40] Our understanding of the depth and breadth of the tradition develops because the Holy Spirit broadens and deepens the memory of the Church in order to guide her 'into all the truth' (John 16:13). According to the Council, growth in the perception (*Wahrnehmung, perceptio*) of what is inherent to the tradition occurs in three ways: through the meditation and study of the faithful, through an interior understanding which stems from the spiritual life, and through the proclamation of those 'who have received the sure charism of truth by succeeding to the office

---

38   I have sought to explain the correct, biblical sense of the concept 'people of God' in my book, *Church, Ecumenism and Politics*. New York: Crossroad, 1988; see also my small book, *Zur Gemeinschaft gerufen*. Freiburg: Herder, 1991, pp. 27–30.

39   Cf., also, in this regard, my *Zur Gemeinschaft gerufen*. Freiburg: Herder, 1991, pp. 70–97. Also noteworthy is the document of the CDF to the bishops of the Catholic Church on 'Some Aspects of the Church as Communio' (Vatican City, 1992).

40   [See the Second Vatican Council's Dogmatic Constitution on Divine Revelation,] *Dei Verbum*, no. 10.

of the bishop.'[41] The following words basically paraphrase the spiritual position of a council as well as its possibilities and tasks: the council is committed from within to the Word of God and to the tradition. It can only teach what is handed on. As a rule, it must find new language to hand on the tradition in each new context so that – to put it a different way – the tradition remains genuinely the same. If the Second Vatican Council brought the notion of *communio* to the forefront of our attention, it did not do so in order to create a new ecclesiology or even a new Church. Rather, careful study and the spiritual discernment which comes from the experience of the faithful made it possible at this moment to express more completely and more comprehensively what the tradition states. Even after this excursus we might still ask what *communio* means in the tradition and in the continuation of the tradition which occurs in the Second Vatican Council. First of all, *communio* is not a sociological but a theological notion, one which even extends to the realm of ontology. [. . .]

Hans Urs von Balthasar described the foundations of what the last Council developed on this point [. . .]. In the first place, we must remember that 'communion' between men and women is only possible when embraced by a third element. In other words, common human nature creates the very possibility that we can communicate with one another. We are not only nature but also persons, and in such a way that each person represents a unique way of being human different from everyone else. Therefore, nature alone is not sufficient to communicate the inner sensibility of persons. [. . .] Being a person is by nature being related . . . . [B]oth in its very depths and in its highest aspirations being a person goes beyond its own boundaries towards a greater, universal 'something' and even toward a greater, universal 'someone.' The all-embracing third, to which we return so often can only bind when it is greater and higher than individuals. On the other hand, the third is itself within each individual because it touches each one from within. Augustine once described this as 'higher than my heights, more interior than I am to myself.' This third, which in truth is the first, we call God. We touch ourselves in him. Through him and only through him, a *communio* which grasps our own depths comes into being.

We have to proceed one stop further. God communicated himself to humanity by himself becoming man. His humanity in Christ is opened up through the Holy Spirit in such a way that it embraces all of us as if we could all be united in a single body, in a single common flesh. Trinitarian faith and faith in the Incarnation guide the idea of communion with God away from the realm of philosophical concepts and locate it in the historical reality of our lives. One can therefore see why the Christian tradition interprets *koinōnía-communio* in 2 Corinthians 13:13 as an outright description of the Holy Spirit.

To put it in the form of a concrete statement: the communion of people with

41 Ibid., no. 8.

one another is possible because of God, who unites us through Christ in the Holy Spirit so that communion becomes a community, a 'church' in the genuine sense of the word. The church discussed in the New Testament is a church 'from above,' not from a humanly fabricated 'above' but from the real 'above' about which Jesus says: 'You belong to what is below, I belong to what is above' (John 8:23). Jesus clearly gave new meaning to the 'below,' for 'he descended into the lower regions of the earth' (Eph 4:9). The ecclesiology 'from below' which is commended to us today presupposes that one regards the Church as a purely sociological quantity and that Christ as an acting subject has no real significance. But in this case, one is no longer speaking about a church at all but about a society which has also set religious goals for itself. According to the logic of this position, such a church will also be 'from below' in a theological sense, namely, 'of this world,' which is how Jesus defines 'below' in the Gospel of John (John 8:23). An ecclesiology based upon *communio* consists of thinking and loving from the real 'above.' This 'above' relativises every human 'above' and 'below' because before him the first will be last and the last will be first. A principal task of the review *Communio* had to be, and therefore must still be, to steer us toward this real 'above,' the one which disappears from view when understood in merely sociological and psychological terms. The 'dreams of the Church' for tomorrow unleash a blind yearning to be committed to forming a church which has disintegrated whatever is essential. [. . .]

Hans Urs von Balthasar has dealt a severe blow to the sociology of groups. He reminds us that the ecclesiastical community appears to quite a number of people today as no more than a skeleton of institutions. As a result, 'the small group . . . will become more and more the criterion of ecclesiastical vitality. For these people, the Church as Catholic and universal seems to hover like a disconnected roof over the buildings which they inhabit.'[42] [. . .]

42   Hans Urs von Balthasar, 'Communio – A Programme', in *International Catholic Review: Communio* 1, no. 1 (1972) p. 10.

CHAPTER 4

CHRISTIAN FAITH, CHURCH AND WORLD

Lieven Boeve

Introduction

In this section, we go deeper into three distinctive aspects of Joseph Ratzinger's thought. First, we take the reception of *Gaudium et Spes*, the Pastoral Constitution on the Church in the Modern World, as a starting point for a presentation of Ratzinger's theological position as regards the dialogue of Christianity with the modern world. A careful analysis shows, as the years go by, his progressively growing discomfort with the dialogue of the Church with the (too) modern world. A second aspect, immediately linked to the first, is Ratzinger's deep concern for the soul of Europe, a worry that he has expressed in several accounts over the last two decades. For Ratzinger, because of the weakening presence of Christianity in European culture and society, Europe is threatened in its very identity. Third, we shed light on his views on the relation between Christian faith and politics.

4.1 The Dialogue of the Church with the Modern World

Both as (conciliar) theologian and as Church leader, Joseph Ratzinger has never been able to muster a great deal of enthusiasm for the notion of dialogue with modernity as it is formulated, for example, in *Gaudium et Spes*, and certainly not for the way in which this document – and Vatican II as a whole in its wake – was received after the Council.[1] Indeed, Ratzinger played an active role in the discussion surrounding what has come to be

---

1   For these paragraphs on Joseph Ratzinger's attitude to (the reception of) *Gaudium et Spes*, see L. Boeve, 'Gaudium et spes and the Crisis of Modernity: The End of the Dialogue with the World?', in M. Lamberigts and L. Kenis (eds), *Vatican II and its Legacy*. Leuven: Peeters Press, 2002, pp. 83–94, and 'Europe in Crisis. A Question of Belief or Unbelief? Perspectives from the Vatican', in *Modern Theology* 23 (2007) pp. 205–227. For an analogous presentation, see H.-J. Sander, 'Theologischer Kommentar zur Pastoralkonstitution über die Kirche in der Welt von heute Gaudium et spes', in P. Hünermann and B.J. Hilberath (eds), *Herders Theologischer Kommentar zum Zweiten Vatikanischen Konzil*, Band 4. Freiburg/Basel/Vienna: Herder, 2005, pp. 581–886, 838–844.

known as *Schema XIII*, one of two preparatory texts for *Gaudium et Spes*. During these discussions, Ratzinger was among the first to point out the potential dangers of making exaggerated overtures towards the modern world.[2] One of the major problems in the discussions consisted in the evaluation of modern technological development and its promises for humankind. Inspired by the work of Teilhard de Chardin, a number of the conciliar Fathers too hastily identified Christian hope with modern belief in the progress of humanity: for such individuals, there was no longer any difference between the process of 'hominisation' and the process of 'Christification' towards the 'omega' point; the reconciliation of Christianity and modernity was complete. In *Schema XIII*, Ratzinger noticed a version of the same naive optimism with respect to technological development and a dangerous confusion of technological progress with Christian hope. In specifying the relationship between Christ and the technical world, the *Schema* tended to consider Christology as a sacralization of technological evolution, instead of applying it at the level of the passion of human life and of human love. In the final text, the recognition of the fruits of technology was accompanied – to Ratzinger's relief – by a warning not to untie the bonds between technology and the primacy of the human person and the broader horizon of meaning opened up in Christian revelation.

In general terms, Ratzinger was afraid that the turn towards the modern world and the positive assessment of modern hopes would, theologically speaking, place too much emphasis on the dynamics of incarnation (God becomes flesh in this world), forgetting the mystery of the cross (Christian faith is not of this world). *Aggiornamento*, as Ratzinger wrote in *Angesichts der Welt von heute*, does not consist in a simple adjustment of Christian faith to the modern world. The Christian individual's 'yes to the world' is always a critical 'yes' – the modern world cannot only be identified with progress toward more humanity, it is also and always characterized by an illegitimate 'will to absolute autonomy', the will to live without God, which is modern *hubris*. Dialogue with the world can only proceed when (through this dialogue) the world is purified,[3] or, as Ratzinger wrote in an extended

2   J. Ratzinger, 'Sentire ecclesiam', in *Geist und Leben* 36 (1963) pp. 321–326; *Ergebnisse und Probleme der dritten Konzilsperiode*. Cologne: Bachem, 1965, pp. 38–39, *Die letzte Sitzungsperiode des Konzils*: Cologne: Bachem, 1966, pp. 25–58, 'Angesichts der Welt von heute. Überlegungen zur Konfrontation mit der Kirche im Schema XIII', in *Wort und Wahrheit* 20 (1965) pp. 493–504 (enlarged and revised as *Dogma und Verkündigung*. Munich: Wewel, 1973, pp. 183–204). He has also written a commentary accompanying the first chapter of Part 1 of *Gaudium et Spes* in the edition of *Lexikon für Theologie und Kirche. Das zweite Vatikanische Konzil. Konstitutionen, Dekrete und Erklärungen. Kommentare*, Teil 3. Freiburg/Basel/Vienna: Herder, pp. 313–354.
3   J. Ratzinger, 'Angesichts der Welt von heute. Überlegungen zur Konfrontation mit der Kirche im Schema XIII', in *Wort und Wahrheit* 20 (1965), pp. 502–503.

version of the aforementioned article published in 1973: when the world is 'exorcised'.[4] In a later version of the same article, Ratzinger added some sections designed to relativize the optimism engendered by the Council and the pastoral Constitution, the following statement being among them: 'The tragic one-sidedness of the final conciliar debates consisted in the fact that they were dominated by the trauma of backwardness and a pathos to catch up with modernity, a pathos which remained blind to the inherent ambiguity of today's world. [. . .] Now, in the post-conciliar Church, we are forced to endure problems that are arising on account of that which did not find expression in the conciliar debates'.[5] We have selected parts from the amended text from 1973.

On several occasions since the Council, Ratzinger has offered further reflection on the post-conciliar reception of the openness to the modern world proposed by *Gaudium et Spes* in an exemplary manner.[6] Over the years, his evaluation of this openness has become more and more negative, especially when he observes that progressive theologians (roughly to be identified with the theologians of the *Concilium*-group, here in particular J.-B. Metz) claim to follow the spirit of Vatican II when they introduce neo-Marxist schemes into their theological reflection.[7] In Ratzinger's opinion, it is wrong to understand *Gaudium et Spes* as a plea for ongoing progressivism, as a never ending process of adjustment to modernity. In this regard, the pastoral constitution should be read within the framework established by the dogmatic constitution *Lumen Gentium*, and not the other way around.[8] Moreover, *Gaudium et Spes* was not meant as a starting point

4   J. Ratzinger, 'Überlegungen zur Konfrontation mit der Kirche im Schema XIII', in *Dogma und Verkündigung*. Munich: Wewel, 1973, p. 201.
5   Ibid., p. 199–200 (translation mine).
6   Cf. J. Ratzinger, 'Der Katholizismus nach dem Konzil – Katholische Sicht', in *Auf Dein Wort hin. 81. Deutscher Katholikentag*. Paderborn: Bonifacius, 1966, pp. 245–266 (enlarged edition: *Das neue Volk Gottes. Entwürfe zur Ekklesiologie*. Düsseldorf: Patmos, 1969, pp. 302–321), 'Weltoffene Kirche? Überlegungen zur Struktur des Zweiten Vatikanischen Konzils', in T. Filthaut (ed.), *Umkehr und Erneuerung. Kirche nach dem Konzil*. Mainz: Grünewald, 1966, pp. 273–291 (=*Das neue Volk Gottes. Entwürfe zur Ekklesiologie*. Düsseldorf: Patmos, 1969, pp. 281–301); *Glaube und Zukunft*. München: Kösel, 1970, pp. 93–106, 'Zehn Jahre nach Konzilsbeginn — Wo stehen wir?', in *Dogma und Verkundigung*. München: Erich Wewel, 1973, pp. 439–447, 'Der Weltdienst der Kirche. Auswirkungen von Gaudium et spes im letzten Jahrzehnt', in *Internat. Kath. Zeitschrift* 4 (1975) pp. 439–454, 395–411, 'Bilanz de Nachkonzilszeit — Misserfolge, Aufgaben, Hoffnungen', in *Theologische Prinzipienlehre*. Munich: Wewel, 1982, pp. 383–395. At the end of this last article, Ratzinger even goes so far as to warn the reader that, from a historical perspective, not all valid councils were also fruitful councils. For an English translation of *Theologische Prinzipienlehre*, cf. *Principles of Catholic Theology. Building Stones for a Fundamental Theology*. San Francisco: Ignatius Press, 1987.
7   Another familiar critique that we have already encountered and will come across again is Ratzinger's other contributions in this volume.
8   J. Ratzinger, *Theologische Prinzipienlehre*. Munich: Wewel, 1982, p. 408. Also cf. Chapter Eight in this volume.

for unrestricted dialogue, it was intended rather to set the boundaries of such a dialogue. Also in the so-called *Ratzinger Report* of 1985,[9] Ratzinger urges Christians to rediscover the courage of non-conformism, the capacity to reject the euphoric post-conciliar solidarity with the world.

On the one hand, modernity, under the ideals of freedom, the humanisation[10] of the world through the power of human reason and justice, runs away from Christianity, and, at the same time, the impression arises that the driving forces behind this running away from the Church have, nevertheless, been taken from the core of the Christian message; the impression arises that it is precisely in this classical movement of modernity that the most essential content of Christianity finds its realisation, and that, therefore, the Christian should immediately leave to join this movement, even helping to drive this movement, in order to become a true Christian through absolute solidarity with the spirit of modernity. On the other hand, the question remains as to whether the Christian should not in fact fulfil a corrective function, thereby protecting man from himself. The path of Christianity in modernity therefore demonstrates a curious zigzagging motion: first, deciding in the Enlightenment to board the train of modernity, then, following the shock of the Revolution and the wars that it triggered, making a rather frightened retreat into properly church-related matters, and then, after finding new strength, increasingly proclaiming the heresy of the alleged ecclesial ghettos of this time (misjudging the great impulse that was then starting to have an effect in social and educational domains in the form of the foundation of new religious orders and lay movements), entering into new, more radical solidarity with the spirit of the present age, and finally facing the dilemma of a division of the present age into different 'presents', and a church internally torn apart. The tragic one-sidedness of the last conciliar debates came about because they were controlled by the trauma of underdevelopment and by a pathos of 'caught-up' modernity, that remained blind to the inner ambivalence of the contemporary world; and because of the all too doctrinaire, scholastically reinforced reaction of the conciliar opposition could not be made to face up to the severity of the real situation. Whatever was not dealt with in the conciliar debates, must now, therefore, be tediously endured in the post-conciliar Church; but perhaps enduring this situation together is also the only way to discovering insights that can take us further. [. . .]

In order to attempt an answer, it seems important to me to distinguish between the situation of the individual Christian as an individual and the task of the Church as Church. Both aspects are complementary to one another, but they are not identical and must therefore be investigated separately.

9   J. Ratzinger and V. Messori, *Rapporto sulla fede*. Torino: Edizioni Paoline, 1985 (E.T.: *The Ratzinger Report: An Exclusive Interview on the State of the Church*. San Francisco: Ignatius, 1986.

10   [Selection from J. Ratzinger, 'Der Christ und die Welt von heute', in *Dogma und Verkundigung*. München: Erich Wewel, 1973, pp. 179–200, here pp. 195–200. Trans. by David Kirchhoffer].

1. The ethos of work, science, and the quest for a just order express the contemporary way that man relates to earthly reality. It is, in this respect, the 'world' that the Christian has to deal with. The question of the relationship of the Christian to the 'world of today' is, thus, more specifically a question of his relationship to these realities, that is, to the behavioural whole that these entail. It is clear that, in this new behavioural entity, elements of human obstinacy and the rejection of God, in other words the world in Johannine sense of 'this world', *could* become operative at anytime, and are in effect, in no small measure, *already* operative. In this respect, the 'world of today' challenges the alertness and the critical faculties of the believer. It seems to me, however, no less clear that this behavioural whole that we have identified as the material content of the 'world of today' actually contains elements that come from that which is central to Christianity. That which Christian love actually wants and should want—to provide every human being with the same opportunities as one has oneself; to ease the burden of being for everyone; to make it possible for every human being to fulfil the talents given to them by the Creator; to lead people from division to unity—is certainly not the only driver of the modern worlds of science and work, a world in which not only Marxist criticism can reveal fatal interests behind pretty masks; but this driver is still present and the 'interests' regarding it should be purified—that is what concrete, creative Christian criticism of the 'world of today' should be.

It must be admitted that we stand, today, before the paradox that the 'curiositas' of science and the world on which it has left its mark can, in many respects, more radically carry out the thrust of Christian caritas than the individual charity of Christian Antiquity and the Middle Ages. Why should the Church, in this situation, shy away from admitting—and from being grateful for—the fact that that which is hers comes to her anew, from the outside, and even challenges her? It should be the task of Christians, not to stand apart from the world of today, negating it, but to purify the worlds of science and work on the basis of the Caritas Christiana, to exorcise them, and so to free them. The Christian, by living in the world from this central core, and only by doing this, can, at the same time, critically help to eradicate that which is always in fact at work in the powers of 'this world' (in the negative sense of the term). If, in light of the undeniable presence of this factor *too*, the Christian's yes to the 'world of today' must be a critical yes, then it can certainly not mean that he may do it only half-heartedly—just because it can't be done otherwise. It cannot mean that he may participate only as one pulled along, and not as one doing the pulling. Half-heartedness is useless. The Christian's answer to the problems of today cannot be to half believe and to half allow himself to be dragged along by the world from which he cannot escape. His answer must rather be to wholly believe, and, from the wholeness of belief, to affirm the wholeness of the world, i.e. in realising technical structures, to do so out of the responsibility to love. Such wholehearted service to the task of today's world also does not then mean a betrayal vis-à-vis the foolishness of the cross in favour of a naïve belief in progress: the practical nature of the services undertaken in such a way is precisely what demands—if we are to understand the inner core of the Caritas Christiana properly—the preparedness to lose oneself every day anew, without which one cannot find oneself. Christian asceticism does not become superfluous even if its forms change. And it is clear: the service of personal love also does not become superfluous, no matter how much the face of the world is changed. Without this service, the fundamental thrust of the Caritas Christiana, of which we spoke, would lose its credibility.

And, finally, the critical yes, which does not exclude but rather longs for the whole heart, will mean that the Christian lives in the world of work in such a way that he makes it a means to greater freedom. This is also the goal of the world of work, but freedom remains empty as long as it is just limited to free time, to a contrast in one's schedule, and therefore ultimately to a disguised form of bondage. Freedom is only fulfilled when it becomes the space of the eternal; this means allowing the physical and the temporal relief brought about by technology to become a real liberation of man, i.e., a new liberation for the eternal. This is a hope yet to be fulfilled, but, precisely for this reason, a task of the first order for the Christian.

2. With regard to the task of the Church, the modern theology of the last decade has followed a curious path. It began with an idea that was developed in the youth movements, that of the 'bringing home' [Heimholung] of the world and its values. But the values 'brought home' proved to be stronger than the house they had been brought into, and so followed the transition from the world brought home to the idea of the worldly world: Christianity should promote the worldliness of the world, not its Christian-ness; to Christianise should mean to secularise, to desacralise, to 'de-taboo-ise', to free the world to be itself. Then the next step brings about the complete reversal of the initial movement. Now the world is no longer taken into the Church, but instead the Church itself must now be become involved in the world. It is her task to function socio-critically, to be an institutionalised critique of the primary institutions. Finally, this critique gets its own dogma, and the Church is seen as a politically important factor, as a part of the political liberation movement of this world.

In this outline of a decade's theological development, the woeful state of theology becomes fully apparent, a state that is extremely evident in the theme of our discussion. A thorough examination of this is among today's most urgent tasks. This cannot be accomplished here, in a reflection on the conciliar dispute surrounding the Church and the world.[11] Instead, I shall only make a small, entirely unguarded comment with regard to the general direction that, in my opinion, the conversation should lead us. From the Gospel, we can easily see that the task of the Church as Church cannot be to root itself in wordly things, by which it would try, in a sense,

11   Cf. J. B Metz, "Politische Theologie in der Diskussion", in *Diskussion zur 'politischen Theologie'*. H.Peukert (ed). Mainz-München: Matthias Grünwald, 1969, pp. 267-301; H. Maier, *Kritik der politischen Theologie*. Einsiedeln: Johannes Verlag, 1970; ders., *Kirche und Gesellschaft*. München: Kösel, 1972; H. Kuhn, *Der Staat*.München: Kösel, 1967.

under its own direction to build a sort of exclusively Catholic world. Rather, the world is one world for all people; the task of the Christian (and therefore the task of the Catholic) cannot be the creation of his own world. His task is, instead, to permeate this one world with the Spirit of Jesus Christ. What the Church has to give the world is not a private ideal world, which would in reality very quickly become a typically human world, as has been demonstrated often enough by all the historical attempts to do so. What she has to offer the world, is really that which only she is able to give: the Word of God, which is no less vital for man as earthly bread is. Man is and remains a creature in which not only the stomach hungers, but also the mind and the heart; a creature that not only hungers for food, but that also hungers for meaning, for love, for infinitude, and that, without these truly human, nay, divine gifts, couldn't live. Moreover, in the technical world, and indeed precisely in it, this hunger remains, and the Church owes it to man not to delay the would-be construction of a better world, which she cannot provide anyway, but rather to answer man's hunger and to reveal this hunger to him in the event that it has been forgotten. She should only opt for institutions, or choose to become rooted in the flesh of the earth, to the extent that these are necessary for this service to the Word. The extent of the concrete institutionalisation and the earthly engagement rests in the needs of the Word of God, and nowhere else.

With this, we have returned to our point of departure: to the tasks that confronted the Council, which sought to develop them in a text about the Church in the world of today. The difficulty of this task is perhaps more clearly demonstrated by the stammering attempts at answers at the end of this contribution than by the development of the questions that preceded them. And yet, here too one should not forget that it could not be the task of the Church (represented in the Council) to create something like an official, intellectual, ideal world—a scientifically produced synthesis of all of the questions of life that face people today, and that should immediately inspire everybody. Looking back, one could reproach the Council for trying too hard to move in this direction (forgetting the modesty of earlier councils) and, in so doing, for wanting too much. In this way, many of the statements in a text that is in itself well-intentioned and on the whole also really useful will rather quickly become outdated. What counts is the attempt to awaken consciences and to call them to responsibility before God, who, in Jesus Christ, revealed himself as Word and Love, which, in the cross, has become both the crisis [or turning point: *Krise*] and the hope of the world.

4.2. The Christian Soul of Europe

Since 1989, Ratzinger's analysis of the opposition between Christian faith and the modern world has become increasingly focused on Europe. In 1991, for instance, he published a collection of articles, titled *Wendezeit für Europa? Diagnosen und Prognosen zur Lage von Kirche und Welt*, dealing with the situation of Europe after 1989 and the role that faith and the Church might continue to play in the region.[12] According to Ratzinger, Europe has been deeply affected by those master narratives of progress and emancipation that we have heard him critique in various writings already. The continent has forgotten what it is to be really human – i.e. what real truth and real freedom are. Truth is not something that is self-made, created, or discussed in terms of majority and minority. Freedom, at the same time, is not something empty, i.e. the freedom to do whatever one wants – arbitrary freedom. The result of the modern abolition of 'humanity' has been the contemporary civilization of death,[13] which has become significantly apparent in the major fatal ills of our time: HIV/AIDS, drugs, terrorism, abortion, suicide, collective violence, ecological disasters, rising nationalism, and also some new forms of religiosity and esoteria (New Age), all of which have come forth from a fundamental misunderstanding of the foundation and roots of real humanity, real truth, real freedom.[14] A civilization in which truth is something one creates and decides upon, in which freedom is something empty, ultimately leads to irrationalism and amorality, to nihilism and relativism.[15] For Ratzinger, truth and freedom are not self-made but given, they are not empty, but bound to something independent of human activity: God and God's revelation. The truth about humanity is revealed in an anthropological and ethical vision of Christianity, which, Ratzinger contends, can be considered a synthesis of the major ethical intuitions of humankind.[16] God revealed the salvific and liberating truth in the Scriptures and the tradition to the Church, which has to guard and proclaim it. Insofar as the Church is able to remind the contemporary world of this liberating truth, it can offer a way out of the modern civilization of death.

Likewise, in a biographical interview with Peter Seewald, published in book form under the title *Salz der Erde* in 1996,[17] Ratzinger once

12   *Wendezeit für Europa? Diagnosen und Prognosen zur Lage von Kirche und Welt.* Einsiedeln: Johannes Verlag, 1991, ²1992 (E.T.: *Turning Point for Europe.* San Francisco: Ignatius Press, 1994).
13   J. Ratzinger, *Wendezeit für Europa? Diagnosen und Prognosen zur Lage von Kirche und Welt.* Einsiedeln: Johannes Verlag, 1991, ²1992, p 92.
14   Cf. also, for example, his 'Jesus Christus heute', in *Internat. Kath. Zeitschrift Communio* 19 (1990) pp. 56–70; 'Die Bedeutung religiöser und sittlicher Werte in der pluralistischen Gesellschaft', in *Ibidem* 21 (1992) pp. 500–512.
15   Again, these themes are encountered in Chapters Three, Five, Six and Seven of this volume.
16   J. Ratzinger, *Wendezeit für Europa? Diagnosen und Prognosen zur Lage von Kirche und Welt.* Einsiedeln: Johannes Verlag, 1991, ²1992, pp. 26–27.
17   J. Ratzinger, *Salz der Erde. Christentum und katholische Kirche an der Jahrtausendwende. Ein Gespräch mit Peter Seewald.* Stuttgart: Deutsche Verlags-Anstalt, 1996 (E.T.: *Salt of the Earth.* San Francisco: Ignatius Press, 1997).

again expressed his evaluation of modernity in crisis and the remedy that the Christian faith has to offer in response thereto. He also referred, for example, to what he perceived to be an erroneous understanding of the concept 'renewal' that many had read in the Second Vatican Council.[18] The book deals in more specific detail with the situation of the Church and theology in a number of different European countries and indicates the concrete problems that he argues are the result of 'too much' modernity.

The name chosen by Joseph Ratzinger as successor to Peter came as something of a surprise, although his clarification thereof during his first general audience revealed its appropriateness. The name not only referred to Benedict XV, who had endeavoured to prevent the First World War and had worked for peace and reconciliation, but also to Benedict of Nursia, founder of the Benedictine order and one of the patron saints of Europe who – according to the Pope – had exercised an enormous influence on Europe's Christian heritage. Benedict of Nursia represents 'a fundamental reference point for European unity and a powerful reminder of the indispensable Christian roots of its culture and civilization'.[19]

Benedict is therefore a name with an explicitly European programme. The Pope's choice becomes even less surprising when one reviews Joseph Ratzinger's speaking engagements and publications in the last few years. Reference should not only be made to *Values in a Time of Upheaval*,[20] which deals explicitly – and in a nuanced manner – with Europe and its Christian heritage (and contains, among other things, the text of a speech addressed to the Italian senate on 13 May 2004), but also, for example, to a – more outspoken – lecture on the cultural crisis in Europe, which he gave on 1 April 2005 in Subiaco (Italy), on the occasion of being awarded the Saint Benedict Prize for the promotion of life and the Christian family in Europe. It is from this text that we have selected a substantial fragment.[21]

---

18 Ibid., p. 74–76.
19 See full text of this audience: www.vatican.va/holy_father/benedict_xvi/audiences///hf_ben-xvi_aud_20050427_en.html (accessed 1st September 2009).
20 J. Ratzinger, *Values in a Time of Upheaval*, New York: Crossroad Publishing, 2006.
21 Published in English as: J. Ratzinger, 'Europe in the Crisis of Cultures', in *Communio: International Catholic Review* 32 (2005) 345-356. A little earlier, on January 19th 2004, Ratzinger entered into a dialogue with the German philosopher Jürgen Habermas, the introductory statements of both thinkers having appeared in *Dialektik der Säkularisierung: Über Vernunft und Religion*, Freiburg/Basel/Vienna, Herder, 2005. A considerable portion of Ratzinger's text is made up of material from the various contributions collected in *Values in a Time of Upheaval*. In addition, the (original) German version of Ratzinger's Subiaco lecture has also appeared in a collection of essays together with a text written by the chair of the Italian senate, Marcello Pera, and followed by a letter from the latter addressed to Ratzinger in which he offers a clear and highly readable response. The title of the collection is nevertheless significant: *Ohne Wurzeln: Der Relativismus und die Krise der Europäischen*

Reflections on today's contrasting cultures[22]

Of course, Christianity did not start in Europe, and so cannot be classified as a European religion, the religion of the European cultural realm. But it was precisely in Europe that Christianity received its most historically influential cultural and intellectual form, and it therefore remains intertwined with Europe in a special way. On the other hand, it is also true that, beginning with the Renaissance, and then in complete form with the Enlightenment, this same Europe also developed the scientific rationality that not only led to the geographical unity of the world, to the meeting of continents and cultures in the age of discovery, but that now, thanks to the technological culture made possible by science, much more deeply places its stamp on what is now truly the whole world, indeed, in a certain sense reduces the world to uniformity. And, in the wake of this form of rationality, Europe has developed a culture that, in a way hitherto unknown to humanity, excludes God from public consciousness, whether he is totally denied or whether his existence is judged to be indemonstrable, uncertain, and so is relegated to the domain of subjective choices, as something in any case irrelevant for public life. This purely functional rationality, to give it a name, has revolutionized moral conscience in a way that is equally new with respect to all hitherto existing cultures, inasmuch as it claims that only what is experimentally provable is rational. [. . .]

Let us take a closer look at this contrast between the two cultures that have marked Europe. This contrast has surfaced in two controverted points of the debate about the Preamble to the European Constitution: shall the Constitution mention God? Shall it mention Europe's Christian roots? Some say that there is no need to worry, since article 52 of the Constitution guarantees the institutional rights of the Church. However, this means that the Churches find room in European life only in the realm of political compromise, but that when it comes to the foundations of Europe, their actual substance has no room to play any formative role. The arguments given for this clear 'No' are superficial, and it is clear that, rather than indicating the real reason, they in fact cover it. The claim that mentioning Europe's Christian roots would offend the feelings of the many non-Christians who live in Europe is unconvincing, since what we are dealing with is first and foremost a historical fact that no one can seriously deny. Of course, this historical observation also implies something about the present, since to mention roots is also to point to residual sources of moral guidance, and so to something that constitutes the identity of this thing called Europe. Who would be offended? Whose identity would be threatened? Muslims, who are typically used as the favorite examples in this regard, do not feel threatened by our Christian moral foundations, but by the cynicism of a secularized culture that denies its own bases. Nor do our

Kultur, Augsburg, Sankt Ulrich Verlag, 2004 (ET: *Without Roots: The West, Relativism, Christianity, Islam*, New York, Basic Books, 2006).

22   [Selection from J. Ratzinger, 'Europe in the Crisis of Cultures', in *Communio: International Catholic Review* 32 (2005) 345-356, here pp. 349-355.]

Jewish fellow citizens feel offended when Europe's Christian roots are mentioned, since these roots go back to Mount Sinai: they bear the mark of the voice that resounded on the Mountain of God and they unite us in the great basic guidelines that the Decalogue has given to humanity. The same holds for the reference to God: it is not the mention of God that offends adherents of other religions, but rather the attempt to build the human community without any relationship to God whatsoever. The reasons for this double 'No' are deeper than the arguments that have been advanced for it would suggest. They presuppose the idea that only radical Enlightenment culture, which has reached its full development in our time, is able to define what European culture is. Different religious cultures, each enjoying its respective rights, can therefore co-exist alongside Enlightenment culture – so long and so far as they respect, and subordinate themselves to, its criteria. This culture is substantially defined by the rights of freedom. Its starting-point is freedom, which it takes to be a fundamental value that measures everything else: the liberty of religious choice, which includes the religious neutrality of the state; the liberty to express one's own opinion, as long as it does not call into doubt this canon of freedom; the democratic ordering of the state, hence, parliamentary control over the organisms of the state; the free formation of parties; the independence of the judiciary; and, finally, the protection of the rights of man and the prohibition of discrimination in any form. In this last respect, the canon is still in formation, since the rights of man can also be in conflict, for example, when there is a clash between a woman's desire for freedom and an unborn baby's right to life. The concept of discrimination is being continually broadened, and in this way the prohibition of discrimination can find itself increasingly transformed into a limitation on the freedom of opinion and the freedom of religion. We are not far from the time when we will no longer be allowed to state publicly that homosexuality is, as the Catholic Church teaches, an objective disorder in the structuring of human existence. And the Church's conviction that it does not have the right to give priestly ordination to women is already considered by some to be incompatible with the spirit of the European Constitution. It is obvious that this canon of Enlightenment culture – which is anything but definitive – contains important values that we, precisely as Christians, cannot, and do not wish to, do without. But it is also obvious that the ill-defined, or even simply undefined, conception of freedom on which this culture rests inevitably entails contradictions. And it is obvious that the actual use of this concept – a use that seems radical – brings with it restrictions on freedom that would have been unimaginable a generation ago. A confused ideology of freedom leads to a dogmatism that turns out to be – more and more – hostile to freedom.

2. The significance and limits of today's rationalist culture.

We must now face these last two questions. With respect to the first question – have we attained the universal, at last fully scientific philosophy that brings to expression mankind's common reason? – we have to answer that we have indeed achieved important gains that can claim a general validity: we have achieved the insight that religion cannot be imposed by the state, but can be welcomed only in freedom; respect for the fundamental rights of man, which are equal for all; the separation of powers and the control of power. We must not imagine, however, that these basic values, though generally valid, can be realized in the same way in every historical context. Not every society has the sociological presuppositions for the sort of party-based democracy that exists in the West. By the same token, complete religious neutrality on the part of the state has to be regarded, in most historical contexts, as an illusion. And with that we come to the problems raised by the second question. But first let us clear up the question as to whether modern Enlightenment philosophies, taken as a whole, can claim to speak the last word for reason as something common to all men. Characteristic of these philosophies is their positivism, hence, their anti-metaphysical posture. Consequently, they end up leaving no room for God. They are based on a self-limitation of positive reason, which is adequate in the technical domain, but which, when it gets generalized, mutilates man. It follows from this that man no longer acknowledges any moral authority outside of his calculations, and, as we have seen, even the concept of freedom, which at first sight might seem to expand here without limit, leads in the end to the self-destruction of freedom. Admittedly, the positivist philosophies contain important elements of truth. But these elements are based on a self-limitation of reason typical of a given cultural situation – that of the modern West – and as such cannot be reason's last word. Although they appear to be totally rational, they are not the voice of reason itself, but are themselves culturally bound; bound, that is, to the situation of today's West. They are, then, not at all the philosophy that, one day, might rightfully claim validity throughout the whole world. But above all we need to say that this Enlightenment philosophy, with its corresponding culture, is incomplete. It consciously severs its own cultural roots, thus depriving itself of the original energies from which it itself sprang, the fundamental memory of humanity, as it were, without which reason loses its compass. Indeed, the principle that reigns today says that man is the measure of his action. If we know how to do it, we are allowed to do it. There is no longer any such thing as knowing how to do something without being allowed to do it – such a situation would be contrary to freedom, which is the supreme, absolute value. [. . .]

The act of setting aside Europe's Christian roots is not, after all, the expression of a superior tolerance that respects all cultures equally, and refrains from privileging any of then, but rather the absolutization of a way of thinking and living that stand in radical contrast, among other things, to the other historical cultures of humanity. The true antithesis that characterizes today's world is not that between different religious cultures, but that between the radical emancipation of man from God, from the roots of life, on the one hand, and the great religious cultures, on the other. If we eventually find ourselves in a clash of cultures, it will not be because of the clash of the great religions – which have always been in conflict with one another, but which, in the end, have always managed to coexist – but it will be because of the clash between this radical emancipation of man and the major cultures of history. In this sense, the refusal to mention God is not the expression of a tolerance that would protect the non-theistic religions and the dignity of atheists and agnostics. It is rather the expression of a mind-set that would like to see God erased once and for all from the public life of humanity and relegated to the subjective sphere maintained by residual cultures from the past. Relativism, which is the starting-point for all of this, thus becomes a dogmatism that believes itself in possession of the definitive knowledge of reason and of the right to regard everything else as a mere stage of humanity's development that has been fundamentally superseded and that is best treated as a pure relativity.[23] What this really means is that we need roots to survive and that we must not lose sight of God, at the cost of the disappearance of human dignity.

3. The permanent significance of Christian faith

Is this a simple refusal of the Enlightenment and of modernity? Absolutely not. From its very beginning, Christianity has understood itself as the religion of the *logos*, as the religion according to reason. It found its precursor, not primarily in the other religions, but in the philosophical enlightenment that cleared the way of traditions in order to devote itself to the pursuit of the true and the good, of the one God who is above all the gods. As a religion of the persecuted, as a universal religion that reached beyond states and peoples, Christianity denied the state the right to regard religion as a part of its own order, and so claimed freedom for faith. It has always defined men, all men without distinction, as creatures of God and images of God, and has always in principle proclaimed their equal dignity, albeit within the inevitable limits of given societies. In this sense, the Enlightenment is of Christian origin and it is not an accident that it came to birth precisely and exclusively in the domain of Christian faith. True, in that very domain Christianity had unfortunately contradicted its own nature by becoming a state tradition and a state religion. Despite the fact that philosophy, as a quest for rationality – including the rationality of faith – had always been the prerogative of Christianity, the voice of reason had been too much tamed. The merit of the Enlightenment was to insist once again on these original values of Christianity and to give reason back its voice. The Second Vatican Council, in its constitution on the Church and the modern world, reasserted this deep correspondence between Christianity and enlightenment. It sought to achieve a true conciliation between Christianity and modernity, which is the great inheritance that both sides are called upon to protect.

That having been said, the two parties need to reflect on themselves and to be ready for self-correction. Christianity must always remember that it is the religion of the *logos*. It is a faith in the *Creator Spiritus*, the source of all reality. This faith ought to energize Christianity philosophically in our day, since the problem we now face

---

23   [For this theme see also Chapter Five (reading 5.5) of this volume].

is whether the world comes from the irrational, and reason is therefore nothing but a 'byproduct,' and perhaps a harmful one, of its development – or whether the world comes from reason, so that reason is the world's criterion and aim. The Christian faith tends towards the second position. From the purely philosophical point of view, then, it has a truly strong hand to play, despite the fact that many today consider the first position alone to be 'rational' and modern. But a reason that springs forth from the irrational and that, in the end, is itself irrational, is no answer to our problems. Only creative reason, which has manifested itself as love in the crucified God, can show us the way.

In the necessary dialogue between Catholics and the secular-minded, we Christians have to take especial care to remain faithful to this basic principle: we have to live a faith that comes from the *logos,* from creative reason, and that is therefore open to all that is truly rational. But at this point I would like, as a believer, to make a proposal to secular folk. The Enlightenment attempted to define the essential norms of morality while claiming that they would be valid *etsi Deus non daretur,* even if God did not exist. In the midst of confessional conflict and the crisis of the image of God, the attempt was made to keep the essential moral values free of contradiction and to undergird them with an evidence that would make them independent of the many divisions and uncertainties of the various philosophies and confessions. The idea was to secure the bases of coexistence and, in general, the bases of humanity. At that time, this seemed possible, inasmuch as the great basic convictions created by Christianity still held and still seemed undeniable. But this is no longer the case. The quest for a reassuring certitude that could stand uncontested beyond all differences has failed. Not even Kant, for all of his undeniable greatness, was able to create the necessary shared certainty. Kant had denied that God is knowable within the domain of pure reason, but, at the same time, he thought of God, freedom, and immortality as postulates of practical reason, without which it was impossible to act morally in any consistent way. Doesn't the situation of the world today make us wonder whether he might not have been right after all? Let me put it differently: the extreme attempt to fashion the things of man without any reference to God leads us ever closer to the edge of the abyss, to the total abolition of man. We therefore have good reason to turn the Enlightenment axiom on its head and to say that even those who are unable to accept God should nonetheless try to live *veluti si Deus daretur,* as if God existed. This was the advice that Pascal gave to his non-believing friends; it is also the advice that we would like to give to our non-believing friends today as well. Thus, no one's freedom is restricted, but everything human gets the support and the criterion it so urgently needs. What we most need at this moment of history are men who make God visible in this world through their enlightened and lived faith. The negative witness of Christians who spoke of God but lived against him obscured his image and opened the door to unbelief. We need men who have their eyes fixed straight on God, and who learn from him what true humanity is. We need men whose intellects have been enlightened by the light of God and whose hearts have been opened by God, so that their intellects can speak to others' intellects and their hearts can open others' hearts. God returns among men only through men who are touched by God.

4.3 Christian Faith and Politics

The previous considerations have already partly indicated Ratzinger's vision of the relation between faith and politics. Despite the fact that politics is related to human salvation, human salvation cannot be realized through politics. Whoever aims at this, contributes instead to the alienation of the modern person rather than his or her liberation.[24] Ultimately, this is one of the main reasons why Ratzinger so criticizes liberation theology, as illustrated, for example, by his confrontation with Gustavo Guttiérez's liberation theology. In this, Ratzinger asserts, Christian hope turns into a political program.[25] Indeed, neither the human person nor history should be identified with God, since this identification results in the distortion of the true human image and to a caricature of salvation. Theology and politics only touch each other via ethics when the biblical human image, which does justice to the freedom and value of each person, is respected. This understanding of politics does not offer exclusively socio-economic projects, nor does it offer a final salvation to be realized through politics. Political salvation then depends on the human ethos, on the formation of conscience, and on the simultaneous rational and moral relation to reality, with its source in empirical and moral reason.

For this reason, Ratzinger calls the domain of politics very broadly 'the state', with which he primarily associates the democratic form of government. The state is the result of human work on behalf of the organization of society, but it does not comprise the entire existence of human beings. If this were indeed the case, then society would become totalitarian. The first contribution of faith to politics is precisely to reveal its limits by collapsing the political myths of humanly achievable utopias. Christians recognize the state but are also aware of its boundaries. They help to build the state by combating evil with good, immorality with morality.[26] This

---

24 Cf. J. Ratzinger, *Dogma und Verkündigung*. Munich: Wewel, 1973, p. 453: 'Man needs politics – social and political planning and action. But where this becomes total, where politics presents itself as the salvation of man, it becomes the total enslavement of man.' (Translation from the German edition.) (E.T.: *Dogma and Preaching*. Chicago: Franciscan Herald Press, 1985).

25 For this, see especially his *Politik und Erlösung. Zum Verhältnis von Glaube, Rationalität und Irrationalem in der sogenannten Theologie der Befreiung*. Opladen: Leske & Budrich, 1986.

26 Cf. J. Ratzinger, *Church, Ecumenism and Politics: New Endeavours in Ecclesiology*. San Francisco: Ignatius Press, 2008, p. 146.

is why the political domain feels the need for Christianity. After all, the state is a *societas imperfecta* and so needs something beyond itself to have access to moral strength. Ratzinger mentions three aspects in this regard. First, Christianity makes possible the acceptance of the state's imperfection through the perspective of the Christian promise that exceeds all politics and underscores the place of politics in the sphere of rationality and morals. Second, faith awakens consciousness and gives a foundation to morals. As such, it provides content and direction to practical reason. Finally, there is the special bond between the state and Christianity. In order that pluralistic democracy might function, there needs to be a balance between the freedom of the Church as a community of believers and bearer of the truth, and the freedom of the state. It should be clear from this that the public dimension of Christian faith should not impose boundaries upon pluralism and the state's religious tolerance. However, that does not imply that the state should be neutral on the level of values: 'It has to learn that there is a fund of truth that is not subject to consensus but rather precedes it and makes it possible'.[27]

The Church's social teaching should also be regarded within this framework. Ratzinger defines this as the making operable of the faith. This involves the ethos of faith challenging scientific and political reason to develop models of action 'which do not produce redemption, but can open up the conditions for a redeemed existence'.[28] Hence, for Ratzinger, the criticisms that liberation theology levels at Church teaching in this matter, as if it were deficient and supportive of the status quo, are incorrect. If the social teaching is at all deficient, then this is because the engagements between the ethos of faith and scientific and political rationality are not implemented energetically enough. The weakness of the Church's social teaching is precisely the plurality of political solutions that it advocates according to its teaching; its strength is that the Church is purely focused on the human, that she is honest and oriented toward the truth.

In the following, we present some paragraphs from a text of 1984, some five years before the fall of the Berlin wall, in which Ratzinger evokes and illustrates similar ideas about faith and politics.

27   Ibid., p. 207.
28   Translated from J. Ratzinger, *Politik und Erlösung. Zum Verhältnis von Glaube, Rationalität und Irrationalem in der sogenannten Theologie der Befreiung.* Opladen: Leske & Budrich, 1986, p 23.

What threatens democracy today? I see three main trends that are leading[29] or could lead to the repudiation of democracy. First, there is the inability to be reconciled with the imperfection of human affairs. The demand for the absolute in history is the enemy of what is good in it. Manes Sperber speaks about a fanaticism that arises from a disgust with the status quo.[30] Disgust with the status quo is on the increase today, along with a delight in anarchy, based on the conviction that there must be a good world some-where after all. No one wants to pay homage to the Enlightenment faith in progress any more, but a sort of secular messianic belief has penetrated deep into the general consciousness. Ernesto Cardenal's remark, 'I believe in history', expresses the secret creed of many. Somehow the general consciousness has latched onto Hegel's idea that history itself will finally bring about the great synthesis. The notion that all history to date has been the history of bondage but that now, finally, the just society can and must be built soon is propagated in various slogans among atheists and Christians alike and even makes its way into bishops' statements and liturgical texts. Strangely enough, the Reich (kingdom) mystique from the period between the two world wars, which then met with such a macabre end, is now making a comeback. Once again, instead of talking about the 'kingdom of God', people like to speak simply about the 'kingdom' as something we are working for and building, which through our efforts has come within our grasp. The 'kingdom' or the 'new society' has become a moralistic slogan that replaces political and economic arguments. That we are working for a new and definitively better world has long been a self-evident commonplace. There is much that is philosophically and politically questionable about such an imminent eschatology, it seems to me, and this can be demonstrated by examining three main aspects of this outlook.

a. In a liberated society, the good no longer depends on the ethical striving of the people responsible for this society; rather, it is simply and irrevocably provided by the structures. The myth of the liberated society is based on this notion, since moral values are always endangered, never perfect, and must be achieved over and over again. Therefore a state upheld by morality, that is, by freedom, is never complete, never entirely just, never secured. It is imperfect, like man himself. For this very reason the 'liberated society' has to be independent of morality. Its freedom and justice must be produced, so to speak, by its structures; indeed, morality is shifted away from man to the structures. The current structures are sinful, the future structures

29 [Selection from J. Ratzinger, *Church, Ecumenism and Politics: New Endeavours in Ecclesiology*. San Francisco: Ignatius, 2008, pp. 195–200. Original: 'Christliche Orientierung in der pluralistischen Demokratie?' in H. Schambeck (ed.), *Pro fide et iustitia. Festschrift für Agostino Kardinal. Casaroli zum 70. Geburtstag*. Berlin: Duncker und Humblot 1984, pp. 747–761. Included in the German edn. of *Church < Ecumenism and Politics, Kirche, ökumene und Politik, Neue Versuche zur Ekklesiologie*. Einsiedeln: Johannes Verlag, [1-2]1987].
30 Quoted in K. Low, *Warum fasziniert der Kommunismus?*. Cologne: Deutscher Instituts-Verlag, 1981, p. 87; for an overview of this question, see R. Spaemann, *Zur Kritik der politischen Utopie*. Stuttgart: Klett, 1977.

will be just. We have to design and construct them the way one builds appliances – but then they are there. It follows that sin, too, becomes social-structural sin and can be mentioned again as such. Therefore salvation depends on an analysis of the structures and on the consequent political-economic activity. The ethos does not support the structures, but rather the structures support the ethos, precisely because the ethos is the fragile thing, while the structures are considered firm and reliable. I see in this reversal, which is at the root of the myth of the better world, the real essence of materialism, which does not just consist of the denial of one sphere of reality but is at bottom an anthropological program that is necessarily connected with a certain idea about the interrelations among the individual spheres of reality. The claim that mind or spirit is not the origin of matter but only a product of material developments corresponds to the notion that morality is produced by the economy (instead of the economy being shaped, ultimately, by fundamental human decisions). But when we look at the presuppositions and the consequences of this seemingly marvellous expedient that lifts the burden of man's inconstancy, we realize that this unburdening – 'liberation' – is based on the renunciation of morality, that is, on the renunciation of responsibility and freedom, on the renunciation of conscience. That is why this sort of 'kingdom' is an optical illusion with which the Anti-Christ dupes us – such a liberated society presupposes perfect tyranny. I think we must make it clear to ourselves again today, in all earnestness, that neither reason nor faith ever promises that there will be a perfect world someday. It does not exist. Constantly expecting it, playing with the possibility and proximity of it, is the most serious threat to our politics and our society, because anarchical fanaticism necessarily proceeds from it. The continued existence of pluralistic democracy (that is, the continued existence and development of a humanly possible standard of justice) urgently requires that we have the courage to accept imperfection and learn again to recognize the perpetual endangerment of human affairs. Only those political programs are moral which arouse this courage. Conversely, that semblance of morality which claims to be content only with perfection is immoral. Those who preach morality in and near the Church will also have to make an examination of conscience in this regard, since their overwrought demands and hopes aid and abet the flight from morality into Utopia.

b. The attempt to make morality, inadequate and endangered as it is, superfluous through the mechanical security (so to speak) of a correctly engineered society has still other roots, however. They lie in the one-sidedness of the modern concept of reason, as it was first explicitly formulated by Francis Bacon and then in the nineteenth century became increasingly predominant: Only quantitative reason, the reason of calculation and experimentation, is considered to be reason at all; everything else is non-rational and must gradually be overcome and likewise brought into the realm of 'exact' knowledge. With Bacon as with Comte – to mention only two proponents of this school of thought – the goal is ultimately to arrive at a physics of human affairs as well.[31] In this connection, Martin Kriele speaks about the reversal of the relationship between science and practical reason, a reduction of ethics and politics to physics.[32] Using terminology that was still provisional and hence in need of critical evaluation, Romano Guardini repeatedly calls attention to the same phenomenon and describes it as a momentous and vital problem in European politics. He says that there is a failure to recognize that what is logical and what is alogical are complementary and form a unity. More accurately we should say that the Logos is being reduced to a particular sort of rationality and everything else is relegated to the category of the alogical. 'Therefore,' he continues, 'no Europe exists yet, in the strict sense of the word, but instead the spiritual and human spheres, despite all the organization, stand side by side, unconnected and hostile.'[33]

We can declare, therefore, that the repudiation of morality in favor of technology is not based primarily on the flight from the difficulty of morality at all; rather, it is based on the suspicion that it is unreasonable. It cannot be deduced rationally in the same way as the functioning of an apparatus. Once this has been set up as the standard for reason, however, classical morality can be assigned only to the category of unreason. Meanwhile, we increasingly read about attempts to give an 'exact' account of morality. It is then explained in one form or another as a type of calculus, as the calculation of the relation between the favorable and unfavorable consequences of a human act. This, however, amounts to a dismissal of morality as such. For what is good in itself and what is evil in itself no longer exist, but only a reckoning of advantages and disadvantages; this does not change the fact that we are assured that in general the outcomes will remain approximately the same as with what had previously been regarded as rules of conduct.

But this also pulls the rug out from under the law. I cannot resist mentioning here an illustration from the judicial system in Munich, which in my opinion is a chilling example of the process whereby our law is losing its substance. At least twice in recent months charges of slandering religion were ultimately dismissed because, it was said, peaceful public order was not disturbed by the misconduct at issue. The question of the justice of the indictment in either case does not concern me here; the only thing that interests me is the reason why they were dismissed. For this reason contains, in fact, an invitation to rule by main force. If the plaintiffs had threatened to provoke a public disturbance on behalf of their cause, then the courts would have had to take the case seriously – that, after all, is what

31   On Bacon, see M. Kriele, *Befreiung und politische Aufklärung*. Freiburg: Herder, 1980, pp. 78–82; on Comte, see Henri de Lubac, *The Drama of Atheist Humanism*. Trans. Edith M. Riley. London: Sheed & Ward, 1949, pp. 77–159. For a general discussion of the set of problems addressed here, see F. H. Tenbruck, *Die unbewaltigten Sozialwissenschaften oder Die Abschaffung des Menschen*. Graz: Styria verlag, 1984, esp. pp. 230–243.

32   M. Kriele, *Befreiung und politische Aufklärung*. Freiburg: Herder, 1980, 76.

33   Romano Guardini, *Religiose Gestalten in Dostojewskijs Werk*, 6th ed. München: Kösel, 1977, p. 427.

the alleged reason implies. But this means that one is no longer protecting the objects of legal protection at all but only trying to avoid the collision of opposed interests. This, of course, is logical if morality as such is no longer recognized as a good worthy of protection under the law because it appears to be a matter of subjective preferences – which becomes cause for legal proceedings only if it poses a threat to peace and public order. When moral reasoning is repealed, the result is that the law can no longer refer to a fundamental notion of justice and instead simply mirrors prevailing opinions. But everyone can see that that is not the way to establish justice. Recourse to an ideologically rigid type of justice that seems to be derived from a scientifically guaranteed interpretation of history thus becomes absolutely unavoidable. Therefore, the question of re-establishing a fundamental moral consensus in our society is at the same time a question of survival for society and the state.

c. Allow me to add yet a third perspective that encompasses and deepens the two just described. Again, I will try to illustrate it by means of an example. Recently I was able to ask a friend from the German Democratic Republic what, in his opinion, was the cause for the intensified push to get out of East Germany and go to the West – whether the resistance of conscience to ideology was the essential motive. He said that there were various reasons for this trend, the last-mentioned certainly among them. One not uncommon reason, though, was of another sort altogether: it had been constantly drummed into the people that this is the only life and that a human being must expect no other happiness than the present one. Assuming this, however, life under socialism appears so colorless, so tedious and empty, that they have to break out and look for a real life somewhere. Now, the need to escape, to 'get out', is also quite prevalent in the West, for ultimately all its novelties and thrills are empty, too, when they claim to be all there is. The loss of transcendence evokes the flight into Utopia. I am convinced that the destruction of transcendence is actually the mutilation of man from which all the other sicknesses spring. Robbed of his real greatness, he can only resort to illusory hopes. Furthermore, this confirms and seals that narrowing of reason, which is no longer capable of perceiving authentically human concerns as reasonable. Marx taught us that one must take away transcendence so that man, finally healed of false consolations, may build the perfect world. Today we know that man needs transcendence so that he can shape his ever-imperfect world in such a way that one can live in it with human dignity.

If we summarize our reflections thus far, we find that they emphatically corroborate Bockenforde's thesis that the modern state is a *societas imperfecta* – imperfect not only in the sense that its institutions always remain as imperfect as its inhabitants, but also in the sense that it needs forces from outside of itself in order to continue being itself. Where are these forces that are indispensable to it?

CHAPTER 5

CHRISTIAN UNITY AND RELIGIOUS DIALOGUE: ON ECUMENISM AND OTHER FAITHS

Gerard Mannion

Introduction

As with so much of his theological corpus,[1] Ratzinger's theological approach to ecumenism and relations with other faiths has been shaped, to a great extent, as a response to developments throughout the Church in the wake of changed perceptions and practices introduced since Vatican II. It must also be set against the background of the context of wider cultural and migratory shifts in the same period. However, his thoughts on these subjects have maintained a degree of consistency in relation to certain fundamental issues that pre-date the Council.

For Ratzinger, the superiority of the Roman Catholic faith as a path to salvation, over and against other paths, has always been something he has upheld, whether implicitly or explicitly, in his theological writings. In the Catholic Church alone is the path towards the *fullness* of salvation to be found.[2] Other paths, including other Christian ones, are perceived as

---

1   A selection of representative books available in English by Ratzinger of relevance to ecumenical and inter-faith relations includes *Principles of Catholic Theology: Building Stones for a Fundamental Theology*. San Francisco: Ignatius Press, 1982; Ratzinger's with Vittorio Messori, *The Ratzinger Report: An Exclusive Interview on the State of the Church*. San Francisco: Ignatius Press, 1983; *Called to Communion: Understanding the Church Today*. San Francisco: Ignatius Press, 1996; *Salt of the Earth*. San Francisco: Ignatius Press, 1997; *Many Religions – One Covenant: Israel, the Church, and the World*. San Francisco: Ignatius Press, 1999; *Truth and Tolerance: Christian Belief and World Religions*. San Francisco: Ignatius Press, 2004; with Marcello Pera, *Without Roots: The West, Relativism, Christianity, Islam*. San Francisco: Ignatius Press, 2005; *Pilgrim Fellowship of Faith: the Church as Communion*. San Francisco: Ignatius Press, 2005. As indicated in our previous chapter, *Das neue Volk Gottes: Entwufe zur Ekklesiologie*. Düsseldorf: Patmos, 1969, (2nd edn., 1977) is among the more significant German works of relevance here yet to be translated *in toto*, although two of our readings in this chapter are translations of sections of that work. One appears for the first time in English, another is a translation of a revised section of that book which appeared in *Truth and Tolerance: Christian Belief and World Religions*. San Francisco, Ignatius Press, 2004.

2   Notwithstanding his thoughts on the 'universal' applicability of the faith, as illustrated in Chapter Two of this volume. Note, also, that he holds the Orthodox Churches in considerably higher esteem than other Christian communities and also regards their faith as valid paths to salvation in Christ. But, even so, the Roman Catholic church is perceived in a superior fashion.

falling short of the way of salvation safeguarded by the Catholic Church. In holding this position, Ratzinger believes that he holds together the essential understanding of both the pre-Vatican II Church and indeed the core meaning and implications of the conciliar documents themselves.

Cardinal Frings, whom Ratzinger served as an advisor at Vatican II, spoke against any dilution of the superior understanding of the Catholic faith and defended conversional mission and evangelization as necessary. Ratzinger, while approving of a more cordial atmosphere in relation to other churches and faiths at the Council as well as moves towards dialogue with them, has consistently reflected Frings' views as well. Obviously, in some instances, Frings would have been voicing the perspectives informed by his theological adviser.

Nonetheless, Ratzinger has regularly affirmed his commitment to the pursuit of a number of ecumenical endeavours, particularly to fostering closer ties between the Roman Catholic and the Orthodox Churches. But it is also the case that Ratzinger's fundamental ecclesiology, which we explored in Chapter Three, has, in turn, led to a very particular under-standing of ecumenism. His preference is for a slower, what he perceives to be more realistic and theologically attentive, approach. This entails a negative assessment of some efforts towards greater Christian unity. Thus Ratzinger has been critical of particular ecumenical practices, as well as joint ecclesial dialogues and documents from recent decades alike. He is therefore frequently associated with the Roman Catholic contribution to what has been termed an 'ecumenical winter' in recent decades.

Just as Ratzinger perceives there to be a hierarchy of validity among the churches and other 'ecclesial communities', so, also, in the salvific economy, he steadfastly maintains the superiority of the Catholic Church and the Christian faith, over and against other faiths as paths towards salvation, perceiving (again, sometimes implicitly, sometimes explicitly or by inference or logical entailment) there to be soteriological deficiencies in such faiths.

For Ratzinger, this all comes down to the fundamentals of what Catholic Christian belief and tradition entails. It is a question of wanting people to come to the truth, which is the God whom Jesus Christ brings Christians into communion with. All religions are not equally valid paths to salvation and Christianity proclaims a saviour who, as God incarnate, is the supreme path to the true God, who is personal in character. When entering into dialogue with those of other churches and faiths, one should assume equal rights to the partners in dialogue but not an equality of the churches or faiths involved. Ratzinger believes that the latter approach is the path to destructive relativism.

In this chapter, then, we encounter another area where the distinc-tion between the theologian and the Church leader become especially blurred. Despite the qualifications that appear throughout his writings that seek to ensure his attitudes towards other churches and faiths are not misunderstood, it is also the case that Ratzinger – both as theologian and Church leader alike – has opposed particular forms of ecumenical and inter-faith dialogue and interaction, along with theological interpretations of the same since the 1960s. Since the 1980s and particularly the 1990s, his personal writings and speeches have held fast to this approach while the actions and documents of the CDF have equally reflected his own theological views on ecumenism and other faiths.

Theologians who have sought to develop a broader sense of ecclesial dialogue, both in Christian ecumenical terms and in relation to other faiths, have been rebuked (sometimes sharply so) in both Ratzinger's private and official writings and addresses. A number of theologians have been publicly disciplined for their pluralistic outlook and the related theological approaches and schools of thought condemned.

Ratzinger understands religious pluralism as a similar threat to (and as erroneous a theological path as) liberation theology. This should be of little surprise, for many of the theologians influenced by one are also open to the other. They stress the importance of the context of the local Church, of the need for renewed and reformed ecclesial structures, and see co-responsibility, participation, collegiality, equality, dialogue and prophecy as themes of fundamental importance for the Church today. So, too, do they stress the need for the Church to be open to greater 'complementarity' of Christianity with other faiths in promoting the 'Reign of God'. Ratzinger has clear positions on each of these areas of ecclesial life. Indeed, complementarity is a concept that Ratzinger finds particularly objectionable.

Ratzinger's relations with other churches and members of other faiths have been the focus of close scrutiny in recent times, even prior to his becoming Pope. According to representatives of other churches and faiths, certain documents issued by Rome while Ratzinger was Prefect of the CDF, as well as personal writings and addresses by him, church documents, addresses and even official actions since he became Supreme Pontiff have caused confusion, anger, hurt or offence. Ratzinger's supporters claim misunderstanding and misrepresentation to be the root cause of such problems. Ratzinger's critics argue that, in those more recent times, the character and tone of 'official' Catholic documents on ecumenism and relations with other faiths would appear to be distinct from the prevailing character, tone, and ecclesiology of the documents of Vatican II and other post-conciliar official documents.[3]

---

3   Cf. the discussion in Gerard Mannion, 'Roman Catholicism and its Religious "Others"': Contemporary Challenges' in Gerard Mannion (ed.), *Church and Religious Other: Essays on Truth, Unity and Diversity*. London: T&T Clark, 2008, pp. 126–153.

Such debates, as well as the conundrum of separating the theologian from the ecclesiastical leader, can be illustrated with reference to the most controversial document to emerge on these issues during Ratzinger's time at the CDF. In 2000, the declaration *Dominus Iesus* led to many disagreements about the interpretation of the Catholic Church's relation-ship with other faiths and with other Christian churches. Indeed, the document appeared to set further explicit and definitive limits to what actually enables a Christian community to be called a church. The text concerns itself with certain aspects central to the faith that Ratzinger and the CDF deemed to be in need of reiteration. These relate to the uniqueness of salvation brought about through God's incarnation in Christ, the place of the Catholic Church in God's plan of salvation, and particular questions relating to religious and ecclesiological pluralism. The threats of relativism and pluralism are closely linked by the document, with religious 'relativism', for the CDF and Ratzinger himself, believed to be a standpoint that tends to perceive all religions as equally valid paths toward salvation. Thus the declaration sought to remind its readers of the importance of the 'Unicity and Salvific Universality of Jesus Christ and the Church.' The document was believed to mark a clear shift in focus – from dialogue back to evangelization (as opposed to the understanding of dialogue *as* evangelization that had emerged in numerous Catholic contexts following Vatican II).[4]

Joseph Ratzinger's views here and in relation to the subject matter of *Dominus Iesus* in general, can be gleaned from a collection of essays which, although published in English in 2004, are largely from the 1990s, thus also from the period when the curial thinking reflected in *Dominus Iesus* was in formation.[5]

At a press conference to mark the actual document's release, Ratzinger stated that it sought to challenge a 'false concept of tolerance' in the field of religious pluralism. He added that nothing contained in the document was actually new Church teaching. However, many have since commented that its *interpretation* of fundamental Catholic teachings, in a post-Vatican II context, was indeed something novel (or even nostalgic,

---

4   As illustrated by one of the document's key paragraphs, *Dominus Iesus* VI, §22.
5   I.e., *Truth and Tolerance*. (2004). This collection also features aspects of his earlier thinking on the same topics. As another example, the document released by the Vatican's CDF in July 2007 – *Responses to Some Questions Concerning Certain Aspects of the Doctrine on the Church* – was also deemed to be controversial and even offensive to millions of other Christians. Of course, much sensationalist reporting and comment followed in its wake, much of it erroneously blaming Pope Benedict for the document, for he neither wrote nor issued it (although he did approve it). But perhaps it is of significance that the document does represent, in a very concise fashion, Ratzinger's views about the Church and about other churches and about what he would term those 'Christian communities' that are somehow not fully churches or are deficient in one form or another.

i.e. reminiscent of preconciliar ecclesial documents). *Dominus Iesus* asserted that the Church's 'missionary proclamation' was under threat from these theories of religious pluralism.

The text goes on to locate the source of the difficulties facing the Church today in 'relativistic attitudes towards truth itself': those who attempt to juxtapose 'western' epistemological categories with those from the 'east', overt 'subjectivism', problematic interpretations of history that limit the universal significance of events at the core of Christian faith, and eclecticism in theological method.

It is significant that these are all familiar sentiments from Ratzinger's own theological writings. Ratzinger was not the author of *Dominus Iesus*, but he obviously assented to all that the document states and he did later confer a curial promotion upon the person believed to be the document's author. Ratzinger also initiated many of the investigations against theologians writing and working in inter-faith contexts and those who are known to be open to forms of pluralism. So the dividing line and actual formative relationship between private theological opinion and official Church teaching here is especially worthy of further consideration and reflection.

A number of commentators on Ratzinger's views here, as well as those documents issued by the CDF and curial authorities during his time in Rome, have deliberated over this shift in focus away from the ecumenical thinking not simply of the various inter-church discussions of recent decades, but also from the spirit of dialogue at Vatican II that gave rise to them, and that of Paul VI, indeed even – it could be argued – of John Paul II. This is the view of those such as Gregory Baum,[6] who sees *Dominus Iesus* – and, in effect, Ratzinger's theological position on relations with those beyond the confines of the Roman Catholic church – as a reversal not simply of the open dialogical spirit of Vatican II but also of documents such as *Dialogue and Mission* (Secretariat for Non-Christian Missions, 1984) and *Dialogue and Proclamation* (Pontifical Council for Interreligious Dialogue, 1991), which along with teachings and pronouncements by John Paul II helped indicate that dialogue is always to be respectful and sensitive and, in the case of the latter document, even hints that in certain situations the Church must limit its mission to dialogue rather than proclamation (although both are seen to be fundamental to the Church's evangelizing mission).[7]

Baum's conclusion aptly goes to the heart of these present debates: 'We note that the dialogue blessed by Cardinal Ratzinger is quite different

---

6   Gregory Baum, *Amazing Church: A Catholic Theologian Remembers a Half Century of Change.* Maryknoll, NY: Orbis, 2005, chaps. 4 (83-100) and 5 (101-134).

7   Ibid., p. 115 (and also pp. 121–122).

from the dialogue across boundaries fostered by John Paul II . . . . In today's ethical horizon, it would be immoral to engage in ecumenical or interreligious dialogue, based on trust and aimed at mutual understanding, in order to persuade one's partners to change their religion. This seems to me quite basic. Ratzinger's proposal reflects an ethical horizon that the Church has left behind. . . . To enter into dialogue for the purpose of proselytizing would instrumentalize dialogue and destroy its profound meaning'[8]. Yet Ratzinger's supporters argue that he has sought, wherever possible, to be publicly courteous and welcoming to other Christians and members of other faith communities. They also speak of his consistent commitment to ecumenism and positive assessment of other faiths and suggest that what critics object to is actually a misunderstanding of his nuanced statements simply because he maintains a critical line throughout all this. As with his approach to intra-Christian relations, Ratzinger believes world religions can come closer together and cooperate greatly in social and moral causes. However, in terms of fundamental doctrinal beliefs, some of the great faiths are essentially occupying different spiritual, epistemological and cultural 'universes'. Ratzinger believes that dialogue must be honest and he maintains it is important to remember that none of the world religions are uniformly homogenous – all have very different branches and expressions of their beliefs and practices. Furthermore, Ratzinger upholds the Church's teaching that the path to salvation is barred to no one who sincerely and correctly follows their conscience (while nonetheless rejecting many interpretations of such a teaching).[9]

Ratzinger's critics would protest that, given the consistently stated theological positions he holds in relation to the same, it is unsurprising that offence has nonetheless been caused and taken. At the very least, they would argue, Ratzinger sends out decidedly 'mixed messages'.

Part of the problem here, of course, as even his aides and loyal supporters have remarked since his elevation to the papacy, is that his views as a theologian, when placed in the public domain, carry much greater weight than in the world of the library, lecture theatre and seminar room. The riposte of critics is that Ratzinger knows this all too well. The view of those occupying the 'safe middle ground' is that if he does not, he certainly ought to and has enough advisors to keep him informed in this field. So the question of whether Ratzinger's theological views are taken out of context here is more complicated than many assume: the context of theological efforts to understand, explicate and influence inter-church and inter-faith dialogue can never be divorced from the relationships it

---

8   Ibid., p. 120.
9   Cf. Joseph Ratzinger with Vittorio Messori, *The Ratzinger Report: An Exclusive Interview on the State of the Church*. San Francisco: Ignatius Press, 1983, pp. 196–197.

comments upon – indeed, many would argue that those relations are the very context of such theologizing itself.

For example, those who have expressed anger and hurt at Ratzinger's theological positions and his writings and addresses here include members of the Anglican church, which he deems to be not even a proper church in the full sense (rather an 'ecclesial community') and whose ministerial orders, he believes, remain null and void – a fact he has stated is a Catholic teaching taught with the charism of infallibility. Lutherans have heard decidedly mixed messages from this German theologian, who on the one hand sees much of value and truth in the writings of Martin Luther, which have personally influenced his own theology in a profound way. Yet, on the other hand, he appears to display an ambiguous attitude towards the status of their 'church' which, for Ratzinger, along with other Protestant communities, is also perceived to be not yet a fully 'authentic' church. Those involved in official ecumenical exchanges, such as the ARCIC talks between Anglican and Roman Catholics and the joint Catholic-Lutheran discussions, have expressed frustration at some of Ratzinger's negative interventions in these processes.

Jewish people have heard and read Ratzinger's denunciations of antisemitism and his detailed reflections upon the Hebrew Bible and the great faith of the Jewish people. Yet he has expressed theological opinions that speak of the Christian faith as pointing towards the ultimate significance and fulfilment of the Jewish faith itself. Ergo, his critics say, conversion to Christianity is the logical path for Jews to follow, if Ratzinger's theological position is to be taken to its obvious conclusions. Ratzinger himself would today express this in eschatological terms – i.e. Jews and Christians being together in Christ, in the end.

Many Hindus, Buddhists, Jains and members of other so-called 'Eastern' religions, have read and heard of Ratzinger's generalizations about the nature of their beliefs and practices. A criticism is that, too often, he appears to lump faiths with Asiatic origins together in an indiscriminate fashion and perceives them to be overtly 'mystical'. He has repeated his warnings of the dangers of mixing Western metaphysics with Eastern epistemology on numerous occasions. Critics would further protest how his warnings against mysticism do not sufficiently take into account the deep similarities between Western Christian forms of this path towards salvation, including among some of the West's most prominent theologians, and those versions found in Asiatic faiths. Ratzinger's criticisms of the introduction of religious practices from these faiths in the 'West', bracketing them alongside 'New Age' religious developments, is again taken as an illustration of an over-generalizing tendency that could be overcome through a deeper knowledge and understanding of diverse religions with rich and ancient traditions. A more sustained engagement with such faiths would be of great value.

With regard to Islam, the mixed messages here have been exacerbated in recent times largely because of a high-profile lecture that he gave in 2006. His understanding of Islam as previously evidenced in his writings as a private theologian proves less controversial than the media frenzy and intemperate reactions to which that lecture gave rise. Nonetheless, even there it has proved controversial enough. Ratzinger does appear to see Islam as a faith that has various manifestations among its followers – some positive, some negative. He admires the steadfastness of true devotees to this faith but calls for greater tolerance of religious minorities in Islamic societies. But critics of Ratzinger say that, in more recent years, he has been poorly-advised and/or -informed with regard to writings and addresses concerning Islam. The protests assert that he has also employed inaccurate, generalized and stereotypical accounts of the Islamic faith and its cultural heritage. With regard to that controversial September 2006 lecture itself, the now infamous 'Regensburg Address'[10] marked an occasion where the Pope was invited to deliver a lecture at the university where he was previously professor. His text included an ill-advised remark from a medieval emperor that was grossly offensive to Muslims. And this despite a number of journalists who had seen the document early in the morning of the day on which it was due to be delivered advising that the offending passage should be removed.

Again, this incident blurs the dividing line between the private theologian and Church leader. Ratzinger apologized for any offence caused and his officials rushed to assuage an angry media, arguing that Ratzinger's address was an academic lecture addressing particular intellectual debates as opposed to being about Islam and inter-faith relations *per se*. But the problem is that, even prior to his election to the papacy, Ratzinger's lectures, speeches and writings have always had interest beyond the dusty libraries and seminar rooms of faculties of theology.

The further into his career one goes, the more this becomes the case and, as we have seen above, as well as in Chapter Three and will especially see in Chapter Six, there have been times when Ratzinger, himself, has been responsible for blurring the lines of distinction between private theological opinion and public Church pronouncement or teaching.

As a further example here, Ratzinger publicly objected to aspects of the gathering of leaders of world faiths that John Paul II called for in October 1986 and tried to ensure that a follow-up meeting in 1999 was a much more low-key affair. And yet he has supported the later,

---

10   Titled 'Faith, Reason and the University: Memories and Reflections'. Subsequently, the lecture has also attracted a great deal of debate concerning the perspective it offers on the relation between faith and reason.

modified, versions of such gatherings, such as the Day of Prayer for Peace on 24 January 2002. Nonetheless, it once again demonstrates how the opinions expressed as private theologian become official Church policy in very important areas.[11] Indeed, even that support in 2002 came in a distinctly qualified fashion, which helps further illustrate the ambiguities encountered in interpreting some of Ratzinger's writings and official pronouncements here: 'For a proper understanding of the Assisi event, I think it is important that we do not see it as a representative array of supposedly interchangeable religions. It was not the affirmation of the equality of the religions, which does not exist. Assisi was more the expression of a journeying, of a seeking, of the pilgrimage for peace that is only possible if peace be united with justice'.[12]

In the aftermath of various controversies in these areas, Ratzinger as Pope Benedict has taken steps to ensure that his intentions towards peoples of other churches and faiths are not misrepresented and has engaged in a number of conversations and visits to promote good will, with a visit to Jordan and the Holy Land in May 2009 being of particular value in efforts to rebuild trust and good relations with those of other faiths. Although critics believe fundamental inconsistencies were clearly emerging into the public arena: ecumenical and dialogical ventures pursued from a private theological perspective whereby one's own path of faith is seen as markedly superior to that of others throws the sincerity and purpose of any inter-church or inter-faith dialogue into doubt. The point here being that, when such private theological opinion informs

---

11   In his official capacity as Pope, many experts in inter-religious dialogue felt dismay when Ratzinger moved the Irish Archbishop Michael Fitzgerald from the Pontifical Council for Interreligious Dialogue to Egypt (as Papal Nuncio and delegate to the Arab League). Again the Vatican said this was a positive step, but it appeared to signal a distinctive shift in focus and policy on interreligious matters in Rome – see Chapter Seven, p. 231 n. 26. Further controversy came in 2009, when moves to lift the excommunication of members of the ultra-Conservative Society of Pius X offended those of other churches and other faiths alike, due to their hard-line exclusivist and anti-Vatican II stance on key issues. But, most of all, the attempted rehabilitation of the English 'bishop' from this society, Richard Williamson, turned into a catastrophe as Williamson, just two days after Rome had briefed journalists about the planned lifting of the excommunications, gave an interview to Swedish television in which he publicly repeated his long-held opinion that the Shoah (Holocaust) of six million Jews never actually took place.

12   Joseph Ratzinger, 'The Assisi Day of Prayer: The Splendor of the Peace of Francis', originally an article in *30 Days* magazine, reprinted in John F. Thornton and Susan B. Varenne (eds), *The Essential Pope Benedict XVI: His Central Writings and Speeches*. New York: HarperOne, 2007, pp. 43–45. Interestingly, this passage was not featured in the account of Ratzinger's address featured by the Zenit News Agency at the time. John L. Allen's article reflecting upon Pope Benedict's visit to a Mosque in November 2006 further illustrates the difficulties involved in discerning the true relation between the theologian and the Church leader, 'Benedict's Prayer by Ratzinger's Criteria', in *National Catholic Reporter* (Dec 15, 2006) available online at http://natcath.org/NCR_Online/ archives2/2006d/121506/121506j.php (accessed September 30 2009).

and shapes Church teaching and policy, then further consideration of these debates becomes necessary. But the best way for readers to discern their own judgment on these issues is to engage with some of Ratzinger's theological writings in these areas themselves and so to a selection of these we now turn.

5.1 Christianity and World Religions

This text addresses the topic of the relationship between Christianity and the other major world faiths. Originally it was written in the midst of the deliberations over this very topic during Vatican II (and perhaps was the result of Ratzinger's reflections upon the same). It appeared in a *Festgabe* for Karl Rahner (and Ratzinger was familiar with and has written upon Rahner's very different understanding of this question). But it was revised for a collection of essays published in 2004 and so also, to a certain extent, allows the reader to discern developments in Ratzinger's position in the subsequent decades. In the text, Ratzinger offers an understanding of other faiths as being 'provisional', and pathways to the truth and salvation only insofar as they point towards Christ and Christianity. He offers this not, as he explains, as a sign of arrogance or dogmatism, but rather to challenge perspectives that see all religions as being paths towards the same ends, i.e. religious relativism. He rejects pluralistic, philosophical and 'mythical' understandings of religion and of its origins and purpose. Ratzinger charts the threefold modern understanding of religious development, from 'mysticism' to monotheism and onto 'enlightenment'.

Ratzinger contrasts the impersonalism of the 'mystical' approach that he particularly identifies with 'Eastern' religions (and 'New Age' forms of religion), where self becomes annihilated, with the form of 'revolutionary' monotheism that arose in Judaism, Islam, and Christianity (and to a lesser extent Zoroastrianism). He believes that instead of contrasting mysticism and monotheism, we should instead speak of mysticism and revelation. In the latter form of religion, a personal relationship with God is central, as is faith.

The critical voices would here point to overt generalizations made about other faiths and would argue that Ratzinger, himself, commits a form of the very approach he criticizes in that he appears to believe that many religions are, in the final analysis, all the same, only here perceived in terms of their deficiencies compared with Christianity and the most closely related other monotheistic faiths, Judaism and Islam. Although, in parts, he claims not to be discussing whether mysticism or monotheism is to be preferred, his tone, language and rhetorical devices make it clear that he regards the former as an inferior mode of religion to the latter.

Critics would again point out that he here, by and large, passes over the wide-ranging mystical traditions in Christianity, Judaism and Islam. For such critics, the schematization of religion that he offers, then, might be judged somewhat crude and/or even forced.

1. The Problem[13]

The position that Christianity assigns itself in the history of religions is one that was basically expressed long ago: it sees in Christ the only real salvation of man and, thus, his final salvation. In accordance with this, two attitudes are possible (so it seems) with regard to other religions: one may address them as being provisional and, in this respect, as preparatory to Christianity and, thus, in a certain sense attribute to them a positive value, insofar as they allow themselves to be regarded as precursors. They can of course also be understood as insufficient, anti-Christian, contrary to the truth, as leading people to believe they are saved without ever truly being able to offer salvation. The first of these attitudes was shown by Christ himself with respect to the faith of Israel, that is to say, the religion of the Old Testament. That this may also, in a way, be done with regard to all other religions has been clearly shown and emphasized only in recent times. We may in fact perfectly well say that the story of the covenant with Noah (Gen 8:20 – 9:17) establishes that there is a kernel of truth hidden in the mythical religions: it is in the regular 'dying away and coming into existence' of the cosmos that the God who is faithful, who stands in a covenant relationship, not merely with Abraham and his people, but with *all* men,[14] exercises his providential rule. And did not the Magi find their way to Christ (even if they did so only by a roundabout way, by way of Jerusalem, and by the Scriptures of the Old Testament) by means of the star, that is, by means of their 'superstition', by *their* religious beliefs and practices (Mt 2:1-23)? Did not their religion, then, kneel before Christ, as it were, in their persons, recognizing itself as provisional, or rather as proceeding toward Christ?

[. . . T]wo attitudes toward the religions of the nations can be found in the Scriptures: a partial recognition, under the heading of preparation, as well as a decided rejection.

The theology of our own day, as we said, has particularly brought to light the positive aspect and, in so doing, has in particular elucidated the extension of the concept of being provisional, preparatory: the fact that even hundreds of years

---

13 [From Joseph Ratzinger, *Truth and Tolerance: Christian Belief and World Religions*. San Francisco: Ignatius Press, 2004, pp. 19–39, a revised translation of the original essay which appeared as 'Der christliche Glaube und die Weltreligionen', in H. Vorgrimler (ed.), *Gott in Welt. Festgabe für Karl Rahner*. Freiburg: Herder, 1964, pp. 287–305].

14 Cf. J. Daniélou, *Essai sur le mystère de l'histoire*. Paris; Éd. du Seuil, 1953 [E.T.: *The Lord of History: Reflections on the Inner Meaning of History*. Trans. Nigel Abercrombie. London: Longmans; Chicago: H. Regnery, 1958; in the German trans., *Vom Geheimnis der Geschichte*, Stuttgart: Schwabenverlag, 1955, pp. 25ff.

'after Christ', from the point of view of history, people may still be living in the historical state 'before Christ' and, thus, legitimately in the provisional, preparatory stage.[15] To sum up, we may say that, according to its own understanding of itself, Christianity stands at one and the same time in both a positive and a negative relation to the religions of the world: it recognizes itself as being linked with them in the unity of the concept of a covenant relationship and lives out of the conviction that the cosmos and its myth, just like history and its mystery, speak of God and can lead men to God; but it is equally aware of a decided No to other religions and sees in them a means by which man seeks to shield himself from God instead of leaving himself open to his demands.[16] [. . .]

The dominant impression of most people today is that all religions, with a varied multiplicity of forms and manifestations, in the end are and mean one and the same thing; which is something everyone can see, except for them. The man of today will for the most part scarcely respond with an abrupt No to a particular religion's claim to be true; he will simply relativize that claim by saying 'There are many religions.'[17] And behind his response will probably be the opinion, in some form or other, that beneath varying forms they are in essence all the same; each person has his own.

If we were to try to extract, from a current intellectual view of that kind, a couple of characteristic opinions, then we might well say: the concept of religion held by 'the man of today' [. . .] is static; he usually does not foresee any development from one religion to another; rather, he expects each person to remain in his own and to experience it with an awareness that it is, in its basic spiritual core, identical with all the others. There is thus a kind of 'worldwide religious citizenship', which does not exclude but rather includes belonging to a given 'province' of religion, which finds any change of religious 'nationality' undesirable, except just in certain exemplary instances, and in any case takes a very reserved attitude toward the idea of any mission and is basically inclined to reject it. There is second factor always involved in what we have been saying. Today's man has a concept of religion that is always very much a matter of symbols, heavily spiritualized. Religion appears as a world of symbols, which despite the ultimate unity of the language of human symbols (as is increasingly demonstrated today by psychology and religious anthropology),[18] vary in many details but nonetheless mean just the

---

15   K. Rahner, *Schriften zur Theologie* [Multi-volume collection translated into English as *Theological Investigations*], 5:140ff [Einsiedeln 1962].

16   It was above all the so-called 'dialectical theology', following the lead of Karl Barth, that most decidedly emphasized this; with regard to world religions, it was probably H. Kraemer who developed this position with the greatest logic and consistency. His last work of some size (*Religion and Christian Faith*. [London: Lutterworth Press, 1956]) is certainly substantially more cautious and more nuanced than the earlier books.

17   This is the title of a little book by J. Thomé, dealing with the problem of the absolutist nature of Christianity.

18   Most impressive on this point are the works collected in the *Eranos-Jahrbuch*, and, besides that, the

same thing and really ought to begin to discover their deep, underlying unity. Once this comes about, then the unity of religions will be achieved without doing away with any of their variety. [. . .]

No one, to date, has been able to offer our generation a more impressive, warmer, or more persuasive picture of a religion of the future, which in its turn would be able to bring about a 'future for religion', than the President of India, Radhakrishnan, whose written works ever and again lead up to a vista of the coming religion of the spirit, which will be able to unite fundamental unity with the most varied differentiation." Over against such prophetic utterances, with their unmistakable weight of human and religious authority, the Christian theologian looks like a dogmatic stick-in-the-mud, who cannot get away from his know-it-all attitude, whether he expresses it in the swaggering manner of apologists in past times or whether in the friendly manner of contemporary theologians, who acknowledge to the other person to what extent he is already a Christian without being aware of it. [. . .]

2. The Place of Christianity in the History of Religion

[. . .] Thus, as we have already seen, out of the impression of complete plurality, which represents, so to speak, the first stage of perception, there develops an impression of all being ultimately the same. Modern philosophers of religion are convinced that they can even specify the basis of this hidden identity. In the way they conceive it, any religion that exists originates – so far as it is 'genuine' – in that form of inner experience of the divine that is experienced in its final common form by mystics of all times and all places. All religion is said to be based in the final analysis on the experience of the mystic, who alone is able to make contact directly with the divine and who passes something of this on to the many, who are not capable of having such experience.[19] In this view, religion would exist among mankind in two (and only two) forms: in the direct form of mysticism as 'firsthand' religion and, then, in the indirect form of knowledge only 'passed on' from the mystic, that is to say, as faith and, thus, as 'secondhand' religion. The articulate and formally expressed religion of the many would thus be secondhand religion, a mere sharing in a mystical experience that is in itself formless. [. . .]

Thus, the starting point for a further theological investigation at last becomes clearer, and we can now formulate it in the quite concrete question of whether the mystical interpretation of religion is correct. It is beyond doubt that a large part of the phenomenon of religion is quite correctly thus conceived – that, as we have said, there is a hidden element of identity in the multiform world of religions. Yet it is equally clear that the whole phenomenon cannot be thus conceived; rather,

---

various particular investigations of M. Éliade, especially *Traite d'histoire des religions*. Paris: Payot, 1948 (E.T.: *Patterns in Comparative Religion*. Trans. Rosemary Sheed. New York: Sheed and Ward, 1958).

19   This is particularly clear in O. Spann, *Religionsphilosophie aufgeschichtlicher Grundlage*. Vienna: Gallus-Verlag, 1947.

any attempt to do so would result in a false simplification. [. . .]

Summarizing what has been said, we find that there is no more an identity of religions in general than there is an unrelated plurality among them; rather, we find that a structural formula emerges that encompasses the dynamic aspect of history (of becoming, development), the aspect of constant relationship, and that of concrete and irreducible variety and differentiation. This historical development could be represented in outline thus:

Primitive experience
↓
Mythical religions
↓
Three ways of moving beyond myth
mysticism　　monotheistic revolution　　enlightenment

[. . . T]he real questions concerning relations between religions arise between the first and the second way ('mysticism' and 'monotheistic revolution'). [. . .] no choice can be made in favor of one or the other on rational grounds [. . .]. This choice is, rather, in the final analysis a matter of faith, albeit of a faith that makes use of rational standards. What can be done in the scientific field is simply this, to try to acquire a more detailed knowledge of the structure of the two ways and of the relationship between them. [. . .] It should have become clear, in what has already been said, that we are not referring simply to a form of religious practice that can also find its place in the Christian faith. 'Mysticism' is here understood in a more radical sense, as one path in the history of religion, as an attitude that does not tolerate any other element superior to itself; rather, it regards the imageless, unmetaphorical, and mysterious experience of the mystic as the only determinative and ultimate reality in the realm of religion. This attitude is just as characteristic of Buddha as of the great religious thinkers of the Hindu group of religions, even if they hold to positions so firmly opposed to each other as that of Shankara on one side and Ramanuja on the other.' This is the way that constitutes, amid multifarious derivations, the unified background to Asiatic higher religion. What is characteristic for this mysticism is the experience of identity: the mystic sinks down into the ocean of the all-one, irrespective of whether this is portrayed, with emphatic *theologia negativa*, as 'nothingness' or, in a positive sense, as 'everything'. In the final stage of such an experience, the 'mystic' will no longer be able to say to his God, 'I am Thine'; the expression he uses is 'I am Thee'. The difference has been left behind in what is provisional, preparatory, and what is ultimately valid is fusion, unity.

[. . .] The dogmatic presupposition of the assertion that all religions are equal, with which the Western man of today has so much sympathy, is revealed here as the claim that God and the world, the Divinity and the depths of the soul, are identical. At the same time it becomes clear why, for Asian religious sensibility, the person is not an ultimate reality, and hence God is not conceived of in personal terms: the person, the contrast between I and Thou, belongs to the sphere of distinctions; in the all-is-one experience of the mystic, these boundaries that separate I from Thou are absorbed, are revealed as provisional.

The model in which the monotheistic revolution is embodied, on the contrary, is not the mystic but the prophet. For him, the decisive thing is, not identifying with, but standing over against the God who calls and who commands. [. . .]

These[20] brief indications should already suffice to show that in 'monotheism' and 'mysticism' we have before us two structures that right from the start are built up in quite different ways. In mysticism, inwardness holds the first place; spiritual experience is posited as an absolute. That includes the view that God is purely passive in relation to man and that the content of religion can only consist of man plunging into God. God does not act; there is only the 'mysticism' of men, the gradual ascent to union. The monotheistic way starts from a conviction that is the opposite of this: here man is the passive element upon whom God acts; here it is man who can do nothing of himself, but instead we have here an activity on the part of God, a call from God, and man opens himself to salvation through obedience in response to the call. To that extent, we could choose, instead of the opposites 'mysticism – monotheistic revolution', the opposites 'mysticism – revelation', purely as a phenomenological criterion, without bringing monotheistic faith into play at all. For the one way, it is characteristic for 'mysticism' to occur as a spiritual experience of man and for this occurrence to be regarded as the ultimate and, in truth, only reality in the history of religion and, hence, as being absolute. If this is our starting point, then there can ultimately be no 'revelation' of God whatever; it would be illogical to speak of it in this context, whereas it is equally characteristic of the other way for 'revelation' to exist, for there to be a call from God, and for this call to be what is absolute among mankind, for it to be from it that salvation comes to man.

[. . .] As we said, we will not discuss here which of these positions is right; it has just been a matter of demonstrating that they are quite independent of one another and quite different. [. . .]

It should be clear that the best way forward for a fruitful dialogue between the two ways is opened up by reflections of this kind, a dialogue that would make it possible to get beyond the unsatisfactory duality of 'monotheism' and 'mysticism' without monotheism being absorbed into an unfruitful mystical syncretism or, contrariwise, making the religions devoted to mysticism subject to a false and petty absolutism on the part of Western historical forms. But for that, a great deal of patience, tact, and integrity in their religious seeking will be needed on both sides.

20   [pp. 36–39].

5.2 No Salvation Outside the Church?

The age-old doctrine *Extra ecclesiam nulla salus est*, that there is no
salvation outside the Church, is explored here by Ratzinger in a text
originally published in 1965, thus again reflecting Ratzinger's thoughts
on the subject during the years of the Council, but it was also revised
for inclusion in his work *Das neue Volk Gottes*, published in 1969. During
the late 1960s, particularly in Germany, questions about the appropriate
understanding and means of relation to other faiths (and therefore of
Christian mission, also) became hotly contested subjects and Ratzinger
himself became involved in the public refutation of a young theologian
(Hubertus Halbfas) who had been denied positions at Catholic universities because of his open and dialogical theological stance towards other
faiths (informed, as Halbfas believed, by the teaching of Vatican II).

In the full essay, Ratzinger explores the biblical, ecclesiastical and
historical backdrop to this doctrine, tracing the development of its fundamental meaning (linked to the obligations of faith) from later Judaism
through the New Testament, the Church Fathers, medieval papacy and
down through the Jansenist controversies (where he suggests it became
equated to the still harsher notion, 'outside the Church, no grace'), and
developments in the teaching of Pius IX, Pius XII and down to Vatican II.
Ratzinger then turns, as our extract details, to the more recent debates
pertaining to the notion.

Ratzinger strongly rejects the notion that each person should follow
their own religious pathway and that, in so doing, all will move towards
salvation in equal measure. The Church, because of its ministry to be the
presence of Christ to the whole world, attains a salvific necessity that
cannot be irrelevant for any human being. The Church as the body of
Christ performs a ministry on behalf of all humanity. The Church, he
claims, is not an 'esoteric circle' but rather an 'open space'.[21] While he tries
to assert that the doctrine only makes sense within an intra-Christian
conversation – for he believes it relates only to the obligations of love
and concerns for the salvation of all human beings – what emerges in
clear terms is Ratzinger's unswerving conviction of the superiority of
Christianity in relation to other faiths.

> [. . .] The Christian religion made a universal claim from the very beginning, a
> claim with which it set itself against the entire world of religions; talking about the
> salvific exclusivity of the Church is just the ecclesiastical concretisation of this claim,

---

21 Critics would see some of Ratzinger's arguments here sitting uneasily with his later neo-exclusivist
    writings and also his oft-stated belief that the Church needs to become smaller but purer.

which, since the second century, arose from the ecclesiastical concretisation of the religion itself. Without this claim to universality, the Christian religion would no longer be itself, but it is precisely this claim that seems to be positively outdated.[22]

[. . .] The primary question is no longer the salvation of others, which is, in principle undoubtedly possible; the real leading question is rather how, in light of this irrefutable certainty, the absolute claim of the Church and its belief ought to be understood.[23] When it is put like this, however, when—in other words—the real question posed by the ancient Christian sentence today addresses not the outsider, but rather primarily us, then such sagacious theories about the salvation of others are still insufficient. Thus, the question should rather be whether there is a compatibility of these historical claims with our contemporary consciousness. It must be made clear how it possible for the religion to stay true to itself under such altered circumstances. [. . .]

The State of the Question Today
[. . .] The question regarding salvation cannot be posed from the perspective of the isolated subject, which does not as such exist; rather, together with the subjective conditions of salvation, its objective enablement must be considered. If this is done, then both the unlimited extent of salvation (universality as hope) and the indispensability of the Christ-event and of believing in it (universality as demand) become self-evidently clear. Thus, we shall try to elaborate on both aspects.

The Subjective Aspect of the Question[24]
[. . . W]ith regard to the question of what is expected of a person so that he can be saved, the New Testament gives two answers, which precisely in their apparent contradiction form a unity. It says simultaneously, 'Love alone suffices,' and, 'Only faith suffices.' Both together, however, express an attitude of self-transcendence,

---

22 [Translation by David Kirchhoffer of sections from 'Kein Heil aßerhalb der Kirche?', in *Das neue Volk Gottes: Entwufe zur Ekklesiologie*. Düsseldorf: Patmos, 1969, pp. 339–361, which is a revised version of an earlier text, 'Salus Extra Ecclesiam Nulla Est' in *Veranderd Kerkbewustzijn*, Documentation catholique dossiers vol. 4., Hiversum/Antwerpen: Uitgeverij Paul Brand N.V., 1965, pp. 42–50].

23 The status of the various systematic investigations into our axiom is largely determined by their awareness of the problem. Where they do not understand it as a question of the meaning and mission of being Christian, but rather naively, objectifyingly only indulge in theories about the other, there can be little mention of a positive contribution to the matter. Therein lies the actual weakness of the analysis by A. Röper, *Die anonymen Christen*. Mainz: Grünewald, 1963. In contrast, in the foundational article by K. Rahner, 'Die Gliedschaft in der Kirche nach der Lehre der Enzyklika Pius' XII, "Mystici Corporis Christi"', in: *Schiften* II, pp. 7-94, which indeed forms the point of departure for the formulation 'anonymous Christian', a comprehensive awareness of the problem is certainly given, which admittedly, in the relevant essays in later volumes (esp. V, pp. 136–158; VI, pp. 13–33 and 537–554), seems to have been softened. The problem of the concept 'anonymous Christian' is that, in its abbreviated form, it points the question in the wrong direction.

24 Here, I make use of ideas that I have already developed in my booklet 'Vom Sinn des Christseins', München ²1966, pp. 53–63.

in which the human being begins to leave his egoism behind and to go forth toward the other. Therefore, the brother, the fellow human being is the actual testing ground of this attitude; in his You, the You of God comes to the human being incognito. If we accordingly approach the neighbour as the primary incognito of God, it nevertheless remains true that he can choose any number of a multitude of other disguises, i.e. that many of the realities of the current religious and profane order can become a call to and a help in the saving exodus of self-transcendence. But it is also clear that there are things that will never be able to be an incognito of God. 'God cannot choose the incognito of hate, hedonistic egoism, or pride.'[25]

This apparently obvious statement allows us to draw several important conclusions. Namely, it shows to be false the widespread notion that says that everyone should live according to their convictions and will be saved based on the 'conscientiousness' that they thereby demonstrate. How? Should, for example, the heroism of the SS man, the terrible fidelity of his perverted allegiance, be considered a kind of 'Votum ecclesiae'? Never!

Only through this extreme example does the whole problematic of this idea and its approach become clear. Because, if it equates the call of conscience with the current convictions that have social and historical status, it leads to the view that a person is saved through conscientiously practicing that system in which he finds himself or to which he has somehow attached himself. Conscience degenerates into conscientiousness; the current system becomes the 'way to salvation.' It sounds humane and broad-minded when one therefore says, a Muslim should, in order be saved, just be a 'good Muslim' (what does that actually mean?), a Hindu should be a good Hindu, and so on.[26] But then, should one not likewise say that a cannibal should just be a 'good cannibal' and a convinced SS man a thoroughgoing SS man? It is obvious: something is not right here. A 'theology of religions' that is developed from this starting point can only lead to a dead-end.

But what is actually wrong here? For a start, there is the idolisation of the systems, the institutions. Theses like the one just mentioned (Muslims should stay Muslim, Hindus should stay Hindus) only seem 'progressive;' in truth they elevate conservatism to an ideology [Weltanschauung]: each becomes blessed through his system. But it is not the system or adherence to a system that saves a human being; rather, he is saved by something that is greater than all systems and that constitutes the opening of all systems: love and faith, which ultimately put an end to egoism and self-destructive hubris. The religions assist in salvation according to the extent to which they lead to this attitude; they hinder salvation according to the extent to which they hinder this attitude in the human being.[27] If just the

25   Y. Congar ['Ecclesia ab Abel' in H. Elfers – F. Hofmann, *Abhandlungen über Theologie und Kirche*, Düsseldorf: Patmos 1952, 79–108], 144.

26   H. Halbfas, *Fundamentalkatechetik*. Düsseldorf : Patmos-Verlag, 1968, p. 241.

27   In light of this approach, one is just as likely to encounter a false dismissal of religion and religions

available religions or ideological systems as such would save a human being, be the way to salvation for him, then humanity would remain eternally trapped in its particularisms. Faith in Christ, on the other hand, means the conviction that there is a call to transcend these particularisms, and that only in this way, in moving towards the unity of the Spirit, does history attain its fulfilment.

This reveals a second problem. The statement that each should live according to his conscience is in itself—obviously—completely correct. The only question is what one understands by 'conscience.' If one uses conscience to justify staying faithfully in the current system, then 'conscience' is evidently not being used to refer to the call of God common to all, but rather to a social reflex, the superego of the respective group. But should one actually conserve this superego, or should one dissolve it because it stands in the way of the true call to human beings, because it falsely identifies itself with this call? Conscience itself, the genuine article, which alone can insist on obedience, surely cannot say something different to each person: that one must be a Hindu, the other a Muslim, another a cannibal. It says to all this, that in the midst of their systems, and not uncommonly in opposition to them, one thing is required, that every person be humane to his fellow human being, that he should love. One has only realised a 'Votum' (the 'longing for Christ'), if one has followed *this* voice. Living according to conscience does not mean enclosing oneself in one's so-called convictions, but following this call that is made to every person: the call to faith and love. Only these two attitudes, which are the basic law [or constitution: *Grundgesetz*] of Christianity, can form something like an 'anonymous Christianity'—if one may, with reservations, use this questionable notion here.[28]

The Objective Aspect

In the above attempt to determine the subjective components of salvation (i.e. of the 'Votum ecclesiae'), the matter of the intrinsic necessity of the objective factor also arose. For, while we were describing love as the truly saving, we already had to acknowledge that in every human love there is the taint of egoism, which pollutes it and ultimately makes it inadequate. That is why the substitutionary ministration of Jesus Christ is necessary, and is the only thing that affords any meaning at all to the reaching out that constitutes the gesture of faith, of declaring one's own inadequacy. Without the ministration of Christ this gesture is reaching into a vacuum. At this point, however, what we can call the salvific necessity of the Church also comes in. First, we can observe that the whole of humanity lives from Jesus Christ's act of love, from the 'for' in which he situated his life (cf. Mk 10:45; 14:23 in view of Is 53:10–12). The Church's calling is to step

as to encounter a false glorification. Cf. in relation to this issue the careful, considerate explanations of H. Fries, *Wir und die anderen*. Stuttgart: Kröner, 1966, pp. 240–272.

28   The problematic of this concept is keenly addressed by H. Schlier, 'Der Christ und die Welt', in *GuL* [*Geist und Leben*] 38 (1965) pp. 416–428, and 427 f.

into this substitutionary ministration of Christ, which is what Christ—as Augustine has beautifully expressed: as 'the whole Christ, head and members'—wanted to do. To put it differently, every time a human being is saved, according to Christian belief, Christ is at work. Where Christ is, however, the Church is also involved, because he did not want to remain alone; instead, in a way, the doubly extravagant occurs, and he includes us in his ministry. Christ is, of course, not an individual that stands apart from the whole of humanity. That Jesus of Nazareth is 'the Christ' also means precisely that he did not want to remain alone, that he created a 'body' for himself. 'Body of Christ' means just that: the participation of human beings in Christ's ministry, so that they become, so to speak, his 'organs' and he can no longer be thought of without them. One could then say, 'Solus Christus nunquam solus'. Christ alone saves, but this Christ, who is alone the saviour, is never alone, and the key feature of his salvific activity is precisely that he does not simply reduce the other to a passive recipient of a self-contained gift, but rather incorporates him into his own activity. The human being is saved when he participates in saving others. One is saved, so to speak, always for others, and, hence, also through others.[29]

In principle, it can only work this way if one once again reflects on the essence of the Christ Event. We said that the existential orientation of Jesus, his actual essence, is characterised by the small word 'for.' If 'being saved' means that one becomes like him, then it must present itself concretely as participation in this 'for.' Then being Christian must imply the constant Pascha of the transition from being for itself into being for one another. With that we can now return to the actual pressing question behind all this: why is one actually a Christian? We can now say that the full ministry of explicitly belonging to the Church is not done *by* all, but *for* all. Humanity lives because this ministry exists. I believe that this idea can be made clear in a very concrete sociological-historical way. If there were no Church anymore, if there were no people anymore who would reveal the full seriousness of the faith in the Church, the world would look quite different. If the Christian faith were to disappear, then indeed—one can say without exaggeration—heaven would collapse all over the world. Not a liberation, but a destruction would be the consequence. [. . .]

This leads to a final comment that takes us back to the beginning. What we can see of the phenomenon of the Church is becoming ever smaller when compared to the whole of the cosmos. [. . .] In order to be salvation for all, the Church does not have to correspond physically to that all. Its nature is far more, in the emulation of he who took the whole of humanity upon his shoulders, to be the few through whom God wants to save the many. Church is not everything, but

29   H. U. von Balthasar, *Wer ist Kirche?* Freiburg: Vier Skizzen, 1965, p. 126 H.f. Cf. also Y. Congar, loc. cit. *Außer der Kirche kein Heil: Wahrheit und Dimensionen des Heils*, Essen 1961, French original: *Vaste monde ma paroisse: Vérité et dimensions du Salut*, Paris: Témoignage Chrétien, 1959, 17, and in the texts mentioned therein, esp. from Simeon the New Theologian.

it stands for everything. Is it an expression of the fact that God builds up history in people's being for one another through Christ. Congar has traced this idea through the entire Bible, in which he constantly finds the principle of the 'pars pro toto', the 'minority at the service of a majority.'[30] He shows the Bible's contempt for the quantitative aspect of things, which is particularly evident in its disdain for statistics.[31] He uses the words of Gustave Thibon, 'Every kind of other transcendental order can only be accommodated in the form of something infinitesimally small.'[32] This strange law is also a law of history and of 'salvation history.' It once more confirms everything that we have just considered.

[. . .] Now, it seems to me that the significance of mission is lost if other religions *as such* are declared to be ways to salvation. We have, however, just countered this idea with what has already been said.[33] Certainly, we have to admit that what has been discussed so far does not of itself offer a justification for mission; it aims at answering a different question that is complementary to the mission problem. Said differently, it is open to the imperative of mission without providing a justification for it itself.

Let us try to elaborate on this inner openness of these ideas more clearly! We have said that the Church is not a circle of the saved that exists only for itself, around which then the condemned would exist; it is rather, in essence, there for others, a magnanimity that is open to others. With that, however, we are already at the idea of mission, which is firstly then simply the necessary expression of every 'for', every openness that the Church has profoundly appropriated from Christ. As a sign of the divine love, that being for each other through which history is saved and led home to God, the Church must not be an esoteric circle, but rather is even essentially an *open space*. One may recall, here, an idea that was particularly emphatically formulated by Pseudo-Dionysius, that then became a favourite of scholasticism. 'Bonum diffusivum sui,' he says—the good must of necessity flow out beyond itself; the desire to share belongs intrinsically and necessarily to the good as such. This first of all refers to the essential openness of God: God as goodness in person, is at once sharing, overflowing, self-transcendent, self-giving. But the sentence also applies to everything that is good because of him, the Good. The Church too can only fulfil itself in the 'diffundere', in the sharing, in the missionary self-transcendence. The Church is a dynamic magnanimity. It only remains true to its purpose, it only fulfils its task, if it does not keep the message given to it to itself but carries it forth to humanity. From the synoptic imagery, one could express the formulation thus: mission is the expression of divine hospitality, it

30   Yves Congar, [*Außer der Kirche kein Heil*], 20-27, esp. 23.
31   Ibid. 20f.
32   Translated here from the German used in the present reading.
33   Which does not, of course, exclude the possibility that the religions, in different ways, serve the cause of faith-hope-love and hence can be 'salvation-containing'. But then they are also moving towards the core of what is Christian.

is the messengers setting out into the world with the invitation to the divine wedding feast. Continually passing on this invitation belongs, indispensably, to the Church's ministry of salvation. Even if it knows that God's mercy has no limit, the following always applies: '. . . woe betide me if I do not proclaim the gospel!'(1 Cor 9:16). For the Church, service to the Gospel is required by that love (2 Cor 5:14) from whence the Church comes; and serving this love is its only justification.

5.3 Discerning the 'Ecumenical Dispute' between Orthodoxy, Catholicism and Protestantism

Taken from a lecture first delivered in Graz, Austria, in 1976 (in response to moves towards a Roman Catholic 'recognition' of the *Confessio Augustana* of the Protestant churches of the Augsburg Confession), Ratzinger follows his interpretation of the two main sources and forms of division within Christianity and picks up on the prospects for ecumenism vis-à-vis Rome and, respectively, the Orthodox churches of the East and the Protestant, particularly Lutheran-inspired, churches of the West.

He first details the four absolutist demands that the differing traditions make of one another before recognizing that none of these are realistically achievable. He then turns to consider some more creative means by which mutual recognition, and eventually greater unity, might come about. In the final analysis concessions appear necessary on all sides. Ratzinger states that what is something only historically related to the fundamental truth of faith, to a lesser or greater degree, should not be mistaken for that truth itself. Nor, however, can ecumenism prosper by the Roman Catholic tradition abandoning fundamental aspects of its life and faith.

In relation to the Orthodox churches, the historical precedents for mutual recognition can lay the foundations for overcoming structural and theological differences. The theological groundwork for closer union has already developed to an advanced stage. What prevents union moving forward is a less-developed spiritual preparation. Formulations and practices should not be allowed to stand in the way of the higher truth of unity in the one faith of the Fathers and the basic form of the Church as they understood it.

In relation to the Protestant (here specifically Lutheran) churches, the recognition of the *Confessio Augustana* by Rome would entail that Church recognizing a certain degree of independence in the manner in which the one faith is lived out, while the Protestant churches would commend the confession's original intention of affirming these communities as part of that one Catholic faith and as being in unity with the one dogma and basic structure of it. A narrow 'confessionalism of separation' must be opposed with 'a hermeneutics of union that sees the confession of faith as that which unites'. Thus there must be an attempt to overcome the two obstacles of confessional chauvinism that should be rejected on the one hand, just as an 'indifferentism to faith', which sees truth as a stumbling block and is driven by a unity of expediency, must be rejected on the other hand.

Ratzinger's supporters would here see refreshing honesty and constructive realism that might actually aid better relations between these differing ecclesial communities. Critics would wonder whether subtle rhetoric masks an essentially 'Roman' agenda of 'return' beneath a veneer of open and dialogical language.

Later theological writings (as well as documents issued under Ratzinger's authority by the CDF) demonstrate that certain non-negotiable 'lines in the sand' in Ratzinger's approach to ecumenical discussions are indeed pronounced to a greater degree than they appear in this more nuanced theological reflection. Whether they were such at the time this essay was composed is open to discussion.

> [. . .] It seems to me that, among the incalculable number of divisions by which Christianity is torn, there are two basic types to which two different models of unity correspond. [. . .] Against this background we [. . .] weigh the possibilities that are open to Christian ecumenism. The maximum demands on which the search for unity must certainly founder are immediately clear. On the part of the West, the maximum demand would be that the East recognize the primacy of the bishop of Rome in the full scope of the definition of 1870 and in so doing submit in practice, to a primacy such as been accepted by the Uniate churches. On the part of the East, the maximum demand would be that the West declare the 1870 doctrine of primacy erroneous and in so doing submit, in practice, to a primacy such as been accepted with the removal of the *Filioque* from the Creed and including the Marian dogmas of the nineteenth and twentieth centuries. As regards Protestantism, the maximum demand of the Catholic Church would be that the Protestant ecclesiological ministries be regarded as totally invalid and that Protestants be converted to Catholicism; the maximum demand of Protestants, on the other hand, would be that the Catholic Church accept, along with the unconditional acknowledgement of all Protestant ministries, the Protestant concept of ministry and their understanding of the Church and thus, in practice, renounce the apostolic and sacramental structure of the Church, which would mean, in practice, the conversion of Catholics to Protestantism and their acceptance of a multiplicity of distinct community structures as the historical form of the Church. While the first three maximum demands are today rather unanimously rejected by Christian consciousness, the fourth exercises a kind of fascination for it – as it were, a certain conclusiveness that makes it appear to be the real solution to the problem. This is all the more true since there is joined to it the expectation that a

Parliament of Churches, a 'truly ecumenical council', could then harmonize this pluralism and promote a Christian unity of action. That no real union would result from this, but that its very impossibility would become a single common dogma, should convince anyone who examines the suggestion closely that such a way would not bring Church unity but only a final renunciation of it.[34]

As a result, none of the maximum solutions offers any real hope of unity. In any event, church unity is not a political problem that can be solved by means of compromise or the weighing of what is regarded as possible or acceptable. What is at stake here is unity of belief, that is, the question of truth, which cannot be the object of political manoeuvring. As long as and to the extent that the maximum solution must be regarded as a requirement of truth itself, just so long and to just that extent will there be no other recourse than simply to strive to convert one's partner in the debate. In other words, the claim of truth ought not to be raised where there is not a compelling and indisputable reason for doing so. We may not interpret as truth that which is, in reality, a historical development with a more or less close relationship to truth. Whenever, then, the weight of truth and its incontrovertibility are involved, they must be met by a corresponding sincerity that avoids laying claim to truth prematurely and is ready to search for the inner fullness of truth with the eyes of love.

On the question of reunion between East and West

How, then, are the maximum demands to be decided in advance? Certainly, no one who claims allegiance to Catholic theology can simply declare the doctrine of primacy null and void, especially not if he seeks to understand the objections and evaluates with an open mind the relative weight of what can be determined historically. Nor is it possible, on the other hand, for him to regard as the only possible form and, consequently, as binding on all Christians the form this primacy has taken in the nineteenth and twentieth centuries. The symbolic gestures of Pope Paul VI and, in particular, his kneeling before the representative of the Ecumenical Patriarch were an attempt to express precisely this and, by such signs, to point the way out of the historical impasse. Although it is not given us to halt the flight of history, to change the course of centuries, we may say, nevertheless, that what was possible for a thousand years is not impossible for Christians today. After all, Cardinal Humbert of Silva Candida, in the same bull in which he excommunicated the Patriarch Michael Cerularius and thus inaugurated the schism between East and West, designated the Emperor and people of Constantinople as 'very Christian and orthodox', although their concept of the Roman primacy was certainly far less different from that of Cerularius than from that, let us say, of the First Vatican Council.[35] In other words, Rome must not require more from the

---

34 Sections from *Principles of Catholic Theology: Building Stones for a Fundamental Theology.* San Francisco: Ignatius, 1987, pp. 193–203.

35 Cf. J. Meyendorff, 'Églises soeurs. Implications ecclésiologiques du Tomos Agapes', in [*Koinonia:*

East with respect to the doctrine of primacy than had been formulated and was lived in the first millenium. When the Patriarch Athenagoras, on July 25, 1967, on the occasion of the Pope's visit to Phanar, designated him as the successor of St. Peter, as the most esteemed among us, as one who presides in charity, this great Church leader was expressing the essential content of the doctrine of primacy as it was known in the first millenium. Rome need not ask for more. Reunion could take place in this context if, on the one hand, the East would cease to oppose as heretical the developments that took place in the West in the second millenium and would accept the Catholic Church as legitimate and orthodox in the form she had acquired in the course of that development, while, on the other hand, the West would recognize the Church of the East as orthodox and legitimate in the form she has always had.

Such a mutual act of acceptance and recognition, in the Catholicity that is common to and still possessed by each side, is assuredly no light matter. It is an act of self-conquest, of self-renunciation and, certainly, also of self-discovery. It is an act that cannot be brought about by diplomacy but must be a spiritual undertaking of the whole Church in both East and West. If what is theologically possible is also to be actually possible in the Church, the theological aspect must be spiritually prepared and spiritually accepted. My diagnosis of the relationship between East and West in the Church is as follows: from a theological perspective, the union of the Churches of East and West is fundamentally possible, but the spiritual preparation is not yet sufficiently far advanced and, therefore, not yet ready in practice. When I say it is fundamentally possible from a theological perspective, I do not overlook the fact that, on closer inspection, a number of obstacles still exist with respect to the theological possibility. From the *Filioque* to the question of the indissolubility of marriage. Despite these difficulties, some of which are present more strongly in the West, some in the East, we must learn that unity, for its part, is a Christian truth, an essentially Christian concept, of so high a rank that it can be sacrificed only to safeguard what is most fundamental, not where the way to it is obstructed by formulations and practices that, however important they may be, do not destroy community in the faith of the Fathers and in the basic form of the Church as they saw her.[36] Because it has two elements, the above-mentioned diagnosis admits of quite opposing prognostications. What is theologically possible can miscarry spiritually and, in consequence, become once again theologically impossible. What is theologically possible can also be spiritually possible and, in consequence, become theologically deeper and

Premier Colloque ecclésiologique entre théologiens orthodoxes et catholiques. Paris: Istina, 1975 – henceforth *Kononia*], pp. 35–46 (German translation in *IKZ* [*Internationale Katholische Zeitschrift: Communio*] 3 (1974) pp. 308–322, esp. 309–310.

36   Louis Bouyer offers a plan for the gradual restoration of unity between East and West in 'Réflexions sur le rétablissement possible de la communion entre les Églises orthodoxe et catholique. Perspectives actuelles', in *Koinonia*, pp. 112–115.

purer. Which prognostication will prove to be the correct one cannot be foretold at the present time: the factors pointing to one or other of them are almost equally strong.

But the opposing prognostications that are expressed in this diagnosis should be construed not just as a theorizing about theoretical possibilities but as a practical imperative: it is the task of every responsible Christian and, in a particular way, of theologians and leaders of the Church to create a spiritual climate for the theologically possible; under the compelling mandate of a unity without sameness, to see and experience the antithetical at all times without specious superficiality; to inquire always not just about the defensibility of union, of mutual recognition, but even more urgently about the defensibility of remaining separate, for it is not unity that requires justification but the absence of it.[37] The fact that opposing prognostications are possible means that the prognostication is also dependent on ourselves, that it exists in the form of a mandate and that to make us aware of this fact should be the sole meaning of any encounter that does not simply impart information but makes known a task and demands an examination of conscience that compels us to action.

On the Question of Catholic-Protestant Ecumenism

Prognostications as to the future of ecumenism – the question is only half answered as long as we have said nothing about the prospects of unity between the Catholic Church and the Protestant denominations. In view of the overwhelming plurality of world Protestantism, the question is admittedly much more difficult to answer than that regarding Catholicism and Orthodoxy, which can be approached uniformly, as it were, from a common and consistent model. In any event, one thing should be clear: unity between Catholicism and Orthodoxy would not hinder but rather facilitate unity with the Protestant churches. Granted, the solution that is being proposed, in this context, in the suggestion of the Ecumenical Institute of the Faculties of German Universities,[38] seeks a healing of the division in the rejection of the dogma and structure of the ancient Church. But we have already seen that such a solution would not lead to unity but would constitute its ultimate rejection. In view of the variety of positions and situations that exist in the individual Protestant denominations, I shall limit my remarks here to those churches that bear the stamp of Luther, but a model that will serve for all Protestant churches should

37 Papandreou shows emphatically that this is the right perspective, in Raymund Erni and Damaskinos Papandreou (eds), *Eucharistiegemeinschaft. Der Standpunkt der Orthodoxie*. Freiburg: Kanisius-Verlag, 1974, pp. 68–96, esp. 91–92.

38 *Reform und Anerkennung kirchlicher Ämter. Ein Memorandum der Arbeitsgemeinschaft ökumenischer Universitätsinstitute*. Munich: Kaiser. 1973; the text of the memorandum is on pp. 11–25. For several responses to this, see *Catholica* 27 (1973), esp. the contribution by Karl Lehmann, pp. 248–262; cf. also Heinz Schutte, *Amt, Ordination und Sukzession in Verstandnis evangelischer und katholischer Exegeten und Dogmatiker der Gegenwart sowie in Dokutnenten ökumenischer Gesprache*. Düsseldorf: Patmos, 1974.

become recognizable in the process. Logically, the search for church unity must begin with the denominational and ecclesial structure, however much it will also respect and appreciate precisely those sources of a quite personal piety and the spiritual strength and depth that are provided for the individual. But if what we are discussing is not a union between individuals but a community of churches, then what is at stake is the confession and faith of the church of which the individual is a member and in which he is opened to a personal encounter with God. That means: the reference point of such an effort must be the confessional writings of the Evangelical Lutheran Church; writings of private theologians will be taken into account only insofar as they contribute to denominational theology.[39] Research in recent years has led to the conclusion that it was not just for diplomatic reasons that the Confessio Augustana [CA] was composed as the fundamental Lutheran confessional text; it was intended to be interpreted under the law of the empire as a Catholic confession; it was understood with inner conviction as a search for evangelical Catholicity – as an effort to filter the seething discontent of the early reform movement in a way that would make it a Catholic reform.[40] Efforts are being made, accordingly, to bring about a Catholic recognition of the CA – or, more accurately, a recognition of the CA as Catholic – that would establish the Catholicity of the churches of the Augsburg Confession and thus make possible a corporate union despite existing differences.[41] Certainly such a recognition of the CA by the Catholic Church would be far more than a theoretical theological action that could be worked out by historians and church politicians. It would be, rather, a concrete historical step on both sides. It would mean that the Catholic Church recognized, in the beginnings thus made, an appropriate form for realizing the common faith with the independence that was its due. On the other hand, it would mean that the Protestant churches would accept and understand this text, which is susceptible of many interpretations, in the way that was originally intended: in unity with the dogma and basic structure of the ancient Church. It would mean for both sides that the open question as to the center of the Reformation would

39   In this context, we must ask ourselves above all what significance Luther's theology has in relation to the confessional writings. Until there is a more or less universally accepted answer to that question, everything else will continue to be uncertain.
40   Cf. Vinzenz Pfnür, Einig in der Rechtfertigungslehre? Die Rechtfertigungslehre der Confessio Augustana (1530) und die Stellungnahme der katholischen Kontroverstheologie zwischen 1530 und 1535. Wiesbaden: Steiner, 1970.
41   A concrete programme in this direction was proposed in the journal Bausteine (1975), vol. 58, pp. 9–20, and vol. 59, 3–22. See also the fundamental article by Vinzenz Pfnür, 'Anerkennung der Confessio Augustana durch die katholische Kirche? Zu einer aktuellen Frage des katholisch-lutherischen Dialogs', in IKZ (1975) pp. 298–307. Objections to this article by Paul Hacker and T. Beer in IKZ (1976) rest on the problematic historical and fundamental ('juridical') relationship of the Confessio Augustana to Luther's work and to the remaining work of Melanchthon (especially the defence [Apologia] of the Augsburg Confession). In any event, the question cannot be solved by a historically favourable interpretation of the CA but only by a spiritual and ecclesial decision that is beyond the competence of historians.

be solved in a spiritual decision that would recognize the Catholic orientation of the CA and that the heritage of that time would be experienced and accepted in accordance with this interpretation.

The question of the practical possibility of such a development – the prognosis on the basis of the diagnosis – is much more difficult than it was with regard to a rapprochement between the Catholic Church and Orthodoxy. This, too, is a question that can be answered better by action than by speculation. What action? Generally speaking, certainly, a manner of thinking and acting that respects the other in his search for the true essence of Christianity; an attitude that regards unity as an urgent good that demands sacrifice, whereas separation demands justification in every single instance. But we can define the required action even more clearly in terms of the above diagnosis. It means that the Catholic does not insist on the dissolution of the Protestant confessions and the demolishing of their churches but hopes, rather, that they will be strengthened in their confessions and in their ecclesial reality. There is, of course, a confessionalism that divides and that must be overcome: on whatever side it occurs, we must speak of confessionalism in a pejorative sense wherever the noncommunal, the anti-, is experienced as an essential constituent and thus intensifies the division. We must oppose to this confessionalism of separation a hermeneutics of union that sees the confession of faith as that which unites. Our interest, that is, the interest of ecumenism, cannot be linked to the precondition that the confession will simply disappear but rather that it will be translated from its banishment to the realm of the nonbinding into the full meaning of a binding community of faith in the Church. For only where this happens is a mutually binding community possible; only thus does an ecumenism of faith possess the necessary stability.

The question about the prognosis for ecumenism is, ultimately, a question about the forces that are operative in Christianity today and that may be expected to leave their mark on the future. Two obstacles are opposed to the realization of Church unity: on the one hand, a confessional chauvinism that orients itself primarily, not according to truth, but according to custom and, in its obsession with what is its own, puts emphasis primarily on what is directed against others. On the other hand, an indifferentism with regard to faith that sees the question of truth as an obstacle, measures unity by expediency and thus turns it into an external pact that bears always within itself the seeds of new divisions. The guarantee of unity is a Christianity of faith and fidelity that lives the faith as a decision with a definite content but precisely for that reason is always searching for unity, lets itself be constantly purified and deepened as a preparation for it and, in so doing, helps the other to recognize the common center and to find himself there by the same process of purification and deepening. It is clear that the first two attitudes are closer and more immediate to man than the third, which challenges him to excel himself and, at the same time, reduces him to utter helplessness, demands from him inexhaustible patience and a readiness to be constantly purified and deepened anew. But Christianity, as a whole, rests on the victory of the improbable, on the impulse of the Holy Spirit, who leads man beyond himself and precisely in this way brings him to himself. Because we have confidence in the power of the Holy Spirit, we hope also for the unity of the Church and dedicate ourselves to an ecumenism of faith.

5.4 Ecumenical Realities Today

This extract was originally a letter to the editor of the German academic journal, *Theologische Quartalschrift*, and a response to a 1986 request for Ratzinger to set down his thoughts on the 'current state' of ecumenical relations. He speaks of the great hopes engendered for the cause of Christian unity by the Second Vatican Council first but then swiftly turns to suggest that there has emerged a polarization between those keen to move ecumenism on more quickly by focusing on a 'grass roots' effort across the churches, as opposed to the more cautious 'official' Church and its authorities.

He rejects that this would lead to a true path towards unity, particularly if it focuses primarily on social issues and projects, and he also criticizes the Protestant and Catholic theologians Heinrich Fries and Karl Rahner for their overt optimism that local communities across the churches would simply accept unity if church leaders proclaimed it. Instead, Ratzinger believes that a unity 'imposed' by human beings would not be the full unity intended by the Gospel of John (ch.17). True unity involves more than 'political' diplomacy and organizational matters. Ratzinger instead suggests that remaining divisions might become a *felix culpa*, a happy fault, if they help lead the Church towards unity through multiplicity and diversity. Some differences may be the will of God. He points to the historical example of the co-existence of Protestantism and Catholicism in Germany, and the fruits of both forms of Christian existence gained from this, as an example of the promise of such a path towards unity.

Ratzinger's preferred model of ecumenism is therefore twofold. For sure, he states, the scholarly and prayerful debates at the official and theological level should continue. But alongside this, he argues that one needs to accept the expression of the Protestant reformer, Philip Melanchthon, 'where and when God has seen fit', and apply it to ecumenical relations today. That is to say, unity will emerge according to God's will, not the will of human beings. He thus proposes a form of receptive ecumenism, of mutually learning from one another's gifts. Furthermore, Ratzinger reminds his readers that Christians already share much in common, the Bible as the word of God, the common profession of faith and the common form of Christian prayer, so, also, the fundamentals of Christian ethics.

He suggests that there are other ways of Christian churches 'sharing' one another's gifts short of inter-communion and lists examples of these. He also suggests that Catholics and Protestants should not force one another's understandings of the Church and its sacraments upon one another. He lays particular emphasis here upon his defence of the Catholic understanding of the Eucharist and the Church both as the body of Christ and he stresses, as in many places elsewhere, that such essentials are a prerequisite for unity, rather than obstacles in the path towards it. He feels that following the path as willed by God, rather than transmutating 'theology into diplomacy and faith into "social involvement"' will further the cause of ecumenism better.

Ratzinger's supporters would here see possible ways beyond ecumenical impasse without risking any fundamental aspects of the Catholic faith being diluted or suppressed simply for the sake of better relations. Others would suggest that the line of argument here effectively stalls ecumenical progress and again point to official statements from the CDF that have set back the cause of ecumenical dialogue by decades in recent years. The notion of 'receptive' ecumenism, as understood here by Ratzinger and taken up and developed by others in recent times, is judged to be a 'safe' and 'risk-free' ecumenism, whereby civility and cordiality are exchanged, while doctrinal and structural stumbling blocks are left untouched. As such, critics wonder whether any genuine progress towards truly greater unity – including forms of partial communion and inter-communion – can actually be achieved through such a process. A further criticism is that, while Ratzinger states that no Christian community should have their way of being forcibly changed by the imposition of the understanding and practices of other churches, his arguments concerning the Eucharist and its relation to the Church entail precisely that.

[. . .] Allow me, first, to review briefly the road that has been travelled over the last twenty years, because today's bearings seem to me to be an indispensable part of tomorrow's prospects. The Second Vatican Council created new foundations for ecumenical activity in the Catholic Church, but that moment had been preceded by a long struggle, a process of joint effort in which much had matured and could now be put into action quickly. Given the tempo at which such new and hitherto unexpected things suddenly became possible, the hope for a speedy complete end to the divisions seemed well founded. But once everything that had become intrinsically possible was actually translated into official forms, a sort of standstill necessarily ensued. For those who had been acquainted with the ecumenical process from its beginnings or had personally been involved in it, this moment was foreseeable because everyone knew where solutions were already in sight and where the borders had not yet been opened up. For outsiders, in contrast, it must have been a moment of great disappointment there were unavoidable attempts to assign blame, and the obvious targets were the ecclesiastical authorities.[42]

Very soon after the initial conciliar enthusiasm had waned, the alternative model of 'grass-roots ecumenism' cropped up, which tried to bring about unity 'from below' if it could not be obtained 'from above'. In one respect, this concept is correct: the 'authorities' in the Church cannot accomplish anything that has not previously matured in the life of the Church by faith through insight and experience. But where such maturation was not intended, but instead the division of the Church into the 'grass-roots church' and the 'official Church' prevailed, no new far-reaching unity could develop. 'Grass-roots ecumenism' of this sort ultimately brings forth nothing but splinter groups that divide congregations and do not even have a deeper unity among themselves, despite a common worldwide propaganda. For a time it may have looked as though the traditional ecclesiastical divisions were now being replaced by a new partitioning and that in the future progressive, 'politically involved' Christians and 'traditionalists' would stand on opposite sides and recruit for their respective parties from the various existing churches. This prospect gave rise then to the suggestion that the 'authorities' should be left out of ecumenism entirely, because an eventual rapprochement or even reunion at that level would only strengthen the traditionalist wing of Christendom and hinder the development of a progressive new Christianity.

Today, of course, such ideas are still not entirely dead, but it seems in any case that their first flowering is a thing of the past. A Christianity that defines itself essentially in terms of social 'involvement' has contours that are too blurred for it to be capable of producing long-term unity and the stability of shared ecclesiastical life. People do not remain in the Church permanently because they find parish socials or political action committees there, but rather because they hope to find answers concerning the things in their lives that are beyond their control – answers that have not been made up by the parish priests or other officials but that come from a higher authority and are faithfully handed down by the pastors . . ..

By this I mean that the stability of the visible religious entity comes from realms that are not encompassed by 'grass-roots ecumenism' and that the search for what is beyond our control also marks the boundary of all 'official' action in the Church. This means that neither an isolated 'grass-roots community' nor an isolated 'officialdom' can be considered responsible for ecumenical action; effective ecumenical action presupposes the inner unity of the authorities' activity with the authentic faith life of the Church. I see herein one of the fundamental errors of the Fries-Rahner project: Rahner thinks that Catholics would follow the authorities anyway, that this can be taken for granted, given the tradition and structure of the Catholic Church. In fact, though, he argues, it is essentially no different with the Protestants; if the authorities declare unity and are sufficiently committed to

42 [From 'On The Progress Of Ecumenism' in Joseph Ratzinger, *Church, Ecumenism and Politics: New Essays in Ecclesiology*. New York: Crossroad 1988 (and also San Francisco, Ignatius Press, 2008), 132-138. Also appearing in a different translation, Slough: St Paul's, 1988, pp. 135–142].

it, there, too, the local congregations will not fail to follow. In my opinion, this is a form of official ecumenism that corresponds to neither the Catholic nor the Protestant understanding of the Church.

Logically, a unity negotiated by men could only be a matter of human right, *iuris humani*. In that case it would not pertain at all to the theological unity referred to in John 17, and consequently it could not be a testimony to the mystery of Jesus Christ but would merely speak in favor of the diplomatic skill and willingness to compromise of those who conducted the negotiations. That, too, is something, but it does not affect at all the genuinely religious plane with which ecumenism is concerned. Even theological joint statements necessarily remain on the level of human (scholarly) insight, which can make arrangements to satisfy essential prerequisites for the act of faith but does not itself pertain to the act of faith as such. Looking to the future, it therefore seems to me important to recognize the limits of 'ecumenical negotiations' and to expect no more from them than they can yield: rapprochement in important human areas, but not unity itself. It seems to me that we could have avoided many disappointments if this had been clear from the start. But after the successes of the early postconciliar period, many people understood ecumenism in political terms as a diplomatic task; just as one expects that after a while good negotiators will arrive at a common agreement that is acceptable to all parties, so too people thought that they could expect this of the ecclesiastical authorities in ecumenical matters. But this was making too great a demand upon them; what they were able to accomplish after the Council was based on a process of maturation that they had not caused but simply needed to transpose into public church organization.

But if this is how matters stand, what are we to do? In addressing this question, I have found very helpful the formula that Oscar Cullmann recently injected into the debate: unity *through* multiplicity, through diversity. Certainly, division is harmful, especially when it leads to enmity and an impoverishment of Christian witness. But if the poison of hostility is slowly removed from the division, and if, through mutual acceptance, diversity leads no longer to mere impoverishment but rather to a new wealth of listening and understanding, then during the transition to unity division can become *felix culpa*, a happy fault, even before it is completely healed. [. . .]

Along the path marked out by Cullmann, therefore, we should first try to find unity *through* diversity, in other words, to accept what is fruitful in our divisions, to detoxify them, and to welcome the positive things that come precisely from diversity – of course, in the hope that in the end the division will cease to be division at all and will just be 'polarity' without contradiction. But any attempt to reach this final stage too directly in a hasty and hectic do-it-yourself rush only deepens the division instead of healing it. Allow me to explain what I mean quite empirically and pragmatically with an example: Was it not a good thing in many respects, for the Catholic Church in Germany and beyond, that Protestantism, with its liberalism and its piety and its internal conflicts and its lofty intellectual standards, existed alongside her? Certainly in the times of the religious wars, division was almost exclusively mutual opposition, but then it increasingly developed also into a positive factor for the faith on both sides, which helps us to understand something of the mysterious 'must' of Saint Paul. And conversely: Could anyone really imagine an exclusively Protestant world? Is not Protestantism instead, in all its declarations, precisely as a protest, so completely connected with Catholicism that it would be scarcely imaginable without it?

This would result in a twofold approach to ecumenical activity One line of action would necessarily consist of continuing efforts to find *complete* unity to devise models of unity while attempting to see oppositions in a fuller light that leads toward unity – not only in scholarly debates but above all in prayer and penance. Alongside this, however, there should be a second field of action, which presupposes that we do not know and cannot determine the hour when and the manner in which unity will come about. In this regard, Melanchthon's expression, 'ubi et quando visum est Deo' [where and when God has seen fit] really holds true in the strictest sense. In any case, it should be clear that we do not *make* unity (any more than we achieve justice by our works); however, we must not twiddle our thumbs. Therefore, it is a matter of receiving again and again from the other as other, while respecting his otherness. Even as separated brethren we can be one.

We can and must promote the continual growth of this sort of unity, without subordinating it to the all-too-human pressure to succeed in reaching the 'final goal'. This sort of unity travels along many different paths and therefore demands many different initiatives. First, it is a question of finding, recognizing, and acknowledging the already existing forms of unity, which are really not insignificant. The fact that we read the Bible together as the Word of God, that we share the profession of faith – formulated by the ancient councils in reading the Bible – in the triune God, in Jesus Christ as true God and true man, as well as in baptism and the forgiveness of sins and, thus, share a fundamental image of God and of man: this fact must be realized over and over again, publicly acknowledged, and deepened as it is realized. Yet another thing that we have in common is the basic form of Christian prayer; one also is the essential ethical instruction of the Decalogue, as read in light of the New Testament. To this fundamental unity of profession should correspond a fundamental unity of action as well. Thus it would be a matter of putting into action the existing unity, making it concrete and extending it. It goes without saying that this involves many forms of encounter at all levels (those in ministry, theologians, the faithful) and forms of joint action; all this must take shape in concrete experiences and be developed further, as is happening now to a great extent, praise God.

This 'unity through diversity' could and should be promoted also by additional symbolic actions, which would constantly bring this cause to the attention of the people in the pews. We might recall in this connection Oscar Cullmann's suggestion of ecumenical collects. The custom in the Eastern Churches of distributing blessed bread would be well suited to the West, also. Even where genuine eucharistic communion is not possible, this is a real and even physical way of being together in our differences and 'communicating', a way of enduring the thorn of being different and at the same time transforming division into a mutual giving.

Another component of this 'unity through diversity', then, is being unwilling to impose on the other party anything that (still) threatens him in the core of his Christian identity. Catholics should not try to force Protestants to recognize the papacy and their understanding of apostolic succession; the insertion of the Word into the sphere of the sacrament and the juridical order defined by the sacrament obviously appears to Protestants to be a manipulation of the Word and a viola- tion of its freedom, and we should respect that. Conversely, Protestants should stop pressuring the Catholic Church to allow intercommunion based on their understanding of the Lord's Supper, since for us the twofold mystery of the Body of Christ – the Body of Christ as Church and the Body of Christ as sacramental gift – is one and the same sacrament, and to tear the corporeality of the sacrament out of the context of the Church's corporeality would mean trampling on both the Church and the sacrament. Such respect for the things that constitute for both sides the 'must' of the division does not delay unity; it is a fundamental prerequisite for it. Pausing respectfully in this way in the presence of the 'must' that we did not invent will produce much more charity and thus much more proximity than that urgent insistence which creates resistance and ultimately aversion. And such respect, consequently, not only will not hinder the search for greater understanding precisely in these core areas, but will rather yield a peaceful maturation and a joyful gratitude for so much closeness despite the mysterious 'must'.

I can imagine that many people will not like the concept when it is put in this way. Whatever might be said against it, one objection should not be raised: that this concept implies stagnation or resignation or even a rejection of ecumenism. It is quite simply the attempt to leave to God what is his business and his alone and to investigate then what our tasks are, in all seriousness. This sphere of our tasks includes doing and suffering, activity and patience. Anyone who crosses out one of the two ruins the whole thing. If we take in hand everything that is assigned to us to do, then ecumenism will continue to be an extremely vital and promising cause, even more so than before. I am convinced that we – delivered from the pressure to do it all ourselves and from its covert and overt timetables – will draw nearer more rapidly and more deeply than when we began to transmute theology into diplomacy and faith into 'social involvement'. [. . .]

5.5 Against Pluralism and Relativism

In this text, Ratzinger addresses particular questions and challenges for the Christian faith and theology that he believes emerged in the 1990s.

Having first revisited the 'crisis for liberation theology'[43], which he identifies as an attempt to try and make political ideology (namely, Marxism), the basis of human redemption and to make human effort and praxis the core of theological reflection, he notes how the political events of 1989 and beyond (the fall of the Berlin Wall and collapse of Eastern European state totalitarianism) pose new challenges and he suggests 'new forms' of the Marxist view of the world will emerge. Liberation theology is blamed for setting in motion a malaise with regard to faith and theology.

In particular he identifies 'relativism' as the new 'dominant philosophy' and the 'central problem of faith for our time'. He admits a certain amount of relativism in the political sphere is no bad thing, but with regard to faith he laments the rise of the pluralistic theology of the religions, forms of such he believed reached their peak in the 1990s. He sees pluralistic theology as being a product of the Western world view and yet echoing much of the 'Asian' understanding of religion: 'postmetaphysical philosophy' from the former combines with the 'negative theology' of the latter.

He singles out the English Presbyterian philosopher of religion and theologian, John Hick, as epitomizing the approach he rejects. Hick believes the different religions are leading towards the same ultimate reality in necessarily different ways. Ratzinger sketches a caricature of such an approach, which he believes requires that all religions' viewpoints become equal and teaches that no particular faith or historically manifested path to God can be deemed superior to any other.

In particular, Ratzinger criticizes relativism in Christology and in ecclesiology, whereby Christ is somehow seen as one saviour or mediator for humanity among others and possibly even just a human being who was not literally divine, and where no particular church is afforded pre-eminence over and against others. Ratzinger equally rejects modified forms of pluralism based on the primacy of orthopraxis over orthodoxy. A further development here is the rise in 'New Age' religions and the revival of older forms of religion and ritual. Furthermore a 'grey pragmatism' has emerged in the Church, with regard to not just faith, but also church organisation, morals and even the liturgy, where local congregations are calling for the right to determine even the form of the mass relative to their context.

Ratzinger's supporters would identify such arguments as marking a turning of the tide in theological understandings of the relations between different faiths. They would point out that Christian uniqueness, particularly that of salvation in Christ, is so fundamental an aspect of the faith

---

43   Which may, at first, appear a little strange in this context until one appreciates Ratzinger's general ecclesiological perspective (see Chapter Three of this volume).

that any theological position that undermines it therefore undermines the faith itself. Liberal political ideas, ideologies and philosophies had infected theological positions within Catholicism for too long, according to such views, and thus what Ratzinger offers is a corrective to such a theological malaise. But his critics say that Ratzinger offers only an exaggerated caricature and 'straw man' portrayal for each of liberation theology, Marxism, relativism, pluralism, Asian religions and philosophy and 'New Age' approaches to life and religion, as opposed to what the proponents of these various standpoints actually argue and believe. For example, John Hick replied at length to Ratzinger in publication, indicating that Ratzinger had misrepresented and misunderstood his work in numerous ways.[44] Indeed, even Ratzinger himself admitted (in a footnote in the original), that his account of both Hick and Paul Knitter was based on his reading of a secondary discussion of their work.

[. . .] *Relativism – The Dominant Philosophy*[45]
[R]elativism has become the central problem for faith in our time. It by no means appears simply as resignation in the face of the unfathomable nature of truth, of course; rather, it defines itself positively on the basis of the concepts of tolerance, dialectic epistemology, and freedom, which would be limited by maintaining one truth as being valid for everyone . . . . In the realm of politics and society, therefore, one cannot deny relativism a certain right. The problem is based on the fact that it sees itself as being unlimited. And now it is being quite consciously applied to the field of religion and ethics. [. . .] The so-called pluralistic theology of religions had in fact been gradually developing since the fifties, but it did not occupy the center of attention for Christians until now. With respect to the ramifications of the questions it raises, and likewise to its being present in the most various cultural spheres, it occupies much the same place as did liberation theology in the past decade; it is also frequently combined with the latter in an attempt to give it a new, updated form. It appears in widely varying forms, so that it is impossible to express it in a short formula and present its essential elements briefly. On the one hand, this is a typical product of the Western world and of its thought forms, yet, on the other hand, it is astonishingly close to the philosophical and religious intuitions of Asia, and especially of the Indian sub-continent, so that in the current historical situation the contact of these two worlds gives it a particular impact.

44   John Hick, *Dialogues in the Philosophy of Religion*. London: Palgrave Macmillan, 1993, pp. 149–168 (Hick's reply being from p. 157 ff.).
45   [From 'The New Questions that Arose in the Nineties: Faith and Theology Today', in Joseph Ratzinger, *Truth and Tolerance: Christian Belief and World Religions*. San Francisco: Ignatius Press, 2004, pp. 115–137].

Relativism in Theology – The Revocation of Christology
That is clearly visible in the work of one of its founders and principal representatives, the English Presbyterian J. Hick, whose philosophical starting point is found in Kant's distinction between phenomenon and noumenon: we can never know ultimate reality in itself but only ever its appearance in the way we perceive things, seeing it through various 'lenses'. Everything we perceive is, not actual reality as it is in itself, but a reflection corresponding to our capacities. This approach, which Hick first tried to apply in a context that was still christocentric, he transformed after a year's stay in India, in what he himself calls a Copernican turning point in his thinking, into a new form of theocentrism. The identification of one single historical figure, Jesus of Nazareth, with 'reality' itself, with the living God, was now rejected as a relapse into myth; Jesus was consciously relativized, reduced to one religious genius among others. There can be no absolute entity in itself, or absolute person in himself, within history, only patterns, only ideal figures, which direct our attention toward the wholly other, which in history cannot in fact be comprehended in itself. It is clear that by the same token Church, dogma, and sacraments must thereby lose their unconditional status. To regard such finite mediations as absolute, or even as real encounters with the universally valid truth of the God who reveals himself, amounts to setting up one's own experience as absolute and thus failing to perceive the infinity of the God who is wholly other.

From such a standpoint, which dominates thinking far beyond the scope of Hick's theories, the belief that there is indeed truth, valid and binding truth, within history itself, in the figure of Jesus Christ and in the faith of the Church, is referred to as fundamentalism, which appears as the real assault upon the spirit of the modern age and, manifested in many forms, as the fundamental threat to the highest good of that age, freedom and tolerance. Thus to a great extent the concept of dialogue, which certainly held an important place in the Platonic and in the Christian tradition, has acquired a different meaning. It has become the very epitome of the relativist credo, the concept opposed to that of 'conversion' and mission: dialogue in the relativist sense means setting one's own position or belief on the same level with what the other person believes, ascribing to it, on principle, no more of the truth than to the position of the other person. Only if my fundamental presupposition is that the other person may be just as much in the right as I am, or even more so, can any dialogue take place at all. Dialogue, it is said, has to be an exchange between positions that are fundamentally of equal status and thus mutually relative, with the aim of achieving a maximum of cooperation and integration between various religious bodies and entities. The relativist elimination of Christology, and most certainly of ecclesiology, now becomes a central commandment of religion. To turn back to Hick: the belief in the divinity of an individual, he tells us, leads to fanaticism and particularism, to the dissociation of faith from love; and this is the thing that must be overcome.[46]

The Recourse to Asian Religions

In the thought of J. Hick, whom we have particularly in mind here as a prominent representative of religious relativism, the postmetaphysical philosophy of Europe converges in a remarkable way with the negative theology of Asia, for which the Divinity can never enter, in itself and undisguised, into the world of appearances in which we live: it only ever shows itself in relative reflections and in itself remains beyond all words and beyond all comprehension in absolute transcendence. In their starting points, as in the direction they give to human existence, the two philosophies are in themselves fundamentally different. Yet they appear nonetheless to support one another in their metaphysical and religious relativism. The a-religious and pragmatic relativism of Europe and America can borrow a kind of consecration from India, which seems to give its renunciation of dogma the dignity of a heightened reverence for the mystery of God and of man. Conversely, the way that European and American thinking has turned back to India's philosophical and theological vision has the effect of further strengthening that relativizing of all religious figures which is part of India's heritage. Thus it now actually seems imperative in India, even for Christian theology, to extract from its particularity the figure of Christ, regarded as Western, and to set it beside Indian redemption myths as if it were of similar status: the historical Jesus, so people now think, is actually no more uniquely the Logos than any other savior figures from history are. The fact that here, in the context of the encounter between cultures, relativism seems appropriate as the true philosophy of humanity gives it (as we have already suggested) such an appreciable impact, both in East and West, that it hardly seems possible to offer further resistance. Anyone who opposes it is not only setting himself against democracy and tolerance, that is the fundamental rules of human intercourse; he is obstinately insisting on the preeminence of his own Western culture and thus refusing to share in that coexistence of cultures which is obviously the order of the day. [. . .]

New Age

The relativism of Hick and Knitter and other related theories is ultimately based on a rationalism that holds that reason in Kant's sense is incapable of any metaphysical knowledge; religion is then given a new basis along pragmatic lines, with either a more ethical or a more political coloration. There is, however, a consciously antirationalist response to the experience that 'everything is relative', a complex reality that is lumped together under the title of New Age. The way out of the dilemma of relativism is now sought, not in a new encounter of the 'I' with the 'Thou' or the 'We', but in overcoming subjective consciousness, in a re-entry into

---

46   Cf., for example, J. Hick, *An Interpretation of Religion: Human Responses to the Transcendent*. New Haven: Yale University Press, 1989; Menke, *Einzigkeit Jesu Christi*. Freiburg: Johannes-Verlag, 1995, p. 90.

the dance of the cosmos through ecstasy. As in the case of Gnosis in the ancient world, this way believes itself to be fully in tune with all the teachings and the claims of science, making use of scientific knowledge of every kind (biology, psychology, sociology, physics). At the same time, however, it offers against this background a completely antirationalist pattern of religion, a modern 'mysticism': the absolute is, not something to be believed in, but something to be experienced. God is not a person distinct from the world; rather, he is the spiritual energy that is at work throughout the universe. Religion means bringing myself into tune with the cosmic whole, the transcending of all divisions . . ..

Objectifying reason, New Age thinking tells us, closes our way to the mystery of reality; existing as the self shuts us out from the fullness of cosmic reality; it destroys the harmony of the whole and is the real reason for our being unredeemed. Redemption lies in breaking down the limits of the self, in plunging into the fullness of life and all that is living, in going back home to the universe. [. . .] The gods are returning. They have become more credible than God. Aboriginal rites must be renewed in which the self is initiated into the mysteries of the universe and freed from its own self.

There are many reasons for the renewal of pre-Christian religions and cults that is being widely undertaken today. If there is no truth shared by everyone, a truth that is valid simply because it is true, then Christianity is merely a foreign import, a form of spiritual imperialism, which needs to be shaken off just as much as political imperialism. If what takes place in the sacraments is not the encounter with the one living God of all men, then they are empty rituals that mean nothing and give us nothing and, at best, allow us to sense the numinous element that is actively present in all religions. It then seems to make better sense to seek after what was originally our own than to permit alien and antiquated things to be imposed on us. But above all, if the 'rational intoxication' of the Christian mystery cannot make us intoxicated with God, then we just have to conjure up the real, concrete intoxication of effective ecstasies, the passionate power of which catches us up and turns us, at least for a moment, into gods, helps us for a moment to sense the pleasure of infinity and to forget the misery of finite existence. The more the pointlessness of political absolutisms becomes obvious, the more powerful will be the attraction of irrationalism, the renunciation of everyday reality.

Pragmatism in Everyday Church Life

Side by side with these radical solutions, and side by side also with the greater pragmatism of the liberation theologies, there is also the gray pragmatism at work in the everyday life of the Church, whereby everything is apparently being done right, yet in reality the faith is stale and declining into a shabby meanness. I am thinking of two phenomena that I regard with some concern. On one hand, there are attempts, some more determined than others, to extend the majority principle to matters of faith and morals and, thus, to 'democratize' the Church in a decided fashion. What is not obvious to the majority cannot have any binding claim upon

us, so it seems. Majority of whom, in fact? Will this majority be different tomorrow
from what it is today? A faith we can decide for ourselves is no faith at all. And
no minority has any reason to allow a majority to prescribe what it should believe.
Either the faith and its practice come to us from the Lord by way of the Church
and her sacramental services, or there is no such thing. [. . .]

The other point I would raise concerns the liturgy. The various phases of liturgical
reform have allowed people to gain the impression that liturgy can be changed
as and how you wish. If there is any unchanging element, people think, then this
would in no instance be anything other than the words of consecration: everything
else might be done differently. The next idea is quite logical: If a central authority
can do that, then why not local decision-making bodies? And if local bodies, then
why not the congregation itself? It ought to be expressing itself in the liturgy and
should be able to see its own style recognizably present there. After the rationalist
and puritan trend of the seventies, and even the eighties, people are tired of liturgies that are just words and would like liturgies they can experience; and these
soon get close to New Age styles: a search for intoxication and ecstasy . [. . .]

The Tasks Facing Theology

Thus, all in all, we are facing a remarkable situation: liberation theology had tried
to give a new practice to a Christendom that was tired of dogma, a practice by
means of which redemption was finally to become an actual event. This practice,
however, instead of bringing freedom, left destruction in its wake. What was
left was relativism and the attempt to come to terms with it. Yet what that offers
is in its turn so empty that the relativist theories look for help from the liberation
theology, so as thus to become of more practical use. Finally, New Age says,
'Let's just leave Christianity as a failed experiment and go back to the gods – it's
better that way.' [. . .]

Prospect

If we look at the current constellation in the history of ideas that I have been
trying to sketch in outline, then it must seem like a real miracle that, despite all
this, people still hold the Christian faith . [. . .] Why has faith still any chance
at all? I should say it is because it corresponds to the nature of man. For man is
more generously proportioned than the way Kant and the various post-Kantian
philosophies see him or will allow him to be. Kant himself ought to have found
a place for this, somehow or other, among his postulates. The longing for the
infinite is alive and unquenchable within man. None of the attempted answers
will do; only the God who himself became finite in order to tear open our finitude
and lead us out into the wide spaces of his infinity, only he corresponds to the
question of our being. That is why, even today, Christian faith will come to man
again. It is our task to serve this faith with humble courage, with all the strength
of our heart and of our mind.

CHAPTER 6

TEACHING AND AUTHORITY: DIMENSIONS OF MAGISTERIUM

Gerard Mannion

Introduction

When it comes to the area of the specific teaching charisms and ministries of the church, along with the wider charism of teaching authority (magisterium),[1] which properly belongs to the Church entire, the borders between Joseph Ratzinger as private theologian and Joseph Ratzinger as Prefect for the CDF are more difficult to discern than in perhaps any other area of his theological corpus. This blurring of the dividing lines is evidenced by the discussions in the public domain as much as it is in the theological and ecclesiastical contexts alike.

Partly this is because when appointed to the CDF, Ratzinger quite naturally brought with him his own understanding of theology, magisterium and discussions in the Church that he had developed over the years (and particularly in the thirteen years or so preceding that appointment). Such an understanding would naturally influence his stewardship at the CDF. Over the course of his career, Ratzinger's perception of the nature and tasks of theology in relation to the articulation and explication of Church teaching entailed a good deal of reflection upon the parameters of what he believed Catholic theologians could and should say, write

---

1   For background to this concept cf. Richard R. Gaillardetz, *By What Authority? A Primer on Scripture, the Magisterium and the Sense of the Faithful.* Collegeville: Liturgical Press, 2003; Richard A. Gaillardetz, *Teaching with Authority.* Collegeville: Liturgical Press, 1997; Francis A. Sullivan, *Magisterium: Teaching Authority in the Roman Catholic Church.* Dublin: Gill & Macmillan, 1985; Michael A. Fahey, 'Magisterium', in Gerard Mannion and Lewis M. Mudge (eds), *The Routledge Companion to the Christian Church.* London and New York: Routledge, 2008, pp. 524–535; Yves Congar's two essays, 'A Semantic History of the Term "Magisterium"' and 'A Brief History of the Forms of the Magisterium and Its Relations with Scholars', both available in Charles E. Curran and Richard A. McCormick (eds.), *The Magisterium and Morality: Readings in Moral Theology.* No. 3. New York: Paulist Press, 1982, pp. 297–313 and 314–331; Ladislas Örsy, *The Church: Learning and Teaching. Magisterium, Assent and Dissent.* Collegeville MN: Michael Glazier, 1988, pp. 47–97; See, also, the collection of texts in Kenneth Wilson, 'The Magisterium: the Church and its Teaching', in Gerard Mannion, Richard Gaillardetz, Jan Kerkhofs and Kenneth Wilson (eds), *Readings in Church Authority.* Aldershot and Burlington VT: Ashgate, 2003, pp. 91–145.

about and teach vis-à-vis the Church's hierarchical authorities and their official pronouncements.

But the relationship also became circular for, as issues and debates arose during his time at the CDF, Ratzinger obviously continued to develop his thinking on the nature and tasks of the Catholic theologian and upon magisterium accordingly. Furthermore, there are numerous instances where Ratzinger would offer public and private commentary and explication of official Church teachings and pronouncements. Through his doing so, the dividing line between private theologian and Church official became blurred to a great extent, generating not a little controversy in the process. The latter was accentuated because the 'authority' of such private reflections, even when uttered in public at official venues, is quite rightly something very far removed from the requisite authority of official Church teachings *per se*. Unfortunately, too many in the Church and beyond fail to appreciate such a very important distinction.

And, as Aidan Nichols, who has authored a particularly sympathetic account of Ratzinger's theology, states: 'the cardinal's actions can hardly be separated from his ideas'.[2] Here, then, more than in most areas, the writings of the private theologian are closely related to the public pronouncements and actions of the Prefect.

Not surprisingly, Ratzinger's understanding of magisterium, including its nature and scope, and of theology and the role of the theologian in particular are, once again and quite naturally, shaped and informed by his ecclesiology. The intentions behind his writings in this area are familiarly focused upon a resolve to safeguard the integrity of Catholic doctrine, protect the Church from what he perceives to be overt accommodation to the 'spirit of the age' and ensure that theologians serve Rome in its teaching mission as opposed to critiquing the hierarchy in a quasi-democratic fashion, and therefore misleading and confusing the wider faithful.

Ratzinger believes Catholic theologians should primarily concern themselves with 'faithfully' explicating the teaching of the Church on behalf of the laity. Thus increasing and renewed centralization of teaching authority upon Rome and an emphasis upon obedience to Church teaching and to Church authorities are further defining features of his theological thought here. This is the case especially in the post-conciliar years, although, as we will see, there is also some consistency stretching back much earlier, despite the well-known more progressive soundings

---

2   Aidan Nichols, *The Thought of Benedict XVI: an Introduction to the Theology of Joseph Ratzinger*, London and New York, Burns & Oates/Continuum, 2005, p. 2 (the reissued edition of his The Theology of Joseph Ratzinger (1998).

made in relation to the rights of free theological enquiry when working for Cardinal Frings at Vatican II and even as late as when he was a signatory to the collective Nijmegen Declaration on those very same rights in 1968.

A synthesis of Ratzinger's understanding of these themes might go something like this. Theology finds its essential locus in the inherent human quest for truth and that truth is to be found in the Word, the revelation of God's own self in the person of Christ and continued to this day in the presence of the Spirit and served through the sacramental mission of the Church. The task of the Catholic theologian is to aid and explicate this quest, the sources of revelation and the means and path to salvation through Christ in the Church.

Theologians are not an alternative or counter magisterium to the papacy, college of bishops or Roman curia. They should not usurp the authority proper only to these other ecclesial entities. They are there to serve the Church. Thus, for example, the International Theological Commission (ITC), established by Pope Paul VI in 1969, is an advisory and consultative body. The ITC does not decide what constitutes Church teaching nor what it should be, but rather advises on how to explain Church teaching. A Catholic theologian has, first and foremost, an ecclesial vocation. They are to serve the Church and its (official) magisterium, not dictate to them. There are clear teachings that all must assent to. Theologians should not confuse the faithful by encouraging a 'pick and mix' attitude towards Church teaching. Rather, they should help explain the provenance and implications of such teaching.

Theological discourse, discussion and debate obviously remain valid but there is no such thing as legitimate 'dissent' from the authentic teaching of the official magisterium. Theologians must submit to the authority of that magisterium and should never seek to exploit the mass media in waging campaigns against Church authorities.

Theologians should be wary of following new trends, schools of thought and ideologies, particularly political ideologies, current in their day. Theology should critique these new cultural developments rather than become infected and enslaved by them. Above all else in recent times, the errors of relativism and pluralism must be resisted.

The task of the Roman Curia and particularly the CDF in 'defending the faith' is to exert vigilance in these times of flux and change. The deposit of the faith, including teaching on morals, must be protected from erroneous and misleading interpretations and novelties that might lead the simple faithful astray.

Where misleading ideas are taught or set down in publications, they must be examined, scrutinized and, where deemed to be at fault, the theologian in question should be investigated and, following due process, disciplined if necessary. Even when theologians become aware they are under investigation by Rome or, following such investigation, have been subject to disciplinary measures (such as being placed under a period of 'silence' for reasons of dissent), they should endure such in respectful acquiescence and try to understand the motives behind this necessary corrective action.

If a theologian proves obstinate in refusing to correct errors identified by the official magisterium, then they should no longer be considered to be a Catholic theologian and should be prevented from teaching and speaking in any institution or place connected with the Church in a fundamental fashion. Where possible, such as in the case of members of religious orders, further disciplinary actions should be taken to ensure such theologians no longer publish their erroneous viewpoints until or unless they admit to their faults and correct their ways.

The primary task of the bishop is to teach and preach the gospel. national Episcopal conferences are artificially created entities that have no teaching mandate as such – they are bodies created for discussion and consultation and have value that is of an administrative and functional nature in the main. There can be no question of Church teaching being decided by majority rule. For this reason the Synod of Bishops is also, in the main, a body that is consultative in character – its juridical nature being simply to advise the Pope. Bishops are urged to exercise in their dioceses the same vigilance that Rome does against erroneous and misleading forms of theology and to speak out against any practices that contravene the Church's teaching on morality.

For Ratzinger, magisterium equates to the central Church authorities and is necessarily hierarchical. Rome, i.e. the Vatican machinery, with the Pope at its head, exists to guide and watch over faith and morals around the world. All other authority to teach in the church is subservient to this. Thus an overview of Ratzinger's understanding of magisterium.

In an area where emotions can run high and where opinions are sharply divided, most would perhaps at least agree that Ratzinger's understanding of theology and magisterium have had a profound effect upon the Church in the post-Vatican II era. This stands true whether one regards Ratzinger as the steadfast defender of orthodoxy[3] (the nickname 'Panzerkardinal' was one accorded him equally by his supporters and critics alike) or whether one perceives his views here to be restrictive

3   A particularly sympathetic account of Ratzinger's understanding of the role and task of theology and of Catholic theologians vis-à-vis magisterium is again given by Aidan Nichols, 'Back to Foundations', in *The Thought of Benedict XVI: an Introduction to the Theology of Joseph Ratzinger*. London and New York: Burns & Oates/Continuum, 2005, pp. 225–240. The following chapter, 'The Prefect', is also of relevance to our discussions in this present chapter, pp. 241–291.

and detrimental to the flourishing of theology and the Church's life in general.

Whatever one's standpoint, what is beyond question is that the significant role that Ratzinger has played in the majority of changes and developments in relation to the understanding and exercise of Church teaching authority (i.e. magisterium) in recent decades has generated much discussion and disagreement.[4] Although once himself a university professor and therefore academic theologian, his relations with many other Catholic theologians would become increasingly strained from the late 1960s onwards. His development of the understanding of what the role and vocation of the Catholic theologian should be, appears to be markedly different from the understanding which many perceived to have emerged in consensus form following Vatican II.

It would be impossible (perhaps even negligent) to study Ratzinger's writings on magisterium and theology without reference to the wider ecclesial and cultural contexts during recent decades. This we shall seek to do below, offering but a sketch of some of the main developments and topics of attention pertaining to the themes of our chapter in this period.

Numerous studies rehearse the developments of how Vatican II marked a period of 'opening to the world' for the Church. Attendant with such an opening came a new era where theological innovation and new enquiry were not simply tolerated but actively encouraged. From the late 1960s onwards, many of those opposed to how Vatican II was being interpreted and implemented throughout the Church began to make their voices heard. Ratzinger's approach to these areas of ecclesial life was shaped by his own experiences of the late 1960s and particularly of the year 1968. This was a year of great upheavals, innovations and liberative developments, even revolutions. Seemingly everywhere, stagnant and life-denying authority was being challenged. But it was also a year of counteraction whereby challenges to authority and dissent began to be suppressed and reactionary forces sought to devise mechanisms and structures to try and ensure such challenges and dissent did not prevail.

As we shall see in one of our texts, shortly after that year Ratzinger argued that the Church had become all too embroiled in the wider trends and development of the world of that time. The Church mirrored in its own life the struggles witnessed in wider society. Thus 1968 signifies a watershed year in the ecclesial outlook of Ratzinger and most of his biographers also point to this fact.

---

4   Cf. Gerard Mannion, '"Defending the Faith": The Changing Landscape of Church Teaching Authority and Catholic Theology', in Gerard Mannion (ed.), *The Vision of John Paul II: Assessing His Thought and Influence*. Collegeville, MN: Liturgical Press, 2008, pp. 78–106, which assesses developments pertaining to these areas during the period 1978–2005.

Of course, by 1968 the aftermath of Vatican II was beginning to make itself felt in the Church, with great optimism in many quarters matched by a fear of the pace and shape of reform in others. One event perhaps encapsulates 1968 for Catholics more than most: the completion of the work of the Papal Birth Commission, which led to the issuing of the papal encyclical *Humanae Vitae*. The controversy over this letter and the open 'rebellion' against the 'official' magisterium that ensued, along with the resignations from active ministry of a large number of priests, led to a hardening of attitudes among the conservative-minded in positions of power in the Church. Further steps against perceived theological 'dissent' would follow throughout the coming decades.

1968 was the year that the Latin American Bishops would meet in Medellín – as growing momentum would set in motion the development and maturation of liberation theology. It was also the year in which the 'Nijmegen Statement' was released by Catholic theologians calling for greater freedom for Roman Catholic theologians. Although, as already noted, Joseph Ratzinger would sign that Statement, for himself, more significantly, 1968 was the year that he would become horrified at the student demonstrations in Tübingen and decide that perhaps too much openness and reform could in fact be bad, and that authority and discipline were as much necessary parts of Church life as they had ever been. Ratzinger abandoned Tübingen because of the student radicalism of the time, moving to the new University of Regensburg.

The understanding and exercise of the official magisterium would gradually be transformed over the coming decades in a very different sense to that envisioned in the Nijmegen document. This would emerge in piecemeal fashion at first, but then, with the advent of the pontificate of John Paul II, in a systematic and programmatic way that would transform the understanding and exercise not simply of the official magisterium, but of the role and task of the Roman Catholic theologian in general. Indeed the character of Catholic episcopal stewardship would equally be transformed.

Post-conciliar developments from the grass roots up to the level of national Episcopal conferences (such as in the Netherlands) had set alarm bells ringing in certain ecclesial quarters. Many believed the pace of reform was being handled badly (particularly in the case of the liturgy) or indeed was moving not only too fast but also in the wrong direction altogether. Indeed the actions of Episcopal conferences would come under similar scrutiny also. Eventually this would culminate in Ratzinger, as Prefect of the CDF, arguing vociferously that national Episcopal conferences have no teaching mandate at all.

The blame for such perceived ills was frequently laid at the door of theologians by disgruntled curial officials, bishops and Catholic pressure groups of a more conservative ecclesial outlook and disposition, some sections of the media and, of course, theologians of a different ilk to those perceived to be 'liberal'.

Thus the election of John Paul II in 1978 and his later appointment of Ratzinger as Prefect of the CDF in 1981 mark further defining moments. In the years which followed, punctuated with regular Roman interventions and documents, the nature and role of the Catholic theologian, the primacy of conscience and the notions of 'dissent' from official teaching would become much debated. A range of alternative assessments, involving concepts now established in a large corpus of literature as part of the discourse in this field, such as 'creative fidelity' and 'loyal disagreement', filled the pages of journals, edited collections and monographs. The emergence of new magisterial 'ways and means', including notions such as 'definitive doctrine', along with new regulations concerning the demand for assent from Catholic theologians become equally discussed, as did concerns about collegiality and the 'infallible' exercise of the teaching office. Joseph Ratzinger's theological perspectives would play a role in each of these debates.

Many scholars have expressed concern over what they perceive to be a more restrictive and renewed centralizing understanding and exercise of magisterium that has emerged in recent decades, and they particularly criticize Ratzinger's central role in these developments. In the opinion of those who hold such views, disagreement, dissent and even debate pertaining to 'official' teaching on many issues have been dealt with in a stern fashion. By the 1980s it became very clear that such 'dissent'[5] from 'official' teachings would not be tolerated in any fashion. An increasing number of scholars found themselves called to account before the Church authorities, following secretive investigations of their works by curial officials. Harsh penalties, even excommunication awaited those who would not, or who believed their consciences *could* not allow them to retract whatever they had said or written that was deemed unacceptable by the 'official Church'.

It was in this period, for example, that the clashes with liberation theology came to a head. It was the same period when Charles Curran was deprived of his licence to teach in a Catholic institution and removed from his post at the Catholic University of America, and relations between many moral theologians and the Vatican became especially strained.[6]

So this was a time of great controversy over the censure of individual

---

5   Cf. Charles E. Curran and Richard A. McCormick, *Dissent in the Church*, vol. 6 of *Readings in Moral Theology*. NY: Paulist Press, 1991.

6   Here see, in particular, Part Five of Curran and McCormick, *Dissent in the Church*, 1988, pp. 357–539 and also Charles E. Curran, *Loyal Dissent*. Washington DC: Georgetown University Press, 2006, *passim*.

theologians and theological schools of thought and the attempt to impose greater controls over Catholic faculties in Church-linked universities. The question of priests being involved in active politics was a further contentious issue, as were the numerous attempts to announce 'closure' on further disputed doctrinal and moral questions. Religious pluralism and the related debates concerning inculturation, and complementarity of different faiths became issues that would preoccupy Rome well into the twenty-first century.[7]

Attempts to exert ever greater control over who could teach in Catholic institutions, as well as over what they could teach and publish, along with a general attempt to bring theological enquiry in Catholic universities and seminaries under still closer scrutiny, were facilitated by documents such as the 1989 release of a new 'Profession of Faith and Oath of Fidelity', which lecturers and teachers of philosophy and theology in Catholic educational institutions were expected to make. In 1990, John Paul II issued a lengthy document on the nature and role of a Catholic university – *Ex Corde Ecclesiae* – which reinforced the obligatory demand that theologians apply for an official 'mandatum' to certify their perceived orthodoxy in line with the official teaching of the day.

One of the most decisive documents of all those issued throughout this period in an attempt to set down the 'official' understanding of these matters in hand was released in 1990, the CDF document, *Donum Veritatis (Instruction on the Ecclesial Vocation of the Theologian)*. This document set forth the CDF's understanding of the nature and task of theology as faith's quest for understanding, informed by reason and the word of God. The *Instruction* strongly asserts that the central Roman magisterium is the supreme authority in all matters pertaining to these quests, that is to matters relating to faith and morals. It defines what is deemed to be appropriate interaction between theologians and various cultures. It provides guidelines concerning the relation of theology and theologians to the ('official') magisterium, including defining when it may be appropriate for theologians to raise questions about elements of 'the' magisterium's teaching and when it would not be. In particular, the CDF here demands the faithful assent of theologians to Rome's magisterium and sets down definite parameters as to what constitutes legitimate areas of inquiry for Catholic theologians, as well as limiting the levels of permissible disagreement with official Church teaching (this document clearly underlines the perspective that 'dissent' is ruled out). Different responses are outlined

---

7   Cf., also, the discussion of these issues in Chapter Five of this volume.

corresponding to different forms of teaching.[8] It was the *Instruction* that gave birth to the highly controversial 'new' category of teaching known as 'definitive doctrine' (which is nonetheless, *not* irreformable). The Church is *not* a democracy, according to the instruction, and those theologians who apply the tenets of philosophical liberalism and political movements for greater democracy within the Church are in error.

The blurred dividing line between Ratzinger the private theologian and Ratzinger the Prefect of the CDF is further demonstrated by the fact that, in essence, this *Instruction* is also a very good summary of Ratzinger's own position on these issues, and was issued following reflection on various clashes between Rome and theologians throughout the 1970s and 80s. The commentary that Ratzinger offered on the *Instruction*, part of which we reproduce below, itself proved controversial and provoked protests about such a blurring of these important lines of division.

Further key documents would emerge in 1998 with the papal 'Motu Proprio' *Ad Tuendam Fidem*[9] and the commentary upon the 'Profession of Faith' (*Professio Fidei*), which the CDF, under Ratzinger, issued at the same time. The latter is a key example of those theological statements by Ratzinger of ambiguous authoritative status.[10]

Thus, essentially, such developments reflected a reinterpretation of the Church's teaching authority, i.e. its magisterium. This, in turn, was informed by the prevailing 'official' normative form of the *communio* ecclesiology.[11]

6.1 The Relationship between the Bishops and the Papacy

This writing comes from the period just before Vatican II and was originally in a collection of essays that Ratzinger co-authored with fellow-German Karl Rahner on episcopacy and primacy. These subjects were being debated widely at the time in both Roman Catholic and also wider Christian circles – Pope John XXIII had already called the Council and this inspired much discussion about the Church in every aspect. In this section, Ratzinger offers an interpretation of what Church teaching

---

8   William C. Spohn, 'The Magisterium and Morality: Notes on Moral Theology 1992', in *Theological Studies* 54 (1993) pp. 95–111. Cf., also, Francis A. Sullivan, 'The Theologian's Ecclesial Vocation and the 1990 CDF Instruction', in *Theological Studies* 52 (1991) pp. 51–68.

9   In effect, *Ad Tuendam Fidem* was designed to incorporate fully the 1989 *Professio Fidei* into canon law, particularly with regards to the juridical penalties relating to one clause of that profession.

10   Joseph Ratzinger and Tarcisio Bertone, 'Commentary On The Profession of Faith's Concluding Paragraphs', 16 July 1998, E.T.: *The Tablet*, (11 July 1998), pp. 920–922.

11   See Chapter Three of this volume.

says about the relations between the papacy and the other bishops across the world.

Set against this background, and that of the wider divisions in Christianity, Ratzinger offers some reflections, in particular, upon the notion of apostolic succession and the ecclesial implications of such. It should be noted that when he refers to the 'Vatican Council' here, Ratzinger means the *First* Vatican Council (1869-70). In his introduction he states that he intends to concentrate only on 'truly open questions' that will aid the ecumenical cause through offering a better understanding of the nature of the Church.

Here Ratzinger argues that the Church's tradition is most faithfully represented by an emphasis upon neither the absolute supremacy of the papacy on the one hand nor upon the episcopacy and conciliarism on the other – rather both elements are fundamental to the right order of the Church, and the First Vatican Council taught as much. Ratzinger also cites the 1875 statement of the German bishops, which made clear that the bishops are far from being the mere pawns of the papacy, a sentiment that the then Pope, Pius IX, agreed with. Both the episcopate and primacy are of divine origin and neither one should be played off against the other, according to the judgement of Ratzinger.

Succession is linked to the early Church notion of *didache*, which meant both tradition and succession. The former is not seen as some static doctrine handed on, but rather a dynamism, the living word that is realized in faith. Succession is also not about inheriting power or office but is particular to the bearer of apostolic authority and responsibility to the word – to serve it. The office-holder is subservient to such a task in every sense, 'only a voice which renders the word articulate in the world'. In fact, tradition is here seen to be the *equivalent* of succession, understood both in terms of service and witness to the word of God. Both define one another: 'The succession is the external form of the tradition, and tradition is the content of the succession'. The word, here, means not simply the written word of scripture, but rather the word that is preached and heard. The sense of the 'living word' existed prior to the formation of the New Testament canon, therefore the notion of apostolic succession, so bound up with tradition as opposed to any notion that written scripture takes precedence over all, is more faithful to the beliefs of the actual New Testament communities and the later early Christian churches. Here Ratzinger delves into the debates about the nature and sources of revelation, although his position in this essay raises interesting questions in relation to the final version of Vatican II's Dogmatic Constitution on Divine Revelation, *Dei Verbum*.

It worth considering the themes discussed in this text at greater length here, for they have are closely related to so many other areas of

Ratzinger's theological corpus. In this reading, Ratzinger anticipates later debates and developments on issues pertaining to ecclesial office and authority which would figure prominently in the discussions throughout Vatican II and beyond.[12] The particular authority and role of the Papacy is discerned. Furthermore, Ratzinger offers pertinent reflections on the ecumenical implications of the Roman Catholic understanding of primacy, episcopacy and apostolic succession.[13] But of especial significance is that here we see, already, Ratzinger's deliberations concerning how the universal church relates to local churches. The very nature and purpose of catholicity looms large in an explicit fashion, just as the issues that would preoccupy Vatican II concerning Episcopal collegiality do so in a more implicit manner.

At the latter Council, the fathers would affirm the two-fold emphasis on Papal and Collegial authority, albeit with much debate leading to the insertion of a famous *Nota Praevia* (a preliminary note) into the Dogmatic Constitution on the Church, *Lumen Gentium*.[14] This note, which sought to clarify the notion of collegiality contained in chapter three of that Constitution, made clear that the College of Bishops exercises its authority only insofar as the Pope assents to it doing so.

Paul VI ordered the inclusion of the *Nota Praevia* to appease those attending the council who wished to downplay collegiality, fearing a dilution of papal authority in the direction of conciliarism. The interpretation of this note has generated a great deal of literature and discussion since. Some have interpreted it as placing rigid limitations upon the exercise of Episcopal collegiality, others perceive it to have been a necessary mode of reassuring council fathers with doubts or who wished to have ambiguities clarified, in order that *Lumen Gentium* could finally be promulgated.[15] But there was certainly opposition to the *Nota Praevia* at the time and many scholars since have suggested that the final text remained ambiguous on these very questions, not least of all *because* of the insertion of the *Nota Praevia*.

---

12   Not surprisingly, given the debates current at the time and the volume in which this essay originally appeared, particularly given the contributions offered by Karl Rahner in the same volume.

13   The volume in which Ratzinger's essay featured was specifically written with ecumenical concerns in mind.

14   Although the *Nota* was actually added to the text as an appendix.

15   Here an excellent discussion on the issue of collegiality is given by Paul Lakeland, 'John Paul II and Collegiality' in Gerard Mannion (ed.): *The Vision of John Paul II: Assessing his Thought and Influence.* Michael Glazier/Liturgical Press: 2008), 184-199 esp. 188-191. See, also, Paul Lakeland, '*Lumen Gentium*: The Unfinished Business', *New Blackfriars*, vol. 90 no. 1026 (March 2009), 146-162. Cf., also, the informative earlier essay by Karl Rahner, 'On the Relationship between the Pope and the College of Bishops' in *Theological Investigations*, Vol. 10, (1973), 50-70. An equally excellent full-length study of the concept of apostolicity for these times is John Burkhardt, *Apostolicity Then and Now: An Ecumenical Church in a Postmodern World.* Collegeville, MN: Liturgical Press, 2004.

There is evidence that Ratzinger voiced opinions against the *Nota Praevia* at the Council, and we have earlier mentioned his essay in the first issue of *Concilium*, which appeared to be assertive in its support of collegiality.[16] But although our text here suggests that Ratzinger is offering, in a number of cases, idiosyncratic definitions and interpretations of key ecclesiological and wider theological concepts, it also demonstrates that there is a most worthwhile debate to be had concerning whether and to what extent his views on the core issues here fluctuated during this period and beyond. Our text shows Ratzinger not so far from the consensus of Vatican II on the dual nature of the church's supreme authority and although there is even a slightly greater emphasis upon the primacy and authority of the papacy, as would be reflected in the *Nota Praevia*.

On the other hand, despite the fact that, in many respects, the *Concilium* article is now adjudged to be the main exception to his thoughts in these areas, it is also significant that the following text which, we must remember, predates the *Concilium* article, has Ratzinger arguing that Rome and the Papacy require the rest of the church in order to be truly Catholic as much as vice-versa. Nonetheless, in the final analysis, the overall emphasis here does appear to remain upon Rome and the Papacy. Perhaps the *Concilium* article reflects the tide of enthusiasm concerning collegiality and synodality that emerged increasingly towards the close of Vatican II.

But Ratzinger's critics would point out how, in later years, he would appear to shift from the dual emphasis upon authority settled upon at Vatican II and reflected in this reading, in practice if not also in spirit, towards an increasingly still greater emphasis upon the priority of papal authority. Such critical voices would point out how, in particular, Ratzinger played down the teaching authority of national Episcopal conferences and how he would have a major part in ensuring that the synods of bishops essentially became gatherings where the agendas and conclusions were, in effect, dictated in advance by Rome (cf. reading 6.2, below). Local bishops were left in no doubt that Rome expected obedience in all matters during his time at the CDF. Furthermore, those of other Christian traditions would protest that this text contains an over-generalizing portrayal of how various Protestant churches perceive tradition, authority and scripture.

Ratzinger's influence on later official church teachings on episcopacy, primacy and collegiality have proved controversial in that the much-hoped for blossoming of Episcopal collegiality at Vatican II has failed to

---

16   'The Pastoral Implications of Episcopal Collegiality', in *Concilium*, vol. 1. Glen Rock, NJ: Paulist, 1964, pp. 39–67. See Chapter Three.

materialise, being supplanted instead by ever-more Roman centralisation of authority. So it is worth considering whether it is possible to see the embryonic standpoint of the later church leader present here already. Certainly, the (negative) ecumenical implications of Ratzinger's later position on these issues are also foreshadowed in our reading, albeit perhaps also reflecting the period during which they were composed. But, at the time of its composition, is it possible that Ratzinger's thought could have gone in another direction, as suggested by interpretations of the *Concilium* article? One can certainly identify continuity on many points between the *Concilium* text and our reading, below. However, Ratzinger, himself, appears to suggest not in his many later contributions on all these issues.[17] Naturally, Ratzinger would have developed his thoughts in the light of the council. But, all in all, the text below is also characterised by a dialectical approach which demands greater hermeneutical reflection still to determine the true position of its author on given issues.[18] And what is of particular further interest here is Ratzinger's statement in the following text, which somewhat foreshadows aspects of John Paul II's groundbreaking invitation to debate concerning the nature of the papacy in *Ut Unum Sint* (1995),

[The Pope] 'is the sign of the true "ecumene" and it in its turn is the sign which authenticates him. Precisely because of the inner nature of his infallibility, he needs the testimony of the "ecumene", of an episcopate which consists not of papal officials, shadows of himself, but of bishops in their own divine right, whose concrete "ecumene" visibly attests and fulfils his inner and essential "ecumene"'.[19]

Perhaps, some forty-five years after the publication of Ratzinger's famous essay in *Concilium*, it is time to consider the pastoral as well as the wider ecclesial implications of the failure for Episcopal collegiality to become an empowering reality in the post-conciliar church. Ratzinger's words in

17 For example, Ratzinger's article, 'Anglican-Catholic Dialogue: Its Problems and Hopes', *Insight*, vol. 1, no 3 (March 1983), 5, would appear to echo his sentiments on page 39f of the original of this reading (see page 194f., below).

18 Here an informative discussion is Charles M. Murphy, 'Collegiality: An Essay toward better Understanding', in *Theological Studies*, 46 (1985), 38-49.

19 Joseph Ratzinger, 'Primacy, Episcopate and Apostolic Succession', in Karl Rahner and Joseph Ratzinger, *The Episcopate and the Primacy*. New York: Herder and Herder, 1962, 62-63. See, below, p. 199-200. Here also cf. the reflections which eventually followed a CDF symposium on papal primacy in December 1996 ('Il Primato del Successore di Pietro, Atti del Simposio teologico', Rome, 2-4 December 1996, Libreria Editrice Vaticana, Vatican City, 1998) in Joseph Ratzinger and Tarcisio Bertone, 'The Primacy of the Successor of Peter in the Mystery of the Church', *L'Osservatore Romano*, English edn. (November 18th 1998), 5-6. The latter text also aids with the hermeneutical discernment of Ratzinger's position on such issues and of the continuity or otherwise with his earlier self.

the following text, that we must avoid playing the papacy and episcopate off against one another and that theologians can help here in helping to make relations between the two more fruitful, perhaps also deserve closer consideration.[20] Certainly his exhortation to attend to 'truly open questions'[21] remains most pertinent in all considerations of teaching and authority in the Church.

[. . .]. *The Teaching of the Church on Primacy and Episcopate*[22]
Let us then first ask what is the certain teaching of the Church, the data which we can and must presuppose in discussion both among Catholics and with others. First, it is the certain teaching of the Church that the pope has immediate, ordinary, truly episcopal power of jurisdiction over the whole Church.[23] The Vatican Council calls the primacy of the pope the apostolic primacy, and the Roman See the apostolic see.[24] Thus in the realm of doctrine the pope, in his official capacity, is infallible, his *ex cathedra* decisions being irreformable *ex sese*[25] and not in virtue of the Church's subsequent confirmation. So far as *communio* is concerned, the other pillar of the Church, it follows that only he who is in communion with the pope lives in the true *communio* of the body of the Lord, *i.e.*, in the true Church.

Contrasted with these certain truths about the pope stand a series of truths, equally certain, about the nature of the episcopal office. If on the one hand the papal see is called the apostolic see and his primacy is called apostolic, it is also true that the bishops '*in Apostolorum locum successerunt*'.[26] While the pope is accorded ordinary episcopal power in the whole Church, so that one might have the impression that the bishops were only executive organs of this power, it is declared on the other hand that they are 'instituted by the Holy Ghost'[27] and that they are 'of divine right'. That is, they are not of papal right; the pope cannot suppress them since they are as much part and parcel of the divinely appointed structure of the Church as he.

20   See pp. 44–45 in the original.
21   Page 39 in the original.
22   [Sections from 'Primacy, Episcopate and Apostolic Succession', in Karl Rahner and Joseph Ratzinger, *The Episcopate and the Primacy*. New York: Herder and Herder, 1962, 37–63, (original: *Episkopat und Primat*. Quaestiones disputatae 11. Freiburg im Breisgau: Herder 1961, 2nd end., 1963). A different translation appears in Joseph Ratzinger, *God's Word: Scripture, Tradition, Office*. San Francisco, Ignatius Press: 2008, pp. 13–39].
23   Dz. [H. Denzinger, *Enchiridion Symbolorum, Definitionum et Declarationum de Rebus Fidei et Morum*, various editions since 1852, with 30th edn. revised by Karl Rahner in 1954 (Freiburg im Breisgau: Herder) – with subsequent revisions following the time of Ratzinger's writing here] 1827, 1831.
24   Dz. 1832, 1836.
25   The two orders of '*communio*' and 'doctrine' are expressly placed side by side in Dz. 1827: '. . . *ita ut, custodita cum Romano Pontifice tam communionis quam ejusdem fidei professionis unitate, Ecclesia Christi sit unus grex sub uno sumtno pastore.*'
26   Dz. 1828.
27   CJC, [*Codex Juris Canonici* (Code of Canon Law)] can. 329, par. 1.

Dom Olivier Rousseau recently drew the attention of theologians to a sadly neglected document, which he rightly judges to be an authentic commentary on the Vatican Council. One could indeed look on it as a sort of postscript to the tract *De episcopo*, which the Council did not embark upon. It is, at any rate, a most important supplement for it provides the key to the full meaning of the Vatican decrees. It is the 'Collective Statement of the German Episcopate concerning the Circular of the German Imperial Chancellor in respect of the Coming Papal Election', of the year 1875, which received the express and unqualified endorsement of Pius IX.[28] Rousseau summarizes the content of this document in seven points.

1. The pope cannot arrogate to himself the episcopal rights, nor substitute his power for that of the bishops;
2. the episcopal jurisdiction has not been absorbed in the papal jurisdiction;
3. the pope was not given the entire fullness of the bishops' powers by the decrees of the Vatican Council;
4. he has not virtually taken the place of each individual bishop;
5. he cannot put himself in the place of a bishop in each single instance, *vis-à-vis* governments;
6. the bishops have not become instruments of the pope;
7. they are not officials of a foreign sovereign in their relations with their own governments.[29]

If, in light of this document, one re-examines the Vatican pronouncements on the primacy, then it cannot be denied that they are much deeper and also much less simple than theological textbooks commonly indicate.

Now if we consider the paragraph *De R. Pontificis et episcoporum jurisdictione*,[30] often lightly passed over, then we see that it brings into the doctrine on the primacy that same dialectic which characterizes the Council's notion of faith and revelation. Once again there are two series of statements confronting each other and not easily brought into a simple unity. Only as they stand can they approximately express the whole, no less complicated, reality. To borrow the expression of Heribert Schauf, the Church is not like a circle, with a single centre, but like an ellipse with two foci, primacy and episcopate.[31]

28 O. Rousseau, 'La vraie Valeur de L'Épiscopat dans l'Église d'après d'importants documents de 1875', in *Irénikon* 29 (1956), pp. 121–150. Rousseau rightly pointed out that this is a text that ought to be included in 'Denzinger'.
29 The German translation from Rousseau in *Una Sancta* 12 (1957) p. 227. (The English was checked with the original French of Rousseau.) In footnote 6 of Rousseau's article a similar statement by Cardinal van Roey is mentioned. Note 4 refers to a corresponding declaration of the English bishops and of Cardinal Dechamps. The texts of the double acknowledgement of the Pope are on p. 225 ff.
30 Dz. 1828.
31 H. Schauf, *De Corpore Christi Mystico*. Freiburg: Herder, 1959, 307.

We can express this in terms of the history of dogma. In the centuries-long struggle between episcopalism-conciliarism on the one side and papalism on the other, the Vatican Council is not at all a clear victory for the latter, as it might well seem to the superficial observer. According to the classical papalism of the Middle Ages, 'the hierarchical culmination of the priesthood in the episcopate, i.e, the jurisdictional superiority of the bishop' was 'a disciplinary measure of the Church', explained by the consideration that 'the pope, simply as a matter of fact, is not in a position to shepherd and govern all the faithful'. The pope can, according to this theory, 'define, narrow or even suppress the jurisdictional power of a bishop at any time'.[32] The Vatican Council stands for a condemnation of papalism as much as of episcopalism. Actually, it brands both doctrines as erroneous and, in place of one-sided solutions stemming from late theology or power politics, it establishes the dialectic of the reality we have from Christ.

In the great historical struggle between the two powerful movements, the Vatican Council takes neither side, but creates a new position, which, transcending all human constitutional thought, formulates the special quality of the Church, which comes not from the discretion of men, but in the final analysis, from the word of God.

Our investigation into the teaching of the Church has thus led us into the midst of the problems connected with these matters of certainty, and, of course, also made clear their limits. Episcopate and primacy in the Church are, according to the Catholic Faith, of divine origin. There can be no question, consequently, of the Catholic theologian playing one off against the other; he can only attempt to understand more deeply the vital relationship between the two.

If now in our quest we begin with the notion of word, we are led to the notion of *successio*. This notion was not derived (at least not primarily) from a consideration of *communio*, but rather from the struggle for the 'word', and is more germane to this context, even though objectively it necessarily connotes the aspect of *communio*. The problem of primacy and episcopate is mirrored in the notion of succession inasmuch as it is said on the one hand that the bishops are the successors of the apostles, while on the other, the predicate *apostolicus* is reserved to the pope in a special way. Thus the question arises whether there is a double succession and therefore a double participation in apostolicity.

2. Reflections on the Nature of the Apostolic Succession in General

The notion of succession, as the German Protestant theologian von Campenhausen has shown, was clearly formulated in the anti-gnostic polemics of the second century.[33] Its purpose was to oppose to the pseudo-apostolic tradition of Gnosis,

---

32   This was the view of one of the earliest advocates of papalism, Herveus Natalis (d. 1323). The quotations are from L. Hoedl, *De Jurisdictione. Ein unveröffentlichter Traktat des Herveus Natalis O. P. über die Kirchengewalt.* Munich, 1959, p. 11.

33   Hans von Campenhausen, *Kirchliches Amt und geistliche Vollmacht in den ersten drei Jahrhunderten.*

the true apostolic tradition of the Church. Thus from the beginning it was very closely connected with the question of true apostolicity. But first and foremost, it is clear that *successio* and *traditio*, as first used, meant practically the same thing, and indeed were expressed by the same word διαδοχή [didache], which meant both tradition and succession. 'Tradition' is never a simple, anonymous passing on of doctrine, but is personal, is the living word, concretely realized in the faith. And 'succession' is not a taking over of official powers, which then are at the disposal of their possessor, but is rather a dedication to the word, an office of bearing witness to the treasure with which one has been entrusted. The office is superior to its holder, so that he is entirely overshadowed by that which he has received; he is, as it were — to adopt the image of Isaiah and John the Baptist — only a voice which renders the word articulate in the world.

The office, the apostolic succession is grounded in the word. That is as true today as then. What was the situation then? To the Christianity of the Church the Gnostics opposed their own tangled philosophy of religion, which they represented as a secret tradition from the apostles. Against this the defenders of the Church declared that it was in the Church that those communities were to be found in which the apostles themselves had laboured, or which had received apostolic letters. In these communities the line of succession could be traced back, as it were, to the lips of an apostle. The men who were now their leaders could trace their spiritual lineage back to the apostles [. . .].

We see here very clearly how in fact succession equals tradition. Succession means cleaving to the apostolic word, just as tradition means the continuance of authorized witnesses. Beyond the instrumental role of Gnosis [. . .], the Church, in formulating the principle of succession (tradition), adapted for herself a method of the ancient philosophers who, in their schools, had first practised a way of drawing up lists of succession.[34] This may be so, though the state of the sources hardly allows a fully definitive judgment. For the rest, must not the word of God and the reality based on it always make use of human relationships in order to express itself among men? However, if by this von Campenhausen meant to show that biblical theology takes precedence over a later, and thus secondary, theology of succession-tradition, then we must regard this as an error. Christians had already formulated the principle of *successio-traditio* before they yet understood the New Testament as 'Scripture'. Therefore they could not formulate this as a biblical principle from the New Testament [. . .].

Let us not be deceived: The existence of writings which concerned the New Covenant and were acknowledged as apostolic, does not yet imply the existence of a New Testament as 'Scripture'. [. . .] Before the idea of New Testament Scripture, as a 'canon', was formulated the Church had already worked out

Tübingen: J. C. B. Mohr (Siebeck), 1953, pp. 163-194.
34   Ibid., p. 183.

another notion of canon. She had her Scripture indeed in the Old Testament, but this Scripture needed a canon, that is, a rule of interpretation, in accordance with the New Christian Covenant. This the Church found in tradition, guaranteed by succession. 'Canon', as von Harnack once drastically formulated it, 'was originally the rule of faith; actually, Scripture entered into it only afterwards.'[35] Before the New Testament itself became Scripture, it was faith which interpreted the 'Scripture,' *i.e.*, the Old Testament. Of course the other extreme, also erroneous, must be rejected. The Church opposed Gnosis with the living διαδοχή which is, as we have seen, *traditio* and *successio* all in one: the word bound up with a witness, and the witness bound to the word. But that did not mean that the Church intended to canonize an oral tradition of doctrine as something parallel to Scripture. Quite the contrary: she formulated the principle precisely to defend herself against the gnostic allegation of a παράδοσις ἄγραφος, (an unwritten tradition). The uninterrupted διαδοχή (παράδοσις) ἀποστολιχή of the Church was for the early anti-gnostic theologians precisely the proof that there was no such thing as the παράδοσις ἄγραφος which the Gnostics preached (at least in the form alleged by the Gnostics). Whatever might be the terminological dependence, παράδοσις (διαδοχή) meant something entirely different on the two sides — in fact the exact opposite. In Gnosis it meant exhaustive doctrines of allegedly apostolic origin. But in the theology of the Church it meant the connection of the living faith with the authority of the Church, embodied in the episcopal succession. The Church did not appeal to the παράδοσις in order to assert unwritten apostolic doctrines as a source of revelation parallel to Scripture; but precisely in order to deny the existence of such a secret heritage. For her, παράδοσις meant that in the community of the New Covenant the 'Scriptures' (*i.e.*, the Old Testament) are subordinate to the living interpretation of the faith which has come down from the apostles. The central instruments of this interpretation are the New Testament Scriptures and the Creed which sums them up, but they are instruments in the service of the living faith, which has its concrete form in the διαδοχή. [. . .]

Thus it emerges that apostolic tradition and apostolic succession define each other. The succession is the external form of the tradition, and tradition is the content of the succession. At the same time this relationship contains the justification of both principles. In fact, there is really only one principle, the decisive one which separates Catholic Christianity (Roman or Greek) from that group of Christians who renounce the *cognomen* Catholic, and are content with the Gospel alone for their title. For to accord priority to the living word of preaching over Scripture alone is genuinely in keeping with the New Testament . [. . .]

But can we really treat succession and the word as opposites? Undoubtedly, only if we take the word to mean exclusively the written word, *i.e.*, a book. But can we really assume that the New Testament is thinking of a book when it speaks

---

35   A. von Harnack, [. . . *Lehrbuch der Dogmengeschichte* I (Tübingen, 5th edn., 1931)], vol. II, p. 87, note 3 [. . .].

of the word? It is true that later generations come to the faith through the word; but in the perspective of the Bible, not as *readers,* but as *hearers* of the word. [. . .]

That is to say that if true apostolic succession is bound up with the word, it cannot be bound up merely with a book, but must, as the succession of the word, be a succession of preachers, which in turn cannot exist without a 'mission', *i.e.*, a personal continuity reaching back to the apostles. Precisely for the sake of the word, which in the New Covenant is not to consist in dead letters but in a living voice, a living succession is necessary. Ultimately the theology of word and Scripture in the New Testament supplies even stronger confirmation of the concept of succession as formulated by early anti-gnostic theology than the increasingly widespread recognition that the rite of conferring an office by imposition of hands, taken over from Judaism, must go back to the Jewish beginnings of Christianity.

Finally, it is precisely and only in such an understanding of the gift of the Word to the Church, that man is forced, continually and in all earnestness, into the position of a 'Hearer of the Word', a hearer who himself has not power over the Word, but remains in that purely receptive frame of mind which is called 'believing'. [. . .]

To sum up, the Church at first opposed to the gnostic notion of secret, unwritten traditions not Scripture but the principle of succession. Apostolic succession is essentially the living presence of the Word in the person of the witness. The unbroken continuity of witnesses follows from the nature of the Word as *auctoritas* and *viva vox*.

3. Papal Succession and Episcopal Succession: Their Relation and Differences

The anti-gnostic theology of succession extends a good deal further than we have shown into the problematic area of the question of 'primacy and episcopate'. In proof of their error the Gnostics were not referred to the Episcopal office as such in the Church, but to the apostolic sees, *i.e.*, those sees where the apostles had once worked or which had received apostolic letters. In other words not every Episcopal see was apostolic, but only that limited number which stood in a unique and special relationship to the apostles. These were centres of apostolic witness with which all other sees had to align themselves. [. . .] From this we can draw a number of important conclusions:

1. Early Catholic theology in the context of the question of succession, uses the word 'apostolic' in a very precise and strictly defined sense. It is used to designate only that very limited number of sees standing in special relation to the apostles, a relation other sees do not enjoy.
2. This is not in any way to dispute the apostolic succession of all bishops. But the majority of bishops, those not in apostolic sees, succeed only by a circuitous route, i.e., through an apostolic see. They are apostolic indirectly, not directly. They are legitimately apostolic only because they are in communion with an

apostolic sees. The practice of 'communion' in the ancient Church which must be considered the means by which Church unity was then effected, worked on this principle. The apostolic sees were the criterion of the true, i.e., the Catholic communion. Whoever was in communion with them was in the Catholic church, for these sees could not, by their very nature, exist outside the Church. Thus the Catholicity of a see was not measured simply by its size, but by its 'weight', or importance: that importance, however, depended on apostolicity.

3. To this extent it can be said that theology draws a very real distinction between two forms of apostolic succession, one direct and the one indirect. The latter needs communion with the former in order to remain Catholic, and, therefore in the full sense of the word, apostolic.

4. Among the apostolic sees, there is in turn *the* apostolic see, Rome, which bears approximately the same relation to the other apostolic sees as they do to those which are not directly apostolic. Thus Rome is the final, proper, and self-sufficient criterion of Catholicity.

Taken together, these points establish that the theology of apostolic succession, at the moment when it was first formulated as such and when the Church thus first undertook consciously to define her own nature, i.e., to formulate the 'canon' of her being, was neither an Episcopal theology nor indeed a papal theology. It was dual, distinguishing the 'episcopate' from the apostolic sees – the latter supremely embodied in the one See of Rome. If succession is the concrete form of the word then from the very beginning it exhibits that most intense (perhaps scandalous) concreteness, which consists in being ultimately bound to the Roman line of succession. Here all anonymity ceases. [. . .]

One further point. It is clear that the duality set up by the earliest theology of succession with its emphasis on apostolic sees has nothing to do with the later patriarchal theory. Confusion between the primitive claim of the apostolic see and the administrative claim of the patriarchal city characterizes the tragic beginning of conflict between Constantinople and Rome. [. . .] The overshadowing of the old theological notion of the apostolic see – an original part, after all, of the Church's understanding of her own nature – by the theory of five patriarchs must be understood as the real harm done in the quarrel between East and West. [. . .]

The actual content of the Roman claim is expressed by the concept of the apostolic see in centripetal fashion, yet the same concept also connotes an orientation to the fullness of the Church. We get, therefore, the following picture: The Church is the living presence of the divine Word. This presence is made concrete in those persons (the bishops) whose basic function is to hold fast to the word, who are, then, the personal embodiment of 'tradition' (παράδοσις) and to this extent are in the apostolic 'succession' (διαδοχή). Conspicuous among the successors of the apostles is the line of the apostolic sees, which ultimately is concentrated in the See of Peter and Paul. This is the touchstone of all apostolic succession. Thus the 'bishops' are first of all referred to Rome, for only communion with Rome gives them Catholicity and that fullness if apostolicity without which they would not be true bishops. Without communion with Rome one cannot be in the *Catholica*. This reference of the bishops to Rome is the primary relationship to be ascertained.

On the other hand, the Episcopal see of Rome itself does not stand in isolation, devoid of relationships. It creates their Catholicity for other sees, but precisely for this reason it also needs Catholicity. It sets up the essential order of Catholicity; and precisely because of this it needs the reality of Catholicity. Just as, on the one hand, it guarantees essential Catholicity, so on the other hand real Catholicity stands warranty for it. Just as the other sees need the apostolic testimony of Rome in order to be Catholic, so Rome needs their Catholic testimony, the testimony of real fulness, in order to remain true. Without the testimony of reality, Rome would negate its own meaning. A pope who would excommunicate the entire episcopate could never exist, for a Church which had become *only* Roman would no longer be Catholic. Both are simultaneously included in the notion of Catholicity properly understood. The universal claim of the pope and the inherent limitation of this claim, which remains bound to the basic law of fulness, and so to the divine right of the bishops.

This opens up another important vista on that question in which the problem of the word is crucially condensed, the question of the infallibility of the Church; or put another way, of the relation between episcopal (conciliar) and papal infallibility. [. . .] It can be established that episcopal-conciliar infallibility, by its nature, can never legitimately conflict with papal infallibility. An 'ecumenical' council which took sides against the pope, would thereby betray its non-ecumenicity, since after all a council held without or against the See of St. Peter is not ecumenical, ecumenicity depending essentially on the participation of Rome, the supreme apostolic see.[36] The majority of the bishops has, from time immemorial in the Church, been determined not simply by the externally greater number, but by the 'weight' of the sees. And there can be no number large enough to counterbalance the weight of the See of St. Peter. Anything else would mean substituting some sort of profane arithmetic for the holy bond of tradition.[37] To this extent a council is never an independent subject of infallibility, distinct from, or even against, the pope. For the pope is himself a bishop, *the* ecumenical bishop, without whom the episcopate would never have its full number, nor above all its 'full weight', but would necessarily have to be judged 'too light'. Thus it is that the decrees of

---

36 [It could be argued that Ratzinger is being ahistorical here, given the nature of the convening of even the councils of Nicaea and Chalcedon but, more specifically, examples such as the Council of Constance and the resolution of the western schism, when at one time there were three different popes at one and the same time].

37 [Note certain parallels here with Ratzinger's later stern rebukes against the notion of democracy in the church].

the pope are *ex sese* irreformable.[38]

On the other hand, since the pope is the ecumenical bishop he cannot and may not, by reason of his office, stand against the 'ecumene'. He is the sign of the true 'ecumene' and it in its turn is the sign which authenticates him. Precisely because of the inner nature of his infallibility, he needs the testimony of the 'ecumene', of an episcopate which consists not of papal officials, shadows of himself, but of bishops in their own divine right, whose concrete 'ecumene' visibly attests and fulfils his inner and essential 'ecumene'. Even after the definition of papal infallibility, indeed because of it, a council has its necessary and immutable meaning.

Let us finally turn once more to the religious-statistical formula 'Roman Catholic' with which we started. Basically it reflects the entire complex of problems which we have gone through in the course of these considerations. In that it says 'Catholic' it is distinguished from a Christianity based on Scripture alone, and instead acknowledges faith in the authority of the living word, i.e., in the office of the apostolic succession. In that it says 'Roman' it firmly refers this office to its centre, the office of the keys vested in the successor of the St. Peter in the city consecrated by the blood of two apostles. By uniting the two in 'Roman Catholic' it expresses the pregnant dialectic between primacy and episcopate, neither of which exists without the other. A church which wished to be only 'Catholic', having no part with Rome, would thereby lose its Catholicity. A church which *per impossible*, wished to be only Roman without being Catholic, would similarly deny herself and degenerate into a sect. 'Roman' guarantees true Catholicity; actually Catholicity attests Rome's right.

But at the same time the formula expresses the twofold breach running through the Church: the breach between 'Catholicism' and the Christianity of the mere written word; the breach between Christianity based upon the Roman office of Peter, and Christianity severed from it. In both cases it is ultimately the 'office' which causes the parting of the ways. Does this not recall in terrible fashion that quarrelling began even among Christ's disciples for the places to the right and to the left of the master, that is, for the offices in the coming messianic kingdom? And ought it not to recall to both sides the words of the Lord, that the greatest must be as the least, and servant of all?[39] This is not to do away with the office; the mandate to Peter and the mandate to the apostles are not withdrawn. But it is a demand of ultimate urgency addressed both to those who, vested with the office, are preachers of the word, and to their listeners. To the former that they should strive to be in very truth *servi servorum Dei*;[40] to the latter, not to refuse to be outwardly the 'last' in order to know, in humble joy, that, precisely thus and not otherwise, they are first. Only if both – those in office and those without

38   Dz. [Denzinger] 1839.
39   Mark. 9: 33ff. Mark 10: 35-45.
40   [Servants of the Servants of God].

– seek the spirit of the Gospel in unconditional integrity can there be hope for a union of those who would never have been torn asunder without a denial of this spirit.

6.2 The Structure and Task of the Synod of Bishops

Our next text is a modified version of Ratzinger's own contribution to the 1983 Synod of Bishops, which discussed the very nature and task of the synod itself. What is offered by Ratzinger is effectively a distinctive blueprint for the functioning of the synod. Ratzinger explores the 'relation between the theological and canonical definitions of the synod' according to canon law – with the canonical definitions being, in his interpretation, especially but necessarily limited. For some time, debates have been active in the Church suggesting an active 'neutering' of the synod so that its effectiveness was never really what had been envisaged when it was proposed. This merits some further consideration in relation to the substance of the following essay. Certainly what is outlined here – with Ratzinger arguing such is dependent upon the Code of Canon Law – is a subordinationist model of the synod. Ratzinger emphasises the subordination of the synod to the Pope at each turn, and interprets its roles as to be concerned with the unity of the Church and at the service of the central authority in all matters. In all, then, the central thrust of the paper is the consideration of the 'rights' and 'power' of the synod vis-à-vis the central Roman ecclesial authorities.

Ratzinger's focus here upon the understanding of the synod offered in the new Code of Canon Law, implies an assumption that this might settle the debates in hand. However, his critics point to the fact that he himself had a decisive influence on the Code's prescription of a limited role for the synod.

Ratzinger offers many arguments concerning the practicalities of why the synod should not be allowed to function differently – he wishes to overcome confusions surrounding the very nature, purpose and organization of the synod itself. But his critics would respond by suggesting that the end result of the model he sketches here is that the synod is reduced to a limited consultative role and subordinated even to the CDF. Although Ratzinger mentions that the college of bishops is not able to delegate its authority to the synod, what in effect has happened, critical voices argue, is that the CDF under Ratzinger actually assumed many roles proper only to the papal office and/or college of bishops itself. The tensions that have arisen in relation to the synod can be illustrated, for example, in relation to Ratzinger's argument that one of the reasons for not granting the synod greater efficacy would be that it would then amount to little more than a second Roman Curia, something that Ratzinger sees no need for. But the real point here, those who would advocate a different understanding of ecclesial governance would respond, is that such a synod would be more representative of the world Church, more pastorally oriented and more open to the signs of the times, in the spirit Vatican II intended the synod to be. Furthermore, an oft-cited riposte to Ratzinger's claim that 'in matters of faith and morals, no one can be bound by majority decisions', is the simple point that popes are elected through a popular vote by the College of Cardinals. Other examples could be furnished here, such as the decisions of Councils or even the disciplinary decisions of the CDF while Ratzinger was at its helm. So it is clear that majority decisions often inform matters pertaining to faith and morals. Critics would suggest that Ratzinger's 'contribution', far from being purely for discussion, could be construed as intended to curtail debate concerning alternative and more expansive models of the synod and therefore to prevent any such understanding of the synod from prevailing at the discussions in 1983. They would therefore question whether Ratzinger's blueprint for the functioning of the synod set down here runs counter to what was intended for the synod by Vatican II and Paul VI.

> Already during the Council one began to hear the question whether there should not be in the Catholic Church, too, something like a 'permanent synod' that would assist the pope in governing the universal Church and constantly unite the collegial principle with the primatial principle. The synod of bishops, a structure created by Paul VI and adopted by the new Code of Canon Law (CIC), does take up the idea of having the bishops of the Church throughout the world participate regularly and communally in deliberations about the major issues facing the universal Church, but canonically and theologically it follows another model. It advises the pope; it is neither a miniature council nor a collegial organ for governing the Church as a whole. Yet by the very nature of the matter, the question came up again and again in the synod of bishops and in the council of the synod whether we should not try to do more. So in 1983 Pope John Paul II invited the synod council to discuss this question thoroughly and eventually to present recommendations. [. . .] [41]
>
> The Synod Of Bishops According To The New Code Of Canon Law
> *Nature and purposes of the synod*
> The canonical form of the synod of bishops that is in force today is described in canons 342-48 of the new Code of Canon Law. [. . . W]e must . . . examine

41   [Sections 'Questions about the Structure and Task of the Synod of Bishops', in Joseph Ratzinger, *Church, Ecumenism, Politics: New Essays in Ecclesiology*. New York: Crossroad, 1988, pp. 51–66. Also published in San Francisco by Ignatius Press, 2008 and appearing in a different translation: Slough, St Paul Publications, 1988, 46–62].

more closely the question of the relation between the theological and canonical definitions of the synod in these canons. A review of the discussion thus far shows that the theological and canonical formulae are not absolutely identical, that the theological framework is, instead, broader in scope than the canonical. The theological definition includes not only the primatial aspect of the Church's constitution, but also the intention of uniting the college of bishops and the pope, as well as a reference to the Church's responsibilities in the world. From the canonical perspective, on the other hand, the synod belongs entirely and exclusively to the juridical sphere of the primacy; it advises the pope, and its own occasional deliberative powers are delegations of papal authority and not derived from the college.

Naturally the question immediately occurs to the critical observer: Does it have to be that way? Or should not the scope of the canonical specifications be as broad as the theological definition of purpose? Is this not perhaps a good start for further expansion and reform? This question can be answered only if we explain why the canonical lines were drawn more narrowly than the theological, pastoral parameters, that is, if we determine the form in which the college can effectively become a source of law in the first place. The answers given by the CIC to these questions are simply those of the Second Vatican Council, which in turn summarizes the conciliar and canonical tradition of the Catholic Church. According to the Council, there are only two ways in which the college can act with juridical power, that is, as a body vested with authority over the whole Church: the ecumenical council and a practical corporate action of all the bishops throughout the world. The Council discussed in depth and declared conclusively the reasons why the restriction to these two manners of acting is not a positive decree subject to modification but rather is based on the very nature of the college and hence cannot be broadened.

Since that is how the matter stands, the college cannot delegate its powers; it can only exercise them itself, that is, corporately as a whole (in a council or for a practical measure). This in turn implies that the college can in a general way have an influence on a course of action as a spiritual reality but cannot be the source of law for any sort of constituency whatsoever. But this means that in fact only the pope can be the juridical source for the synod and that the dichotomy between the theological-pastoral and the canonical specifications is inevitable.

The underlying cause here, then, is the decisive fact that responsibility for the whole Church, which belongs to the college only as a whole and as a unity, cannot be delegated. [. . .]

Meanwhile, we can say the following about it, based on the ground rules of ecclesiology. The essential ecclesiological purpose of the college of bishops is not to form a central ecclesiastical government, but precisely the reverse: to help build up the Church as an organism that grows in living cells and is alive and one. The individual bishops participate in leading the whole Church, not by being represented in a central organ, but rather by leading as shepherds their particular Churches, which make up the whole and bear it within themselves, and by leading therein the whole Church, the health and proper governance of which depends not simply on a central authority but rather on the upright living of the individual cells internally and with respect to the whole. The bishops share in governing the whole Church by governing their respective particular Churches and in no other way. The notion that only representation in the center would make them important for the whole is a fundamental misunderstanding of the nature of the Church; it is the expression of the very centralism that the Second Vatican Council wanted to overcome. If we were to act upon this notion so as to overcome papal centralism, it would only introduce a new and much cruder centralism that would cause the authentic nature of the Church to fade away and would subject her to the logic of modern theories about the state. To overcome a one-sided centralism, we must proceed in precisely the opposite direction: not by concentrating every-thing in the center, but rather by affirming the intrinsic bipolarity of the Church's nature. This nature consists in the association of the full primatial authority, which expresses the unity of the Church in multiplicity, with the living multiplicity of the local Churches, each of whose bishops is an *episcopus ecclesiae catholicae* precisely because in his Church he leads the Catholic Church and leads her as catholic.

Questions About Synodal Reform
[. . .] *Unusable models*

a. By far the simplest model for raising the status of the synod and investing it with more importance is the suggestion to grant it decision-making authority in general and not only in individual cases. On closer inspection, it becomes apparent that nothing would be gained thereby, either from the theological or from the practical viewpoint.

    [i]. The theological reason has already been made evident. Such decision-making authority would – inevitably, as we have seen – be delegated papal authority, not authority proper to the synod. In reality such a synod would simply amount to a second Roman Curia, and it is incomprehensible what would be gained by that.

    [ii]. The practical reason is that, within the short time during which the synod can meet, it is not possible to prepare documents or decrees thoroughly. Only one synod – the one held in 1971 – has managed thus far to issue its own documents, which are by all means respectable yet have gained little influence on ecclesiastical life as a whole. One might reply: Well, that is true – four weeks is too little. But why do we not just extend the duration of the session accordingly? Now it is important here to note the difference between a council and a synod. The council, being a rare event in the life of the Church, can justify for that special case a rather

long absence of the bishop from his diocese . [. . .] Setting up the synod as a regular component of ecclesiastical life would therefore encroach on the very nature of the episcopal ministry if the sessions were of the appropriate length. [. . .]

In this sense, the practical reason for this suggestion coincides essentially with the theological reason;[42] one could formulate it – a bit schematically – in the following syllogism:

Within the limited time of a synod – aside from special cases – deliberative power cannot be exercised responsibly.

Lengthening the session so that this becomes possible is incompatible with the intrinsic nature of the episcopal ministry ('iuris divini').

Consequently, the use of deliberative power cannot be the normal canonical form of the synod of bishops. In other words, bishops remain bishops, responsible to their particular Churches. It is not an optional feature of the Church's constitution to erect a second central power within it; that would be much less detrimental to the importance of the papal ministry than to the ministry of the bishops; indeed, it would go so far as to rescind the latter.

b. The same is true for the suggestion that the council of the synod secretariat be expanded into a perpetual synod. For once again, either its members stay in Rome or they do not. If they stay, then they cease to be residential bishops and become a second Curia with an international composition. Or else they do not stay in Rome, and then they cannot do the necessary work and do not constitute a permanent synod. In this respect, the recommendation is unrealistic. One positive note that we can take from the idea is that it is desirable to appoint members to the Curia so as to make it as international as possible (with opportunities for rotating prefectures); this would bring about in practice what is intended (with the wrong labeling) by such a permanent synod. Another aspect of the recommendation that we should note is the demand for a more lively and intensive ongoing exchange between the Curia and the world episcopate. However deserving of criticism the Curia may be, we can say that things are developing in this direction.

42 [Note that in an alternative translation this clause reads as follows 'In this way the practical reason against this proposal in fact coincides with the theological reason', trans. Robert Nowell, St Paul's, Slough, 1988 edn., pp. 46–63 at 54. The original German version would appear to concur with the former translation and reads as follows: 'In diesem Sinn fällt der praktische Grund dieses Vorschlags sachlich mit dem theologischen zusammen; man könnte ihn – ein wenig schematisch – in folgendem Schlußverfahren darstellen', in *Kirche, Ökumene und Politik: Neue Versuche zur Ekklesiologie*. Einsiedeln, Freiburg im Breisgau: Johannes Verlag, 1987, 49–63 at p56].

[C]larification of fundamental elements of the Church's constitution
[. . .] Here we confront once again the question of whether it might not be possible
after all to make it a genuine organ of the episcopal college. Our considerations have shown that the real reason why that will not work is the fact that the
college's right to govern cannot be delegated, because by its nature it cannot
be centralized. Yet there are other ideas about how to get around this inability
to delegate; we must turn to them now. The suggestion has been made that the
individual conferences of bishops should discuss the topics for the synod, make
decisions about them as conferences, and then bind their representatives to present
and advocate only the decisions of their own bishops' conference. According
to the reasoning of the suggestion, the delegates would then be plenipotentiary
representatives of their conferences; taken all together, therefore, they would
necessarily represent the whole college of bishops, and thus the assembly of
delegates could regard themselves as a genuine council and act on the canonical
basis of the ecumenical council.

At first glance, the suggestion is tempting. Upon closer inspection, it becomes
evident that it is neither tenable in theory nor feasible in practice, whereby – just
as before – the practical and theoretical arguments are only two sides of the
same coin.

α. The suggestion assumes that the individual delegates are authorized by a
    so-called imperative mandate. But if the decisions of the individual bishops'
    conferences are not identical (as we may readily assume), then the gathering
    is doomed to be a complete deadlock. No one can allow himself to be
    convinced by someone else, because he is bound by his mandate; all real
    debate and all rapprochement are ruled out. For this reason, even though
    certain ideologues demand the imperative mandate, democratic practice
    rejects it in the political sphere, because it would mean the end of democracy.
    Although synod and council are something different from a parliament, they,
    too, require genuine debate; they, too, could not continue under the rule of
    the imperative mandate.

β. In matters of faith and morals, no one can be bound by majority decisions.
    This is also the reason why bishops' conferences have no teaching authority
    and cannot, as conferences, make doctrines binding. Because this is so, even
    ecumenical councils can make decisions in questions of faith and morals only
    with moral unanimity, since one cannot produce the truth by a decision-making
    process but only recognize and accept it. The form in which truths as such
    are defined is not the majority decision, but rather the collectively manifested
    acknowledgment that the defenders of the faith who have joined in sacra-
    mental communion collectively recognize a statement to be the consequence
    of this, their faith. When such unity comes about, it can be deemed a sign
    that the Church's faith is really being expressed, since the Church as such
    and as a whole cannot err in faith. That is the intrinsic basis of theological

definitions. To bind consciences to doctrine by majority decision is impossible, both anthropologically and theologically.

γ.   Because the conscience is the place in which faith dwells, the best representative of both the local Church and the whole Church is the one who follows his conscience – of course this does not mean the ego taken as an absolute, but rather the conscience of faith that has been formed to be open from within, alert and listening. For this reason, the habit of listening to conscience contributes more to real 'representation' than majority decisions, which are frequently prepared by a few persons and are often accepted by many people more for the sake of keeping the peace than out of deep, inner conviction. This is by no means to imply that the collective work of the conferences is meaningless or superfluous. But their significance cannot consist of hammering out imperative mandates; rather it is one of collectively informing the conscience so that it is alert and hears distinctly; in this way unity is found from within. I think that the work of the conference, by its very nature, should aim, not to issue a lot of decisions and position papers, but rather to make consciences clearer and thus more free on the basis of the truth. Only in that way can they bring about at all the true liberation of mankind to which the Church is called. Therefore the synod discussion, by its very nature, cannot be partisan rhetoric aiming to convince others, as is often the practice in parliaments. It ought to be the effort of communal listening to the conscience of faith and thus help the members to understand the faith better with one another, so that they might also give better witness to it, based on such a communal understanding. [. . .] Therefore synod decisions acquire their importance, not so much from the large number of those who vote for them (which can and most often will be an indication yet is not decisive simply as a number), but rather from the emergence and verbalization of the truth that is already present in the conscience. [. . .]

If one reflects a little more deeply on the duties of the synod briefly outlined here, it automatically becomes clear that the synod's primary concern cannot be how it can expand its own rights over against central Roman authorities that appear to be far too powerful. Our common work on behalf of the gospel in this time demands all our strength, and the people who live in today's world look to us, not for debates about the relation between our respective rights, but rather for the contribution that we can make toward the salvation of the world, thanks to the gospel: that is what God has called us to do.

6.3 Free Expression and Obedience in the Church

Our next text was also composed during the early stages of Vatican II and concerns another issue much debated at the time and in the run-up to the Council – *viz.*, whether it is permissible to criticize the Church itself and, if so, to what extent. Although Ratzinger's style here appears to be that of the scholastic disputation, in fact there is a consistency to the line of argumentation he wishes to put across in the service of a very particular conclusion. In the full text he begins with a reflection upon the relation of the Old Testament to the New, and then moves on to remind his readers that holiness and sin co-exist in the Church and always have done so.[43] He therefore urges that criticism of the Church should only ever be voiced out of love for the Church. He rejects any criticism coming from outside of the Church, including from those who cut themselves off from truly belonging to it.[44]

Although Ratzinger here states that he does not wish to place limitations upon the 'prophetic' spirit in the Church, he warns that what such voices say must be tested against the truth and the doctrine of the faith, which is of an infinitely greater importance than particular criticisms offered by these voices themselves.

One might say that we see here, in embryonic form, not only the understanding of the relation between theologians and the Roman elements of official magisterium that would form the focus of much of Ratzinger's later theological reflections, but also of elements of the policy that would inform Ratzinger's stewardship of the CDF.[45] Note how, in the early 1960s, Ratzinger was already railing against 'relativism, skepticism, and doctrinaire independence'.

> . . . [H]ow can there be a Council without responsible exchange of views, without frank discussions? And how can there be frank discussion without freedom? Now in the early stages of Vaticanum II, we should earnestly inquire as to precisely in what sense debate, criticism, protest, and the right of dissent can be said to arise legitimately from the Church's very nature, and where the line is to be drawn in such matters. [. . .][46]
>
> The simple fact which emerges from this tradition is that it is impossible to contemplate the Church independently of the men who make up the Church; the idealization of a Church divorced from the human element corresponds to no historical reality. The Church lives through men in a temporal world; she lives in a truly human manner despite the divine mystery she bears within herself. The

---

43   Cf. Chapter One of this volume.

44   One of the popular biographies of Ratzinger, writing about events much later than this piece, notes that such an attitude was reflected in Ratzinger's overall approach to defending the Catholic faith. Cf. David Gibson, *The Rule of Benedict: Pope Benedict XV and His Battle with the Modern World*. New York: HarperOne, 2006, pp. 187–188

45   One might even imagine a younger Karol Wojtyla reading this essay and recalling it when, as John Paul II, the time came to appoint a new Prefect of the CDF.

46   [From 'Free Expression and Obedience in the Church', in Hugo Rahner et al., *The Church: Readings in Theology*. New York: P. J. Kenedy, 1963, pp. 194–217].

institution as institution also bears its burden of humanity; it too shares the human vanity of the stumbling block. And who is not perfectly aware of the fact? Yet, the Church remains the holy-sinful Church, both witness to and realization of God's unconquerable grace, of his gracious favor whereby he loves us in our very unworthiness. [. . .]

How, then, is the Christian to conduct himself with regard to the historically living Church? Critically (for the sake of the Church's integrity)?; or how? We are tempted to state simply: He must love her, the Church, and all else will ensue from the 'logic of love.' *Dilige et quod vis, fac,*[47] applies here as well. [. . .]

Nevertheless, the theologian does wish for something more definite. He wants to investigate the structure of this *sentire Ecclesiam,* this 'empathy towards the Church.' He needs this in order to obtain a more precise indication of the proper direction to follow even though, when it comes to the actual decision, one is forced to rely on oneself, on subjective faith, hope and love, and cannot depend simply on an objective rule.

To summarize, then: the Church has assumed the mantle of the prophets, the heritage of those who suffered for truth's sake. She herself entered into history as the Church of martyrs. She, as a whole, has borne the prophetic burden of suffering for truth. Therefore the 'prophetic' in her cannot be dead. On the contrary, it makes its true abode in her. However, one may object that the 'prophetic' has won its victory in the Church and subsequently has lost its critical function. But to do so would be to misconstrue the essence of human history as well as the particular mode by which the New Covenant, indeed the Spirit and the divine, exist in the world.

For [. . .] the recall of the Church from Babylon, the transformation from 'whore' to 'bride,' from 'stumbling block' to 'cornerstone' is not a distant event that occurred once and for all at the dawn of her history. There is much more to it than that. She is summoned ever anew. She stands, as it were, ever upon the threshold. And the *pascha,* the 'passing-over' from this world's existence into newness of spirit, remains first and last her vital primary principle. In this sense, the Easter mystery is the abiding form of the Church's existence in this world.

The Church lives and thrives on the call of the spirit, in the 'crisis,' that tension aroused by the transition from the old to the new. Was it by chance alone that the great saints had to struggle not only with the world but also within the Church as well; that they wrestled with the temptation of the Church to become 'world' and suffered within the Church and at the hand of the Church? A Francis of Assisi, for example, or an Ignatius of Loyola who, arrested for the third time during the Inquisition, rotted in a Salamanca prison, chained for twenty-two days to his companion Calisto. And yet Ignatius retained enough courage and cheerful faith

---

47 ['Love and do as you will', Augustine of Hippo, *Homily no. 7 on the First Epistle of John,* §8],

to say: 'In all of Salamanca there are not so many shackles and chains that I would not put up with more for the love of God.'[48] Thus he renounced no part of his mission and none of his obedience to the Church.

A summary of what thus far has been established shows the Christian median between freedom of speech and submissive obedience to lie within two fundamental polarities.

1. The Christian enjoys the knowledge that the voice of the prophets has so triumphed in the Church that it wondrously surpasses and transfigures the prophetic mission. How? Not through final fulfillment of the covenant by men, but though the gratuitous goodness of God who, despite human failures, remains gracious toward them and demands nothing more than their trusting acceptance of his graciousness. The Christian realizes that the definitive character of God's new people in the Church has its foundation not in human achievements, but in that divine favor whose revocation no human failure can effect.

Thus in the Church the Christian discerns the finality of God's mercy as well as his own obligation to acquiesce. This sets a limit to his critical protest, a limit which should not be exceeded. Yet he realizes as well that this Church, precisely because she exists through the obstinacy of God's grace, also stands amid ceaseless temptation and failure. He knows that she is constantly in the throes of the chasmic strain between rock and stumbling stone, between 'petra' and 'Satan.' Only faith can surmount this existential tension to which the Christian is destined in his obedience to the Church.

It stands to reason, then, that in this way obedience *as* obedience takes on a new aspect: the obligation of 'bearing witness,' the duty to strive for the integrity of the Church, to battle against the 'Babylon' within her that raises its head not only among the laity, not only among individual Christians, but even higher up within the very core of the Church's structure. Not only does it appear but it does so necessarily in that mysterious 'must' through which the Church originated: 'Did not the Christ *have to* suffer thus before entering into his glory?' (Luke 24:26). Therefore it is evident that even within the Church such bearing of witness will now as ever prove painful, open as it is to misunderstanding, suspicion, even condemnation.

Meanwhile, the servility of the sycophants (branded by the genuine prophets of the Old Testament as 'false prophets'), of those who shy from and shun every collision, who prize above all their calm complacency, is not true obedience. The true obedience is that which remains obedient even while bearing witness in suffering; it is that obedience which is forthright truthfulness and which is animated by the persistent power of love. It is this obedience that has fructified the Church throughout the centuries and has drawn her away from the temptations of 'Babylon' to the side of her crucified Lord.

---

48   L. von Matt and H. Rahner, *Ignatius von Loyola*. (Würzburg: 1955), p. 187.

A schooling in *sentire Ecclesiam* should lead us to none other than just such an obedience which is born of truth and leads to truth. What the Church needs today, as always, are not adulators to extol the status quo, but men whose humility and obedience are no less than their passion for truth; men who brave every misunderstanding and attack as they bear witness; men who, in a word, love the Church more than ease and the unruffled course of their personal destiny.

2. We can also look at the matter from the moral point of view. He who feels himself impelled to give critical witness ought to consider various aspects of the question. He must inquire of himself whether or not he has the necessary assurance to justify such a course of action. Secondly, his earnestness in the matter should be determined by the importance his protest can claim according to the scale of theological value. This scale indicates the degree to which the Church *qua* Church agrees with an assertion or movement, and consequently the degree to which this movement or assertion may or may not be criticized. Obviously, when one confronts the deposit of faith as such, criticism must cease.

Further, since criticism never enjoys the invulnerability of a doctrine of the faith, it is clear that of itself criticism is open to reassessment and the criticism of others. Therefore, one should subject his own opinion to thorough and relentless inspection before attempting to criticize another. In an age of relativism, skepticism, and doctrinaire independence, it is a relief to find in the midst of intellectual chaos one last refuge demanding of one a respectful, obedient attitude rather than summoning one to debate. That is one restriction which must be kept in mind.

There is another and of equal importance: we must take into consideration the brother weak in faith, the unbelieving world surrounding us, and, too, the infirmity of our own faith, so capable of withering once we retreat behind the border of criticism and of deteriorating into the self-pitying rancor of one misunderstood.

On the other hand, however, there exists in contrast to discretion, another factor which must be taken into consideration. Truth, as well as love, possesses a right of its own and over sheer utility it takes precedence – truth from which stems that strict necessity for prophetic charisma, and which can demand of one the duty of bearing public witness. [. . .]

Therefore the restrictions listed above are not meant to muzzle the prophetic element within the Church. Such restrictions are worthwhile only in so far as they serve to integrate this element into the organism of Christ's body where the law of truth is equal to that of love: But again in these matters, all things taken into consideration, there is no absolute norm except for the necessity of an obedient decision made in the light of the faith.

At present we must waive specific questions in regard to the nature of 'free speech in the Church' – for example, what part does the layman play in it, and what is its significance to the relationship between layman and clergy, etc. – in order to establish a final and fundamental point. Until now we have been considering the individual in relation to the whole. Now we can say something concerning the 'whole,' concerning the role of the institution and of office as such. The Church needs the spirit of freedom and of sincere forthrightness because she is bound by the command, 'Do not stifle the Spirit' (1 Thess. 5:19), which is valid for all time.

Upon hearing such words, who can help but recall Paul's account of his collision with Peter: 'But when Cephas came to Antioch, I rebuked him to his face, for his own conduct condemned him. [. . .] But when I say they were not straightforward about the truths of the good news, I said to Cephas, right before them all, "If you live like a heathen and not like a Jew, though you are a Jew yourself, why should you try to make the heathen live like Jews?"' (Gal. 2:11-14).

Yet, if it was a weakness in Peter to have compromised the freedom of the gospel for fear of James' supporters, it was his greatness which enabled him to accept the liberty of Paul, who 'rebuked him to his face.' And today the Church owes her life to this liberty which paved the way for her entry to the heathen world.

But where could the like of it occur today? In our day and age, one would not dare reproach the Church as did Guillaume d'Auvergne the Church of his time. Naturally today the Church cannot be accused of being so degenerate and monstrous that 'all who behold her stiffen in horror.' And it can hardly be claimed, 'that nowadays the chariot of the Church' runs 'not forward but backward since the horses run backward pushing her in reverse.'[49] But might she not be taken to task for holding the reins a bit too tightly, for the creation of too many norms, so that not a few of these helped abandon the century to disbelief rather than save it? In other words, might she not be rebuked for trusting too little that power of truth which lives and triumphs in the faith, for entrenching herself behind exterior safeguards instead of relying on the truth, which is inherent in liberty and shuns such defenses?

Perhaps we of today need a reminder that boldness is one of the basic Christian attitudes referred to most frequently in the New Testament. Boldness it was that made Peter step forward and preach to the Jews (Acts 2:29; 4:13, 29, 31). What would it not mean for the Church in the world of today – in a century that thirsts after freedom, in an era which walked out of the Church for the sake of freedom, illusory though it may have been – if the words of Paul could ring with the force of old, could actually mature until veritably visible: those magnificent words into which Paul poured the full expression of his faith: 'But wherever the spirit of the Lord is, there is freedom' (2 Cor. 3:17).

6.4 The Vocation of the Catholic Theologian

Here Ratzinger addresses the subject of what it means to be a 'Catholic' theologian. This essay is Ratzinger's response to widespread criticisms made of the Instruction published by the CDF on 24 May 1990 – (*On*

---

49   Cited in H. U. v. Balthasar, 'Casta meretrix', in *Sponsa Verbi*. Einsiedeln: Johannes Verlag, 1961 p. 205.

the Ecclesial Vocation of the Theologian). As Ratzinger points out, the early part of the full essay summarizes an explanatory text he produced for the media at the time of the Instruction's release. He then moves on to explore objections to the Instruction. The document proved to be very controversial and was seen as part of a wider process of 'clamping down' on Catholic theologians whom the Roman authorities felt were straying too far from official Church teaching in their researches. Responses came from around the globe and from differing schools of theological thought.

In our reading, Ratzinger unpacks and further explicates the Instruction. He states that he is keen to ensure the Instruction is not misunderstood, as its release generated a wealth of articles, debates and conferences in the theological community. Both the Instruction and Ratzinger's commentary on it, below, represent defining moments in the shift in ecclesial thinking that took place in the 1980s and 90s, with regard to the role of the Catholic theologian vis-à-vis the official teaching authority (magisterium) of the Church. Those in favour of the Instruction's sentiments saw it as part of a process of clarification made necessary by errant scholars leading the faithful astray. They welcomed this as upholding the authority of the Church and its doctrine, as well as offering guidance with regard to the limits of criticism of official Church teaching, following a turbulent period in relations between theologians and Rome. Critics saw a rigid, 'reigning in' of theologians who dissented from the official 'party-line' prevalent in Rome.

Ratzinger's attempt here to respond to the Instruction's critics also steers the debate in a particular direction, namely, towards a focus upon the *ecclesial* role and service that Catholic theologians must provide and away from what he perceives to be a misleading concentration upon the rights of individuals, intellectual freedom and conscience. For Ratzinger, 'the Church enters into the nature of theology' hence 'A theology wholly bent on being academic and "scientific" according to the standards of the modern university, cuts itself off from its great historical matrices and renders itself sterile for the Church'.[50]

The significance of the theologian and of theology for the whole community of believers became evident in a new way at the Second Vatican Council. Before the Council, it had been usual to consider theology as a pursuit reserved to a small circle of clerics, as an elitist and abstract affair which could hardly lay claim to the interest of the Church at large. The new mode of seeing and expressing the faith which prevailed at the Council was the fruit of the dramatic, and until then practically unnoticed, history of a new theological sensibility which had made its

50   See p. 116 of the original text.

debut after the First World War in conjunction with new spiritual movements. The regnant mood of liberalism, with its naïve faith in progress, had collapsed in the horror of the war, carrying with it theological Modernism, which has attempted to assimilate faith to the liberal worldview. The liturgical movement, the biblical and ecumenical movements, finally, a strong Marian movement shaped a new spiritual climate favourable to the growth of a new theology, which later bore fruit for the whole Church at the Second Vatican Council. [. . .][51]

After the Council, the dynamic of this development continued apace. Theologians increasingly felt themselves to be the true teachers of the Church and even of the bishops. Moreover, since the Council they had been discovered by the mass media and had captured their interest. The Magisterium of the Holy See now appeared in the public eye to be the last holdover of a failed authoritarianism. The impression was that the insistent claim to competence on the part of a non-academic authority threatened to keep thought under tutelage, whereas in reality the path to knowledge could not be prescribed by authority but rather depended solely upon the force of argument. In these circumstances, it has become necessary to reflect anew on the position of theology and of the theologian as well as on their relationship to the Magisterium. Such a reflection would attempt to understand both theology and the Magisterium in accord with their inner logic and, in so doing, would contribute not only to peace in the Church but, above all, to a correct way of relating faith and reason.

It is this task which the [CDF 'Instruction on the Ecclesial Vocation of the Theologian', issued in May 1990,] tries to serve. Hence, it is ultimately concerned with an anthropological problem: if religion and reason cannot be brought into the proper correspondence, man's spiritual life disintegrates into a flat rationalism dominated by technique, on the one hand, and into a dark irrationalism, on the other. [. . .] For this reason, the Instruction places the subject of theology within the broad horizon of the question of man's capacity for truth and of his true freedom. The Christian faith is not a pastime, and the Church is not one club among others of a similar or even of a different sort. Rather, faith responds to the primordial question of man regarding his origin and goal. It bears on those basic problems which Kant characterized as the essential core of philosophy: What can I know? What may I hope for? What is man? In other words, faith has to do with truth, and only if man is capable of truth can it also be said that he is called to freedom.

[. . .] But what distinguishes theology from the philosophy of religion and from secular religious science? The answer is that man's reason knows that it has not been left to its own devices. It is preceded by a Word which, though logical and rational, does not originate from reason itself but has been granted it as a gift

51   [From 'On the "Instruction concerning the Ecclesial Vocation of the Theologian"' in Joseph Ratzinger, *The Nature and Mission of Theology*. San Francisco: Ignatius Press, 1993, 101–120, (translation of 'Zur Instruktion über die kirchliche Berufung des Theologen', in *Internationale Katholische Zeitschrift: Communio* 19 (1990) pp. 561–564)].

and, as such, always transcends it. It remains a task which we never completely fulfil in history. Theology is pondering what God has said and thought before us. If it abandons this secure ground, it annuls its own constitution. [. . .]

Let us return to our Instruction. It treats of the task of the theologian in this broad context and thereby manifests plainly the greatness of his mission. A striking feature of the division of the text is that it does not begin with the Magisterium but with the truth, which it presents as a gift of God to his people. The truth of faith, in fact, is not bestowed upon the isolated individual, for God has willed instead to build history and community with it. It has its place in a common subject: the people of God, the Church. The vocation of the theologian is presented next, and the Magisterium and the mutual relation of the two are discussed only afterward. This implies two things:

a) Theology is not simply and exclusively an ancillary function of the Magisterium: it is not limited to gathering arguments for a priori magisterial decisions. If that were so, the Magisterium and theology would draw perilously close to an ideology whose sole interest is the acquisition and preservation of power. Theology has a specific origin of its own. The document, borrowing from Saint Bonaventure, designates two roots of theology in the Church. The first is the dynamism toward truth and understanding inherent in the faith; the second is the dynamism of love, which desires to know the beloved more intimately. Correspondingly, there are two directions in theology, which, however, continually cross and recross each other. The first, more outwardly moving direction devotes its efforts to dialogue with every reasonable search for truth; the second, which moves predominantly inward, strives to fathom the inner logic and depth of the faith.

b) The document treats the ecclesial mission of the theologian, not in the context of the dualism Magisterium-theology, but rather in the framework of the triangular relationship defined by the people of God, understood as the bearer of the *sensus fidei* and the common locus of all faith, the Magisterium and theology. The development of dogma in the last 150 years is a clear index of how closely these three elements hang together: the dogmas of 1854, 1870 and 1950[52] became possible because the *sensus fidei* had discovered them, while the Magisterium and theology followed its lead and tried slowly to catch up with it.

This is already a statement of the essentially ecclesial identity of theology. Theology is never simply the private idea of one theologian. If it were, it could count for little, for as a private idea it would sink rapidly into insignificance. On

---

52   [Respectively, the definitions of the dogmas of the Immaculate Conception, Papal Infallibility and the Assumption of the Blessed Virgin Mary].

the contrary, the Church, as a living subject which endures amid the changes of history, is the vital milieu of the theologian; the Church preserves faith's experiences with God. Theology can remain historically relevant only if it acknowledges this living environment, inserts itself into it and attains an inner participation in it. It follows that the Church is not an organization which the theologian must regard as alien and extrinsic to thought. Insofar as the Church is a corporate subject which transcends the narrowness of individuals, she is the condition which makes theological activity possible. It is thus evident that two things are essential for the theologian. First, the methodological rigor which is part and parcel of the business of scholarship; in this regard, the document refers to philosophy, the historical disciplines and the human sciences as privileged partners of the theologian. But he also has need of inner participation in the organic structure of the Church; he needs that faith which is prayer, contemplation and life. Only in this symphony does theology come into being.

This also makes for an organic understanding of the Magisterium. We said that the Church enters into the nature of theology. But the Church is more than an exterior organization of believers only if she has her own voice. Faith precedes theology; theology is the quest to understand the Word which, not having been devised by us, elicits the utmost effort from our thought but is never engulfed by it. This Word which precedes theological research is the measure of theology and requires its own organ – the Magisterium, which Christ committed to the apostles and, through them, to their successors. I do not wish to discuss in detail here how the document explains the relationship between the Magisterium and theology. Under the title 'reciprocal collaboration', it sets forth the task proper to each and explains how they ought to live and work together. The priority of faith, which lends the Magisterium authority and a final right of decision, does not obliterate the independence of theological research but guarantees it a solid basis. The document does not conceal the fact that there can be tensions even under the most favourable circumstances. These tensions, however, can be productive, provided that each side sustains them in the recognition that its function is intrinsically ordered to that of the other. The text also presents the various forms of binding authority which correspond to the grades of the Magisterium. It states – perhaps for the first time with such candor – that there are magisterial decisions which cannot be the final word on a given matter as such but, despite the permanent value of their principles, are chiefly also a signal for pastoral prudence, a sort of provisional policy. Their kernel remains valid, but the particulars determined by circumstances can stand in need of correction. In this connection, one will probably call to mind both the pontifical statements of the last century regarding freedom of religion and the anti-Modernist decisions of the beginning of this century, especially the decisions of the then Biblical Commission. [. . .] Nevertheless, with respect to particular aspects of their content, they were superseded after having fulfilled their pastoral function of the time.

In contrast to these healthy forms of tension, a defective variety is treated in the second part of the final chapter under the heading 'dissent', wherewith the Instruction avails itself of a catchword which came into vogue in the United States in the 1960s. When theology organizes itself according to the principle of majority rule and constructs a countermagisterium which offers the faithful alternative modes of behaviour, it misses its own essences. It sets itself up as a political factor, utilizes channels of power to represent its interests and appeals to the political model of majority. By disavowing the Magisterium, it forfeits the firm ground under its feet and, by stepping out of the realm of thought into the play of power, it also falsifies its scientific character. It thus loses the two foundations of its existence.

The Instruction was published in the hope that the distinction between constructive kinds of tension and a perverse and unacceptable form of antithesis between theology and the Magisterium will help to relax the strained atmosphere in the Church. The Church needs a sound theology. Theology needs the living voice of the Magisterium. May the Instruction contribute to a renewal of dialogue between the Magisterium and theology and thereby be of service to the Church at the close of this second millennium and, with her, to humanity in its struggle for truth and freedom.

Toward a Discussion of the Text
The Institution briefly presented here has kindled a controversy, which in part has proceeded in a vehement tone. It has been shown that the Instruction aimed to call attention to the specific role of theology in the Church and thus to the particular responsibility of the theologian. Yet theologians, especially in German-speaking Countries, together with a group of Latin American theologians, claimed to see in the text the precise opposite – a constriction of theological inquiry which posed a threat to its authentic nature. [. . .] Individual scholars like P. Hünermann and D. Mieth, on the other hand, engaged in a fierce polemic. Nor is a commentary undersigned by a good one hundred Latin American Theologians exactly delicate in its appraisals when it condemns the text as 'incriminatory' and 'intellectualistic'. The Congregation is charged with repudiating what Rome had supposedly repudiated in the nineteenth century: the people, democracy, and public opinion.[53]

[. . .] The stock clichés customarily employed by the forces of protest to authenticate themselves as the bearers of prophecy in contrast to the ministerial office are untenable. [. . .] In the end, it is never definitely clear except in retrospect who was an authentic prophet. There is no doubt that truly prophetic figures have also been given to the Church in every age [. . ..] Nor is there any doubt that the ministerial office of the Church is exposed to the risk of disregarding prophetic voices on account of their being uncomfortable. In consequence, we must allow ourselves, in an attitude of vigilance, to be called into question again and again by such challenges and must remain open to the presence of the Spirit, who can

53 'A Missao eclesial do teólogo: Subsidios de leitura e elementos para un diàlogo em torno á Instruçao sobre a vocaçao eclesial do teólogo', in *Revista. Eclesiastica Brasileira* 50, fas. 200 (December 1990) pp. 771–807.

be altogether uncomfortable. [. . .] Both the acceptance of justified criticism and
the protection of the faithful from falsifications of the Gospel, from an adulteration
of the faith by the spirit of the world which passes itself off as the Holy Spirit, are
integral parts of this discernment. We can learn it only in a deep interior union
with Christ, in an obedience to the Word of God which finds ever-new expression
in our lives and in an inner rooting in the living Church of all places and all times.
But we are all in constant need of forgiveness and correction.

6.5 Magisterium and Morality

Here Ratzinger explores the relationship between the teaching authority
of the Church (magisterium) and Christian guidance on moral matters.
Surveying the situation first, he touches upon familiar themes that we
find throughout many of his writings. These include recurring targets of
Ratzinger's attention, such as liberalism, left-wing political movements
and political theology and the influence all have had in the Church. In
particular, he here, as in many places, decries the misappropriation of the
'prophetic' stance in the Church and a shift in focus from 'orthodoxy'
(right belief or worship) to 'orthopraxis' (right action or practice). The
latter distinction, he observes, has received particular attention in ecumenical discussions and in the theologies of liberation. Even the notion
of truth itself, Ratzinger argues, seemed to be subject to flux and change
(here his target appears to be materialist critiques of bourgeois 'truth').

Ratzinger argues that such positions leave little room for the role of the
Church's official magisterium. But he is particularly concerned that such a
movement would also deny the existence of a specific Christian morality
and instead would subject the moral norms of the Christian community
to the passing whims and customs of a given time and place. According to
this approach, reason, not faith, should be the guide in morals. Even the
Bible, adherents of such a position would argue, simply reflects the moral
codes, norms and modes of ethical reasoning of the particular contexts of
the biblical communities as opposed to anything distinctive.

In opposition to such a position, in the full essay Ratzinger embarks
upon a lengthy series of counter-arguments, drawing upon biblical and
doctrinal testimony as he proceeds. In our extract, he focuses upon how
the New Testament, and particularly Paul, demonstrates a distinctive
Christian moral tradition and that Paul exercises his apostolic authority
in order to uphold that moral tradition. Therefore something like magisterium, linked to apostolic succession, is already present in the New
Testament and it is exercised there both in relation to the morality of
Christian individuals and their communities.

Thus, Ratzinger argues, while the practice of faith is always necessary, a one-sided emphasis upon orthopraxis alone actually leads towards a denial of the objective nature of Christian morality. These positions share culpability in a 'heresy against reason'. For Ratzinger, it is rather the higher form of reason informed by faith, as illustrated in exemplary fashion by St Paul, which must be preferred: 'Faith comprises . . . fundamental objective decisions in the moral field.'[54]

Supporters of Ratzinger's approach to such matters would welcome these arguments as a timely reminder of the distinctiveness of the Christian approach to morality, grounded as it is upon faith and a personal relationship with Christ. Ratzinger consistently denounces neo-Pelagian tendencies and moralism in favour of an ethics grounded in living faith. Critical voices would again point to the generalized accounts of those positions Ratzinger attacks here as being misrepresentative of particular schools of theological and moral thought. Furthermore Ratzinger's understanding of ethics and the nature of moral discernment appears to critics as a rather rigid and particular one, which passes over much of the vast history of ethics and even the numerous developments within the Catholic moral tradition – as reflected in the magisterial teachings of the Church itself – across history but in the second half of the twentieth century in particular. Even the biblical hermeneutics being employed here, those critical voices with expertise in the relevant sub-disciplines here might continue runs the risk of lapsing into eisegesis and so reading into the texts a justification for a contemporary understanding of the nature and exercise of Church teaching authority that was simply not manifest in early Christian times in such a form.

Survey of the Problem[55]

The crisis of faith, which is making itself increasingly felt in Christendom, is more and more clearly seen to be also a crisis in awareness of the fundamental values of human life. On the one hand it is nourished by the moral crisis of mankind and on the other hand it has repercussions on the latter, making it more acute. When the attempt is made to survey the panorama of the present discussions on this matter, strange contradictions are met with, which, however, are closely connected with one another. On the one hand, particularly since the meeting of the World Council of Churches at Uppsala, there is an increasingly clear tendency to define Christianity primarily as 'orthopraxis' and not as 'orthodoxy.' There are various reasons for this. Reference should perhaps be made to the seriousness of the racial problem for American Christian communities. Their religion has not

---

54   See below, page 222.
55   [From Joseph Ratzinger, 'Magisterium of the Church, Faith and Morality', in Charles E. Curran and Richard A. McCormick (eds), Readings in Moral Theology Nr. 2: The Distinctiveness of Christian Ethics. New York: Paulist, 1980, pp. 174–189].

succeeded in breaking down the barriers of separation and therefore the validity of faith itself seems to be questioned, since it has not been able to bring to life the love that is the root of the Gospel. In this way a practical question becomes the touchstone of the intrinsic value of doctrine, the proof of what is Christian: where 'orthopraxis' is so glaringly absent, 'orthodoxy' seems questionable.

Another origin of the trend towards 'praxis' lies in the various movements of 'political theology,' which on their side have different motives. Common to them all is great perplexity due to the questions raised by Marxism. The concept of 'truth' is regarded here with suspicion or at least as being without value. To this extent this theory is identified with the fundamental feeling that gives rise to positivism.

Truth is considered unattainable and its proclamation only an alibi for group interests, which are thus consolidated. Only praxis can decide (still according to this view) the value or lack of value of theories. So if Christianity wishes to make some contribution to the construction of a better world, it should create a better praxis – not seek truth as a theory, but reestablish it as a reality.

The claim that Christianity should become 'orthopraxis' of joint activities for a more human future and leave orthodoxy aside as unfruitful or harmful, takes on here a far more fundamental character than in the case of the pragmatic standpoint described above. It is clear at the same time that both positions tend to unite and strengthen each other. In both cases there remains little room for a magisterium, although if these principles were applied consistently it should appear again in a different form. Certainly, a magisterium that wished to formulate a preconstituted truth with regard to correct human praxis and wished to measure praxis by this truth, would fall on the negative side of reality as an obstacle to creative, forward-looking praxis. It would appear as the expression of interests concealed under the label of 'orthodoxy' and opposed to the advance of the history of freedom. [. . .]

The movement that would like to define and realize Christianity as orthopraxis is opposed at the other end (and in fact often passes into it suddenly) by the position that maintains there is no specific Christian morality; on the contrary Christianity must take its norms of behavior every time from the anthropological knowledge of its own age. Faith does not offer any independent principle of moral norms but on this point refers strictly to reason; anything that is not guaranteed by reason would not be supported by faith. This assertion is justified with the statement that, even in its historical sources, the faith did not develop any morality of its own but followed the practical reason of contemporaries in the different periods.[56] This can be seen already in the Old Testament, where value concepts from the time of the patriarchs to sapiential literature were in continual change, conditioned by contact with the development of the moral concepts of collateral cultures. Nowhere can there be found, they say, a moral sentence limited only to the Old Testament, of which it

---

56   H. Küng; *On Being a Christian.* Trs. by Edward Quinn. New York: Doubleday & Co, 1974.

could be said that it is the result exclusively of faith in Jehovah; in the moral field everything was borrowed elsewhere. According to this theory, this applies also to the New Testament: the virtues and vices listed in the Pauline epistles reflect Stoic morality and in this way are the acceptance of the rational canons of human behavior at that time. For this reason their value lies not in the content, but in their structure: as a reference to reason as the only source of moral norms.

It need hardly be said that also with this point of departure there is no room for an ecclesiastical Magisterium in the moral field. For norms essentially based on the tradition of faith would, according to this thesis, spring from the misunderstanding that the teachings of the Bible are absolute and perennial indications while they are only a reference to the positions reached at different moments by the knowledge attained by reason. [. . .]

Faith–Morality–Magisterium

The reference to apostolic teaching with the connection between faith and morality brings up the matter of the Magisterium. For the apostolic epistles are an exercise of the teaching authority. In them Paul takes up a position 'magisterially' also on the moral aspect of faith. The same applies to all the epistles in the New Testament and to the Gospels, which are full of moral instructions, and also to the Apocalypse. In his teaching, Paul does not theorize about human rationality, but sets forth the inner necessity of grace, as H. Schlier has pointed out forcibly in his fine article on the originality of Christian teaching.[57] Actually, although the apostle is convinced he has the authority (2 Cor. 8:8), he does not use the form of explicit command too often (1 Thess. 4:10 f.; other texts in Schlier, p. 342). He does not want to correct the Christian communities with reproofs and the rod, as teachers corrected children in ancient times – he prefers fatherly persuasion in the Christian family. But precisely by doing so he makes it clearly understood that behind his words is the mercy of God himself calling. In his exhortation it is grace that exhorts, it is God that exhorts; it is not a variable accessory to the Gospel, but is guaranteed by the authority of the Lord, even when it is not presented in the form of a command or doctrinal decision.[58] The same can be said when the central themes of his doctrine are considered: salvation in Christ, baptism, the communion of the Body of Christ, the last judgment. The line of demarcation drawn by grace in regard to the life of those who do not know God is quite clear: it is abstention from wantonness, greed, envy and quarrelsomeness; inclination to obedience, patience, truth, trust and joy: in these attitudes the fundamental command of love is unfolded.

What we see in Paul is continued in the writings of the successors of the

57 Heinrich Schlier, *Besinnung auf das neue Testament*. Freiburg: Herder, 1964, pp. 141–144.
58 Ibid., pp. 344–352. Paul acknowledges here the 'teleological' motive (the future judgment and reward) as much as he argues 'deontologically' in terms of the implications of being a member of the body of Christ.

apostles, in which the apostolic doctrine is explained in a way suited to the situation. This means that, for the New Testament, the ecclesiastical Magisterium does not end with the time of the Apostles. The Church therefore remains apostolic also in the post-apostolic era, and it is her permanent task to see to it that the legitimate successors of the apostles defend the unchangeability of the apostolic doctrine. Luke sets this forth expressly in the crisis of transition, taking as the model of the Church of all times the original community of Jerusalem, which 'remained faithful to the teaching of the apostles' (Acts 2:42), and indicating the elders as overseers of this faithfulness (Acts 20:17-38).

It is not necessary to develop in this connection a detailed theory of the ecclesiastic Magisterium and its centralization in the Magisterium of Peter's successor, although it would not be hard to present the lines that run in this direction in the New Testament: on the one hand the concept of tradition and succession that is made increasingly clear and on the other hand the theology of Peter. It is evident that the fundamental value of the apostolic succession consists precisely in the authority to preserve the apostolic faith, and that the consequent magisterial authority essentially comprises also the duty to show concretely the moral necessity of grace and specify it in the different periods.

With this the circle of our thought returns to the beginning again. The practice of faith belongs, in fact, to Christian faith. Orthodoxy without orthopraxis loses the essence of Christianity: the love that comes from grace. At the same time, however, it is admitted that Christian practice is nourished by Christian faith: by the grace that appeared in Christ and was attributed to the *sacramentum Ecclesiae*. The practice of faith depends on the truth of faith, in which man's truth is made visible through God's truth and is raised one step higher. It therefore radically contradicts a practice that seeks first to produce facts and through them establish the truth; against this complete manipulation of reality it defends God's creation. Man's fundamental values, which it gets to know from the example of Jesus Christ, are withdrawn by it from all manipulation. Defending the creation, it protects man. It is the irrevocable task of the successors of the apostles to keep the apostolic teaching present in this way. Since grace is in relation to the creation and the creator, the apostolic doctrine (as continuation of the teaching of the Old Testament) has to do with reason. [. . .]

The faith of the Apostle, as is seen from Rom. 1 and 2, has a higher concept of reason. St. Paul is convinced that reason is capable of truth and that therefore the faith cannot be constructed outside the rules of reason, but finds its way of expressing itself by communicating with the reason of peoples, accepting and refusing. This means that both the process of assimilation and the process of negation and criticism must start from the fundamental decisions of faith and has its firm points of reference in the latter. Reason's capacity of truth means at the same time the objective constancy of truth, which agrees with the constancy of faith.

The task of the Magisterium of the Church in the moral field follows from what has been said. Faith comprises, as we have seen, fundamental objective decisions in the moral field. The task of the Magisterium is first and foremost to continue apostolic teaching and defend these fundamental principles should reason yield to time or capitulate before the omnipotence of practice. The value of these principles is that they correspond to the fundamental knowledge of human reason, purified, deepened and amplified in contact with the life of faith. The positive-critical dialogue with reason must, as has been said, be extended to all times. On the one hand it is never completely clear what is really reason and what is only apparently 'rational'; on the other hand there exist at all times both phenomena, the apparently rational and the appearance of truth through reason. In the process of assimilating what is really rational and rejecting what only seems to be rational, the whole Church has to play a part. This process cannot be carried out in every detail by an isolated Magisterium, with oracular infallibility. The life and suffering of Christians who profess their faith in the midst of their times has just as important a part to play as the thinking and questioning of the learned, which would have a very hollow ring without the backing of Christian existence, which learns to discern spirits in the travail of everyday life. The whole Church's experience of faith, thinkers' researches and questionings, are two factors; the watchful observation, listening and decision of the Magisterium is the third. That correct doctrine is not exercised automatically but requires the 'exhortation and reprimanding' of the responsible pastors of the Church, was experienced by the Church in the first century, and for that very reason she formed the office of those who, with prayer and the laying on of hands, are called to the succession of the apostles. For the Church this office is indispensable today, too, and where her competence is challenged as regards essential decisions for or against an interpretation of morality following upon grace, the fundamental form of apostolic tradition itself is shaken.

CHAPTER 7

LITURGY, CATECHESIS AND EVANGELIZATION

Gerard Mannion

Introduction

There is an interlocking character to the theology of Joseph Ratzinger. This volume as a whole is intended to demonstrate this but, in particular, this chapter will also help readers appreciate that the connections between the writings of Ratzinger on different areas of theological and ecclesial enquiry are usually intentional. In other words, because Ratzinger believes that the doctrine of the Christian faith constitutes a unified whole in a coherent and consistent fashion, one of the intentions behind his own theology is to illustrate such an inter-connected character.[1] Of course, as we have seen throughout this volume, this does not mean that there has not been also change and development as well as revision in Ratzinger's theological thinking across the decades.

The interlocking character of Ratzinger's understanding of God, of history, of salvation, of the world, of the Church and of its mission, all of these elements are brought together and illustrated especially well in his thoughts on the liturgy, and his closely related Eucharistic theology (particularly the Eucharistic sense of ecclesiology) and thus, also his understanding of catechesis and evangelization.

As we have seen earlier in this volume, with so much of his theologising it is Ratzinger's reaction to the perceived ills of first the modern, then postmodern world[2] that feeds his writings on liturgy, catechesis and evangelization. Ratzinger posits faith in general, but the liturgy in particular, as an antidote to the ills of the world, thereby necessitating evangelization and catechesis.

With regard to each of the three themes covered in this chapter, Ratzinger's intentions are to safeguard what he believes to be fundamental to the practice and celebration of the Catholic faith. To such ends, he has denounced innovations that he perceives to be passing cultural

---

1   And this, despite Ratzinger's own statements about a 'new integralism' as detailed in the following chapter (cf. the Introduction to Reading 8.2).
2   See, also, Chapters One, Three and Four of this volume on this theme.

and societal trends.[3] He asserts that essential aspects of the faith have been distorted and neglected in these areas. As with other perceived ecclesial ills, here he frequently blames national Episcopal conferences and academic theologians for many such changes. In Ratzinger's opinion, Vatican II, by and large, did not advocate change and innovation but rather a revitalization of the age-old faith. For Ratzinger, radical change in relation to these areas was neither necessary nor welcome. Rather, lesser adjustments and refinements would have been preferable.[4]

The familiar antipathy to relativism and pluralism, which one finds throughout many of his writings (as we have also seen in earlier chapters), is present in each of these areas, also. Hence his belief that attention to liturgical practice and devotion, to better catechesis, to more explicit evangelization can serve as an antidote to the ills of today's world.

With particular regard to the liturgy, he has written extensively on the topic throughout his long career. Indeed, when the first volume of the ongoing publication of an edition of Ratzinger's complete works[5] was published in 2008, the subject of that very first volume was the theology of liturgy.[6] This was a deliberate choice, and one made, as Ratzinger himself explained in the preface, because he wanted to 'allow God to come first', a further consistent theme throughout much of his theology. Indeed, as Ratzinger's biographer and long-time Rome correspondent for America's *National Catholic Reporter*, John Allen, states, 'There are few subjects about which Ratzinger writes today more passionately than the liturgy.'[7]

For Ratzinger, the liturgy makes sense of the Church and the understanding of the Church he espouses makes sense of the liturgy. The heart of both these doctrines underlines the need for catechesis, mission and evangelization. The incarnation of the word stands behind all of these and feeds into moral and social teaching alike.[8]

---

3   Indeed, during his time at the CDF and since elevation to the papacy, documents and directives have been issued that have sought to counter those changes in each of the areas that he deems to have been misguided.

4   For example, cf. his 'Epilogue: on the Status of Church and Theology Today', in *Principles of Catholic Theology: Building Stones for a Fundamental Theology*. San Francisco: Ignatius, 1987, pp. 367–393 and 'A Company in Constant Renewal', in *Called to Communion: Understanding the Church Today*. San Francisco: Ignatius, 1996, 133-156.

5   Joseph Ratzinger, *Theologie der Liturgie*, (vol. 11 of *Joseph Ratzinger Gesammelte Schriften*. Freiburg: Herder, 2008).

6   I.e. the first volume to appear in print was actually volume 11 and not volume 1 of the series.

7   *Pope Benedict XVI: a Biography of Joseph Ratzinger*. New York: Continuum, 2005, p. 71. See, also, Aidan Nichols, 'The Liturgist', chapter 10 of his *The Thought of Benedict XVI: an Introduction to the Theology of Joseph Ratzinger*. London and New York: Burns & Oates/Continuum, 2005, pp. 207–224.

8   When Ratzinger's work, *The Spirit of the Liturgy*, appeared (trans. by John Saward, San Francisco: Ignatius Press, 2000), Joseph Fessio (publisher of most of Ratzinger's and now Pope Benedict's works

This feeds naturally into his understanding of the Eucharist, which brings together his doctrine of God and theological interpretation of history (and so incarnation),[9] atonement, salvation, and ecclesiology[10] in an especially vivid fashion. This all then works outwards into his understanding of mission, catechesis and evangelization. From here he implies that his understanding of other churches, of other faiths and of secular culture is really only a logical progression from these other areas of theological interpretation of the faith and as such, he would argue, is therefore a perspective ultimately grounded in a theology of revelation itself.

With particular regard to that theology of history, time and again Ratzinger claims that the Christian faith's specificity is its foundation upon real historical events, *viz.* the incarnation and life, mission and death and resurrection of Jesus of Nazareth. A recent study of Ratzinger's theology surmises that its defining characteristic is that theology only makes sense in the light of faith in the God of love:

> For Ratzinger, this love of God for his creatures is constant, and His Revelation, once given, is for ever. Christianity is therefore not a project to be updated throughout history. The challenges faced by Christians will differ from generation to generation but the general 'plot' or 'script' does not change. The principles within which this theo-drama unfolds are not determined by human beings. The Scriptures are authoritative, and cannot be deconstructed into a pile of theologically irrelevant historical facts. History in general, but especially the history of Israel and the early Church, is a rich treasury of theological truths.[11]

Concerning his theology of the Eucharist, we hear (in the subtitle of one volume from Ratzinger's corpus), that the Eucharist is the very 'heart of

---

in English), stated that it was, in effect, the only proper 'book' Ratzinger had written in the previous three decades, with his other publications being interviews or collections of papers, sermons and talks. Fessio's comments were made prior to the publication of Ratzinger's *Jesus of Nazareth* (New York: Doubleday, 2007).

9   Here cf. Chapter Three of this volume.

10   The Protestant theologian, Wolfhart Pannenberg states that 'According to Ratzinger, the Eucharistic basis of the Church's reality as the body of Christ underlies the way in which the Church is the people of God. Christians are the people of God only as they are the body of Christ', *Systematic Theology*, Vol. 3. Trans. by Geoffrey W. Bromiley (Grand Rapids, Micigan, Eerdmans, 1998), p. 468 (see, also, p. 102 and n. 14). He is here particularly referring to Ratzinger's *Das neue Volk Gottes* (Düsseldorf: Patmos, 1969, 2nd edn., 1977), p. 82 and also p. 108. Although Pannenberg believes the concept of the people of God is 'more comprehensive than that of the church' (ibid.), and he discusses how Vatican II also made this point clearly.

11   Tracey Rowland *Ratzinger's Faith: the Theology of Pope Benedict XVI*. Oxford: OUP, 2008, p. 148. Rowland continues by arguing that it is ironic that Ratzinger's 'stance on the theological significance of history and Scripture' has entailed positions that others have seemed to believe are 'merely' conservative.

life'.[12] The Eucharistic ecclesiology he espouses is one of the key conceptual means of forging the integral doctrinal whole that he seeks to promote: all of the Church's fundamental teaching hangs together for him as a self-evidently coherent whole.[13] So Ratzinger has stated that 'the Church is not merely an external society of believers; by her nature she is a liturgical community; she is most truly church when she celebrates the Eucharist and makes present the redemptive love of Jesus Christ'.[14] He then goes on to offer a statement that illustrates well the integrated nature of his ecclesiological perspective and his thinking on wider theological and doctrinal issues:

> Now at last we have reached the inmost core of the concept 'Church' and the deepest meaning of the designation 'sacrament of unity'. The Church is *communio*; she is God's communing with men in Christ and hence the communing of men with one another – and, in consequence, sacrament, sign, instrument of salvation. The Church is the celebration of the Eucharist; the Eucharist is the Church: they do not simply stand side by side; they are one and the same. The Eucharist is the *sacramentum Christi* and, because the Church is *Eucharistia*, she is therefore also *sacramentum* – the sacrament to which all other sacraments are ordered.[15]

Nonetheless, Ratzinger's various critics offer evidence to suggest how the apparently seamless character of this integral theological and doctrinal vision is open to question in certain areas. And it is in relation to his writings on the liturgy that we find one of those areas where Ratzinger has appeared to change his mind in a particularly significant fashion. So, for example, while he spoke during the period of Vatican II of how alienating the use of Latin could be in the liturgy and in seminary education, eventually he would come to see the Latin liturgy as a bulwark against ecclesial reforms too wedded to the spirit of the age. Ratzinger would encourage and rehabilitate the wider celebration of the Tridentine rite and, once Pope, he would reach out to welcome back to the Church

12   Joseph Ratzinger, *God is Near Us: the Eucharist, the Heart of Life*. San Francisco: Ignatius Press, 2003.
13   Although in relation to Eucharistic ecclesiology he was building upon the work of Henri De Lubac and likewise the sense of the Church as the 'sacrament of salvation' (which also owes much to the Belgian theologian, Gerard Phillips), here, as elsewhere, it is not so much that he uniformly agrees with or even accurately portrays the work of the authors whom he draws upon. Rather, Ratzinger takes the ideas of others and employs them frequently as rhetorical flourishes in the service of what are often his own somewhat different conclusions.
14   Joseph Ratzinger, 'The Church as Sacrament of Salvation' in his *Principles of Catholic Theology: Building Stones for a Fundamental Theology*, San Francisco, Ignatius Press, 1982, 250. Here cf. also his study *The Meaning of Christian Brotherhood*, San Francisco: Ignatius Press, 1993.
15   *Principles of Catholic Theology*, 53. On the integrated nature of his theological writings here, see, also, *Pilgrim Fellowship of Faith: the Church as Communion*. San Francisco: Ignatius Press, 2005.

extremist conservative groups such as the Society of St Pius X, whose members had consistently denounced Vatican II and had eventually been excommunicated.[16]

Indeed, Ratzinger would come to lament the direction in which the post-conciliar liturgical reforms would develop in general, seeing them as impositions at the expense of true tradition. He has argued that the emphasis upon the community in the 'new' mass has hindered the openness of the individual to God. The prohibition of the old missal was especially regrettable. Indeed, he has also suggested that the demise of the liturgy is responsible for many of the problems in the Church today. For Ratzinger, innovation, improvisation and particularly inculturation in the liturgy have replaced the sense and meaning of the gift at the heart of the liturgy and have confused anthropology, theology and liturgy alike. Sociological and aesthetical priorities were allowed to take over. He has come to denounce forms of the 'active participation' he once commended and has even shown enthusiasm for the reordering of the altar back towards its pre-reform location.

John Allen has suggested that Ratzinger's long-standing 'campaign' against the post-conciliar liturgical reforms[17] might appear a little disingenuous given that, despite his declaration that his views on the liturgy 'evolved' over the years, he nonetheless was party to and in support of the conciliar energies that brought such reform about. To Allen's mind, what is clearly missing here, to accompany those reservations about the reforms, is 'honest self-disclosure' for,

> Ratzinger was not a passive bystander when the new direction of the liturgical movement was set by Vatican II; he helped put it on that course. He cannot blame anonymous 'liturgical experts' who foisted their private agenda on the church. The principles that guided their work were developed in full public view and approved by the bishops at the council, with Ratzinger's support.[18]

Turning to Catechesis, we encounter another theme that features throughout much of his theology, also, and the overall character of his internationally successful (yet initially incomplete) book, *Introduction to*

---

16   Cf. the introduction to Chapter Five of this volume.

17   Cf. John L. Allen, *Pope Benedict XVI: A Biography of Joseph Ratzinger.* New York: Continuum, 2005, pp. 71–74.

18   Ibid., p. 74. An author who latterly finds much to credit in Ratzinger's liturgical thought is the church historian, Eamon Duffy, cf. his 'Benedict XVI and the Eucharist', *New Blackfriars* Volume 88, no. 1014 (March 2007) p 195-212, which is a quite different perspective to that adopted by the earlier Duffy in his 'Urbi, but not Orbi . . . The Cardinal, the Church and the World', in *New Blackfriars*, vol. 66, no. 780 (June 1985), 272-278 (see chapter 3 of the present volume, 82 n4).

Christianity,[19] helps illustrate this very well. The fact that he personally presided over the production of the new universal *Catechism of the Catholic Church*, released in 1993,[20] is of further significance to understanding Ratzinger's theology. It set forth a presentation of Catholic teaching on faith and morals that was fully intended to be taken as normative.[21]

In his writings and addresses alike, Ratzinger has repeatedly lectured bishops on their catechetical duties and stressed the disciplinary aspects of such obligations as much as any other. So, in many ways, his theological ideas here have fed into his work on that *Catechism*, itself, as well as into the character of the finished product. This is also demonstrated by his various writings and addresses concerning both the *Catechism* itself (a shorter compendium version followed in 2005 – with, one might argue, some debt to Luther's model of catechesis) and catechesis in general. These offer a further clear illustration of the inter-locking character of his understanding of the faith itself and the doctrine that transmits, explains, defends and proclaims it.[22]

Ratzinger places fundamental importance upon the concept of the 'Deposit of Faith' (*Fidei Depositum*),[23] and of its 'faithful' interpretation, transmission, and proclamation alike. Scripture, tradition and the Church are bound together in their common witness to the revelation of God. Likewise, for him, faith and morals constitute a single continuum, not two distinct areas that can or should be kept apart, be it in Church teaching or theological undertakings alike.[24]

---

19   *Introduction to Christianity.* San Francisco: Ignatius, 1990.
20   Cf. Joseph Ratzinger and Christoph Schönbern, *Introduction to the Catechism of the Catholic Church.* San Francisco: Ignatius, 1994, and Joseph Ratzinger, *An Invitation to Faith: An A to Z Primer on the Thought of Pope Benedict XVI.* San Francisco: Ignatius, 2007; also his *Credo for Today.* San Francisco: Ignatius, 2009.
21   In the opening address of a conference to mark the tenth anniversary of the release of the Catechism, Ratzinger stated that 'Whoever looks for a new theological system or new surprising hypotheses in the Catechism will be disappointed . . . This type of current issue is not the concern of the Catechism [. . .]. Appealing to sacred Scripture and to the global richness of Tradition in its multiple forms, and inspired by the Second Vatican Council, [the Catechism] offers an organic view of the totality of the Catholic faith, which is beautiful precisely because of its totality, a beauty that highlights the splendor of truth [. . .]. The present importance of the Catechism is the importance of truth expressed and thought out once again [. . .]. This importance will remain despite the criticisms it may receive.' From 'Cardinal Ratzinger Says Catechism Is a Manual for Happiness', *Zenit* New Agency, available at: www.zenit.org/article-5531?l=english (accessed 1 October 2009).
22   Cf., for example, his 'Current Doctrinal Relevance of the Catechism of the Catholic Church: *The Catechism of the Catholic Church* - Ten Years Since its Publication' (address from 9 October 2002). Available at: www.vatican.va/roman_curia/congregations/cfaith/documents/rc_con_cfaith_doc_20021009_ratzinger-catechetical-congress_en.html (accessed 19 January 2009)
23   Indeed, *Fidei Depositum* was the very title of the Apostolic Constitution that marked the release of the Catechism itself.
24   Here, cf. Reading 6.5 in our previous chapter.

Ratzinger laments the popularization and professionalization of catechesis, which he believes has been overrun by concerns from practical
theology more focused upon anthropology than theology. Catechesis
is, he states, now in crisis. Although he once spoke in favour of certain
aspects of the innovative Dutch catechism of 1966, he was also critical
of many features of the same and would later, as Prefect of the CDF,
condemn similar innovations in France and the United States. Ratzinger
would openly commend the catechetical approach of the Council of
Trent and offer it as a corrective to the failings of more recent approaches.

For Ratzinger, catechism naturally serves, aids and leads into evangelization. In relation to his specific understanding of evangelization,
once again following the line taken by his mentor at Vatican II, Cardinal
Frings, Ratzinger has resisted any watering down of the need for evangelization and of the understanding of Christian mission. In particular,
since Vatican II, he has strongly rejected arguments that would move
away from evangelization being seen in terms of conversion in favour
of seeing dialogue with people of other churches, faiths and of no faith
as being, in itself, a proclamation of the gospel. Ratzinger is vehemently
opposed to such a notion.[25] As we saw in Chapter Five of this volume,
Ratzinger believes that the sense of mission and evangelization as entailing conversion to Catholic Christianity should be neither downplayed
nor neglected. He consistently insists on the priority of evangelization
and mission over dialogue in his writings.[26]

Ratzinger has clashed with various theologians and even Episcopal
conferences (particularly in relation to Asia where Christians are a clear
minority amongst other faiths), who have argued for a more harmonious
approach in emphasizing dialogue as proclamation, as opposed to conversion. We have seen (in chapter 5) how Ratzinger insists on the unicity
and uniqueness of the path to salvation through Jesus Christ as understood and taught by the Roman Catholic Church, which, he believes,
is the custodian and means towards obtaining such salvation. He rejects
attempts to shift the focus away from the Church (i.e. an ecclesio-centric
focus) towards an emphasis upon building the kingdom of God (i.e. a
regno-centric focus). He sees such attempts as divisive and a separation

---

25   Cf. Chapters Three and Five of this volume. The CDF document of 2000, *Dominus Iesus*, made
     objections to such perspectives unambiguously clear.

26   Commentators suggest this was demonstrated clearly in relation to Ratzinger's official capac-
     ity, when the importance of the Pontifical Council for Interreligious Dialogue appeared to be
     downgraded in 2006, being subsumed under the authority of the Pontifical Council for Culture.
     When the furore broke over Benedict's 2006 'Regensburg Address', and partly in response to the
     accusations that dialogue was being perceived as being of lesser importance under this papacy, the
     Council for Interreligious Dialogue was eventually granted its own President, Cardinal Jean Louis
     Tauron, once again.

of two salvific realities that are necessarily entwined and which cannot be divorced for practical and political purposes.

Ratzinger has actively encouraged particular new movements for evangelization in both his theological writings and public addresses and activities.[27] These movements are mainly gathered around what are generally acknowledged as conservative perspectives of the faith and ecclesial life. Ratzinger has had close relations with some of these movements since the 1960s.[28] He encourages the formation of small Christian communities, devotional practices and pilgrimages. World Youth Day is something he especially encourages. He urges Christians to withstand the tide of corruption and decadence that contemporary culture (often referred to by him in the singular) has unleashed against the faith. The Church has a distinctive message, mission and path towards salvation to offer to the wider world.

Those of differing theological, ecclesial and ecumenical persuasions would here argue that rhetorical and dialectical nostalgia informs and shapes aspects of the thought of Joseph Ratzinger on each of these three areas, just as it does aspects of his ecclesiology. Ratzinger's writings in the areas with which this chapter is concerned also work in the service of a normative ecclesiology and towards re-emphasizing the primacy of the universal Church over the local.

But Ratzinger's work in relation to each of these areas has also attracted a great deal of support, admiration and gratitude – including from non-Catholics. Many see him as restoring focus, priorities, order, mystery and awe to fundamental aspects of the faith – its worship, proclamation and explication. He is perceived to be standing up for the core elements of what it means to be a Christian and leading a battle against the erroneous and/or detrimental reforms of recent decades. He has become a figurehead for traditionalists in relation to each of these areas. Ratzinger does, indeed, seek to place the focus back on God, rather than on human individuals.

On the other hand, Ratzinger's critics would point to a potentially ironic problem in his theologizing in that his ecclesiology leads towards and strengthens a more individualistic and less communal form of Catholicism: it is one where the 'communion' is understood not in terms of the local Church and *then* in terms of the universal communion shared

27   E.g. cf. his *New Outpourings of the Spirit*. San Francisco: Ignatius Press, 2007 – an earlier version of part of this volume appeared as 'The Theological Locus of Ecclesial Movements', in *Communio* vol. 25, no. 3 (1998) pp. 480–504.

28   Cf. Stanislav Rylko, 'Introduction', to Joseph Ratzinger, *New Outpourings of the Spirit*. San Francisco: Ignatius Press, 2007, p. 2. This contact continued with renewed fervour in the early 1970s, as Ratzinger confirms himself in *New Outpourings of the Spirit*. San Francisco: Ignatius, 2007, p. 19.

across the world, but rather it leapfrogs the vitality and indeed authority of the local communion and accentuates the diachronic, 'Roman', and universal elements. So, for example, this means that the liturgy itself becomes a more private and personal experience. Eurocentric liturgical interpretations and practices are privileged over local inculturation and contextual vitality. In Ratzinger's understanding of catechesis, critics see a lack of realism and an undermining of decades of innovative and fruitful work by experts in this field. They say Ratzinger's understanding of catechesis is too rigid and can thus prove counter-productive. Ratzinger's sense of evangelization and mission has likewise been criticized for being both too Eurocentric and misguided. The notion of dialogue that was one of Vatican II's key gifts to the Church and which formed a core concept of Paul VI's own teaching, is seen by critics as being relegated and rendered of lesser importance in Ratzinger's thought,[29] and Ratzinger's notion of evangelization poses more problems to bearing witness to the Gospel in many contemporary contexts and cultures than it could hope to solve.

7.1 Change and Permanence in the Liturgy

This reading comes from a dialogue between Ratzinger and the editor of the International Catholic Periodical, *Communio*, in which the editor put a series of forthright questions and perspectives to Ratzinger in relation to the liturgy and developments pertaining to it in recent decades and asked him to elucidate his own opinion on these matters.

Ratzinger uses the opportunity to express his opposition to many academic theologians and to national Episcopal conferences in relation to the impact they have had upon the liturgy since the Council. Ratzinger seeks to portray greater continuity between the 1570 Missal and rite of Pius V in the wake of the Council of Trent and the earlier Church and so, also, between these and the liturgical reforms of Vatican II. The latter, he argues, did not introduce a new sense of the faith, it rather sought to revitalize and reaffirm the same faith under changed circumstances. He laments a lack of attentiveness to how the Vatican II reforms would and should be implemented, towards questions of active participation and continuity etc. In fact, his criticisms of the reforms here, as elsewhere, underlie the thrust of his core thesis.

But while, to the champions of Vatican II's reforms, he plays down the sense of change and innovation, to the 'Tridentinists', here at least,

---

29   Cf. Chapter Five of the present volume.

he issues a reminder that the Church's liturgy has always evolved, albeit in continuity.

Yet he also downplays the sense of inculturation understood as entailing adaptation, just as he rejects the perceived carelessness of the reform of the liturgical calendar and the incursion upon liturgical celebrations of what he perceives to be banal societal niceties. He warns of the dangers of new interpretations of the Eucharist and particularly of the real presence of Christ therein. Ratzinger laments how the Latin rite seems to have almost disappeared as people make up their own liturgies from week to week and from place to place. He is particularly concerned about what he calls a 'breakdown in liturgical consciousness'. As so often, he returns to the sense of *communio* to underpin his own preferred normative understanding and celebration of the liturgy offered here.

Many who lamented the liturgical reforms initiated by Vatican II and those which have followed since, rallied around Ratzinger's increasingly vociferous challenges to how the liturgy was being transformed. In recent times, the Tridentine Rite has become something of a cause célèbre amongst conservative Catholics. On the other hand, critics would say that, while Ratzinger seeks to downplay the sense of innovation in the Vatican II liturgical reforms, here and in numerous other places, he is essentially rejecting much of the spirit as well as the letter of those reforms and wishing to restore an older form, understanding and practice of the liturgy, which is less attentive to contextual needs and realities, and which could have numerous negative consequences through placing less emphasis upon the active participation on the part of the lay faithful. Such critical voices would also wonder if a rhetorical device is in play here both with regard to Ratzinger's account of the post-Trent liturgical reforms, as well as those of Vatican II, which were both more innovative and universally normative in a novel fashion than he suggests. His repeated criticisms of the role that 'professors' played in the Vatican II liturgical reforms and his railing against innovations could be seen as sitting ill at ease with the facts surrounding his own involvement in the debates concerning liturgy during the period of Vatican II and his somewhat different perspectives then, just as it masks his own particular form of innovation in interpreting the liturgy and recommending new norms and guidelines for its celebration.

[On Inculturation, Innovation and the Liturgy][30]

[. . .] First of all it must be said that both [Vatican II's] Constitution on the Liturgy and

---

30   [From 'Change and Permanence in the Liturgy' in Joseph Ratzinger, *Feast of Faith*. San Francisco: Ignatius Press, 2000, pp. 79–96].

the Decree on the Church's Missionary Activity explicitly allow for the possibility of far-reaching adaptations to the customs and cultic traditions of peoples. To that extent the new Missal is only providing a framework for mission lands. It is a feature of the new Missal that its very many *ad libitum* provisions give a great deal of scope for local variations. On the other hand, we must beware of seeing things too naively and simplistically. Only very slowly and with the greatest of caution did the growing Church take up certain of the external forms of pagan liturgies. At the beginning the Church operated within the form of the Jewish synagogue service – an extremely modest form from the point of view of ritual. She joined this to the celebration of the Eucharist, the basic structure of which was equally Jewish, namely, the great prayer of thanksgiving. At the core of this thanksgiving, she placed the account of the institution of the Eucharist. Hence this prayer also mediates the idea of sacrifice insofar as it is attuned to the prayer of Jesus Christ in his self-surrender to the Father and makes this self-offering present in time. These simple elements have constituted the basic structure of every Christian Eucharist right up to the present day. In the course of a gradual development they have been furnished with various cultic forms, ultimately giving rise to the individual ritual genres. But this development presupposes the existence of a Christian identity that was able to create its own fundamental liturgical form. Only on the basis of a Christian consciousness of this kind could the existing elements be refashioned in a fruitful way and made to express Christian realities. In other words, the whole process presupposes the struggle to vindicate what was distinctively Christian, a struggle carried on by the martyrs over three centuries. Only once this had been done could the door be opened to the use of pagan customs, suitably purified. Moreover, much of what we are inclined to see as adaptation from the Roman sphere of influence was in fact the product of the Old Testament renaissance which began in the early Middle Ages, i.e., here too it was far more a case of Christianity returning to appropriate its own distinct origins.

Therefore it seems to me very dangerous to suggest that missionary liturgies could be created overnight, so to speak, by decisions of Bishops' Conferences, which would themselves be dependent on memoranda drawn up by academies. Liturgy does not come about through regulation. One of the weaknesses of the postconciliar liturgical reform can doubtless be traced to the armchair strategy of academies, drawing up things on paper which, in fact, would presuppose years of organic growth. The most blatant example of this is the reform of the Calendar: those responsible simply did not realize how much the various annual feasts had influenced Christian people's relation to time. In redistributing these established feasts throughout the year according to some historical arithmetic – inconsistently applied at that – they ignored a fundamental law of religious life. But to return to the missionary situation: conversion to Christianity means, initially, turning away from pagan forms of life. There was a very clear awareness of this in the first Christian centuries, even long after the so-called Constantinian settlement. Not until a strong Christian identity has grown up in the mission countries can one begin to move, with great caution and on the basis of this identity, toward christening the indigenous forms by adopting them into the liturgy and allowing Christian realities to merge with the forms of everyday life. It goes without saying that expressions which have no meaning in a particular country, or which have a contrary meaning, have been altered. I would not call this liturgical 'reform', however, but the appropriate application of the existing form, something which is always necessary. What is more, I am convinced that a superficial or overhasty adaptation, far from attracting respect for Christianity, would only raise doubts as to its sincerity and the seriousness of its message. Then, too, we must remember that nowadays all indigenous cultures are overlaid by features of the technological world civilization, a fact which should caution us against haste and too much attention to externals.

[The Old Belief and the New?]
[. . .] I must take up the distinction [. . .] between 'the old belief' and 'the new'. I must emphatically deny such a distinction. The Council has not created any new matter for belief, let alone replaced an old belief with a new one. Fundamentally, the Council sees itself as continuing and deepening the work of earlier councils, in particular those of Trent and Vatican I. Its sole concern is to facilitate the same faith under changed circumstances, to revitalize it. That is why the reform of the liturgy aimed at making the faith's expression more transparent. But what we have is a renewed expression of the one faith, not a change in faith.

As to what led up to the reform: there seemed to be more going on in Germany, in terms of preparatory work, than anywhere else. Germany was the heartland of the liturgical movement, which had a great impact on the declarations of the Council. Many of the measures taken by the Council had long been anticipated here. Moreover, Pius XII had already carried out certain elements of liturgical reform – one thinks of the refashioning of the Easter Vigil. All the same I must admit that in the wake of the Council a lot of things happened far too quickly and abruptly, with the result that many of the faithful could not see the inner continuity with what had gone before. In part it is simply a fact that the Council was pushed aside. For instance, it had said that the language of the Latin Rite was to remain Latin, although suitable scope was to be given to the vernacular. Today we might ask: Is there a Latin Rite at all any more? Certainly there is no awareness of it. To most people the liturgy seems to be rather something for the individual congregation to arrange. Core groups make up their own 'liturgies' from week to week, with an enthusiasm which is as amazing as it is misplaced. The really serious thing, in my view, is this fundamental breakdown of liturgical consciousness. Imperceptibly, the distinctions between liturgy and conviviality, liturgy and society become blurred. Thus many priests, following the etiquette of polite society, feel that they must not receive Communion until all the others have been 'served'; or they no longer feel able to say 'I bless *you*' and so dissolve the basic liturgical relationship between priest and people. Here too is the origin of all those tasteless and banal forms of greeting – which many congregations endure with polite stoicism. In the period before the appearance of the new Missal, when the old Missal was already stigmatized as antiquated, there was a loss of the awareness of 'rite', i.e., that there is a prescribed liturgical form and that liturgy can only be liturgy to the extent that it is beyond the manipulation of those who celebrate it. Even the official new books, which are excellent in many ways, occasionally show far too many signs of being drawn up by academies and reinforce the notion that a liturgical book can be 'made' like any other book.

In this connection I would like to make a brief reference to the so-called Tridentine liturgy. In fact there is no such thing as a Tridentine liturgy, and until 1965 the phrase would have meant nothing to anyone. The Council of Trent did not 'make' a liturgy. Strictly speaking, there is no such thing, either, as the Missal of Pius V. The Missal which appeared in 1570 by order of Pius V differed only in tiny details from the first printed edition of the Roman Missal of about a hundred years earlier. Basically the reform of Pius V was only concerned with eliminating certain late medieval accretions and the various mistakes and misprints which had crept in. Thus, again, it prescribed the Missal of the City of Rome, which had remained largely free of these blemishes, for the whole Church. At the same time it was felt that if the *Missale typicum* printed in Rome were used exclusively, it would help to get rid of the uncertainties which had arisen in the confusion of liturgical movements in the Reformation period, for in this liturgical confusion the distinction between Catholic and Reformed had been widely obscured. This is clear from the fact that the reform explicitly made an exception of those liturgical customs which were more than two hundred years old. In 1614, under Urban VIII, there was already a new edition of the Missal, again including various improvements. In this way each century before and after Pius V left its mark on the Missal. On the one hand, it was subject to a continuous process of purification, and on the other, it continued to grow and develop, but it remained the same book throughout. Hence those who cling to the 'Tridentine Missal' have a faulty view of the historical facts. Yet at the same time, the way in which the renewed Missal was presented is open to much criticism. We must say to the 'Tridentines' that the Church's liturgy is alive, like the Church herself, and is thus always involved in a process of maturing which exhibits greater and lesser changes. Four hundred years is far too young an age for the Catholic liturgy – because in fact it reaches right back to Christ and the apostles and has come down to us from that time in a single, constant process. The Missal can no more be mummified than the Church herself. Yet, with all its advantages, the new Missal was published as if it were a book put together by professors, not a phase in a continual growth process. Such a thing has never happened before. It is absolutely contrary to the laws of liturgical growth, and it has resulted in the nonsensical notion that Trent and Pius V had 'produced' a Missal four hundred years ago. The Catholic liturgy was thus reduced to the level of a mere product of modern times. This loss of perspective is really disturbing. Although very few of those who express their uneasiness have a clear picture of these interrelated factors, there is an instinctive grasp of the fact that liturgy cannot be the result of Church regulations, let alone professional erudition, but, to be true to itself, must be the fruit of the Church's life and vitality. Lest there be any misunderstanding, let me add that as far as its content is concerned (apart from a few criticisms), I am very grateful for the new Missal, for the way it has enriched the treasury of prayers and prefaces, for the new eucharistic prayers and the increased number of texts for use on weekdays, etc, quite apart from the availability of the vernacular. But I do regard it as unfortunate that we have been presented with the idea of a new book rather than with that of continuity within a single liturgical history. In my view, a new edition will need to make it quite clear that the so-called Missal of Paul VI is nothing other than a renewed form of the same Missal to which Pius X, Urban VIII, Pius V and their predecessors have contributed, right from the Church's earliest history. It is of the very essence of the Church that she should be aware of her unbroken continuity throughout the history of faith, expressed in an ever-present unity of prayer. This awareness of continuity is destroyed just as much by those who 'opt' for a book supposed to have been produced four hundred years ago as by those who would like to be forever drawing up new liturgies. At bottom, these two attitudes are identical. [. . .] The fundamental issue is whether faith comes about through regulations and learned research or through the living history of a Church which retains her identity throughout the centuries. [. . .]

[Active Participation in the Liturgy]

Perhaps I can begin by saying something about the idea of *participatio actuosa* – 'active participation' – which is indeed a key phrase in the Constitution on the Liturgy of Vatican II. What lies behind it is the awareness that Christian liturgy, of its very nature, is something performed in the context of a community. It involves prayer dialogues, greetings, proclamation, praying together. People are referred to as 'we' and 'you'; the 'I' occurs in only a few relatively late prayers. Here we are involved in an action, a 'drama', in which we all play our part. This being so, the liturgical celebration, from its very structure, calls for the interplay of words and acts between the participants. Otherwise there would arise an inner conflict between the text and what actually takes place. This was the discovery made by the liturgical movement, and it gave a new immediacy to the old words and gestures. At this point the Council was simply lending its authority to something which was self-evident. Generally speaking, this insight proved most fruitful. If one were to remove the active involvement which exists in today's liturgy – and the Council facilitated this involvement – it would immediately be obvious how much growth there has been. No one would want to be without it. But it is always possible for any true insight to be diminished, interpreted one-sidedly or distorted. Many protagonists of liturgical reform seemed to think that if we only did everything together and in a loud voice, the liturgy would automatically become attractive and effective. They forgot that the spoken words also have a *meaning*, and part *of participatio actuosa* is to carry out that meaning. They failed to notice that the *actio* does not consist only or primarily in the alternation of standing, sitting and kneeling, but in inner processes. It is these which give rise to the whole drama of the liturgy. 'Let us pray' – this is an invitation to share in a movement which reaches down into our inner depths. 'Lift up your hearts' – this phrase and the movement which accompanies it are, so to speak, only the 'tip of the iceberg'. The real action takes place in the deep places of men's hearts, which are lifted up to the heights. 'Behold the Lamb of God' – here we have an invitation to a special kind of beholding, at a much deeper level than the external beholding of the Host. Where this inner dimension was neglected, the liturgy still seemed 'boring' and 'unintelligible', with the result that ultimately the Bible was replaced by Marx and the sacrament by a kind of 'party' atmosphere. People wanted to 'turn on' an immediate effect, as it were, from outside. Compared with the merely external busyness which became the rule in many places, the quiet 'following' of Mass, as we knew it in former times, was far more realistic and dramatic: it was a sharing in the action at a deep level, and in it the community of faith was silently and powerfully mobilized. Of course, to say this is not to impugn 'active participation' as I have defined it; the criticism only applies where this participation has degenerated into mere externals. There is simply no way of ensuring that everyone, always and on all occasions, is involved in the *actio*. Indeed, I think it is one of the crucial insights we have gained in the wake of the Council that the liturgy's effect cannot be achieved in a purely external manner. Faith requires a continual process of education, otherwise the words of faith begin to lose their meaning. [. . .]

[On the Relation between Form and Content in the Celebration of the Mass]
Receiving Christ must involve all the dimensions of Christ; so it cannot be limited to a physical process. It also implies belief in the Real Presence. It is so hard to define this adequately because nowadays we no longer have a philosophy which penetrates to the being of things. We are only interested in function. Modern science only asks 'How does it work? What can I do with it?' It no longer asks 'What *is* it?''; such a question would be regarded as unscientific, and indeed, in a strictly scientific sense, it is insoluble. The attempts to define the Eucharist by reference to the level of meaning and the goal (transsignification, transfinalization) were intended as a response to this new situation. Although these new concepts are not simply wrong, they are dangerously limited. Once sacraments and faith are reduced to the level of function, we are no longer speaking of God (for he is not a 'function'), nor are we speaking of man either (for he is not a function, although he *has* many functions). Here we can see how important it is, in a philosophically impoverished era, for sacramental faith to keep alive the question of being. This is the only way to break up the tyranny of functionalism, which would turn the world into one vast concentration camp. When nowadays we affirm that Christ

is present at the level of being in the transformed gifts, we are doing something which, up to a point, is not backed up or 'covered' by philosophy; therefore the affirmation becomes all the more significant as a human act.

On the relationship of the sacrifice and meal elements [. . .] I will say this: modern theology is rather against drawing parallels between the history of religions and Christianity. All the same I regard it as significant that, throughout the entire history of religions, sacrifice and meal are inseparably united. The sacrifice facilitates *communio* with the divinity, and men receive back the divinity's gift in and from the sacrifice. This is transformed and deepened in many ways in the mystery of Jesus Christ: here the sacrifice itself comes from the incarnate love of God, so that it is God who gives himself, taking man up into his action and enabling him to be both gift and recipient. Perhaps I can illustrate what I mean here by taking up another [. . .] question 'Do we need a priest with the power to consecrate?' I would prefer not to speak of 'power', although this term has been used since the early Middle Ages. I think it is better to approach it from another angle. In order that what happened then may become present now, the words 'This is my body – this is my blood' must be said. But the speaker of these words is the 'I' of Jesus Christ. Only he can say them; they are his words. No man can dare to take to himself the 'I' and 'my' of Jesus Christ – and yet the words must be said if the saving mystery is not to remain something in the distant past. So authority to pronounce them is needed, an authority which no one can assume and which no congregation, nor even many congregations together, can confer. Only Jesus Christ himself, in the 'sacramental' form he has committed to the whole Church, can give this authority. The word must be located, as it were, in sacrament; it must be part of the 'sacrament' of the Church, partaking of an authority which she does not create, but only transmits. This is what is meant by 'ordination' and 'priesthood'. Once this is understood, it becomes clear that, in the Church's Eucharist, something is happening which goes far beyond any human celebration, any human joint activity, and any liturgical efforts on the part of a particular community. What is taking place is the mystery of God, communicated to us by Jesus Christ through his death and Resurrection. This is what makes the Eucharist irreplaceable; this is the guarantee of its identity. The reform has not altered it: its aim was simply to shed new light upon it.

7.2 The Crisis of Catechesis

In this article from the journal *Communio*, and originally a paper delivered at Notre-Dame de Fourvière (Lyon) and Notre-Dame de Paris, on 15th and 16th of January 1983, Ratzinger speaks about catechesis as a 'vital function of the faith' and yet identifies it as a function that is in crisis. He laments the increasing professionalization of catechism and the excessive experimentation that this has led to. He particularly criticizes the turn towards practical theology, which has become something deemed of value in its own right, instead of being understood as 'a concrete development of dogmatic or systematic theology'. Ratzinger also laments what he perceives to be a further area witnessing a capitulation to modern and contemporary culture, an excessive focus upon method, particularly the triumph of anthropology over theology, which was then followed by what he believes was an invasion by the social sciences into the realm of theology and faith, resulting in the primacy of experience coming to be seen as central to understanding the faith. He commends the model of catechism offered by the Council of Trent, which, he suggests, offered ample scope for flexibility in application in differing contexts. He reflects upon the fundamental sources of the faith and the four 'master components' of catechism (*viz.*, the Apostles' Creed, the Seven Sacraments, the Ten Commandments and the Lord's Prayer), synthesized therein. Ratzinger wishes to return the focus of catechism to this 'simple structure' in order to overcome the perceived crisis brought about by the experimentation of recent decades. He also reflects upon the new opening to the study of the Bible but reminds readers that even scripture itself points towards and comments upon revelation, rather than being revelation *in toto*, itself. Catechism that purports to be taking the Bible as its direct source, without recourse to dogma, will err. He reminds his readers that there is no faith without the Church and hence communion must be accentuated over individual experience. A further fundamental problem with catechesis today, he suggests, is a failure to distinguish adequately between text and commentary.

The article obviously reflects the currents of thought in the mind of Ratzinger as he was engaged in co-ordinating the composition of the new *Catechism of the Catholic Church* and, therefore, demonstrates his own methodological thinking in progress, along with his own analysis of the problems and challenges in this area that needed to be addressed.

Critical voices would question whether the theological outlook which permeates this article fully resonates with the older traditional Roman Catholic thinking that Ratzinger suggests it is portraying. They would further argue that this article might even offer some statements that sit ill at ease alongside one another, for example, denouncing a reliance upon religious experience and yet then focusing upon the individual's own personal faith as being fundamental. Such critics would see an agenda leading towards the promotion of what is, in effect, a form of neo-integralism, where everything in the faith is understood in terms of a seamless whole and this entails that there must also be a normative way of teaching, understanding and explaining this integral faith, regardless of context.

1. The Crisis of Catechesis and the Problem of Sources: General Characteristics of the Crisis[31]

The present difficulties of catechesis are too well known to need any detailed description. The causes and consequences of the crisis have been often and abundantly described. In the world of technology, which is a creation of man, it is not the Creator whom one first encounters; rather, man encounters only himself. The basic structure of the world of technology is to be 'practical.' Its certitudes are those of the calculable. That is why the question of salvation is not posed in terms of God, who appears nowhere, but in function of the power of man who wants to become his own constructor and the master of his own history. He no longer looks for the criteria of his ethics in a discourse on creation or the Creator, for these have become unknown to him. Creation no longer has an ethical resonance for him, but only speaks to him in a mathematical language in terms of technical usefulness, except when it protests against the violence to which creation has to submit. Even then the moral appeal which creation addresses to man remains indeterminate. In the final analysis morality is identified in one or another way with sociability, that of man to man and that of man with his milieu. From this point of view, ethics has become also a question of calculating the best conditions for future development. Society, too, has been deeply changed. The family, the nurturing cell of Christian culture, appears in the process of dissolution. When metaphysical bonds no longer count, other kinds cannot long maintain themselves. On the one hand, this new image of the world is reflected in the mass media, and on the other hand, it is fed by them. The representation of the world by the mass media makes a bigger impact today on consciousness than does personal experience of reality. All of this influences catechesis, for which the classical supports of a Christian society have been destroyed. Catechesis can no longer lean on a lived experience of the faith in a living Church; the faith seems condemned to remain dumb in a time when language and consciousness are nourished only from the experience of a world which thinks it is its own creator.

Practical theology has devoted itself energetically to this problem in the last decades, in order to work out new and better adapted ways for the transmission of the faith. Meanwhile, many indeed have become convinced that these efforts have contributed more to worsening than to resolving the crisis. It would be unjust to accept such a sweeping condemnation, but it would be just as wrong to deny it purely and simply. It was an initial and grave error to suppress the catechism and to declare obsolete the whole idea of catechisms. To be sure, the catechism as a kind of book only became common at the time of the Reformation, but the transmission of the faith, as a fundamental structure born of the logic of the faith, is as old as the catechumenate, that is to say, as old as the Church itself. It flows

---

31   [From Joseph Ratzinger, 'Sources and Transmission of the Faith', in *Communio*, vol. 10, no. 1 (1983) pp. 17–34. Trans. by Thomas Langan].

from the very nature of the Church's mission, and so one cannot give it up. The rupture with the transmission of the faith as fundamental structure drawn from the sources of a total tradition has had as a consequence the fragmentation of the proclamation of the faith. The faith was arbitrarily dealt with in the way in which it was explicated, and some of its parts were called into question, despite the fact that they belong to a whole, separated from which they appear disparate and meaningless.

What lay behind this erroneous decision, so hasty and yet so universal? There are various reasons which up until now have hardly been looked at. It certainly has something to do with the general evolution of teaching and pedagogy, which is itself characterized by an excess of method in relation to the content of the various disciplines. The methods become criteria for the content rather than just the vehicle. The offer is determined by the demand; it is in these terms that the ways of the new catechesis were defended in the debate over the Dutch catechism. Thus it was necessary to limit oneself to questions for beginners instead of looking for ways to go beyond to things not yet understood. Yet this latter is the only method which positively modifies man and the world. Thus, the faith's potential for change was paralyzed. From that point, practical theology was no longer understood as a concrete development of dogmatic or systematic theology but as having a value in itself. This corresponds perfectly with the new tendency to subordinate theory to praxis, which, in the context of Neo-Marxist and positivist philosophies, was making headway even in theology. All these things have the effect of a restricting anthropology: the priority of method over content means the domination of anthropology over theology, in the sense that theology has to find a place for itself in a radical anthropocentrism. The decline of anthropology in its turn causes new centers of gravity to appear: the reign of sociology, again with the primacy of experience as new criteria for the understanding of the traditional faith.

Behind these and other causes one can find that, for the refusal of the catechism and for the collapse of classical catechesis, there is hidden a more profound process. The fact that one no longer has the courage to present the faith as an organic whole in itself, but only as selected reflections of partial anthropological experiences, is founded in a certain distrust of the totality. It is to be explained by a crisis of the faith, or more exactly, of the common faith of the Church of all times. The result was that one left dogma out of catechesis and attempted to reconstruct the faith directly from the Bible. Now, dogma is nothing other than interpretation of Scripture, but that interpretation, born of the faith of centuries, seemed unable to be accorded with the understanding of the texts to which in the meantime the historical method had led. So two apparently irreducible forms of interpretation seem to coexist: historical interpretation and dogmatic interpretation. But the latter, according to contemporary conceptions, could only be taken for a pre-scientific stage on the way to the new interpretation. Thus it seemed difficult to accord it a proper place. When scientific certitude is considered the only valid form of certitude, indeed the only possible one, then the dogmatic form had to be seen as either archaic or as something imposed by the will-to-power of surviving institutions.

Catechesis, Bible and Dogma

We are now at the central point of our subject, the problem of the proper place of the 'sources' in the process of the transmission of the faith. A catechesis which develops the faith directly from the Bible, without passing through dogma, pretends to be especially derived from the sources. [. . .]

In fact this process, the theological evolution of which Schweitzer thought he had stopped almost a century ago, repeats itself in a new way and with various modifications in modern catechesis. For the documents that one has tried to read without any other intermediary than that of the historical method get farther away as they become more distant from the historical fact. An exegesis which lives and understands the Bible no longer with the living organism of the Church becomes archeology, a museum of past things.

Concretely, this is seen in the fact that the Bible falls apart as Bible, to become nothing more than a collection of heterogeneous books. This then raises the questions of how to assimilate that literature and by what criteria choose the texts with which to build a catechesis. [. . .] If before it was the case that the Bible entered into the teaching of the faith only under the aspect of a doctrine of the Church, now one tries to have access to Christianity by means of a direct dialogue between present experience and the biblical word.

[. . .] A central question poses itself today, then, and this question focuses our subject: how is the water of the sources to be conserved pure during the transmission of the faith? With that question two essential problems appear for the present situation: the relation of dogmatic exegesis to historical-critical exegesis and relationships between method and content, between experience and faith.

The first question, on the relation of dogmatic to historical-critical exegesis, is also the question of the relationship which needs to be established between the living tissue of the tradition on the one hand, and rational methods of reconstituting the past on the other. However, it is also the question of the two levels of thought and life: what is then in fact the place of the rational articulation of science in the whole of human existence and its encounter with the real?

The second question seems to us to consist in the determination of the relationship between method and content, between experience and faith. It is clear that faith without experience can only be verbiage of empty formulas. The reverse is also evident: to reduce faith to experience is to rob it of its kernel. [. . .]

2. Towards Overcoming the Crisis: What is the Faith?

[. . .] Faith is itself *anticipation* of that which is presently inaccessible. It is thus that it rejoins the inaccessible in our lives and leads us to surpass ourselves. To put it another way: for a proper renewal, both theoretical and practical, of the transmission of faith and a true renewal of catechesis, the questions which have just been posed have to be recognized as real questions and brought to some kind of a conclusion. [. . .]

Our reflections have brought us to think about what we might call the personal character of our faith. But that is only half of the story. The other half is also described in the First Letter of St. John. In the first verse, the Apostle characterizes his experience as a 'Vision' and a 'contract' with the Word, who is life and who offers himself to the touch because he became flesh. Hence the mission of the Apostles, which is to transmit what they have seen and heard 'in order that you, too, with us, can enter into communion' with that Word (1 John 1:1-4). The faith is not then just an encounter with God and the Christ, but it is also this contact which opens a contact with those to whom God has communicated himself. This communion, we should add, is the gift of the Spirit, who throws down a bridge for us towards the Father and the Son. Faith then is not only an 'I' and a 'Thou,' it is also a 'We.' In this 'we' lives the memorial which makes us rediscover what we had forgotten: God and the One he has sent.

To put it another way, there is no faith without Church. Henri de Lubac has shown that the 'I' of the Christian confession of faith is not the isolated 'I' of the individual but the collective 'I' of the Church. When I say, 'I believe,' it means that I go beyond the frontiers of my subjectivity, in order to integrate myself with the 'I' of the Church, which at the same time means integrating myself with its knowledge which goes beyond the limits of time. The act of faith is always an act by which one enters into communion with a whole. It is an act of communion through which one lets oneself be integrated into the communion of witnesses, so that through them we touch the intangible, hear the inaudible, see the invisible. Cardinal de Lubac has also shown that we do not believe in the Church as we believe *in* God, but that our faith is fundamentally an act accomplished with the whole Church.[32] Every time one thinks he can neglect the faith of the Church to be able, in catechesis, to draw directly from the Scriptural source a more direct and precise knowledge, he enters into the domain of abstraction. For then he no longer thinks, lives and speaks in function of a certitude which goes beyond his own personal possibilities and which is founded on a memory anchored in the bases of the faith and derived from it. One no longer speaks then in virtue of a delegation which goes beyond the powers of the individual; on the contrary, one plunges into that other kind of faith which is only opinion, more or less founded on the unknown. Under these circumstances, catechesis is reduced to being only one theory alongside others, a power like the others. It can no longer be the study and reception of true life, of eternal life. [. . .]

---

32 Henri de Lubac, *La Foi chrétienne, Essai sur la structure du symbole des apôtres.* Paris: Aubier-Montaigne, 1969, pp. 201–234. See also J. Ratzinger, *Theologische Prinzipilenlehre.* Munich: Wewel, 1982, pp. 15–27. Important and illuminating in this regard is what Louis Bouyer underlines in *Le métier de théologien.* Paris: Editions France-Empire, 1979, pp. 207–227.

The structure of catechesis: the four master components
The internal cohesion between the Word and the organism which bears it prepares the way for catechesis. Its structure appears through the principal events in the life of the Church, which correspond to the essential dimensions of Christian existence. Thus is born from the earliest time a catechetical structure, the kernel of which goes back to the origins of the Church. Luther used that structure for his catechism just as naturally as did the authors of the Catechism of Trent. That was possible because it was not a question of an artificial system, but simply of the synthesis of mnemonic material indispensable to the faith, which reflects at the same time elements vitally indispensable to the Church: the Apostles' Creed (also known as the Symbol of the Apostles), the Sacraments, the Ten Commandments, and the Lord's Prayer. These four classical and master components of catechesis have served for centuries as the depository and résumé of Catholic teaching. They have also opened access to the Bible as to the life of the Church. We have just said that they correspond to the dimensions of Christian existence. [. . .]

I do not see why anyone wants simply to abandon this simple structure, just as correct theologically as it is pedagogically. At the start of the new movement in catechetics this structure was taken to be naive. It was thought they could build a Christian systematization which would be utterly logical and convincing. But such research belongs to theology, not to catechetics, which rarely lasts much longer than its authors. At the opposite extreme they proposed abolition of all structure, and the blind choice made in function of the present situation was an inevitable reaction to the excesses of systematic thought. [. . .]

7.3 The Teaching Office of the Bishop

In March 1989, at the Vatican, Pope John Paul II, along with curial officials, met with thirty-five bishops from the United States. Joseph Ratzinger was asked to address the gathering with a reflection on 'The Bishop as Teacher of the Faith'. In his strongly worded paper, Ratzinger observes that the proclamation of the word does not seem to have received much commentary in the post-Vatican II Catholic discourse. He notes that while bishops do appear to preach in recent times more than they did prior to Vatican II, they have also become somewhat cowed in their exercise of their teaching office. He suggests that many bishops appear to have handed over their teaching duties to professional theologians instead of meeting such obligations themselves.

Here, Ratzinger once again argues that an increasing 'professionalization' of catechism in the Church is also at fault and has led to excessive experimentation.[33] Ratzinger rejects arguments such as those of Hans Küng, which propose a separation of the teaching function from that of shepherds in the Church and he chastises the bishops for their failure to exercise 'their teaching authority in opposition to theologians'. Instead, he asserts, bishops have been too content to concern themselves, in the main, with 'pastoral issues' as opposed to confronting people 'with the authority of the truth'. Here Ratzinger appears to be outlining an aggressive agenda against particular schools of theology and against particular models of episcopacy. This agenda would increasingly dominate his work at the CDF in the following decade and a half. Ratzinger even appears to denounce *aggiornamento* – the watchword of Pope John XXIII and Vatican II.[34] The relation between the Gospel and culture must, he argues, be put into proper perspective. We hear (yet again) that relativism must be resisted and that, as evangelization is the primary task of the bishop, this office must be carried out even to the point of martyrdom. Vigilance is further commended as an urgent contemporary Episcopal task.

Critics would suggest that the tone of Ratzinger's address was both polemical and even coercive. Furthermore, as bishops had long been kept 'out of the loop' on major decisions by the CDF, of which Ratzinger was head, particularly those in relation to Catholic theology and theologians, it should not be surprising that they had chosen to refrain from adding to the divisions in the Church by attacking theologians themselves.[35] Such critical voices would perceive the rhetoric employed here as epitomizing the divisive line that Ratzinger increasingly pursued not only in his theological writings since the late 1960s, but also in his official pronouncements and actions during his time at the CDF.

In the Book of Revelation, it is said of the new city, Jerusalem: 'The walls of the city stood on twelve foundation stones, each one of which bore the name of one of the twelve apostles of the Lamb' (21:14). This grand vision of the end time has to be kept before our eyes in order to understand fully what the Second Vatican Council teaches concerning the office of bishop: 'This sacred synod teaches that by divine institution bishops have succeeded to the place of the apostles as shepherds of the church, and he who hears them, hears Christ' (*Lumen Gentium*, 20). It is of

---

33 As we have already seen, above, see Reading 7.2.
34 Cf. Chapter Six of this volume.
35 To a certain extent, gradual changes began to appear in subsequent years until, under Pope Benedict XVI and Cardinal William Levada at the CDF, the 'disciplining' of theologians deemed errant seemed increasingly to be handed over to local ordinaries and/or Episcopal conferences once the CDF had pronounced judgment upon their work. Obviously, by this stage, Ratzinger's perspective in the following text had long held sway throughout much of the church and the make-up of the episcopacy itself had considerably changed.

'the essence of the episcopal office, then, that the bishops have succeeded to the place of the apostles.' The meaning of this is made clear by the fact that they are called 'shepherds of the church'. Reference to the word of Christ sheds further light upon this expression: He who hears you hears me (Lk. 10:16). This is important: 'The pastoral ministry,' the shepherd's office, is explained through the notion of hearing. One is a shepherd according to the mind of Jesus Christ, then, inasmuch as he brings people to the hearing of Christ. In the background here the words of the prologue of John's Gospel calling Christ the Logos can be heard; resonant too is the ancient Christian idea that it is precisely the Logos who is the shepherd of men, guiding us sheep who have gone astray to the pastures of truth and giving us there the water of life. To be shepherds, then, means to give voice to the Logos, voice to the redeeming Word.[36]

These basic thoughts come back again in practical form when *Lumen Gentium*, No. 25, describes in concrete terms what the bishop is to do. The Second Vatican Council stated it in this way: 'Among the principal duties of bishops, the preaching of the Gospel occupies an eminent place,' which, incidentally, is the repetition of a formula coined by the Council of Trent (Session 24, *De Reform*. IV, eds. Alberigo et al., Bologna 1973, p. 763). First and foremost, the bishop is an evangelist, and we might put it this way: It is as an evangelist that he is a successor of the apostles.

If we as bishops examine our consciences upon the words of that sentence and ask ourselves whether our actual priorities correspond to this ideal, there are within the developments of this post-conciliar era certainly many positive elements according with this image of the bishop which one could adduce: In general, bishops do actually preach more today than was formerly the case – perhaps sometimes too much. It is surely a positive development that bishops themselves almost always preach at pontifical functions and thus take precedence over their priests in proclaiming the word of God. Along the same line, we find intensified efforts on the part of many bishops and bishops' conferences to comment by means of well-prepared pastoral letters upon the great issues of the day and to respond to them in the light of the faith. The balance is seen to tip much less toward the positive, however, as soon as we begin to think about the developments in catechesis in the post-conciliar period. To a large extent, this area has been turned over to the so-called professional. This, in turn, has led to an excess of experimentation, which often makes the actual topic vanish from sight, and to a confusion of voices, making it all the more difficult to recognize that of the Gospel. The problem becomes more evident if we think about the relationship between bishop and theologians who are no longer active in just the quiet realm of academic research and teaching. They frequently perform their quite dissonant

---

36 [Taken from Joseph Ratzinger, 'The Bishop as Teacher of the Faith', in *Origins* vol. 18 (1989), pp. 681–682].

concert for all the public with the instruments of the mass media in such a way that their voice drowns out that of the bishop-evangelist. Despite all the indisputable efforts by bishops to proclaim the word, theologians in many parts of the world have taken the place of the bishop as teacher. Although much good has also come to pass in this way, on the whole the result has to be seen predominantly as one of uncertainty and confusion: The contours of the faith are vanishing behind reflections which ought to be illuminating it.

In this context, I have to mention a particular development of this post-conciliar time which calls for our special attention. We heard how the Second Vatican Council gave precedence to the bishop's mission of proclaiming the word. If we would look now at the theological literature of the period after the council on this question, we would discover surprisingly that this statement has remained practically without commentary. What we find instead in the literature are explanations which attempt to reduce the episcopate to a kind of spiritual administration. Thus J. Colson asserted an equivalence between the early Christian bishop and the *mebaqqer* of the Qumran community, and he strove to verify that this was the model James and the other early Christian leaders followed. After the manner of Qumran, they were only 'supervisors.' The patrologist, A. Hamman, takes a similar position regarding the Greek world: The bishops were called *episkopoi*, which means inspectors according to the linguistic usage current in the civil administration of that time. Hans Küng established the same etymological and genealogical point, and from it draws his distinction between bishops and teachers, his separation of teaching from the function of shepherds. All these theses have not remained in the academic realm, rather they have been transformed into a kind of pressure which is exerted upon the bishop: It would be his task to avoid polarizations, to appear as a moderator acting within the plurality of existing opinions, but he himself is not to become 'partisan' in any substantive way. Now this is always correct, if the question is just one of scholarly differences. But it is wrong, if what comes into issue is the faith itself. For the faith, entry into the church does not constitute a 'partisan act.'

Actually, we have to confess that bishops have submitted in large measure to this scheme of things and have little exercised their teaching authority in opposition to theologians. This course, however, has at the same time caused their own preaching activity to depreciate because the preached word is consigned to the category of the simply 'pastoral' and is not invested with the authority of decision. But this is precisely when it is not pastoral, for pastoral activity consists in placing man at the point of decision, confronting him with the authority of the truth. What is preached conforms to the norm of the psalmist's words: 'You have made known to me the path of life.' (Ps. 16:11).

The German philosopher, Robert Spaemann, made a sarcastic comment upon this psalm verse some time ago: 'To dally long in a Catholic bookstore does not encourage one to pray with the psalmist: "You have made known to me the path to life". There we have learned that in no way did Jesus change water into wine, insights into the art have actually succeeded instead in changing wine into water! This new brand of magic bears the name *aggiornamento.*'

In making our examination of conscience, the question now arises: Why to so large an extent have we bishops acquiesced in this reduction of our office to the inspector, the moderator, the *mebaqqer?* Why have we gone back to Qumran when it comes to this essential point of the New Testament? This is where we encounter the background of our modern culture, the issue of the proper relationship between this culture and the Gospel. Modern culture tells us first of all that it is not possible to distinguish clearly between faith and theology and, even if it should be possible, it can only be the specialist in any case, the theologian not the shepherd, who is competent. How should the shepherd be able to find his way in such a thicket? The shepherd, then, cannot determine whether theological reflection has begun perhaps to erode the faith itself and has forfeited his role of service.

This is just the first stage of the problem. The real question is more radical. Our modern world makes a distinction between two spheres of life, that of action and that of reflection. In the sphere of action, a person needs something like authority which is functionally based and which becomes active within the framework of its area of operation. In the sphere of reflection, there can be no authority. Reflection follows solely the laws of thought. Its essence, however, is such that it recognizes no final validity to its process, just the ever new hypothesis, which must be tested and which, at given times, has to be overhauled. What this means, though, is this: The church can exercise a functional authority within the sphere of her dealings, for authority is based upon functional contexts, nothing else. The church cannot interfere in the course of thought, in the scientific reflection of theology. Theology is not a matter of authority, but rather one of being professional. These notions have attained such a degree of plausibility in the world of today that it is well nigh impossible for bishops not to succumb to them. However, if these notions hold sway, this means that the church, while surely able to dispense pious advice, will not be able to bear witness to the truth in a way that is binding and, thereby, to call people to a commitment.

Involved with this, there is a final problem: In the hierarchy of values of today's world, the free rights of the individual and those accorded to the mass media take highest place while the objective moral values, about which there is no agreement anyway, are banished to the realm of the individual, where they merit no public defense from the community. There is, to put it bluntly, a right to act immorally, but morality itself has no rights. In contrast to the one-sidedness of former epochs, this can have its advantage. On the other hand, the commission of witnessing to the truth of the Gospel brings one also to suffering for it.

But this is at the same time the very positive conclusion toward which our deliberations have been leading: It is the hallmark of truth to be worth suffering for. In the deepest sense of the word, the evangelist must also be a martyr. If he is unwilling to be so, he should not lay his hand to the plough. It goes without saying that the bishop, as messenger of the Gospel, has to be generous in giving space for intellectual disputation. He has to be ready to learn himself and to accept correction. But he must also realize that the faith, which is expressed in the baptismal symbol and which he has inherited from the witnesses of all the centuries preceding, calls him to a responsibility. The word with which Paul bade farewell to the presbyters in Ephesus touches us too: 'Keep watch over yourselves and over the whole flock over which the Holy Spirit has appointed you as bishops that you might care for it as shepherds of God's church which he acquired for himself through the blood of his Son. . . . Be on guard therefore' (Acts 20:28, 31).

7.4 The New Evangelization

Asked to address a colloquium on 'Gospel and Culture', sponsored by the Italian Episcopal conference, Ratzinger's remit was to offer some reflections upon the interrelation between communication, culture and evangelization. The middle term was his chosen area of key focus. He acknowledges that there is more to culture than the Gospel, but presents, in the light of challenges facing the Gospel in the third millennium, particularly in Western cultures, a picture of the Gospel as an educator of cultures. The Gospel is thus understood as something that draws out of particular cultures gifts and potential that they could not realise if they remained solely reliant on their own internal resources. Ratzinger uses the patristic imagery of the notion of cutting a sycamore tree in order to let it bear fruit as a vivid picture of his understanding of the faith-culture dichotomy.[37]

In this text, we encounter another familiar theme found throughout Ratzinger's discourse – *viz.*, that of the superiority of the Gospel over particular cultures , indeed over and against culture in general. Elements of his ecclesiology again supplement his notions of mission and evangelization. In the postmodern climate the 'true' Christians may be few in number, but they are to act as a leaven in their wider society to try and convert it to the truth of the Gospel. Ratzinger's distaste for inculturation – which he perceives to be a dilution of the Gospel for the sake of expediency, is especially evident here. As a uni-directional influence appears to shape his understanding of the relationship between Gospel and culture, then, *a fortiori*, the task of the 'new evangelization' becomes for him unambiguous.

We thus come to learn more of the rationale behind Ratzinger's commendation of new forms of evangelization and, in particular, of lay

---

37   On the relation between the faith and culture cf., also, chapter 4 of the present volume.

apostolic movements, as well as his more recent enthusiasm for pilgrimages and shrines, and World Youth Day. In what might be read by his critics as a thinly veiled directive, Ratzinger warns Episcopal conferences and their agencies to embrace these developments as the way forward for the Church in accordance with how they are understood by the CDF. He makes it clear that Christianity will not only bring gifts to a culture, but it will also, at times, have to oppose elements of it. Despite the pressures contemporary cultures place upon Christians, Ratzinger believes that the grace of God enables them to be true to the faith as a counter-cultural force. As with the patristic era, he adds, the 'useless junk' of contemporary secular culture can be transformed by evangelization into 'magnificent fruit'.

> The topic that was assigned to me includes three main concepts: communication – culture – evangelization. It is quite evident, first of all, that the two concepts 'communication' and 'evangelization' go together: evangelization is the announcement of a Word that is more than a word – it is a way of life, indeed, life itself. So the question initially posed by the topic is: How can the gospel cross the threshold from me to someone else?[38]
>
> [. . .] Man is never alone, he bears the stamp of a community that provides him with patterns of thinking, feeling, and acting. This system of notions and thought patterns that preconditions the individual human being goes by the name of culture. The first and foremost component of culture is the common language; then comes the constitution of the society, that is, the government with its subdivisions, then law, custom, moral concepts, art, forms of worship, and so on. 'Culture' is the system of life into which the Word of the gospel enters. It must make itself understood within it, and it should have some effect in it, make an impression on this entire pattern of life, be the leaven within it, so to speak, that permeates the whole thing. The gospel to a certain extent presupposes culture; it never replaces it, but it does leave its mark upon it. The nearest equivalent to our concept of culture in the Greek world is the word *paideia* – education in the highest sense, which guides a human being to genuine humanity. [. . .]
>
> The topic assigned to me, however, goes on to qualify the general question about the communication of the gospel in the medium of culture by specifying a time: the third millennium. We are dealing, therefore, not with the relationship between gospel and culture in the abstract, but rather with the challenge of how the gospel can be made communicable within today's culture.
>
> [. . .] Yet it has always been true, even in the Middle Ages, that this Christian culture exists side by side with non-Christian and anti-Christian elements. Ever

---

38   [From 'Communication and Culture: New Models of Evangelization in the Third Millennium', in Joseph Ratzinger, *On the Way to Jesus Christ*. San Francisco: Ignatius Press, 2004, pp. 42–52 (a translation by Michael J. Miller of *Unterwegs zu Jesus Christus*, Augsburg, Sankt Ulrich Verlag, 2004)].

since the Enlightenment, Western culture has been moving away from its Christian foundations with increasing rapidity. The disintegration of the family and marriage, the escalating attacks upon human life and its dignity, the confinement of faith to the realm of the subjective and the consequent secularization of public awareness, as well as the fragmentation and relativising of ethical values demonstrate this all too clearly. To this extent contemporary culture [. . .] is a culture torn apart by internal contradictions. Christian culture is there, asserting its ways or developing new ones, but models contrary to Christian *paideia* are there, too, in an ever-growing conflict with it. The evangelization that speaks to this culture, therefore, is not addressing a monolithic group. In this contradictory setting it has to practice the art of discernment, and it must also find inroads into the secularized zones of this culture that have been left open to the faith.

[. . .] I would like to present an image for this path of cultural encounter and conflict, a metaphor that I found in the writings of Basil the Great (d. 379), who in struggling with the Greek culture of his time found himself faced with a task quite similar to the one that confronts us. Basil alludes to the self-concept of the prophet Amos, who said, 'I am a herdsman, and a dresser of sycamore trees' (Amos 7:14). The Greek version, the Septuagint (LXX) translation of this prophetic book, renders the latter expression more vividly as follows: 'I was one who slits the fruit of the sycamore.' The translation is based on the fact that the fruit or 'figs' of the sycamore must be slit before they are picked, so that they will ripen within a few days. In his commentary on Isaiah 9:10, Basil presupposes this practice, for he writes:

> The sycamore is a tree that bears very plentiful fruit. But it is tasteless unless one carefully slits it and allows its sap to run out, whereby it becomes flavorful. That is why, we believe, the sycamore is a symbol for the pagan world: it offers a surplus, yet at the same time it is insipid. This comes from living according to pagan customs. When one manages to slit them by means of the Logos, it [the pagan world] is transformed, becomes tasty and useful.[39]

Christian Gnilka comments as follows upon this passage:

> 'In this symbol are found the plenteousness, the wealth, the luxuriance of the pagan world . . ., but its deficiency is found therein as well. As it is, it is insipid, unusable. It needs a complete transformation, whereby the change does not destroy its substance; rather, it gives to it the qualities that it lacks . . .

---

39 Basil, *In Is* 9, 228 (commentary on Isaiah 9:10), PG [J-P. Migne, ed: *Patrologia Graeca*, 161 vols. (1857ff)] 30, 516D/517A. The attribution of this commentary on Isaiah to Basil has been disputed. The passage is cited in Christian Gnilka, *Chrêsis: Die Methode der Kirchenväter im Umgang mit der antiken Kultur*, vol. 2 of *Kultur und Conversion*. Basel: Schwabe, 1993, p. 84. In the following paragraphs I also rely on Gnilka, whose book is a fundamental study of the question of gospel and culture.

> The fruit remains fruit; its abundance is not diminished; rather it is recognized as an advantage . . .. On the other hand, the necessary transformation can scarcely be more keenly evident in this image than through the fact that what formerly could not be enjoyed now becomes edible. In the "running out" of the sap, furthermore, the process of purification is suggested'.[40]

One other point: The necessary transformation cannot come from the tree itself and its fruit – an intervention of the dresser, an intervention from outside, is necessary. Applied to the pagan world, to what is characteristic of human culture, this means: The Logos itself must slit our cultures and their fruit, so that what is unusable is purified and becomes not only usable but good. [. . .] Yes, ultimately only the Logos himself can guide our cultures to their true purity and maturity, but the Logos makes us his servants, the 'dresser of sycamore trees'. The necessary intervention requires understanding, familiarity with the fruit and its ripening process, experience, and patience. Since Basil is speaking here about the entire pagan world and its customs, it is obvious that this image is not about individual spiritual direction but rather about the purification and maturation of cultures, especially since the word for 'customs' is one of the words that, in patristic writings, correspond more or less to our concept of culture. Thus in this text is portrayed precisely what we are asking about: the way of evangelization within the realm of culture, the relations between the gospel and culture. The gospel does not stand 'beside' culture. It is addressed, not merely to the individual, but to the culture itself, which leaves its mark on the spiritual growth and development of the individual, his fruitfulness or unfruitfulness with respect to God and to the world. Evangelization is not simply adaptation to the culture, either, nor is it dressing up the gospel with elements of the culture, along the lines of a superficial notion of inculturation that supposes that, with modified figures of speech and a few new elements in the liturgy, the job is done. No, the gospel is a slit, a purification that becomes maturation and healing. It is a cut that demands patient involvement and understanding, so that it occurs at the right time, in the right place, and in the right way; a cut, then, that requires sympathy and understanding of the culture from within, an appreciation for its dangers and its hidden or evident potential. Thus it is clear also that this cut 'is not a momentary effort that is automatically followed by a ripening process'.[41] Rather, an ongoing and patient encounter between the Logos and the culture is necessary mediated by the service of the faithful.

It seems to me that the foregoing remarks state the essential requirements for the encounter between faith and culture that is demanded today. They also correct the one-sided notion that we often associate today with the term 'inculturation'. Perhaps, though, it will be useful to explain again what is meant in three short propositions.

---

40   Ibid., p. 85
41   Ibid., p. 86.

1. The Christian faith is open to all that is great, true, and pure in world culture, as Paul explicitly says in the Letter to the Philippians: 'Whatever is true, whatever is honorable, whatever is just, whatever is pure, whatever is lovely, whatever is gracious, if there is any excellence, if there is anything worthy of praise, think about these things' (Phil 4:8). In this passage Paul is probably referring first of all to the essential elements of the Stoic morality that, in his opinion, closely resembled Christianity but also, in general, to everything that is great in the Greco-Roman culture. The remarks that he addressed to that realm are universally true. Anyone who evangelizes today will start by looking in our culture for those features in it that are open to the gospel, the 'seeds of the Word', so to speak, and will strive to develop them further. Naturally he will also take into consideration the sociological or psychological commonplaces that today are opposed to the faith or that could become starting points for its reception. Christianity once began in an urban culture and only slowly managed to spread to the country. The inhabitants of rural areas remained pagan. Then the Christian religion became associated with agrarian culture, and today it must again find places in urban culture where it can dwell. The lay apostolic movements, the new forms of 'being on the way' to the faith in pilgrimages, and so on, gatherings at shrines, and the World Youth Days present models, to which the conferences of bishops and their experts will have to give some thought.

2. Faith is acquainted with bridge-building [Anknüpfung]; it accepts what is good; but it is also a sign of opposition to whatever in the culture bars the doors against the gospel. It is a 'cut', as we have heard. Therefore it has always been critical of culture also, and it must continue fearlessly and steadfastly to critique culture, especially today. Easy compromises benefit no one. [. . . T]his baptismal renunciation is the epitome of the culture-critical character of Christianity and a sign of the 'cut' that it involves. [. . .]

3. No one lives alone. The reference to the connection between gospel and culture is meant to make this clear. Becoming a Christian requires a lived context in which cultural healing and transformation can be accomplished. Evangelization is never merely intellectual communication; it is a process of experience, the purification and transformation of our lives, and for this to happen, company along the way is needed. That is why catechesis necessarily assumes the form of the catechumenate, in which the requisite recoveries can take place, in which especially the connection between thinking and living is established. The report that Cyprian of Carthage (d. 258) gave concerning his conversion to the Christian faith is eloquent testimony to this. He tells us that before his conversion and baptism he could not even imagine how anyone

could ever live as a Christian and overcome the customs of his time.[42] [. . . This] recalls the context in which young people have to grow up today and makes the reader wonder: Can anyone be a Christian in that situation? Is it not an outmoded way of life? [. . .] Yet the impossible, Cyprian tells us, became possible through God's grace and the sacrament of rebirth, which naturally is intended for the concrete setting in which it can take effect: in the company of believers, who set up an alternative way of living and demonstrate that it is possible. With that we return to the topic of culture, the topic of the 'cut'. For Cyprian is speaking, after all, precisely about the force of 'habits', that is, of a culture that makes faith appear impossible. [. . .] Precisely because he changed the culture of his world by way of conversion, through the cut of the Logos, he 'brought over' whatever was substantial and true in it. By cutting the sycamore fig of the culture of antiquity, the Church Fathers have brought it over to us in its entirety and have transformed it from useless junk into a magnificent fruit. That is the task set before us today in our confrontation with the secularized culture of our time – namely the evangelization of the culture.

42 Cyprian, *Ad Donatum 3* (CSEL 3, 1, 5); here, too, I am following Gnilka, *Chrêsis*, pp. 93–94.

CHAPTER 8

INTERPRETING THE SECOND VATICAN COUNCIL

Lieven Boeve

Introduction

As has become clear from the previous chapters, the Second Vatican Council and its correct interpretation runs as a red thread through Ratzinger's theological career. There was of course first the event of the Council itself. It offered a platform for a whole generation of theologians to engage in dialogue about the presence of God, Christian faith and the Church in the world of today. It is, however, the question of the 'correct' reception of the Council that was constitutive for Ratzinger's further theological development – how to interpret the Council's *aggiornamento*. As mentioned in the Introduction, and in the fourth chapter on the Church and the world: whether or not there is really a case to be made for a 'Ratzinger I' and 'Ratzinger II', it remains true that the prudent opening of his theology to the modern context develops into a theology of safeguarding Christian faith against the threats of modernity. In this chapter, we first draw our attention to Joseph Ratzinger's contribution to *Dei Verbum*, the constitution on divine revelation, and the way in which he interprets the events regarding this document as illustrative for the dynamics of the Council as a whole. We then present his criticism of the reception of Vatican II – even thirty years after the Council, he still claims that the real reception of the Council has not yet begun. In the third of the selected texts, Ratzinger sheds light on the right interpretation of conciliar documents and critically engages the difference, made by some, between the spirit and the texts of the Council. In a postscript, we briefly comment on Ratzinger's conciliar hermeneutics, and in as much as this runs as a red thread through his theological work, we necessarily enter into conversation with his theological approach.[1]

---

1   The text of this chapter is in part an elaboration in English of my 'Joseph Ratzinger, révélation et autorité de Vatican II', in *Ephemerides Theologicae Lovanienses* 85 (2009) nr. 4.

8.1 *Aggiornamento* and Vatican II

Ratzinger, who was professor of fundamental theology in Bonn from 1959 until 1963, participated in the preparations and sessions of the Second Vatican Council first as personal advisor of Cardinal Frings of Cologne and then, at the end of the first session, as an official *peritus*. The constitution on divine revelation *Dei Verbum*, approved at the last session on 18 November 1965, John L. Allen writes, is the conciliar document on which Ratzinger 'has exercised the greatest personal influence'.[2] As Frings' most important advisor, he had a hand in the rejection of the schema prepared by the Curia on the 'sources of revelation'. In his report on the first period, Ratzinger describes this preparatory scheme as anti-modernist, constrained, and testifying to an anti-compromise conflictive attitude, 'a theology of negations and prohibitions'.[3] For Ratzinger, the question at stake here was the following:

> Should the Church continue the antimodernist frame of mind and the policy of exclusion, of condemnation, of defensive attitude, pursued to the point of an almost pathological refusal to do anything?[4] Or will she, after seeing to certain necessary fundamentals, open a new page, and go out in a fresh and positive manner to make contact with her origins, her brothers and the world of today?[5]

In addition, he says that precisely because the Council has opted for the second option, it is more than the continuation of Vatican I, which, together with Trent, rather had the purpose to lock and secure; it is a new

2   John L. Allen, *Cardinal Ratzinger*. New York: Continuum, 2000, p 56. For Ratzinger's personal and actual memories of this, cf. among others: *Salz der Erde*. Stuttgart: Deutsche Verlags-Anstalt, 1996, *Christentum und katholische Kirche an der Jahrtausendwende. Ein Gespräch mit Peter Seewald*. (E.T.: *Salt of the Earth*. San Francisco: Ignatius Press, 1997) pp. 75–79 and *Aus meinem Leben. Erinnerungen (1927–1977)*. Stuttgart: DVA, 1998, pp. 100–102, 106–107, 128–132.

3   Cf. J. Ratzinger, *Die erste Sitzungsperiode des Zweiten Vatikanischen Konzils: ein Rückblick*. Köln Bachem, 1963, pp. 38–41 (E.T.: ‚The Second Vatican Council: The First Session', in *The Furrow* XIV (1963) pp. 267–288, esp. p. 281). A majority of the bishops disapproved of the preparatory schema on 20 November 1962; however, there was no two-thirds majority so the official text remained in effect. It was Pope John XXIII who withdrew the text a day later and who installed a mixed commission, including Cardinal Frings, to draft a new text. Strikingly, 35 years later in 1998, Ratzinger minimizes the extent of the conciliar rejection of the preparatory schemas in *Aus meinem Leben* (Heyne, 2000) moreover, he underlines the quality of the original schemata. What was lacking was not the basic theological solidity but the lack of pastoral involvement. 'Evidently, I had a lot to explain, but as to a radical rejection, which was then claimed and put forward by many at the Council, I found no ground.' (p. 101, translation mine).

4   [Selection from J. Ratzinger, *Theological Highlights of Vatican II*. New York: Paulist Press, 1966 pp. 20–30. (*Die erste Sitzungsperiode des 2. Vatikanischen Konzils*. Köln:1963, pp. 38–50)].

5   J. Ratzinger, 'The Second Vatican Council: The First Session, in *The Furrow* XIV (1963) p. 280.

task. Additionally, Ratzinger helped Karl Rahner to edit an alternative text that eventually heavily influenced the final text of the constitution.[6] He also belonged to the sub-commission of the extended theological commission that, in 1964, did the groundwork on a thoroughly reworked schema in preparation for discussion during the third Council session later that year; and was again in attendance of the fourth and last session in which the Constitution on Divine Revelation was finally promulgated on 18 November 1965. In the introduction of his commentary on *Dei Verbum* in the *Lexikon für Theologie und Kirche*,[7] Ratzinger already underscores the pertinence of the saying by Archbishop Florit (Florence), who indicated that the genesis of *Dei Verbum* both in the discussion (in terms of content) and in the factual occurrences strikingly expresses the Council event itself. The constitution carries the traces of this history, Ratzinger observes. However, even if it is the result of many compromises, its meaning is nevertheless significant. 'The text ties faithfulness to church tradition with the yes to critical science and thereby introduces for the first time the way for faith to enter into the present day.'[8] Ratzinger thereby emphasizes that the constitution aims at a re-reading of both Trent and Vatican I: '. . . in which the past is read in the manner of today, and is thereby, at the same time, reinterpreted with regard to what is essential as well as to what is inadequate.'[9]

The text below illustrates Ratzinger's attitude during the conciliar years toward the unfolding events of Vatican II. The text originates from an English compilation of four small German booklets in which Ratzinger gives an account of events and proceedings during the Council and reports on the opening and the first session.

Early Debate on Revelation

The Council faced a more difficult situation when . . . the schema dealing with 'the sources of revelation' was presented to the fathers. The text was, if one may use the label, utterly a product of the 'anti-Modernist' mentality that had taken shape about the turn of the century. The text was written in a spirit of condemnation and negation, which, in contrast with the great positive initiative of the liturgy schema, had a frigid and even offensive tone to many of the fathers.

6   K. Rahner and J. Ratzinger, *Offenbarung und Überlieferung* (*Quaestiones disputatae* 25), Freiburg im Breisgau: Herder, 1965 (E.T.: *Revelation and Tradition*. New York: Herder and Herder, 1965).
7   'Dogmatische Konstitution über die göttliche Offenbarung', in *Lexikon für Theologie und Kirche. Das Zweite Vatikanische Konzil. Konstitutionen, Dekrete und Erklärungen. Kommentare*. Freiburg: Herder, 1967, pp. 497–583 (for the commentaries of J. Ratzinger: cf. pp. 498–528 and 571–581).
8   Translated from: Ibid., p. 503.
9   Translated from: Ibid., p .505. Cf. also p. 521 on a revision of what comprises tradition and the development of tradition.

And this despite the fact that the content of the text was new to no one. It was exactly like dozens of textbooks familiar to the bishops from their seminary days; and in some cases, their former professors were actually responsible for the text now presented to them.

In order to understand the intellectual mentality behind this text, it is necessary to recall the embattled atmosphere of the Church during the previous hundred years. This atmosphere is first clearly marked in the Syllabus of Pius IX (1864) in which the Church decisively and uncompromisingly detached itself from the growing error of the 'modern mind.' As with every historical necessity, however, it undoubtedly went about this with excessively one-sided zeal. This development reaches its zenith in the various measures of Pius X against Modernism (the decree Lamentabili and the encyclical Pascendi [1907], and, finally, the 'oath against Modernism' [1910]).

During these years, there arose an embittered discussion that found expression in such tragic figures as Loisy and Tyrrell, men who thought they could not save the faith without throwing away the inner core along with the expendable shell. Such figures and their tragic schizophrenia show forth the mortal danger that threatened Catholicism at the first outbreak of the modern mind. They explain Pius X's uncompromising opposition to the spirit of novelty which was stirring everywhere. It must be said that, in sifting it out, much real wheat was lost along with 'the chaff.' This historical perspective helps explain, then, that secret fear and mistrust of any theological expression of modern historical and philosophical thought.

This same anxiety persisted until its last reverberation sounded in the encyclical *Humani generis* of Pius XII. This document pursued once more the line of thought of Pius IX and Pius X. The schemata of the theological commission, the first of which now lay before the fathers for consideration, breathed this same spirit. The same cramped thinking, once so necessary as a line of defence, impregnated the text and informed it with a theology of negations and prohibitions; although in themselves they might well have been valid, they certainly could not produce that positive note which was now to be expected from the Council. In any case, none of this could appear strange or startling to the bishops. Familiar with the origins of these opinions and aware of the struggles they themselves had been through they found it easy to recognize in the text the very sentiments many of them had brought to the Council But everything that had happened since the Council began had basically changed the situation. The bishops were no longer the same men they had been before the Council. First of all, they had discovered themselves as an episcopate, with their own powers and their own collective responsibility. Secondly, the passage of the liturgy schema had given rise to a new possibility foreign to the old pattern of 'anti-ism' and negativity, the possibility of abandoning the defensive and really undertaking a Christian 'offensive.' They could now think and act in a positive manner. The spark was ignited. The words of Pope John's opening speech now acquired meaning, became understandable. He had insisted that the Church was no longer to condemn but rather to dispense the medicine of compassion, that the Council was not to speak negatively but to present the faith in a new and positive way, and finally that the Council must refrain from pronouncing anathemas. These very words, previously considered as an expression of the pope's personal temperament, words that had puzzled many, now made sense. And so it could happen that, without prior agreement, Cardinals Liénart, Frings, Léger, König, Alfrink, Suenens, Ritter and Bea, each from his own point of view, delivered sharp criticisms of the schema, something surprising to both its authors and its opponents.

What was the central issue? Among the theological questions open to serious discussion were the relationship of scripture to tradition and the way in which faith is related to history. Also under discussion was a proper understanding of inspiration and of the historicity of events narrated in scripture. The whole question which contemporary historical scholarship raised, and which was postponed rather than solved by Modernism, stood open once more to debate. Beyond these specific questions dealing with the interpretation of faith which cannot be treated here in detail, there was at issue a more fundamental conflict of attitudes of mind that amounted to more than a mere quarrel about theological differences. The real question behind the discussion could be put this way: Was the intellectual position of 'anti-Modernism' — the old policy of exclusiveness, condemnation and defence leading to an almost neurotic denial of all that was new — to be continued? Or would the Church, after it had taken all the necessary precautions to protect the faith, turn over a new leaf and move on into a new and positive encounter with its own origins, with its brothers and with the world of today? Since a clear majority of the fathers opted for the second alternative, we may even speak of the Council as a new beginning. We may also say that with this decision there was a major advance over Vatican Council I. Both Trent and Vatican Council I set up bulwarks for the faith to assure it and to protect it; Vatican Council II turned itself to a new task, building on the work of the two previous Councils.

Two main arguments were used to defend the new position. They rested upon the intention of Pope John that the texts should be pastoral and their theology ecumenical. It must be granted that both arguments employed by the progressive interests at the Council are open to misinterpretation. They can in fact be unobjective, open to misunderstanding and ambiguity. What they did mean, and the sense in which they were actually used under given circumstances, may well be surmised from what we have thus far said. 'Pastoral' should not mean nebulous, without substance, merely 'edifying' – meanings sometimes given to it. Rather what was meant was positive care for the man of today who is not helped by condemnations and who has been told for too long what is false and what he may not do. Modern man really wishes to hear what is true. He has, indeed, not heard enough truth, enough of the positive message of faith for our own time, enough of what the faith has to say to our age. 'Pastoral' should not mean something vague and imprecise, but rather something free from wrangling, and free also from entanglement in questions that concern scholars alone. It should imply openness to the possibility of discussion in a time, which calls for new responses and new obligations. 'Pastoral' should mean, finally, speaking in the language of scripture, of the early Church Fathers, and of contemporary man. Technical theological language has its purpose and is indeed necessary, but it does not belong in the kerygma and in our confession of faith.

'Ecumenical' must not mean concealing truth so as not to displease others. What is true must be said openly and without concealment; full truth is part of full love. 'Ecumenical' must mean that we cease seeing others as mere adversaries against whom we must defend ourselves. We have pursued such a course long enough. 'Ecumenical' means that we must try to recognize as brothers, with whom we can speak and from whom we can also learn, those who do not share our views. 'Ecumenical' must mean that we give proper attention to the truth, which another has, and to another's serious Christian concern in a matter in which he differs from us, or even errs. 'Ecumenical' means to consider the whole, and not to single out some partial aspect that calls for condemnation or correction. 'Ecumenical' means that we present the inner totality of our faith in order to make known to our separated brothers that Catholicism clearly contains all that is truly Christian. 'Ecumenical' and 'Catholic' in their very etymology say the same thing. Therefore, to be a Catholic is not to become entangled in separatism, but to be open to the fullness of Christianity. It was precisely this attitude which the fathers had to assert against the proposed text. The texts almost exclusively relied upon the Latin theology of the last hundred years in continuation of the fight against Modernism, and in so doing, these texts were obviously threatened by a narrowness in which the wide scope of Catholicism could scarcely be detected. It is clear, therefore, from what we have said about the very basic division of mind involved in the revelation schema, that in subsequent debates important specific details of the schema were of comparatively secondary importance. It is also clear that in the fathers' debates there was no fundamental division of dogmatic viewpoint; there was rather an important difference in the basic spiritual approach to the problem of how the Church was to meet its present responsibilities. The voting on November 20 proved that the great majority of the Council opted for the positive position and had made up its mind to abandon an outmoded negative defensiveness.

As the press made abundantly clear, the question to be voted on was so worded that for the moment the issue was obfuscated. According to normal procedure the schema would have been presented to the fathers to pass or reject; two-thirds of all the votes would have been required for passage, while a good one-third would have been sufficient to kill the schema. But instead, the Council was asked to vote whether the present schema should be withdrawn or not. Now the text's opponents had the burden of mustering two-thirds of the vote, and a good one-third was quite enough to save the schema. The result is well known: 1,368 of the fathers voted for the withdrawal of the schema — in other words; opposed the text — while 813 voted for keeping the schema. Another 100 votes or so would have provided the two-thirds necessary to kill the schema. Thus only about one-third of the fathers had voted for the proposed text. Nevertheless, this device had saved the schema despite the fact that quite obviously it ran counter to the will of the majority. The deep dismay and even anger that resulted dissolved on the following day when the pope himself set aside the text of the schema and turned it over to a mixed commission, headed by Cardinals Ottaviani and Bea, for thorough revision. Thus the will of the majority was carried out. The pope had asserted his authority in favour of the Council majority. This decision was obviously of great fundamental importance. The Council had resolutely set itself against perpetuating a one-sided anti-Modernism and so had chosen a new and positive approach. In this sense, we may consider November 20 or November 21, 1962, as a real turning point. It was a turning point, too, in the sense that, in contrast to Trent and Vatican Council I, the pope had rejected curial dominance and sided with the Council.

Last Phase of the First Session

[. . .] Despite the many climaxes that followed, it became increasingly evident that a certain fatigue was spreading over the Council. In my opinion, this was ultimately due to the fact that everyone felt clearly that, in the voting of November 20 and the discussions on the liturgy, the Council had done its work for the time being. Further, the fathers seemed to feel that, for all practical purposes, what was needed now was new preparation. This work would have to be done in a completely new spirit differing from the spirit of the earlier proposals, and, the model for this reworking would have to be the spirit and language of the liturgy schema. The earlier preparatory work had been done in the defensive, anti-Modernistic tradition of the curia, most of whose offices had come into being during the battles of the last hundred years. The Council's decision meant nothing less than a basic overhauling of the view manifested in the preparatory work. It had initiated, in the concentrated effort and thought of the early weeks, a new beginning which now had to be carried forward. The job of working out details was not the business of the plenary assembly. What the plenum and only the plenum (the bishops from all over the world) could do had been done. They had reversed course and had given their orders.

We would like to make clear once more just what all this meant. The Council had asserted its own teaching authority. And now, against the curial congregations which serve the Holy See and its unifying function, the Council had caused to be heard the voice of the episcopate – no, the voice of the universal Church. For, with and in the bishops, the respective countries, the faithful and their needs and their concerns were represented. What the bishops said and did was far more than an expression of a particular theological school. It was rather the expression of another school which they had all attended, the school of their very office, the school of communion with their faithful and with the world in which they lived.

There is much talk today in theological circles of the Church's 'sense of faith' as a source of dogma. Such a source is not always fully trustworthy. Who can really determine what this 'sense of faith' is? Here, however, the consciousness of faith of the whole Church had become genuinely concretized and energetically effective — so much so that, without denying the value of the three-year work of preparation, the Council had nevertheless unmasked it as largely inadequate and had demanded that the preparation be done all over again on a new basis. And so it was clear that a rather long adjournment was needed so that the texts, which had to be so thoroughly revised, might be presented again to the Council in a manageable form.

[. . .] Some may have been discontent because no text emerged from the session, nor any really palpable result. Yet the response to this should be clear from all that has been previously said, for it was precisely in this apparently negative outcome that the greatness, the surprise and the truly positive effect of the first session lie. For it was in this negative outcome that the spirit of the Preparatory work was completely reversed. Here lay the truly epochal character of the first session.

8.2 The Reception of Vatican II: 'The Real Time of Vatican II is Still to Come'

As we have already seen in various readings included in this volume, Ratzinger's discomfort concerning its impact and reception increased soon after the formal ending of the Council. It is by no means certain, he argued, that the Second Vatican Council would prove to be fruitful from the point of view of Church history.

It is to the Council's merit, Ratzinger stated in 1966,[10] that the Church at Vatican II distanced itself from any 'secondary' scandal that veils the 'primary scandal' of God's incarnation in history; to defend positions of power under the pretext of safeguarding God's rights, to maintain unmodified forms of belief from the past in order to preserve the integrity of faith, to canonize scholastic theological opinions under the guise of defending the fullness of the truth, etc.[11] However, the primary scandal of God's love is put under pressure in the post-conciliar period. And, in a paradoxical way, the Council's fundamental openness to the world seems to be the cause of this.[12] After all, this openness should not

---

10   Cf. J. Ratzinger, 'Der Katholizismus nach dem Konzil – Katholische Sicht', in *Auf Dein Wort hin. 81. Deutscher Katholikentag.* Paderborn: Bonifacius, 1966, pp. 245–266 (rewritten in extended version in *Das neue Volk Gottes. Entwürfe zur Ekklesiologie,*.Düsseldorf: Patmos, 1969, pp. 302–321, here pp. 317–18.

11   In his *Einführung in das Christentum.* Munchen: Kösel-Verlag, 2000 Ratzinger talks about the scandal of Christian faith (p. 30 ff.) Cf. Chapter One of this volume.

12   Cf. J. Ratzinger 'Weltoffene Kirche? Überlegungen zur Struktur des Zweiten Vatikanischen Konzils',

be misunderstood: 'The Council marks the transition from a conserving to a missionary attitude, and the conciliar opposite to conservative is not progressive, but missionary.'[13] Besides, turning to the world does not detract from the non-conformism of the Gospel.

As we saw in Chapter Four of this volume, for Ratzinger the struggle over the interpretation of the Council began at the very Council itself, and precisely with the discussion surrounding *Gaudium et Spes*. In 1973, he wrote in a general evaluation of the Council, ten years after it convened, that this debate was a prescient image of the crisis in which the Church finds itself.[14] The theological discord that surfaced only deepened:

> This means that the struggle for the true inheritance of the Second Vatican Council[15] cannot be conducted today on the basis of texts alone. Whether an intellectual backing can be found not just for a counter-historical utopian interpretation of the Council, but also for a creative-spiritual understanding in union with the true tradition, will be decisive for its further progress.[16]

By the former, Ratzinger again referred to, among other things, the political theology of J.-B. Metz that, according to him, has ultimately more to do with neo-Marxism than with theology. The theological movement that actually made the Council possible and that is in continuity with Scripture, the Church Fathers, and the liturgy was all too soon afterwards overwhelmed by modernity, according to Ratzinger: 'At the Council, it was important for this theology to nourish faith not only from the thought of the last hundred years, but from the great tide of the entire tradition.'[17] However, confronted with the consequences of neo-clerical progressivism, this movement gradually regained vigour. He concluded: 'The inheritance of the Second Vatican Council has not yet awoken. But it is waiting for its hour. And this will come; of that I am certain.'[18] Still, two years later the balance was certainly no more positive for

---

in T. Filthaut (ed.), *Umkehr und Erneuerung. Kirche nach dem Konzil*. Mainz: Grünewald, 1966, pp. 273–291 (= *Das neue Volk Gottes*, 281–301)

13 J. Ratzinger, '*Weltoffene Kirche?*', in *Das neue Volk Gottes. Entwürfe zur Ekklesiologie*. Düsseldorf: Patmos, 1969, p. 300.

14 J. Ratzinger, 'Zehn Jahre nach Konzilsbeginn – Wo stehen wir?', in *Dogma und Verkündigung*. Munchen: Sankt Ulrich Verlag, 1973, pp. 439–447.

15 [Selection from V. Messori and J. Ratzinger, *The Ratzinger Report*. San Francisco: Ignatius Press, 1985, pp. 28–40].

16 Translated from: Ibid., p. 443.

17 Translated from: Ibid., p. 445.

18 Translated from: Ibid., p. 447. What is interesting in this regard is the last chapter of J. Ratzinger, *Glaube und Zukunft*. Munchen: Kosel, 1970, pp. 107–125: 'Wie wird die Kirche im Jahre 2000 aussehen?' – 'How will the Church look in the year 2000?'

Ratzinger.[19] Ten years after the Council, Christian faith was still trapped in the tension between the reduction to an earthly messianism and a new integralism, and the middle way remains elusive. The historical value of Vatican II will depend upon the successful attainment of this. Ratzinger finally concluded with the warning that not all valid councils in the history of the Church have been 'fruitful councils'.[20]

Ratzinger's critique culminated in *Ratzinger Report* in 1985, an interview with V. Messori[21] published immediately prior to the extraordinary synod on the reception of Vatican II, twenty years after its closure. In the second chapter, on the necessity of rediscovering the Second Vatican Council, he defends the Council and the conciliar documents both against left-wing and right-wing interpretations of it, which appeal to the character of the Council as a rupture to either reject it, or to radicalize the renewal. 'To defend the true tradition of the Church today means to defend the Council.' Instead of a break with tradition, Ratzinger claims: 'There is, instead, a continuity that allows neither a return to the past nor a flight forward, neither anachronistic longings nor unjustified impatience.'[22] Consequently, there is an urgent call for a 'restoration' – only this can constitute genuine reform today. The following text is a longer extract from *The Ratzinger Report*. The interviewer, V. Messori, introduces the then Cardinal Ratzinger.

[. . .]. Thus ten years before our conversation, he [Card. Ratzinger] had already written: 'Vatican II today stands in a twilight. For a long time it has been regarded by the so-called progressive wing as completely surpassed and, consequently, as a thing of the past, no longer relevant to the present. By the opposite side, the "conservative" wing, it is, conversely, viewed as the cause of the present decadence of the Catholic Church and even judged as an apostasy from Vatican I and from the Council of Trent. Consequently demands have been made for its retraction or for a revision that would be tantamount to a retraction.'[23]

Thereupon he continued: 'Over against both tendencies, before all else, it must be stated that Vatican II is upheld by the same authority as Vatican I and the Council of Trent, namely, the Pope and the College of Bishops in communion with him, and that also with regard to its contents, Vatican II is in the strictest continuity with both previous councils and incorporates their texts word for word

---

19 Cf. J. Ratzinger, 'Bilanz der Nachkonzilszeit – Misserfolge, Aufgaben, Hoffnungen', in *Theologische Prinzipienlehre*. Munchen: Wewel, 1982, pp. 383–395.

20 Cf. ibid., p. 395

21 J. Ratzinger and V. Messori, *Rapporto sulla fede*. Torino: Edizioni Paoline, 1985 (translated as *The Ratzinger Report: An Exclusive Interview on the State of the Church*. San Francisco: Ignatius, 1986).

22 Ibid., p. 31.

23 'Thesen zum Thema 'Zehn Jahre Vaticanum II', 1f. Typewritten manuscript.

in decisive points.'[24]

From this Ratzinger drew two conclusions. *First:* 'It is impossible ("for a Catholic") to take a position *for* Vatican II but *against* Trent or Vatican I. Whoever accepts Vatican II, as it has clearly expressed and understood itself, at the same time accepts the whole binding tradition of the Catholic Church, particularly also the two previous councils. And that also applies to the so-called "progressivism", at least in its extreme forms.' *Second:* 'It is likewise impossible to decide *in favor* of Trent and Vatican I, but *against* Vatican II. Whoever denies Vatican II denies the authority that upholds the other two councils and thereby detaches them from their foundation. And this applies to the so-called "traditionalism", also in its extreme forms.' 'Every partisan choice destroys the whole (the very history of the Church) which can exist only as an indivisible unity.'[25]

Let Us Rediscover the True Vatican II

Hence it is not Vatican II and its documents (it is hardly necessary to recall this) that are problematic. At all events, many see the problem—and Joseph Ratzinger is among them, and not just since yesterday—to lie in the manifold interpretations of those documents which have led to many abuses in the post-conciliar period.

Ratzinger's judgment on this period has been clearly formulated for a long time: 'It is incontestable that the last ten years have been decidedly unfavorable for the Catholic Church.'[26] 'Developments since the Council seem to be in striking contrast to the expectations of all, beginning with those of John XXIII and Paul VI. Christians are once again a minority, more than they have ever been since the end of antiquity.'

He explains his stark judgment (which he also repeated during the interview—but that should not cause any surprise, whatever judgment we might make of it, for he confirmed it many times) as follows: 'What the Popes and the Council Fathers were expecting was a new Catholic unity, and instead one has encountered a dissension which—to use the words of Paul VI—seems to have passed over from self-criticism to self-destruction. There had been the expectation of a new enthusiasm, and instead too often it has ended in boredom and discouragement. There had been the expectation of a step forward, and instead one found oneself facing a progressive process of decadence that to a large measure has been unfolding under the sign of a summons to a presumed "spirit of the Council" and by so doing has actually and increasingly discredited it.'

Thus, already ten years ago, he had arrived at the following conclusion: 'It must be clearly stated that a real reform of the Church presupposes an unequivocal turning away from the erroneous paths whose catastrophic consequences are already incontestable.'

24   Ibid.
25   Ibid.
26   Ibid.

On one occasion he also wrote: 'Cardinal Julius Dopfner once remarked that the Church of the post-conciliar period is a huge construction site. But a critical spirit later added that it was a construction site where the blueprint had been lost and everyone continues to build according to his taste. The result is evident.'

Nevertheless the Cardinal constantly takes pains to repeat, with equal clarity, that 'Vatican II in its official promulgations, in its authentic documents, cannot be held responsible for this development which, on the contrary, radically contradicts both the letter and the spirit of the Council Fathers.'

He says: 'I am convinced that the damage that we have incurred in these twenty years is due, not to the "true" Council, but to the unleashing *within* the Church of latent polemical and centrifugal forces; and *outside* the Church it is due to the confrontation with a cultural revolution in the West: the success of the upper middle class, the new "tertiary bourgeoisie", with its liberal-radical ideology of individualistic, rationalistic and hedonistic stamp.'

Hence his message, his exhortation to all Catholics who wish to remain such, is certainly not to *'turn back'* but, rather, 'to *return to the authentic texts of the original Vatican II.'*

For him, he repeats to me [V. Messori], 'to defend the true tradition of the Church today means to defend the Council. It is also our fault if we have at times provided a pretext (to the "right" and "left" alike) to view Vatican II as a "break" and an abandonment of the tradition. There is, instead, a continuity that allows neither a return to the past nor a flight forward, neither anachronistic longings nor unjustified impatience. We must remain faithful to the *today* of the Church, not the *yesterday* or *tomorrow*. And this today of the Church is the documents of Vatican II, without *reservations* that amputate them and without *arbitrariness* that distorts them.'

A Prescription Against Anachronism

Although critical of the 'left', Ratzinger also exhibits an unmistakable severity toward the 'right', toward that integralist traditionalism quintessentially symbolized by the old Archbishop Marcel Lefebvre. In a reference to it, he told me: 'I see no future for a position that, out of principle, stubbornly renounces Vatican II. In fact in itself it is an illogical position. The point of departure for this tendency is, in fact, the strictest fidelity to the teaching particularly of Pius IX and Pius X and, still more fundamentally, of Vatican I and its definition of papal primacy. But why only the popes up to Pius XII and not beyond? Is perhaps obedience to the Holy See divisible according to years or according to the nearness of a teaching to one's own already-established convictions?'

The fact remains, I observe, that if Rome has intervened with respect to the 'left', it has not yet intervened with respect to the 'right' with the same vigor.

In reply, he states: 'The followers of Msgr. Lefebvre assert the very opposite. They contend that whereas there was an immediate intervention in the case of the respected retired Archbishop with the harsh punishment of suspension, there is an incomprehensible toleration of every kind of deviation from the other side. I don't wish to get involved in a polemic on the greater or lesser severity toward the one or the other side. Besides, both types of opposition present entirely different features. The deviation toward the "left" no doubt represents a broad current of the contemporary thought and action of the Church, but hardly anywhere have they found a juridically definable common form. On the other hand, Archbishop Lefebvre's movement is probably much less broad numerically, but it has a well-defined juridical organization, seminaries, religious houses, etc. Clearly everything possible must be done to prevent this movement from giving rise to a schism peculiar to it that would come into being whenever Msgr. Lefebvre should decide to consecrate a bishop which, thank God, in the hope of a reconciliation, he has not yet done. In the ecumenical sphere today, one deplores that not enough was done in the past to prevent incipient divisions through a greater openness to reconciliation and to an understanding of the different groups. Well, that should apply as a behavioral maxim for us too in the present time. We must commit ourselves to reconciliation, so long and so far as it is possible, and we must utilize all the opportunities granted to us for this purpose.' [. . .]

His prescription for cutting the ground from under the Lefebvre case and other anachronistic resistances seems to re-echo that of the last popes, from Paul VI to today: 'Similar absurd situations have been able to endure up to now precisely by nourishing themselves on the arbitrariness and thoughtlessness of many post-conciliar interpretations. This places a further obligation upon us to show the true face of the Council: thus one will be able to cut the ground from under these false protests.'

Spirit and Anti-spirit

But, I say, opinions differ as regard the 'true' Council. Apart from the cases of that irresponsible 'neo-triumphalism' to which you referred and which refuses to look at reality, there is general agreement that the present situation of the Church is a difficult one. But opinions come to a parting of the ways with respect to diagnosis as well as therapy. The *diagnosis* of some is that the appearances of crisis are only the salutary fevers of a period of growth. For others, instead, they are symptoms of a grave illness. As regards the *therapy,* some demand a greater application of Vatican II, even beyond the texts. Others propose a minor dose of reforms and changes. How to choose? Who is to be declared right?

He answers: 'As I shall explain in great detail, my diagnosis is that we are dealing with an authentic crisis and that it must be treated and cured. Thus, I confirm that even for this healing process, Vatican II is a reality that must be fully accepted. On condition, however, that it must not be viewed as merely a point of departure from which one gets further away by running forward, but as a base on which to build solidly. Today, in fact, we are discovering its "prophetic" function: some texts of Vatican II at the moment of their proclamation seemed really to be ahead of the times. Then came the cultural revolutions and the social convulsions that the Fathers in no way could have foreseen but which have shown how their answers—at that time anticipatory—were those that were needed in the future. Hence it is obvious that return to the documents is of special importance at the present time: they give us the right instrument with which to face the problems of our day. We are summoned to reconstruct the Church, not *despite*, but *thanks* to the true Council.'

Continuing his diagnosis, he recalls that this 'true' Council, 'already during its sessions and then increasingly in the subsequent period, was opposed by a self-styled "spirit of the Council", which in reality is a true "anti-spirit" of the Council. According to this pernicious anti-spirit [*Konzils-Ungeist* in German], everything that is "new" (or presumed such: how many old heresies have surfaced again in recent years that have been presented as something new!) is always and in every case better than what has been or what is. It is the anti-spirit according to which the history of the Church would first begin with Vatican II, viewed as a kind of point zero.'

'Not rupture but continuity'

On this point, he insists, he wants to be very precise. 'This schematism of a *before* and *after* in the history of the Church, wholly unjustified by the documents of Vatican II, which do nothing but reaffirm the continuity of Catholicism, must be decidedly opposed. There is no "pre-" or "post-"conciliar Church: there is but one, unique Church that walks the path toward the Lord, ever deepening and ever better understanding the treasure of faith that he himself has entrusted to her. There are no leaps in this history, there are no fractures, and there is no break in continuity. In no wise did the Council intend to introduce a temporal dichotomy in the Church.'

Continuing his analysis, he recalls that 'in no way was it the intention of the pope who took the initiative for Vatican II, John XXIII, and of the pope who continued it faithfully, Paul VI, to bring up for discussion a *depositum fidei* which was viewed by them as undisputed and already assured.'

Do you wish, perhaps, as some do, to stress the primarily *pastoral* concerns of Vatican II?

'I should like to say that Vatican II surely did not want "to change" the faith, but to represent it in a more effective way. Further, I should say that dialogue is possible only on the foundation of a clear identity. One can, one must be "open", but only when one has something to say and has acquired one's own identity. This is how the Popes and the Council Fathers understood it. Some of them no doubt harbored an optimism that from our present-day perspective we would judge as not critical or realistic enough. But if they thought that they could open themselves with confidence to what is positive in the modern world, it was precisely because they were sure of their identity, of their faith. Whereas on the part of many Catholics in recent years there has been an unrestrained and unfiltered opening to the world, that is to say, to the dominant modern mentality, which at the same time brings up for discussion the very foundations of the *depositum fidei* which for many were no longer clear.'

He continues: 'Vatican II was right in its desire for a revision of the relations between the Church and the world. There are in fact values, which, even though they originated outside the Church, can find their place—provided they are clarified and corrected—in her perspective. This task has been accomplished in these years. But whoever thinks that these two realities can meet each other without conflict or even be identical would betray that he understands neither the Church nor the world.'

Are you proposing, perhaps, a return to the old spirit of 'opposition to the world'?

'It is not Christians who oppose the world, but rather the world which opposes itself to them when the truth about God, about Christ and about man is proclaimed. The world waxes indignant when sin and grace are called by their names. After the phase of indiscriminate "openness" it is time that the Christian reacquire the consciousness of belonging to a minority and of often being in opposition to what is obvious, plausible and natural for that mentality which the New Testament calls—and certainly not in a positive sense—the "spirit of the world". It is time to find again the courage of nonconformism, the capacity to oppose many of the trends of the surrounding culture, renouncing a certain euphoric post-conciliar solidarity.'

Restoration?

At this point —here, too, as during the whole interview, the tape recorder whirred in the silence of the room overlooking the seminary garden—I posed to Cardinal Ratzinger the question whose answer aroused the liveliest reactions. Reactions which were also due to the incomplete ways in which it has often been reported, as well as to the emotion-laden content of the word involved ('restoration'), which hearkens back to times long past and which are certainly neither repeatable nor—at least in our view —even desirable.

Accordingly I asked the Prefect of the Congregation for the Faith: 'Considering what you are saying, it would seem that those who assert that the Church hierarchy intends to close the first phase of the post-conciliar period are not wrong. And that (even though it certainly would not be a return to the pre-conciliar period but to the 'authentic' documents of Vatican II) the same hierarchy intends to set a kind of "restoration" in motion.'

This is the Cardinal's reply, in his own words: 'If by "restoration" is meant a turning back, no restoration of such kind is possible. The Church moves forward toward the consummation of history, she looks ahead to the Lord who is coming. No, there is no going back, nor is it possible to go back. Hence there is no "restoration" whatsoever in this sense. But if by restoration we understand the search for a new balance after all the exaggerations of an indiscriminate opening to the world, after the overly positive interpretations of an agnostic and atheistic world, well, then a restoration understood in this sense (a newly found balance of orientations and values within the Catholic totality) is altogether desirable and, for that matter, is already in operation in the Church. In this sense it can be said that the first phase after Vatican II has come to a close.' [. . .]

Unforeseen Effects
In his view, as he explains to me, 'the situation has changed, the climate has changed for the worse with respect to that which sustained a euphoria whose fruits now lie before us as a warning. The Christian is held to that *realism* which is nothing but complete attention to the signs of the times. Therefore I exclude the possibility that any thought can be given (unrealistically) to go back along the road as if Vatican II had never been. Many of the concrete effects, as we see them now, do not correspond to the intentions of the Council Fathers, but we certainly cannot say: "It would have been better if it had not been". John Henry Cardinal Newman, the historian of the councils, the great scholar who was converted to Catholicism from Anglicanism, said that a council was always a risk for the Church and that, consequently, it should only be called to discuss a limited number of issues and not be overly protracted. True, reforms require time, patience, and a readiness to take risks, but it is still not permissible to say: "Let's not convoke councils because they are dangerous." I believe, rather, that the true time of Vatican II has not yet come, that its authentic reception has not yet begun: its documents were quickly buried under a pile of superficial or frankly inexact publications. The reading of the *letter* of the documents will enable us to discover their true *spirit*. If thus rediscovered in their truth, those great texts will make it possible for us to understand just what happened and to react with a new vigor. I repeat: the Catholic who clearly and, consequently, painfully perceives the damage that has been wrought in his Church by the misinterpretations of Vatican II must find the possibility of revival in Vatican II itself. The Council is *his*, it does not belong to those who want to continue along a road whose results have been catastrophic. It does not belong to those, who, not by chance, don't know just what to make of Vatican II, which they look upon as a "fossil of the clerical era".'

8.3 Interpreting Vatican II: Between the Spirit and the Letter[27]

In later writings, Ratzinger's position regarding Vatican II sees no substantial change. On the question of what went wrong with (the reception of) Vatican II, he states in *Salz der Erde*[28] for instance, that to begin with, the Council had probably raised expectations too high and that there was a strong (and eventually wrong) sense that one could 'make' the Church.

27	[Selection from, J. Ratzinger, *Principles of Catholic Theology: Building Stones for Fundamental Theology*. San Francisco: Ignatius Press, 1987, pp. 389–391].

28	J. Ratzinger, *Salz der Erde. Christentum und katholische Kirche an der Jahrtausendwende. Ein Gespräch mit Peter Seewald*. Stuttgart: Deutsche Verlags-Anstalt, 1996 (E.T.: *Salt of the Earth*. San Francisco: Ignatius Press, 1997).

In the years following the Vatican II, there was (and still is) a struggle for defining and claiming the heritage of the Council. Apart from reactionary responses that reject the Council, Ratzinger makes a distinction between an interpretation that sees the Council in continuity with the whole tradition, and another that sees it rather as a starting point for ongoing change. In this regard, he refers repeatedly to the importance of the reception of the pastoral constitution *Gaudium et Spes*. For Ratzinger, the classic argument that it is precisely the spirit of the Council that should take us beyond its letter is clearly false. In a text included in his *Theologische Prinzipienlehre* (1982)[29] he formulates his opinions as follows:

> It is perhaps too soon to say that for some time now the era of crisis has been changing into an era of consolidation. Let us ask, first, what we are to think of what has taken place thus far. [. . .] Was the Council a wrong road that we must now retrace if we are to save the Church? The voices of those who say that it was are becoming louder and their followers more numerous. Among the more obvious phenomena of the last years must be counted the increasing number of integralist groups in which the desire for piety, for the sense of the mystery, is finding satisfaction. We must be on our guard against minimizing these movements. Without a doubt, they represent a sectarian zealotry that is the antithesis of Catholicity. We cannot resist them too firmly. But we must likewise ask ourselves, in all earnestness, why such contractions and distortions of faith and piety have such an effect and are able to attract those who, by the basic conviction of their faith as well as by personal inclination, are in no way attracted by sectarianism. What drives them into a milieu in which they do not belong? Why have they lost the feeling of being at home in the larger Church? Are all their reproaches unfounded? Is it not, for example, really strange that we have never heard bishops react as strongly against distortions in the heart of the liturgy as they react today against the use of a Missal of the Church that, after all, has been in existence since the time of Pius V? Let it be said again: we should not adopt a sectarian attitude, but neither should we omit the examination of conscience to which these facts compel us.
>
> What shall I say? First of all, one thing seems to me to have become abundantly clear in the course of these ten years. An interpretation of the Council that understands its dogmatic texts as mere preludes to a still unattained conciliar spirit, that regards the whole as just a preparation for *Gaudium et spes* and that looks upon the latter text as just the beginning of an unswerving course toward an ever greater union with what is called progress—such an interpretation is not only contrary to what the Council Fathers intended and meant, it has been reduced *ad absurdum* by the course of events. Where the spirit of the Council is turned against the word of the Council and is vaguely regarded as a distillation from the development that

---

29 *Theologische Prinzipienlehre*. Munchen: Wewel, 1982.

evolved from the 'Pastoral Constitution', this spirit becomes a specter and leads to meaninglessness. The upheavals caused by such a concept are so obvious that their existence cannot be seriously disputed. In like manner, it has become clear that the world, in its modern form, is far from being a unified entity. Let it be said once for all: the progress of the Church cannot consist in a belated embrace of the modern world—the theology of Latin America has made that all too clear to us and has demonstrated thereby the rightness of its cry for liberation. If our criticism of the events of the decade after the Council has guided us to these insights, if it has brought us to the realization that we must interpret Vatican Council II as a whole and that our interpretation must be oriented toward the central theological texts, then our reflections could become fruitful for the whole Church and could help her to unite in sensible reform. The 'Constitution on the Church' is not to be evaluated in terms of the 'Pastoral Constitution', and certainly not in terms of an isolated reading of the intention expressed in the prefatory paragraphs, but vice versa: only the whole in its proper orientation is truly the spirit of the Council.

Does this mean that the Council itself must be revoked? Certainly not. It means only that the real reception of the Council has not yet even begun. What devastated the Church in the decade after the Council was not the Council but the refusal to accept it. This becomes clear precisely in the history of the influence of *Gaudium et spes*. What was identified with the Council was, for the most part, the expression of an attitude that did not coincide with the statements to be found in the text itself, although it is recognizable as a tendency in its development and in some of its individual formulations. The task is not, therefore, to suppress the Council but to discover the real Council and to deepen its true intention in the light of present experience. That means that there can be no return to the *Syllabus*, which may have marked the first stage in the confrontation with liberalism and a newly conceived Marxism but cannot be the last stage. In the long run, neither embrace nor ghetto can solve for Christians the problem of the modern world. The fact is, as Hans Urs von Balthasar pointed out as early as 1952, that the 'demolition of the bastions' is a long-overdue task. The Church cannot choose the times in which she will live. After Constantine, she was obliged to find a mode of coexistence with the world other than that necessitated by the persecutions of the preceding age. But it bespeaks a foolish romanticism to bemoan the change that occurred with Constantine while we ourselves fall at the feet of the world from which we profess our desire to liberate the Church. The struggle between *imperium* and *sacerdotium* in the Middle Ages, the dispute about the 'enlightened' concept of state churches at the beginning of the modern age, were attempts to come to terms with the difficult problems created in its various epochs by a world that had become Christian. In an age of the secular state and of Marxist messianism, in an age of worldwide economic and social problems, in an age when the world is dominated by science, the Church, too, faces anew the question of her relationship with the world and its needs. She must relinquish many of the things that have hitherto spelled security for her and that she has taken for granted. She must demolish longstanding bastions and trust solely to the shield of faith. But the demolition of bastions cannot mean that she no longer has anything to defend or that she can live by forces other than those that brought her forth: the blood and water from the pierced side of the crucified Lord (John 19:31-37). 'In the world you will have trouble, but be brave: I have conquered the world' (John 16:33). That is true today, too.

Finally, on 22 December 2005, two weeks after the fortieth anniversary of the close of the Second Vatican Council, Ratzinger – now Pope Benedict XVI – in his Christmas address to the Curia returned once more to the problem of the reception of the Council.[30] In line with the theological evaluation he had previously offered, he again discerns the problem of the Council's double hermeneutic: on the one hand a hermeneutics of discontinuity and rupture, on the other hand a hermeneutics of reform. Ratzinger holds the former responsible for the confusion of the post-conciliar period. Again, he repeated that this hermeneutics turns to the spirit of the Council to criticize the conciliar texts as compromises, and beyond the texts, continues to promote the élan for renewal. In this way, this hermeneutics forces a rupture between the pre- and post-conciliar Church. The hermeneutics of reform, by contrast, opts essentially for continuity. Also, the apparent discontinuity, which would emerge in a revised discernment on the relation between the Church and the modern world, is embedded in a much more fundamental continuity: 'the continuity of the principles has not been abandoned!' The Pope continues:

In this process of innovation in continuity we must learn to understand more practically than before that the Church's decisions on contingent matters – for example, certain practical forms of liberalism or a free interpretation of the Bible – should necessarily be contingent themselves, precisely because they refer to a specific reality that is changeable in itself. It was necessary to learn to recognize that in these decisions it is only the principles that express the permanent aspect, since they remain as an undercurrent, motivating decisions from within. On the other hand, not so permanent are the practical forms that depend on the historical situation and are therefore subject to change.[31]

To contextualize his words here in terms of the bigger picture of his thought across the decades: Ratzinger was already wondering in 1966 whether the Council, understood in its relation to the councils throughout history, meant a rupture or a continuation. His answer then was that,

30 Cf. www.vatican.va/holy_father/benedict_xvi/speeches/2005/index_en.htm (accessed 1 September 2009).
31 Ibid.

compared to the nineteenth and the beginning of the twentieth centuries, 'it without doubt represents a break, but it is nevertheless a break within a common basic intention.'[32]

Postscript: Which 'hermeneutics of reform'?

At the end of this chapter, we delve a little deeper into the problem of Vatican II's reception. Because of the importance of this for the development of Ratzinger's theological career, it offers us an opportunity to reflect a little further on his whole theological project. At the same time, it offers us the possibility to introduce a contemporary theological question. Indeed, today the actual problem concerning the reception of Vatican II does not appear to be a hermeneutics of discontinuity over and against a hermeneutics of reform. It is certainly true that theologians that are more modern allow further room for discontinuity in the concrete development of tradition; nevertheless, they do this without abandoning a more fundamental continuity. Edward Schillebeeckx, for instance, once stated that it is only 'thanks to shifts and breaks in formulations of dogma, the dogma remains true.'[33] Nonetheless, he too speaks about a lasting truth and he chose to develop a hermeneutical understanding of tradition that – from the perspective of revelation – posits a principle of identity between the different stages in the tradition that the Church has known in its history.[34] It is certainly true as well that a number of contemporary theologians, by reading and interpreting the texts of the Council, give more weight to these texts on the relation between the Church and world than does Joseph Ratzinger. Which is why they have difficulties with his rhetorical question 'Are we to read the dogmatic constitutions as the guiding principle of the pastoral constitution, or have even the dogmatic pronouncements been turned in a new direction?'[35] This is because they see a more dynamic relation between dogmatic theology and pastoral theology. Moreover, they see the reciprocal involvement of pastoral and dogmatics fundamentally present in *all* council texts. It is necessary to recall here that it was precisely the pastoral argument that was important

---

32 Translated from: Ratzinger, 'Weltoffene Kirche?', in *Das neue Volk Gottes. Entwürfe zur Ekklesiologie*. Düsseldorf: Patmos, 1969, p. 300.

33 E. Schillebeeckx, "Breuken in christelijke dogma's," in *Breuklijnen: Grenservaringen en zoektochten*, Fs. T. Schoof. Baarn: Nelissen, 1994, pp. 15–49, here at p. 26. (My translation).

34 Cf. E. Schillebeeckx, *Mensen als verhaal van God*. Baarn: Nelissen, 1989 (E.T.: *Church: The Human Story of God*. New York: Herder and Herder, 1993).

35 Ratzinger, *Principles of Catholic Theology: Buildling Stones for a Fundamental Theology*. San Francisco, Ignatius, 1987, pp. 378–379.

in the rejection of the first schema on revelation. Even more, it is the dynamic understanding of revelation that inspires these theologians. It is undoubtedly true for them that the texts of Vatican II in a special way – because they are conciliar texts – belong to the tradition, but also that these texts – however authoritative – are to be seen in the context of the reality of revelation, which exceeds them. As Joseph Ratzinger himself pointed out in his commentary on *Dei Verbum*, the tension between the 'spoken' and the 'unspoken' needs to remain respectful to revelation: the inclusive, all-encompassing nature of tradition (teaching, life, and worship of the faith community) and the recognition of the development of tradition, and this is not only through the proclamation of the teaching authority, but also in the contemplation and study of the faithful and the insight gained in spiritual experience.[36] The discussion regarding the reception of Vatican II therefore is not one of plain opposition between the Spirit and the text. Nonetheless, precisely in line with *Dei Verbum*, the dynamics between Spirit and letter remains constitutive for any legitimate understanding of the Council. In this regard, the role of the teaching authority is of great importance, but is at the same time embedded in the broader life and thinking of the Church.

That is why it is probably more important for the contemporary theological situation to conduct a debate on the term 'hermeneutics' in the expression 'hermeneutics of reform', rather than focusing on continuity versus discontinuity. This may be very fruitful in light of more recent developments in hermeneutical philosophy that make clear that it is too easy to attribute 'the discontinuity in tradition development' merely to time-related and contingent factors – and this then mainly in the relation between Church and world – while the principles to this would be exempt in principle. After all, we have no access to these principles except through language and interpretation. In that sense, the distinction between truth as enduring content and language as mere form or design is not sustainable (nor realizable). Such an 'essentialist' hermeneutics is not conscious enough of the hermeneutical circle of any human – and hence also theological – understanding of the truth. Language and history are at least co-constitutive for truth. That is why each development and renewal of tradition – precisely why it is continuous – also involves some form of discontinuity. Contrary to what is sometimes feared, this by no means necessarily leads to hermeneutical relativism: precisely because the distinction between truth and language cannot be so construed, tradition remains binding, while at the same time it opens up a process of tradition

36   See his comments in this regard: *Dogmatische Konstitution über die göttliche Offenbarung*, in *Lexikon für Theologie und Kirche. Das zweite Vatikanische Konzil. Konstitutionen, Dekrete und Erklärungen. Kommentare*. Freiburg: Herder, 1967, pp. 497-583.

hermeneutics. Moreover, on the basis of the doctrine of the Incarnation, this point can be made not only philosophically but also theologically. It is precisely in his humanity, that Jesus' incarnation makes God's revelation in history possible, it is co-constitutive of it, and it cannot be disconnected from it: indeed no assimilation but no separation either.[37]

It is also at this point that Joseph Ratzinger's own theological principles feature prominently in the picture. The providential character that he attributes to the synthesis between Jewish-Christian faith and Greek thinking, the structural-Platonizing truth concept that typifies his thinking on truth in relation to time (and hence language), thus brings him quasi-automatically to a more essentialist hermeneutics. Continuity and discontinuity cannot be thought fundamentally together and therefore discontinuity must essentially be able to be reduced to continuity. Whether this is the case by reserving discontinuity for the contingent or by seeing dogmatics as normative for the pastoral – every time there appears an asymmetrical relation between truth and time/language that does not allow us to give a place to the co-constitutive contribution of language, context, and history, to (our coming to) the saving truth. That is why the dynamic understanding of tradition of Vatican II, for Ratzinger, refers fundamentally to a dynamics of the eternal *in* the temporal, not of the eternal *and* the temporal. But even more, to him, to hold the latter position signifies the handing over of the eternal to the temporal. That is why there is no talk about a real dialogue with modernity, and certainly not when this modernity radicalizes.

However, the question is whether this is the only legitimate theological hermeneutics. Even when one accepts that the synthesis between Greek thinking and Jewish-Christian faith is providential, and hence that the result of this involvement of faith and reason is normative, still the question remains as to how this providential and normative nature should be understood: as closed – 'the special right of patristics' – or as a principle and/or paradigm for the way in which revelation and faith produce history. In the latter case, this original synthesis remains providential in a twofold way for the manner in which the Christian faith involves itself intrinsically in the context in which it incarnates itself. First, as the expressed truth of faith of the Church Fathers, it remains primarily a starting point for hermeneutics (to be sure, 'revelation' is not available in a 'disembodied' form). Second, as a methodological paradigm, it also impels this hermeneutics to a true re-contextualization,[38] i.e. the ongoing

37   Cf. L. Boeve, 'Christus Postmodernus: An Attempt at Apophatic Christology', in T. Merrigan and
      J. Haers (eds), *The Myriad Christ: Plurality and the Quest for Unity in Contemporary Christology*. Leuven:
      Peeters Press, 2000, pp. 577–593.

38   For the concept of 're-contextualization', see L. Boeve, *Interrupting Tradition. An Essay on Christian*

critical-productive entering into relation with the context, so that God's revelation can also speak today. Moreover, as regards this, even Thomas Aquinas – to whom the Pope refers in his Christmas address[39] – provides a striking testimony; a testimony that, as history teaches, was not quite appreciated wholeheartedly by everyone immediately.[40]

Faith in a Postmodern Context (Louvain Theological and Pastoral Monographs, 30). Leuven: Peeters / Grand Rapids: Eerdmans, 2003; *God Interrupts History: Theology in a Time of Upheaval*. New York: Continuum, 2007.

39   Cf. Ibid.

40   How Thomas is a striking example of re-contextualization is elaborated on in my *Interrupting Tradition. An Essay on Christian Faith in a Postmodern Context* (Louvain Theological and Pastoral Monographs, 30). Leuven: Peeters / Grand Rapids: Eerdmans, 2003, pp. 28–32.

INDEX OF NAMES

Adam, Alred 22n.16
Adorno, Theodor 3
Alfrink, Bernardus Johannes, Cardinal 261
Allen, John L. 82n.4, 147n.11, 229, 258
Athenagoras I, (Aristocles Spyrou), Patriarch of Constantinople 163
Augustine of Hippo (Aurelius Augustinus Hipponensis) 2, 13, 23, 42, 69n.43, 81, 85, 158, 209n.47

Bacon, Francis 136, 137
Balthasar, Hans Urs von, 3, 54n.13, 86, 94n.24, 113, 114–18, 158n.29, 212n.49, 274
Barth, Karl 25, 150, 241
Basil the Great 253–4
Bauer, Johannes B. 18
Baum, Gregory 143
Bea, Augustine Cardinal 261–2
Behm, Johannes 56
Benoît, André 23, 26
Bertone, Tarcisio 187n.10, 191n.19
Boff, Leonardo 5, 92, 100, 110
Bonaventure (Giovanni di Fidanza) 2, 13, 38, 42, 215
Bouyer, Louis 115, 163n.36
Braun, François-Marie 89n.19
Bromiley, Geoffrey W. 227n.10
Brunner, August 70n.44
Buchmann, Frank 54

Bultmann, Rudolf 17, 33, 35, 76

Campenhausen, Hans von 194
Camus, Albert 59
Cardenal, Ernesto 135
Colson, Jean 249
Comte, Auguste 136
Congar, Yves Marie-Joseph, 156n.25, 159
Cullmann, Oscar 170
Curran, Charles 5, 82n.4 179n.1, 185nos. 5, 6, 219n.55
Cyprian of Carthage (Thascius Caecilius Cyprianus) 255–6

Daniélou, Jean 25n.23, 149n.4
Dibelius, Martin 35
Dionysius the Areopagite, (aka Pseudo-Dionysius or Pseudo-Denys) 160
Dopfner, Julius, Cardinal 4, 268
Döring, Heinrich 4
Duffy, Eamon 82n.4, 229n.18
Dupuis, Jacques 5

Eliade, Mircea 150
Erni, Raymond 164n.37
Evdokimov, Paul 90n.21

Fahey, Michael 179n.1
Fessio, Joseph 226n.8
Fichte, Johann Gottlieb 77
Fitzgerald, Michael, Archbishop 147n.11

Florit, Ermenegildo, Cardinal 259
Frings, Josef Cardinal 2, 140, 181, 258
Fries, Heinrich 4, 156n.27, 167, 169
Francis of Assisi (Giovanni Francesco di Bernardone) 209
Freud, Sigmund 63

Gaillardetz, Richard R. 179n.1
Gese, Harmut 40
Gibson, David 208n.44
Gnilka, Joachim 36, 253
Guardini, Romano 1, 47n.54, 49n.56, 96, 137
Guillaume d'Auvergne 212
Guttiérez, Gustavo 133

Haag, Herbert 42
Habermas, Júrgen 127n.22
Hadot, Pierre 56n.17
Haers, Jacques 278n.37
Halbfas, Hubertus 154, 156n.26
Hamman, Adalbert 249
Harnack, Adolf von 17n.9, 195
Hebblethwaite, Peter 10nos.32, 35
Hegel, Georg Wilhelm Friedrich 8
Heidegger, Martin, 33, 77
Heim, Maximilian Heinrich 83n.6, 85n.10
Hemmerle, Klaus 64, 65n.36
Hick, John 173–4, 175, 176

Hilberath, Bernd Jochen 119n.2
Hoedl, Ludwig 194n.32
Hoffmann, Paul 56
Hommes, Ulrich 73, 51n.2
Humbert of Mourmoutiers (aka of Silva Candida), Cardinal 162
Hünermann, Peter 119n.2, 217

Ignatius of Loyola 209
Instinsky, Hans Ulrich 60n.24

Jaspers, Karl 39
Jeremias, Joachim 92
Joachim of Fiore 75
John XXIII (Angelo Roncalli), Pope 187, 247, 258n.4, 260–1, 267, 270
John Paul II, Pope (Karol Wojtyla) 4, 5, 6, 10, 143, 146, 184–6, 191, 202, 208n.45, 246

Kant, Immanuel 175, 177
Kasper, Walter Cardinal 84
Kattenbusch, Ferdinand 89n.20
Kenis, Leo 119
Kerkhofs, Jan 179n.1
Keßler, Hans 64
Knitter, Paul 174
Kolvenbach, Peter-Hans 72n.47
König, Cardinal 261
Kraemer, Hendrik 150
Kriele, Martin 137
Kuhn, Helmut 125
Küng, Hans 4, 220n.56, 247, 249

Lamberigts, Mathijs 119
Le Guillou, Marie-Joseph 115
Leeuw, Gerardus van der 70
Lefebvre, Marcel 268–9
Léger, Paul-Émile Cardinal 261
Lehmann, Karl, Cardinal 3, 164n.38
Leicht, Robert 84
Lennan, Richard 86
Levada, William 247n.35
Levinas, Emmauel 54
Liénart, Cardinal 261
Linde, Gisela 59n.22

Loisy, Alfred 87, 92, 260
Löw, Reinhardt 35n.36
Lubac, Henri de, Cardinal 3, 25n.23, 102, 104, 115, 228, 245n.32
Luther, Martin 82, 85, 145, 165, 246

Maier, Hans 4, 124
Marcel, Gabriel 61n.26
Marcuse, Herbert 3
Marx, Karl 138, 238
McCormick, Richard A. 179n.1, 185nos.5, 6, 219n.55
McDonnell, Kilian 84n.8
Medina Estévez, Jorge, Cardinal 115
Melanchthon, Phillip 167, 171
Merrigan, Terence 278n.37
Messori, Vittorio 10, 51n.4, 85n.13, 139, 144n.9, 264n.10, 266n.21
Metz, Johann-Baptists 4, 121, 124
Meyendorff, John 163n.35
Michael Cerularius I, Patriarch of Constantinople, 162
Mieth, Dietmar 217
Mudge, Lewis S. 179n.1
Murray, Gilbert 54n.14

Natalis, Herveus 194
Newman, John Henry 102, 272
Nichols, Aidan 180, 182n.3
Nietzsche, Friedrich 54

Origen (aka Origen Adamantius) 114
Örsy, Ladislas 179n.1
Ottaviani, Alfredo, Cardinal 261

Panneberg, Wolfhart 227n.10
Papandreou, Damaskinos 164n.37
Pascal, Blaise 132
Paul VI, Pope (Giovanni Battista Montini) 4, 162, 189, 202, 233, 238, 267, 269–70
Pera, Marcello 139

Peterson, Erik 69n.43, 92n.22
Peukert, Helmut 124
Phillips, Gerard 228
Pieper, Josef 62–4
Pius V (Antonio (Michele) Ghislieri), Pope 223, 237, 238
Pius IX (Giovanni Maria Mastai-Ferretti), Pope 154, 188, 193, 259–60, 268
Pius X (Giuseppe Melchiorre Sarto), pope 147, 229, 238, 260, 268
Pius XII (Eugenio Maria Giuseppe Giovanni Pacelli), Pope 154, 155, 236, 260, 268

Rahner, Karl 2, 4, 14, 148, 150n.15, 155n.23, 167, 169, 187, 189n.12, 258, 259n.6
Ritter, Joachim, 56n.17
Ritter, Joseph Cardinal 261
Rohrmoser, Günter 63
Rousseau, Olivier 192
Rowland, Tracey 227n.11
Rylko, Stanislav 232n.28

Saier, Oskar 90
Sander, Hans-Joachim 119
Schaeffler, Richard 74n.54
Schambeck, Herbert 133
Schauf, Heribert 193n.31
Scheffczyk, Leo 57n.18, 66n.41
Schillebeeckx, Edward 5, 276
Schlier, Heinrich 16n.8, 36n.38, 92, 157n.28, 221
Schmaus, Michael 1
Schönborn, Christoph 70–1, 230n.20
Schutte, Heinz 164
Schweitzer, Albert 246
Seeber, David 10
Šeper, Franjo, Cardinal 4
Söhningen, Gottlieb 2
Spaemann, Robert 35n.36, 48n.55, 63, 249
Spann, Othmar 151n.19
Sperber, Manes 135
Spohn, William C. 186n.8
Suenens, Léon-Joseph, Cardinal 261

Sullivan, Francis A. 109n.32,
  179, 186n.8

Tauron, Jean Louis 231n.26
Teilhard de Chardin, Pierre
  120
Tenbruck, Friedrich H 137
Tertullian (Quintus Septimius

Florens Tertullianus) 20
Thibon, Gustave 159
Thomas Aquinas 13, 36, 279
Thomé, Josef 150n.17
Tillard, Jean-Marie 90n.21
Tracy, David 86
Tura, Roberto 11
Tyrrell, George 260

Urban VIII (Maffeo Barberini),
  Pope 237–8

Vorgrimler, Herbert 84, 149

Wellhausen, Julius 23
Williamson, Richard 147
Wilson, Kenneth 179n.1

INDEX OF SUBJECTS

abortion 71, 126
Abraham 149
aggiornamento 2, 30, 120, 250
  and Vatican II 258–79
anthropology/anthropological
  51, 76–9, 81, 126, 150, 214,
  241, 243
apostolic succession 188,
  194–7
  papal and episcopal
  succession 197–200
Arius 70

baptism 44, 171, 221, 255
being 8, 19–22, 71, 77, 225,
  263, 269, 271, 273–4
  and time 8
Bible, scripture 22–4, 25, 33,
  34, 36, 37, 40, 43, 48, 49,
  55–7, 76, 82, 89–91, 145,
  159, 167, 171, 179, 218,
  221, 238–9, 241, 243,
  244–6, 275
bishops 116, 187–207
  teaching office of 246–51
body of Christ 16, 83, 85,
  93
Buddhism, Buddhists 145,
  152

canon law 104, 187n.9, 201–2
catechesis/catechism 229–31,
  240–6
christology 34, 51, 66, 92, 93,
  120, 174–6

Church
  as communion 5, 83–7,
    112–18, 192, 221, 228,
    229 (*see also* 'communion'
    and 'ecclesiology, of
    communion')
  Eastern Churches 22, 171
  memory of 91
  as mystical body of Christ
    85, 94, 101–2, 154, 172,
    221
  nature of the Church 88–94
  as people of God 93, 104–6
  Roman Catholic 86,
    109–10, 143, 161, 163, 164,
    165–6, 168–70, 172, 198,
    202–4, 230–1, 241, 266–7
  and salvation 154–60
  and the world 124
Communio (journal) 3, 84,
  118, 223, 240 (*see also*
  '*Communio* (project)')
Communio (project) 95, 114–18
  (*see also* 'ecclesiology, of
  communion')
communion 83, 85, 115–18,
  192, 194, 206, 232, 234, 240
Concilium (journal) 2, 3, 113,
  121, 189–91
Congregation for the Doctrine
  of the Faith (CDF) 4, 5, 9,
  95, 100, 110, 108, 113, 141,
  143, 161, 179–80, 181,
  184, 191, 201–2, 207, 212,
  214, 226, 247

conscience 206–7
continuity 81, 88, 91
  and discontinuity 266–79
conversion 44, 46, 53–7, 64, 69,
  102, 145, 161, 175, 231,
  235, 255
covenant 57, 75, 93, 103,
  149–50, 195–7, 209, 212
creation 35, 52, 64, 65, 70, 74,
  102, 107–8, 125, 212, 222,
  242
cross 12, 102, 120–6
culture 52, 67, 71, 82, 113, 119,
  127–30, 176, 227, 232 241,
  242, 247, 250–6, 271

death 39, 71, 72, 74, 78, 98,
  102, 126, 227, 240
decalogue 129, 171
Dei Verbum 258–64
dialogue 140, 142–4, 233
didache 188, 194
dogma 26–8, 124, 160, 161,
  215, 244–6
  as historical 26–8, 73, 193
Dominus Iesus 100, 142, 143

ecclesial 45–8, 122, 140
  teaching office (*see*
    'magisterium')
ecclesiology 81–5, 108, 142, 203
  of communion 85, 87,
    106–10, 113–14, 187
  euchariatic ecclesiology
    102–4

ecumenism 139, 140, 160–72, 261

Enlightenment, the 19, 39, 66, 122, 128–32, 135, 148, 152, 253

eschatology/eschatological 51–2, 72, 87, 90, 92, 99, 105–7, 111, 135, 145

ethics 5, 6, 65, 167, 174, 219, 242

eucharist (see also 'eucharistic ecclesiology') 44, 83, 93, 94, 99, 103, 227–9, 239, 240

evangelization 140, 142, 225–56

exegesis 18, 25, 32–7, 48, 82, 88, 89, 244

Exodus 67–70, 156

Fathers of the Church 22–5, 36, 70, 102, 154, 256, 261, 265, 278

faith 18–22, 29, 41, 44, 51, 53–8, 99, 131–8, 248, 255, 278
   and modernity 28–33, 120
   and reason 8, 12, 18, 20, 28, 34, 37–42, 47, 122, 129–34, 136–8, 162, 176–7, 186, 200, 204–5, 214, 218–23, 278
   and freedom 207–12
   and politics 119

freedom (see also 'faith and freedom') 30, 60–2, 69–71, 124, 126, 129, 130–3, 207–12

Galileo Galilei 43

Gaudium et Spes 12, 84, 119–22, 265, 273

gnosis 23, 47, 72, 177, 194–6

God 31–2, 39–40, 43–5, 55–6, 60–71, 77–9, 126, 128, 131–3, 141, 221, 254
   'of the philosophers'/ philosophical conceptions God 18–22

gospel 20, 23, 40, 48, 54, 75, 88, 93, 95, 97, 118, 124, 160, 167, 182, 207, 248, 250–6

grace 76, 81, 83, 104–5, 154, 209–10, 221–3, 253, 256, 271
   and nature 81

Greek antiquity 54, 55, 56

Greek thought, Greek enlightenment 18–22, 39, 40, 56, 249, 252, 253, 255, 278

heaven 72–4, 158

hell 72, 74

hellenistic 13, 22, 55

hermeneutics 13, 17, 28, 33, 166, 275–9
   and tradition 42–5

Hinduism 145, 152, 156–7

historical method 33, 243–4

history 57, 74, 75, 76–9, 128, 160, 165, 215, 227, 256

HIV/AIDS 71, 126

Holy Spirit 117, 192

hope 72–5

Humanae Vitae 184

incarnation 11–12, 76, 83, 100, 120

inculturation 186, 229, 233–40, 251–6

individualism 90

infallibility 185, 192, 199

Islam, Muslims 128, 129, 146, 148, 149, 156–7

Jainism, Jains 145

Jansenist 154

Jewish 43, 129, 145, 212, 278

John the Baptist 93

Judaism 148, 154, 197

kingdom of God 17, 91, 92, 93

last Supper/lord's Supper 87–8, 102, 172

liberalism 48, 52, 90, 99, 101, 170, 187, 213, 214, 218, 274–5

liberation 68–9, 99, 124, 133, 158, 207, 274

liberation theology 5, 51, 133, 134, 141, 173, 174, 177–8, 184–5, 218

liturgy/liturgical acts 23–4, 44, 99, 173, 227, 233–40, 263, 265

logos 19–21, 41, 131, 132, 136, 176, 248, 254

love 19–22, 42, 59–65, 71–2, 208–11, 215, 220, 221–2, 227–8, 240, 260

Lumen Gentium 83–4, 101, 103, 108, 110, 121, 189, 248

magisterium 18, 33, 45–8, 179–223
   and free expression 207–12
   magisterium: faith and morality 221–4
   and morality 212–21

manichean 82n.4

Marxism/Marxist 51, 53, 77, 90, 99, 123, 173, 243, 265, 274

mediaeval theology 17

metanoia 8, 46, 51, 53–7

metaphysics 39, 76, 145, 242
   anti-metaphysical 130

Middle Ages 17, 23–4, 36, 97, 99, 123, 193, 235, 240, 252

mission 83, 87, 93, 94, 96, 107, 140, 143, 150, 154, 159, 175, 180, 181, 197, 210, 215, 225–7, 231–2, 235, 243, 245, 249, 251

modernity 13, 81, 83, 121, 122, 127
   and faith (see 'faith and modernity')
   modern context 51, 119
   modern theology 124
   modernization 2, 30

monotheism 56, 148, 153

moral theology 54, 218–23

Muslims (Islam) 128, 129, 146, 148, 149, 156–7

mysticism 43, 145, 148, 151, 152, 153, 171

mythology 19–21

National Episcopal Conferences 4, 81, 182, 184, 225, 231, 235, 252

'New Age' religions 126, 145, 148, 176–7, 178
New Testament 16, 34, 43, 55, 73, 75, 87, 91, 92, 103–4, 117, 154, 155, 171, 173, 188, 195, 212, 218, 221–2, 270

Old Testament 16, 17, 22, 34, 43, 55, 75, 87, 93, 108, 195–6, 207, 221, 235
Orthodox Churches and ecumenism 160–4
Orthodox theology/ theologians 103, 105, 107
orthodoxy (in Catholicism) 4, 45, 173, 182, 186, 218, 219, 220, 222
orthopraxis 173, 218–19, 220, 222

Papacy 88, 144, 146, 154, 172, 181, 187–200
Paul/Pauline 16, 28, 211–12, 218, 221–2
penance 53, 54
philosophy 18, 20, 22, 32–4, 37–40, 47–8, 70, 74, 111, 129–31, 173–4, 176, 186, 195, 214, 216, 239–40, 277
Plato 19, 56
platonism/neo-platonism 56, 175, 278
pluralism 95, 134, 141–3, 162, 172–8, 181, 186, 226
polytheism 56, 177
positivism 51, 130, 243
postmodern/postmodernity 52, 81–4, 86–7, 225, 251
practical theology 240, 242
pragmatism 31, 54, 173, 177
progress 30
'protestant orthodoxy' 15
protestant theology 86, 103
protestantism/protestant Christians 23, 89, 103, 145, 160, 161, 164, 167, 170, 171
and ecumenism 160–2
providential 19, 278

Qumran Community 92, 249–50

rationalism 25, 44, 176, 214
redemption 51, 57–8, 65, 76, 134, 173, 176, 177–8
relationality 53
relativism 52, 95, 131, 140, 142, 148, 172–8, 181, 208, 211, 226, 247, 277, 278
ecclesiological relativism 111
religion 19, 20, 39, 47, 55, 68, 89, 128–31, 137, 140, 144, 148–55, 173–7, 195, 214, 216, 219, 255
renaissance 128
repentance 54, 55, 94, 97, 104
resurrection 28, 32, 39, 66, 68–9, 72–4, 98, 102–3, 111, 227, 240
revelation 2, 13–49, 66, 77, 102, 120, 126, 148, 153, 181, 188, 193, 196, 227, 230, 241, 247, 254–64, 276–9
Roman Curia (see also 'CDF') 181, 202, 204, 261

sacraments 8, 69, 76–9, 83, 85, 89, 104, 172, 228, 239, 240, 256
salvation 3, 8n.23, 9, 17, 51, 28, 57–75, 83, 85, 94, 97, 105, 133, 136, 139–73, 181, 207, 221, 225, 227–8, 231–2, 242
and Church, see Church and Salvation
and history 159
Scripture (see, also, Bible) 126, 195, 197, 265
and tradition 13–49, 126
and revelation 188
canon of scripture 195
sin 42, 45. n50, 53, 54, 55, 73, 76, 112, 136, 208, 271
subsistit in 108–12
substitutionary ministration 157–8
symbola, early church, 23–4
synod of bishops 81, 182, 201–7

theologians 179–87, 212–21
theology 1–10, 12, 16, 18, 22, 25, 28–9, 32, 37, 38, 40–2, 45–8, 99, 172, 177–8

of liberation (see 'liberation theology')
patristic theology 19–25
and philosophy 38–42
political theology 3, 4, 52, 218, 229, 265
and politics 133
tradition 2, 8, 12, 13–49, 65, 66, 82, 90, 93, 96, 111, 116, 117, 126, 131, 140, 160, 169, 175, 188, 190, 194–9, 203, 208, 218–19, 221–3, 229–30, 243–4, 259, 261, 263, 265–8, 273–9
and hermeneutics, (see 'hermeneutics and tradition')
Trent, (Trento), Council of, 236, 246, 258, 261
Tridentine rite 228, 237
truth 7, 8, 9, 12, 18, 20, 21, 26, 28, 32, 33, 34, 38, 41, 42, 45–7, 52–3, 56, 62–71, 91, 97, 112, 115–17, 126, 130, 134, 140, 142, 143, 145, 148–9, 53, 156, 160, 161–3, 174, 175, 177, 181, 206, 207, 208–9, 211, 212–23, 247–51, 261–2, 264, 271–2, 276–8

Utopia 136, 138

Vatican I (First Vatican Council) 95, 115, 188, 192–4, 236, 258, 261, 266–7
Vatican II (Second Vatican Council) 2, 6, 12, 13, 83–6, 90, 94, 95, 100, 101, 102, 103, 111–13, 115, 116, 119–21, 127, 139–40, 141, 143, 148, 167, 168, 181, 183, 187–91, 201–3, 207, 213, 225–6, 229, 231, 233–4, 238, 246–9, 257–79
post-Vatican II period 12, 86, 95, 114, 115, 121, 122, 141, 142, 180, 182, 184, 191, 229, 235, 248–9, 257–9
pre-Vatican II period 140

Zoroastrianism 148